Beth Lee
1981

Better Homes and Gardens®

Treasury of Christmas Crafts & Foods

©1980 by Meredith Corporation, Des Moines, Iowa.
All Rights Reserved. Printed in the United States of America.
First Edition. Fourth Printing, 1981.
Library of Congress Catalog Card Number: 79-55159
ISBN: 0-696-00025-3

BETTER HOMES AND GARDENS® BOOKS

Editor in Chief: James A. Autry
Editorial Director: Neil Kuehnl
Executive Art Director: William J. Yates

Editor: Gerald M. Knox
Art Director: Ernest Shelton
Associate Art Directors: Neoma Alt West, Randall Yontz
Copy and Production Editors: David Kirchner,
Lamont Olson, David A. Walsh
Assistant Art Director: Harijs Priekulis
Senior Graphic Designer: Faith Berven
Graphic Designers: Linda Ford,
Sheryl Veenschoten, Thomas Wegner

Crafts Editor: Nancy Lindemeyer
Craft Books Editor: Joan Cravens
Associate Crafts Editor: Ann Levine
Food and Nutrition Editor: Doris Eby
Senior Food Editor: Sharyl Heiken
Associate Food Editor: Rosemary C. Hutchinson

Treasury of Christmas Crafts and Foods

Crafts Editors: Joan Cravens, Ann Levine
Food Editor: Rosemary C. Hutchinson
Copy and Production Editor: David A. Walsh
Graphic Designers: Faith Berven, Sheryl Veenschoten

Christmas is to Remember

Every family album has pictures that bring back warm memories of loved ones and friends celebrating Christmas in their special way. To help create your own Christmas traditions, fun, and festivities, we give you this treasure house of ideas. In it are Christmas ornaments, decorations, playthings and gifts, and holiday foods for dinners and parties. All will help make this Christmas the happiest one for you, your family, and your friends.

Contents

A Spirited Family Christmas

With Wonderfully Simple Things

Christmas is a festive time in American families: The tree is trimmed, decorations are made, gifts are lovingly done up in pretty packages, and joy and laughter abound amid the hustle and bustle of our celebrations. It is, above all, a time when young and old alike delight in sharing the activities that give their Christmas its own unique and special spirit.

Homey simplicity is the heart of this family's holiday, from the down-to-earth naturalness of burlap, brown paper, and wooden trims to the old-fashioned charm of the cookie-cutter shapes of the ornaments, the simple stamp-pad designs on the wrapping paper and "ribbons," and the bright fabric bows tied onto the tree. It all adds up to an easy and beautiful Christmas that everyone in the family will enjoy.

Many of the craft projects in this section can be holiday happenings that involve the entire family. Others are so quick and easy you'll be able to pull them off single-handedly—leaving you plenty of time to be with the folks you hold dear.

Instructions for all projects begin on page 16.

Wonderfully Simple Things

Santa's elves couldn't be happier in their work than our spoon doll makers (right). They are transforming ordinary wooden spoons and bits of fabric and trims into whimsical and imaginative gifts for all the children on their Christmas gift list.

1 Use acrylic paints or ink to create your doll's features. Extra touches include powdered rouge for rosy cheeks, and beads and buttons for bright eyes.

2 The clothing pattern is a very easy one. It's so simple, in fact, that after a few demonstrations of how to position the pattern on the fabric, your youngsters can cut their own.

3 Designing costumes for the dolls puts all your creativity into play. Use bits of lace, eyelet, rickrack, ribbon, and even embroidery to spruce up the outfits.

Notice the striking resemblance between our young doll makers and two of their finished products (left). The girls obviously made these dolls "for keeps," but they also made a bunch more for other kids (whatever their ages) to enjoy, too.

The dolls (above) would be perfect one-of-a-kind presents for everybody: nieces, nephews, cousins, school chums, even grandmas and grandpas. To personalize these adorable dolls, design their features to match the recipient's hair and eye colors.

After painting your doll's facial features, paint on the doll's hair, too. Or get fancy and make hair from yarn, cotton balls, or just about anything you can dream up. For bonnets, try bits of lace gathered and glued on, or search craft, hobby, and miniature shops for tiny straw hats to glue on at a jaunty angle.

The three-piece pattern for the doll dress is included in the how-to instructions on page 16. Clothing is made from as little as ⅜ yard of fabric. Arms and legs are cut from unbleached muslin.

You can use the doll clothes as a guide, or turn your artists loose to design their own fashions.

Attach trims to clothing by hand-stitching or gluing them in place. After decorating, stitch up the clothing, and hem and trim the dress bottom. Stuff arms and legs with batting, then attach arms and sleeves to dress. Stitch legs to the lower edge of the dress. Draw "shoes" on the leg pieces with felt pens. Snug the dress to the spoon with a ribbon bow.

For a doll man, stitch the costume front to form pant legs.

Wonderfully Simple Things

Christmas Eve is a time to enjoy the specialness of families and the excitement of children who just can't wait until tomorrow's wee hours. Perhaps the most-treasured moment of all is when good-night kisses are exchanged and final guesses made as to what will be under the tree come morning.

The candle holders on the table (left and above) are the easiest ever, made from chunks of end-grain 4×4 fir lumber. A finishing nail driven into the center of each block of wood will hold your candle firmly in place. Make a bunch in a variety of heights so you can have your own smashing display of candlelight as your family gathers together this Christmas Eve.

The tablecloth here and on page 14 is so clean, crisp, and cheery, you'd know at a glance it was made just for Christmas. Gather family and friends around a holiday table dressed like this one—and ENJOY.

The cloth is made of un-bleached muslin that has bright red borders. Prim Early American designs are stamped on with acrylic paints. To make fabric-printing stamps for the pattern shown here, cut foam rubber stamps the same way as for our printed paper (shown on page 13).

Wonderfully Simple Things

On Christmas morning ordinary homes can look like palaces, filled with all manner of wonderful things. Stockings and packages are part of the trappings—to be enjoyed as much for their cheery Christmas charm as for the treasures they hold.

Christmas stockings are well worth a little extra effort because many of them are used and enjoyed from year to year. In some families, stockings are almost heirlooms, and it simply wouldn't be Christmas unless familiar ones were hung by the fireside or wherever family tradition dictates.

These burlap stockings (below) are cross-stitched in knitting worsted yarns, so they work up very quickly. You can use the patterns (on page 18) for the decorative bands across the foot and along the top, or you can design your own.

Why purchase expensive gift wrappings when you can organize a work party at your house some

pre-Christmas afternoon and have a ball printing your own? If big sheets of paper prove too much of a task, make paper "ribbon" with quaint designs. Simply "tie" it around a brown paper package.

To print on paper like this (right) use a simplified form of old-fashioned eraser printing, but substitute foam rubber to make your custom stamps. Everything else you'll need—such as small scraps of wood, stamp pads and ink, and white glue—is easy to assemble for your paper makers.

The shapes on our gift wrappings are not difficult to duplicate. Use any designs you like, but keep your patterns as simple as possible for best results.

Wonderfully Simple Things

Add zest and joy to your holiday decorating with simple but unexpected touches, such as a little stand of Christmas pines; an apron, pot holder, and paper wall "tiles" (below); and crèche figures that nestle in the manger.

Pine trees (opposite), mixed with Christmas greenery and displayed atop a small chest, are super simple holiday decorations that you can use in dozens of ways. Cut as many trees as you wish from one-inch pine, sand lightly, and arrange in groves.

Handcrafted wall tiles and the apron and pot holder are easy to make—if you plan your design first, then print according to directions for printed paper.

This nativity scene (above and right) is as simple and beautiful as the Christmas story itself. All the figures have been made from one-inch clear pine with just enough detail to identify them. Sanded smooth and waxed slightly, they are as exquisite as many more-elaborate crèches.

Instructions for a Spirited Family Christmas With Wonderfully Simple Things

The instructions below and on the following pages are for the ornaments, decorations, and gifts shown on pages 6–15. For directions for enlarging and transferring designs, see the glossary, pages 370–371.

Pine Ornaments
page 7

Materials: 1-inch C-select white pine (for alternative woods, see page 18); tissue or brown paper; yarn for hanging loops; medium- and fine-grade sandpaper; lacquer thinner.

Instructions: Enlarge the patterns (below) onto tissue or brown paper. Cut out the patterns and trace them onto pine using a pencil.

Cut around outlines of ornaments with a jigsaw and drill a hole at the top of each one. Remove pencil marks with lacquer thinner, if desired, then sand.

Attach a yarn loop through the hole in the top of each ornament and hang.

Note: For additional designs, trace around cookie cutters or cut simple shapes from paper.

Fabric Bows
page 7

Materials: 1 yard of 44/45-inch-wide red print fabric (enough for 24 bows); starch; sharp scissors.

Instructions: Starch fabric until crisp (spray starch works well) and iron smooth. Using sharp scissors so edges of fabric don't fray, cut fabric into 3×22-inch strips. Tie strips into bows on tree branches.

Spoon Dolls
pages 9–10

Materials: Wooden spoons (see note below); fine-grade sandpaper; small scraps of muslin; assorted small scraps of prints, ginghams, and plain fabrics; scraps of lace, ribbon, eyelet, rickrack, and braid; yarn or pompons; acrylic paints in assorted colors, or colored inks; small paintbrush or pen; tissue paper; glue; pillow stuffing.

Instructions: (*Note:* The dolls shown are made from spoons 10 to 12

inches long. For smaller dolls, made with shorter spoons, adjust clothing patterns proportionately.)

Make each head by lightly sanding the spoon and sketching the facial features onto the inside or outside of the "bowl." Refer to page 9 for ideas.

Paint facial features using a small brush, or draw them with a pen. Practice pen strokes on a spare spoon until you know how much pressure to use, because the ink can bleed, making the lines uneven.

Add freckles or beauty marks using a toothpick dipped in paint. Add rosy cheeks using paint or powdered rouge. Paint eyes, or glue on small beads or buttons. Then, paint the hair, or make it from scraps of yarn, cotton balls, or pompons glued to the spoon. For braids, stitch yarn to a piece of felt, making a part in the center. Glue the felt to the head, and braid the yarn.

Enlarge the clothing pattern and transfer it to tissue paper, adding ¼-inch seam allowance. Cut dress and sleeves from about ⅜ yard of fabric, and arms and legs from muslin.

With right sides facing, sew 2 arm

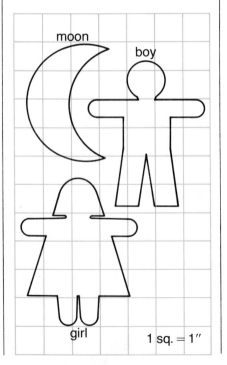

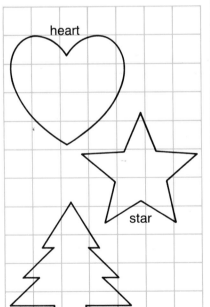

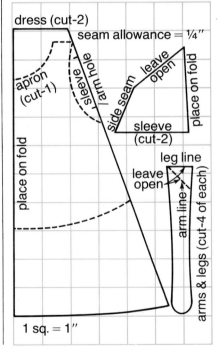

pieces around 3 sides. Clip curves, turn, and stuff lightly. Repeat for all arms and legs.

Sew one side seam on the dress to the armhole. Trim dress with lace sewn along neck and hem, around waist, or on bodice. Trim with beads.

Sew lace to the ends of the sleeves, or gather sleeves into tiny lace-covered cuffs, as shown on page 9.

Assemble the dress by stitching the second seam to the armhole opening. Sew the underarm seam on the sleeve. Slide the sleeve over the muslin arm and pin them together into the armhole. Stitch the remainder of the dress' side seams, catching the sleeve and arm into the seam as you stitch.

Sew muslin legs to the lower edge of the dress. Draw shoes with felt pens.

For a male doll stitch a center seam in the costume to make legs of pants.

Slip the finished dress on the spoon handle, and gather it at the neck with elastic. Tie a ribbon bow at the neckline.

Printed Fabric
pages 10–11

Materials: Good-quality muslin in sufficient quantity for your project; ½-inch-thick scraps of wood; ⅛-inch-thick latex foam (such as Dr. Scholl's Adhesive Foam, available in most drugstores); sharp scissors; white glue; pencil erasers for printing dots; mat knife; red and green acrylic or fabric paints; watercolor brush or small rubber brayer (available in art supply stores).

Note: Foam carpet backing or linoleum scraps may be substituted for the latex foam, but printing surface must be smooth and firm.

General Instructions: To make printing stamps, cut foam pieces into shapes (boys, girls, trees, hearts, houses, etc.) and glue them to small blocks of wood using white glue. Make sure that the edges of each figure are cut cleanly. Use a mat knife to trim small areas if necessary. For easier handling, blocks should be slightly larger than figure to be stamped.

Prepare fabric by sprinkling it with warm water and wrapping in a damp towel. Wait one hour. Stretch fabric flat, straightening out any wrinkles. Lay muslin over a plastic tablecloth on a flat surface, and cover fabric with a damp terry towel. Mix acrylic paints with water to thin them to the consistency of heavy cream.

Fold a corner of the damp towel back to expose the muslin. Place a paper towel underneath the muslin.

If using a brush, wipe excess paint from the brush, and paint rubber stamp surface with acrylic. To use a brayer, pour a little paint onto a sheet of glass or a smooth piece of tinfoil on a cookie sheet. Run the brayer through the paint to coat brayer evenly, then roll paint onto the printing stamp.

Press the stamp onto the damp fabric. If the paint bleeds, then the fabric is too wet. (Practice this technique on muslin scraps before beginning an actual project.) Print larger figures first, then fill in with pencil-eraser dots and other small shapes. Continue unfolding areas and printing.

When fabric is dry, press on wrong side over an old towel; iron slowly to set paint. Fabric may be hand- or machine-washed in warm water.

● *Tablecloth*

Plan a tablecloth to fit your table. Confine the printed area to the overhang of the table in order to make an effective border. To make printing easier decorate a wide fabric strip to stitch to the main section of the tablecloth, as shown in the photograph.

Start printing the design in the center of the border; repeat the design on either side of the center figure as you work to ensure an even border design. Straight lines above and below the pattern are applied freehand with a brush along a penciled guideline.

● *Apron* (see page 14)

For printed apron, use a purchased apron pattern; print each fabric piece before the apron is made up. Print a wide border pattern along the skirt (allowing excess for hemming). Plan pocket and bodice designs from the center out, to make sure design is centered on the pattern piece. Pockets and bodice may be lightly quilted.

● *Pot Holder* (see page 14)

Cut two 9-inch squares of muslin and two 8-inch squares of quilt batting or polyester fleece. Print design on one or both squares of muslin (work design from the center of the square out to the edges). Allow ½ inch for seams.

With right sides together, stitch printed fabric together on three sides (½-inch seam). Turn and press. Insert the batting or fleece and slip-stitch the fourth side closed. Quilt the pot holders by hand or machine, following the lines of the printed pattern. Add a muslin loop for hanging.

Printed Paper and Ribbons
page 12

Materials: Foam printing stamps (see "Printed Fabric" instructions, this page); red and green ink stamp pads; red and green felt-tip pens; brown wrapping paper; ruler; pencil.

Instructions: Using a ruler, lightly pencil a guideline on brown paper. Press a stamp firmly and evenly on the stamp pad, and print a row of figures along the penciled line, re-inking the stamp as necessary.

Draw more lines and print other figures along the rows, alternating patterns and colors as fancy dictates. Work from the top of the sheet down to avoid smudging preceding rows.

Straight lines between rows of figures are drawn with thick and thin strokes of marking pens.

For "ribbons" print rows of figures along a sheet of paper; cut rows into strips. Use double-faced tape for bows.

Cross-Stitched Burlap Stockings
page 12

Materials: (for one stocking) 11×22 inches of natural-colored craft burlap; 11×22 inches of dark green cotton; ⅔ yard of contrasting print fabric for lining; knitting worsted yarn in red, light, and dark green, and in light and dark gold.

Instructions: Enlarge the pattern (below). Add a 1-inch seam allowance to the pattern and cut the stocking front from burlap and the back from green fabric. Stay-stitch along seam lines.

continued

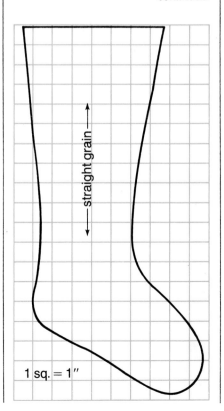

straight grain

1 sq. = 1"

Continued from page 17
Wonderfully Simple Things

Using green or red yarn, work 6 rows of cross-stitches in the toe and 9 rows of cross-stitches across the top. These straight, single rows of stitches should cross 3 threads of burlap. Patterned bands and designs should cross only 2 threads of burlap.

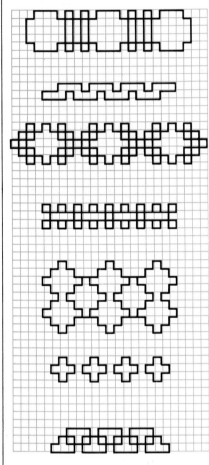

To work the bands above the toe, skip 3 horizontal threads of burlap and begin working the design. Alternate 1 or 2 straight rows of cross-stitches with patterned bands, allowing 3 or 4 horizontal burlap threads between bands and rows. Select band patterns from among diagrams above, or design your own. Patterns may be worked in any color combinations.

The central motif (tree *or* partridge) starts 2 inches above the heel. Top off the central design with a straight row of stitches followed by a trio of bells *or* pears. Add bands and straight rows to fill in the area remaining below the 9 top rows of cross-stitches.

With right sides together, stitch the burlap front to the green cotton back, leaving top edge open. Clip curves and turn. Hem stocking top, line with print fabric, and add loop.

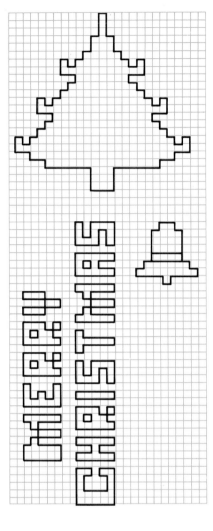

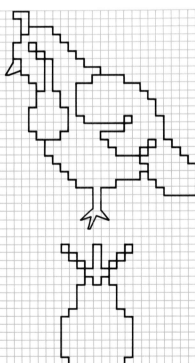

Pine Trees
page 14

Materials: 1-inch C-select pine; medium and fine sandpaper.

Instructions: Using the tree pattern on page 16 as a guide, cut additional tree shapes of different sizes from brown paper. Trace trees onto pine, cut out with a jigsaw, and sand smooth.

Woodworking Tips

If you live in an area where fine furniture woods are available, you may wish to substitute poplar, willow, or basswood for pine in the ornaments and decorations shown in this section. These woods are slightly harder and heavier than pine, so they're wonderfully *easy* to work with—and they frequently have the added bonus of being less expensive than pine.

They're very white woods, which adds to the beauty of a clear finish, and they have fine, even, and generally knot-free grains. Furniture makers like these woods because their grains don't rise during finishing—which makes finishing easier.

Some of the most beautiful wood finishes are also the simplest to apply—such as a coat of old-fashioned paste wax or even clear shoe polish rubbed into wood that's been sanded glass smooth. If you have small children, choose a nontoxic wax.

Or, use a coating of clear shellac. It's quicker and easier to apply than varnish and won't raise the grain of the wood. Dilute it with alcohol, according to the manufacturer's directions. Brush on the first coat; let dry about 10 minutes, then sand with 320-grade sandpaper. Recoat. When the second coat is dry, wax with paste wax and polish to a soft glow.

A word to the wise: Penetrating oil finishes are quick and easy to apply and excellent for hardwoods, but steer clear of them for pine and other softwoods. These woods absorb so much oil that they're apt to be muddy looking and slightly sticky to the touch, a real disappointment when you've put your time and effort into a handcrafted project.

Pine Crèche
page 15

Materials: Two ¾×13¼×11-inch pieces of clear white pine (for alternative woods, see tips, opposite); jigsaw or coping saw; awl, or ⅛-inch drill or drill bit; fine-grade sandpaper; ½-inch-diameter metal tubing, or pocketknife; wood glue; C-clamps or vise.

Instructions: Enlarge pattern (below); trace onto one board. Stack boards atop each other, pattern facing up; clamp. Cut boards along outer edge of pattern, so both are same size.

Cut around the inside perimeter of the top board only, as marked on the pattern. All the crèche figures will be cut from this top piece of wood and will fit together, like a puzzle, inside the frame when the crèche is assembled (the bottom board holds pieces in place).

Glue together the bottom board and the outline of the top board; clamp until glue dries, approximately 3 hours.

Cut out the puzzle pieces (as drawn on the wood) with a jigsaw or coping saw. Lightly sand the pieces until they are smooth; lightly round all corners.

Make the eyes on the people's faces with an awl, or lightly touch the wood with an ⅛-inch drill. Drill the animals' eyes all the way through the wood.

Using a sharpened piece of ½-inch metal tubing, indent small halos above the eyes on Joseph, Mary, and the baby. Press a shallow ridge in the wood as if you were using a linoleum cutter. Curve the ridge into a half circle so ridge looks as if it's a small, narrow halo.

Make 4 shallow cuts in heads of wise men (2 in each direction) to form crowns.

The crèche may be left unfinished, waxed, or shellacked.

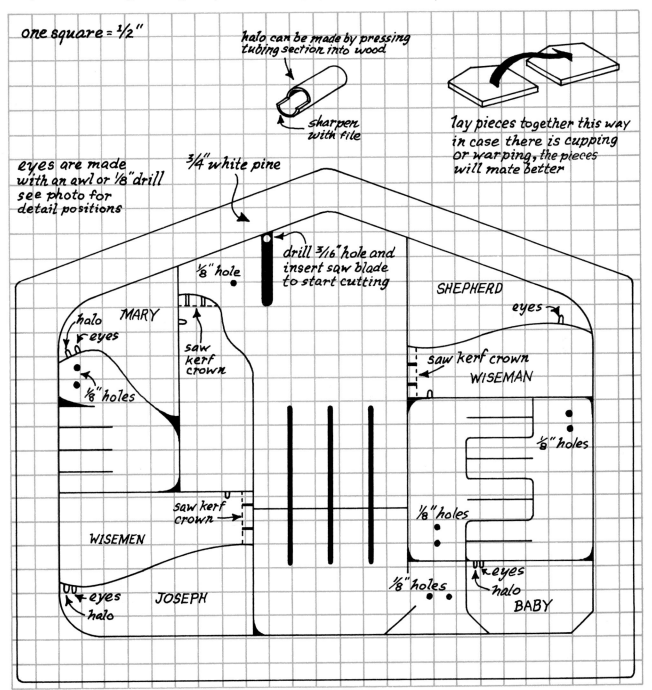

one square = ½"

halo can be made by pressing tubing section into wood

sharpen with file

lay pieces together this way in case there is cupping or warping, the pieces will mate better

eyes are made with an awl or ⅛" drill see photo for detail positions

¾" white pine

⅛" hole

drill ³⁄₁₆" hole and insert saw blade to start cutting

SHEPHERD

eyes

halo
eyes
MARY

saw kerf crown

saw kerf crown
WISEMAN

⅛" holes

⅛" holes

saw kerf crown

⅛" holes

WISEMEN

⅛" holes

eyes
JOSEPH
halo

⅛" holes

eyes
halo
BABY

A Spirited Family Christmas

With A Joyful Celebration of Nature

As free and fanciful as a butterfly, and as colorful as all the flowers in the field, that's the happy spirit of this Christmas celebration. The spectacular tree is bedecked with bread-dough birds and butterflies and yarn-wrapped balls in rainbow colors; the paper-flower wreath and appliquéd crèche banner brighten the fireplace wall. Candle holders (below) are made of rolls of colored jute or macrame cord. Together these decorations are a joyful way to bring the outdoors inside at Christmas. Instructions begin on page 32.

A Joyful Celebration of Nature

Take your cue from Mother Nature and trim your Christmas tree with dozens of bird and butterfly ornaments (above and right). The tree is laden with easy-to-make bread-dough ornaments that you can turn out by the batch. The yarn-wrapped balls add to the dashing display of color, and these ornaments are very simple. Make them by gluing splashy rug and knitting yarns onto plastic foam balls or old glass or satin ornaments that you're ready to recycle.

To make the birds and butterflies, use the recipe for dough on page 34. Roll and cut it into the appropriate shapes, then add antennae to the butterflies and sprightly clove eyes to the birds. Bedeck the birds' necks and tails with additional layers of dough, as shown above. When the ornaments are dry, paint them with bright colors. You can use our birds and butterflies as a guide, or ask your own young artists for their very special designs to duplicate.

Everyone in the family can make yarn-wrapped ornaments. Start with plain or striped ones, then graduate to more elaborate loops and swirls.

To make a patterned ball, plan your design first, then mark the ornament in quadrants with a pen so scallops, circles, or other designs will be evenly spaced. Start with a few stripes at the bottom, then work the pattern around the center, widest, part of the ball, and finish with a few more stripes on top. Or, duplicate the designs on the ornaments at right.

A Joyful Celebration of Nature

We hope the mortar won't fall from the fireplace on Christmas morning if you follow our suggestion to substitute homemade fabric baskets for stockings. These unconventional containers (below and opposite) have two terrific advantages: Santa will be able to stack a lot more inside, and woven baskets like these can be used throughout the year to stash all sorts of things.

Our Christmas baskets can be made in small, medium, and large sizes—although the kids may want theirs big enough to hold a king's ransom! Whatever size you make, if you top off the goodies inside with the lovable lion (above) you're sure to hear some roars of approval. The lion's frizzy rope mane and soft terrycloth body make him wonderfully friendly instead of ferocious.

You can stitch up the lion from a large velour bath towel, and make his mane with just five feet of sisal rope. Use black buttons for eyes or, if your lion tamer is very young, substitute embroidery floss.

When you're stuffing Dad's Christmas basket, include a machine-appliquéd landscape tie like the ones pictured. (Another appears on page 30.) The designs are as fresh as all outdoors and miles away from store-bought tie motifs.

Make these ties using a purchased tie pattern. Cut appliqués from bits of fabric and satin-stitch in place. Then assemble the tie following the directions with the pattern. When you've finished the tie, sign your creation by embroidering your name on the back.

A Joyful Celebration of Nature

Brace yourself for a rafter-rocking "WOW" when you put this whopper of a brontosaurus (opposite) under the Christmas tree. About six feet long, this prehistoric critter is huggable from the tip of his tail to the top of his nose. Two-foot versions of this dinosaur and others, including a stegosaurus (below) and a triceratops, are shown on the following pages.

Was there ever a child who didn't grow wide-eyed at the prospect of meeting a dinosaur? Or who couldn't recite all the names of these fabulous creatures—and their favorite foods? Everything about them seems so much larger than life that it's no wonder they bestir the imaginations of children. If you've been wondering what to give the budding naturalist in your family, one of these magnificent and colorful stuffed animals may be just the thing.

You can make any—or all three—of our dinosaurs in a size to suit your own child simply by enlarging or reducing the pattern on page 38 as much or as little as you wish. Directions on page 37 explain how, and suggest the amount of fabric you'll need for small or large sizes.

After cutting out the pattern pieces, assemble these prehistoric playthings according to the directions below.

To make a brontosaurus, pin both of the body pieces to the mid-bottom section of the dinosaur, right sides together. Stitch them in a ½-inch seam, leaving one side open for turning. Turn the dinosaur right side out and press the seams. Then stuff the dinosaur and slip-stitch the opening closed. (If you use polyester fiberfill for stuffing, the dinosaur will be machine washable and dryable. Shredded foam stuffing can be washed in a machine but should be air-dried. Kapok also is a good stuffing material, but it cannot be washed or dry-cleaned.)

Sew button eyes to the head, and stitch the mouth and feet of the dinosaur with embroidery floss or pearl cotton.

For the stegosaurus, cut the back and tail spikes from felt or fabric. Stitch and stuff the spikes, and then baste them along one body piece of the dinosaur, matching the raw edges. Sew up the dinosaur, turn it right side out, and finish assembling as for the brontosaurus.

To make the triceratops, shown on page 29, cut two horn and collar pieces. Stitch them together, right sides facing, leaving a small opening for turning. Turn the collar right side out, stuff, and slip-stitch the opening closed. Then stay-stitch along the line indicated on the collar pattern and pull the thread tight to make the collar pucker and stand upright. To make the horns stand up, use tight whipstitches to pull the horns upright and secure them to the collar. Stitch, turn, stuff, and complete the triceratops as for the brontosaurus. Finish by hand-stitching the collar to the neck as the pattern indicates.

A Joyful Celebration of Nature

A breakfast table bedecked with fruits, a riot of flowers everywhere, and an abundance of decorations and gifts inspired by nature carry the happy spirit of this family's Christmas all through the house.

Nature lovers will be delighted to discover that the striking abstract designs on the giant pillows (right) are not Picassos but animal tracks that have been enlarged and painted on fabric. To find equally fascinating natural patterns, consult any field guide.

Enlarge the designs you like and paint them on muslin using fabric dyes. Frame the finished paw prints with bright fabrics and assemble them into large, puffy cushions to turn the prints into "natural" winners.

The brightly colored bread-dough butterflies adorning the small tree are another way to bring the world of nature inside this Christmas. And still another is to stencil friendly frogs and insects onto flowerpots and an apron. Purchased stencils were used for these projects, but you could easily design your own dragonflies, grasshoppers, and jumping frogs from a field guide or a child's coloring book. Transfer the motifs to clay pots or fabric using acrylic paints.

The stuffed toys are "naturals," too, but instead of the expected teddy bear, a trio of gem-colored dinosaurs roams the floor. Any of these patterns can be enlarged to create a whopping big dinosaur like the one shown on page 27. Or they can be made up in perky patterned fabric, as was the dinosaur stitched in the ribbon print shown on page 21.

28

A Joyful Celebration of Nature

Why not greet your guests with a feast of color and creativity? To add zest to your entertaining, we dipped into nature's endless paint-pots and produced this brilliant array of projects for you to make.

The needlepoint baskets on the table are stitched from Swistraw ribbon in colors that are as vibrant as a spectacular sunset. Plastic canvas is perfect for these simple-to-stitch bargello designs. It's flexible but sturdy, so baskets hold their shape.

Behind the baskets is a free-form contemporary needlepoint piece in softer, more muted shades. The shapes, colors, and stitches in this project are left to you, so your design will be entirely original.

To create your own free-form design, make an abstract drawing—of a favorite object, perhaps—or close your eyes and gently "scribble" with a pencil on a sheet of paper. Fill sections of the drawing with light, medium, and dark pencil shading. When you're pleased with the balance and shape of the design, transfer it to canvas and work it in assorted light and dark colors and a variety of stitches, including some lacy, pulled-thread patterns. Mount the finished canvas between two sheets of clear acrylic so light can shine through the openwork in the design.

Above the table, our "Rejoice" banner mixes colors and patterns in the same joyful, unrestrained way Mother Nature does. The banner is a stunning 30×84 inches in size, but because it's machine appliquéd, you can make it in just a few evenings.

Instructions for a Spirited Family Christmas With a Joyful Celebration of Nature

The instructions below and on the following pages are for the ornaments, decorations, and gifts shown on pages 20–31. For directions for enlarging and transferring designs, see the glossary, pages 370–371.

Appliquéd Crèche Banner
page 20

Materials: 2¼ yards drapery-weight muslin; 2¼ yards quilt batting; 1½ yards fusible webbing; 1½ yards red fabric; ½ yard each of yellow, white, and red calico fabrics; 1 yard purple polka-dotted fabric; scraps of pink, purple, red, orange, and blue fabric; red and black sewing thread; 1 skein black embroidery floss; 8 yards red hem facing; tissue paper; zigzag sewing machine; brown wrapping paper.

Instructions: Enlarge the pattern (opposite) to size and transfer to brown wrapping paper to use as a placement guide. Think of the pattern as a jigsaw puzzle: All the pieces should be fused into place without overlapping or seam allowances. Careful cutting and placing are important. Use tissue paper to make individual pattern pieces.

Cut 3 main pieces to be appliquéd to the background. From white, cut the whole outline of baby (including head, halo) and Mary's hands. From red, cut Mary's figure, including head, halo, feet, extended arm to wrist. From purple, cut whole outline of Joseph. All smaller pieces are appliquéd to these major shapes, and then the shapes are appliquéd to the background.

Fuse smaller shapes to larger shapes with fusible webbing. Draw facial features and drapery lines with light pencil. Stitch all details, following stitch guide and color suggestions on pattern.

Lay the 3 figures in place on the background fabric and zigzag stitch around all edges. Add manger. Cut and fray yellow woven-fabric rectangles for straw and fuse in place.

Baste polyester padding to the back of the banner and quilt by hand around all shapes, attaching all 3 layers of fabric together. Add red hem tape for trim and make casings for hanging. Insert curtain rod and attach to wall with small hooks or nails for hanging.

Crepe Paper Flowers and Wreath
page 21

Materials: Crepe paper in assorted colors; #16-gauge wire for stems; #26-gauge wire for tying off; scissors; pliers; wire cutter; white glue.

Instructions: Cut one stem wire to desired length, one 6-inch piece of tying wire for flower center, and one 12-inch piece of tying wire for flower.

With crepe paper still folded as it comes in the package, cut strip of paper, cross grain, to desired width (finished flowers are approximately twice as big as width of strips).

Make petals by cutting top edge of folded strips in rounded, pointed, or fringed petal pattern (cut 3 or 4 petals across width of folded strip).

Unfold strip and roll or flute petals to give them shape (hold top edges of paper between thumbs and forefingers and stretch gently). Set aside.

To prepare center, cut a strip of paper about ⅔ the width of the strip used for flower. Prepare edges the same as for flower, or cut a variation. Unfold strip and hold the long uncut edge. Twist and roll paper with one hand while gathering paper and folding it into the center with the other. Make sure bottom edges are even. Increase number of gatherings if center is too tight and decrease gatherings if center is loose. Cut excess paper when center reaches desired fullness, and tie off with several wraps of wire.

Insert end of stem wire 1 inch up between gathered paper and tying wire; secure.

Next, take up petal strip and begin to gather and turn paper (about 6 tight gathers to 1 slight turn) around center, holding the stem wire, the center, and gathers firmly. Use the entire paper strip or cut off when desired fullness is reached.

Wrap base of flower with wire. Pull both ends of wire tight with pliers; twist and wrap excess wire around stem.

Using 3 layers of green crepe paper, cut and shape simple leaf shapes. Large leaves can be gathered at the bottom of flower with #26 wire. Small leaves can be glued to the underside of the flowers, if desired.

Cut 1¼-inch strip of green paper across the grain. Dab glue around the base of the flower and wrap the base and stem with the green strip, stretching downward as you wind. Glue at end.

To make a wreath of crepe-paper flowers, make an assortment of flowers in various colors and sizes. Insert wire stems on flowers into a ready-made wreath of Christmas greens.

Yarn Spool and Macramé Knot Candle Holders
page 20

Note: These candle holders are appropriate only for dripless candles.

Materials: Assorted large spools of yarn (the kind that comes stored on hollow cardboard tubes—available at craft and weaving shops); extra-heavy jute or nylon macramé cord in assorted colors; straight pins; white glue.

Instructions: For yarn spool candle holders, gently push the core tube of a yarn spool from the bottom until the cardboard tube extends about 1½ inches above the top of the roll of yarn. Coat the exposed cardboard tube with a thin film of white glue and wrap the tube with coils of yarn until it is completely covered. Secure the loose end of the yarn with a straight pin.

For woven knot candle holders, simply tie a Turk's-head knot around a 3-inch-high piece of cardboard tubing (cut from a paper towel core or similar tube). If you are unfamiliar with the Turk's-head knot, refer to a good macramé handbook.

Use giant nylon or jute macramé cord, and instead of pulling the ends of the knot tight to form a closed ball or knot, just pull them tight enough to secure the knot around the cardboard tube. Secure the ends of the cord onto the tube with straight pins or white glue. Trim away any excess cardboard.

continued

The actual size of the finished banner is approximately
30x50 inches. Ours was designed to fit beneath a slanted
roof, but the background fabric can be sized to fit any wall
space you choose.

COLOR KEY

Pink	P
Red-Orange	RO
Orange	O
Purple	PL
Dark Orange Dot	DOD
Light Orange Dot	LOD
Red	R
Maroon	M
Pink-Purple	PP
Yellow-Orange	YO
Orange Calico	OC
Lavender	L
Pink Dot	PK
Purple Dot	PLD
Light Beige	LB
Yellow	Y
Black	B

〜〜〜〜 = stitching colors

Black	b
Red	r
White	w

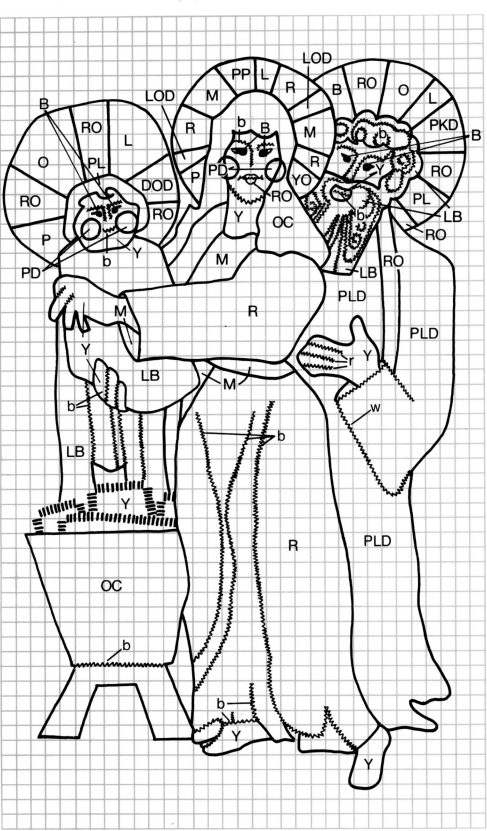

Continued from page 33
A Joyful Celebration of Nature

Bread-Dough Bird and Butterfly Ornaments

pages 22–23

Materials: All-purpose flour; salt; rolling pin; cookie sheet; whole cloves; needle-nose pliers; fine wire; aluminum foil; sandpaper, acrylic paints in assorted colors; watercolor brushes; ½-inch paintbrush; varnish; turpentine.

Instructions: For patterns, use the full-size drawings (opposite) and the photograph of the large bird on page 22. To make the dough, mix 2 cups flour, 1 cup salt, 1 cup water. Knead the dough 2 or 3 minutes until pliable. Roll a portion of dough ⅛ inch thick on a floured board. (Store remainder of the dough in a covered bowl to avoid drying out.)

Using a sharp knife point, cut out dough according to full-size bird and butterfly patterns. Cut bodies and wings of birds separately; cut a pair of butterfly wings as one piece; cut body separately.

For butterflies, cut 2 pieces of 1-inch-long wire and use needle-nose pliers to curl one end of each wire to form antennae. Dip uncurled ends of wires into water and insert about ⅛ inch into center of butterfly, between wings. Moisten the back of the butterfly body, and place it firmly over the middle areas between the wings, with the "head" placed slightly over the inserted antennae. Bend a ¾-inch length of wire into a U shape and insert it into the top of either wing for hanging.

For birds, first cut out body shape. Then bend a 1¼-inch length of wire into a U shape and insert into upper back of bird, halfway between head and tail. Leave at least ½ inch of wire extended beyond the body (loops can be bent to right or left to ensure balanced hanging).

Insert the top of a whole clove into the head for the eye. For the design around the neck area, cut small strips or beads of dough; moisten and press into place. (See the photograph on page 22.) Cut wings, moisten fingers, and smooth edges. Moisten bird's body where wing is to be attached; and press wing in place.

Using spatula move all ornaments onto a cookie sheet. Tips of each bird's wings may be slightly propped away from body with a piece of foil folded several times into the shape of an open matchbook. Wings of butterflies may be similarly propped. Bake ornaments at 200 degrees for 8 to 10 hours, so they dry rather than cook. Allow ornaments to cool thoroughly. Sand edges.

Paint wings and bodies of birds and butterflies with desired acrylic colors. Use 2, 3, or 4 colors, leaving the background neutral. Make butterfly wings symmetrical; paint antennae white. Varnish when paint is dry.

Yarn-Wrapped Ornaments

page 23

Materials: Glass, plastic foam, or satin ornaments; white glue; rug or knitting yarns in assorted bright colors; transparent tape; toothpicks; felt marking pen; gesso (optional).

Instructions: Before beginning to wrap ornaments, paint plastic foam balls with gesso, if desired, so glue will adhere better.

Using tape, anchor yarn to the base of the ornament. Spread glue around base and wind yarn around the center and toward the top. Use wet paper towels to keep fingers clean.

For one-color ornaments, wind same-color yarn from the bottom to the top. For stripes, wind the first color about halfway up, cut the yarn, and start second color. End stripes on same side of ball—this becomes back.

For a more complicated design, wrap ⅓ of the ball as above. Then change colors to make a stripe. Choose a third color and wind yarn into a small circle. Or make scallops, waves, or teardrops. Fill gaps with short pieces in different colors, using a toothpick to push yarn into small spaces. Finish the ornament with another stripe or two above the design.

For a glass or satin ball, glue a metal cap to the top and tie a yarn bow around it. For foam balls, dip the ends of a U-shaped piece of wire in glue and insert them into the ball.

Stuffed Lion Toy

page 24

Materials: 1 gold velour-type bath towel (approximately 24×42 inches) with one rough surface and one velvety side; 1-pound bag of polyester fiberfill; scraps of black and brown felt; 2 buttons for eyes; 5 feet of ½-inch bleached sisal rope; inexpensive rouge; three 6-inch pipe cleaners; pins; adhesive tape; white glue; long needle.

Instructions: Enlarge pattern (right) to size and cut out pattern pieces.

Cut lion top and bottom. Mark eyes, ears, tail, and mane positions on *rough* side of lion top. Mark mane position on *smooth* side of bottom. Pin chin pleat, rough sides together; stitch. Pin nose

pleat, smooth sides together; stitch. Sew lion's rough top side and smooth bottom side together at side seams in a ½-inch seam; trim.

continued

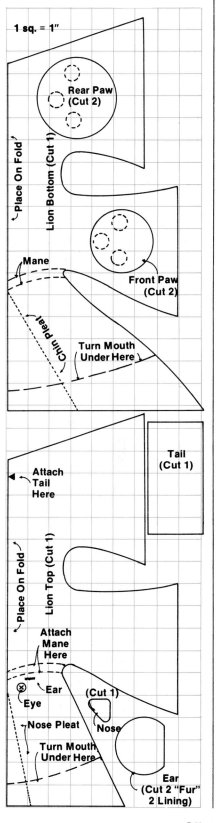

1 sq. = 1"

Rear Paw (Cut 2)

Lion Bottom (Cut 1)

"Place On Fold"

Mane

Front Paw (Cut 2)

Chin Pleat

Turn Mouth Under Here

Tail (Cut 1)

Attach Tail Here

Place On Fold

Lion Top (Cut 1)

Attach Mane Here

Ear

Eye

(Cut 1)

Nose Pleat

Nose

Turn Mouth Under Here

Ear (Cut 2 "Fur" 2 Lining)

Continued from page 35
A Joyful Celebration of Nature

Cut and mark smooth side of paws. Pin paw to inside leg, smooth sides together; pin and stitch paws in place. Turn lion through head opening; stuff.

Loosely stuff head area and chin-pleat cone. Flatten nose pleat to form snout; stitch down. Tuck in raw edges of mouth and pin; hand-stitch mouth into permanent position. Remove pins.

Cut rope into 7-inch lengths. Set aside small amount of rope for end of tail. Untwist rope to make kinky fibers for mane.

Cut one 15×1-inch and one 13×1-inch strip of toweling for mane. Beginning 1 inch from end of 15-inch-long strip, double-stitch fibers of mane down length of strip to within 1 inch of end. Place loose fibers perpendicularly to fabric strip and stitch close together. Glue a scrap strip of toweling over seam line to conceal stitches. Repeat for 13-inch-long mane strip.

Use pins to attach the longer mane piece onto the lion where marked on pattern. Encourage the mane to stand up as you hand-stitch the piece into place. Sew shorter mane strip in place to fill out center portion of mane. Use fingertips to fluff and separate the completed mane. Remove pins.

Cut nose and glue it onto face where marked. Cut out pattern piece for tail. Fold in half. Stitch 3 sides; turn. Braid 3 pipe cleaners and insert them into tail to stiffen. Turn raw edges of tail; insert tuft of rope fiber; stitch to secure fibers and pipe cleaners. Sew tail to body where marked.

Cut ears, stitch round edges, and turn. Fold under raw edges. Pin ears to head, pleating slightly to make ears stand. Hand-stitch in place.

Rub rouge into ears, around mouth and on cheeks, as shown in the photograph on page 24. Cut footpads from felt and glue to paws as marked. Add button or embroidered eyes.

Woven Fabric Baskets
page 24

Note: Materials list and instructions given below are for a 13×13×8-inch basket. Once you have mastered the procedure for making one basket, adapt the instructions to make any size basket you choose.

Materials: 2½ yards of 45-inch-wide fabric; 150 yards of upholstery cord; heavy-duty sewing machine needle; zipper foot; matching thread; large safety pins.

Instructions: Cut fabric into the following lengths: 9 strips of fabric 50½ inches long and 2½ inches wide; 21 strips of fabric 45 inches long and 2½ inches wide.

With right sides together, sew each strip with a ¼-inch seam and turn strips right side out, using a large safety pin. Press tubes flat, so that seam runs down the center of each strip. This will be the *wrong* side of each strip and should always be woven so it faces toward the inside of the basket.

Take one 50½×1-inch stitched strip; set aside for top border of basket.

Cut 2 pieces of upholstery cord for each strip of fabric. Each piece of cord should be *twice* the length of the fabric strip. Fold one piece of cord in half, and run it through a tube of fabric using a large safety pin. With your fingers, spread the cord to each side of the fabric strip, and stitch down the strip using a zipper foot so cord is forced against either edge of the fabric tube. Next, fold the second strip of cording in half, attach to a safety pin, and draw up through the center channel of the fabric tube. Repeat for each tube of fabric. (See diagram.)

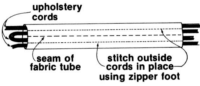

upholstery cords

seam of fabric tube

stitch outside cords in place using zipper foot

On a flat surface, using a simple basket weave (one over, one under), form the base for the basket. Weave eleven 45-inch-long corded strips back and forth across the 10 remaining 45-inch strips. Leave a small space between the strips, and be sure the wrong sides of the strips are facing up so that when the basket is finished all seam lines will be on the inside of the basket. Center the strips to form the bottom of basket.

When you have finished weaving bottom of basket, stitch around the woven area to hold strips in place. Next, take 1 of the 50½-inch-long corded strips of fabric and weave over and under around all 4 sides of the basket, pulling all the side strips of the basket up into a vertical position. Adjust tension and weaving on the 50½-inch strip, trim, and slip-stitch ends together. Weave the remaining seven 50½-inch-long corded fabric strips through the vertical sides of the basket and finish off the same way.

Trim top edges of the vertical strips. Fold remaining, uncorded 50½-inch strip in half; pin over edges of basket. Slip-stitch in place. Remove all pins;

square up basket by creasing strips at corners and bottom edges.

Size of basket may be altered by adjusting length and number of corded strips used to weave it.

Appliquéd Ties
page 26

Materials: Purchased standard tie pattern; 1 yard firmly woven cotton or cotton-blend fabric for each tie; scraps of medium-weight to lightweight cotton for appliquéd scenes; assorted colors of machine thread; zigzag sewing ma-

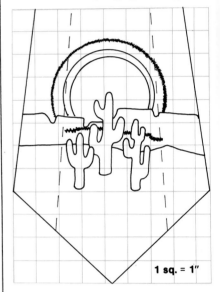

1 sq. = 1"

1 sq. = 1"

chine; pins; small scissors. Tissue paper and interfacing are optional.

Instructions: Cut out the tie pattern according to the pattern directions. Enlarge patterns (below and opposite) for scenes and cut pattern pieces for appliqué design from fabric scraps.

Assemble the appliqué design on the tie, overlapping the pieces where indicated. (Do not turn under raw edges of appliqué pieces; machine satin-stitch will completely bind them.) Center details such as trees, sheep, or cacti on

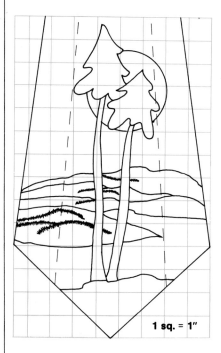

1 sq. = 1"

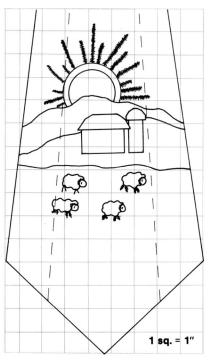

1 sq. = 1"

the tie so they won't be folded to the back. Place bottom appliqué piece over lower fold line so piece wraps around the fold when the tie is completed.

Set zigzag machine for close satin stitch. Sew over the raw edges of the fabric pieces with matching or contrasting colored thread. (If fabric puckers as you sew on the appliqué design, place tissue paper under tie for reinforcement. Tear away paper when you've finished.) Vary width of zigzag stitch to add detail, such as contour lines in mountains, tree branches, additional bands of color around sun and birds.

When all pieces are appliquéd, finish the tie according to pattern directions.

Soft Sculpture Dinosaurs
pages 26–27

Materials: 1 yard cotton or double knit fabric for each small dinosaur; 3 to 4 yards fabric for each larger dinosaur; contrasting fabric or felt scraps for horns, spikes, etc.; buttons for eyes; cotton embroidery thread; fiberfill.

Instructions: Enlarge pattern pieces on page 38 to desired size (small or large version). For small size, 1 square in the grid equals 1 inch; for large size, each square on the grid equals 2 inches. Cut 2 body pieces and 1 bottom section for each dinosaur. Use same or contrasting fabric for bottom section and horns, collars, and back ridges.

To assemble, see page 26.

Paw Print Pillows
pages 28–29

Note: Finished pillow measures approximately 30 inches square.

Materials (for each pillow): 1 package of fabric dye in color of your choice; paintbrush; ½ yard of 100 percent cotton muslin; 2 yards of 36-inch-wide background fabric (we used handkerchief square print); fiberfill; matching thread; handbook of animal tracks.

Instructions: Prewash all fabric. Cut one 16-inch square from muslin and two 31-inch squares from background fabric. Select an animal paw print from your handbook and enlarge it to fit inside a 15-inch square. With a very light pencil, trace outlines of the paw print onto the muslin square.

Prepare fabric dye according to the package instructions. Paint dye within pencil lines and let dry.

Fold raw edges of muslin square under ½ inch and baste. Then, center paw print on background square and topstitch ¼ inch from edge of square.

Make a second stitching line ½ inch from the edge. Back the pillow with the matching square of fabric, then stuff.

Bargello Baskets
pages 30–31

Materials: Several sheets of Columbia Minerva plastic needlepoint mesh (available in 10½×13½-inch sheets); Swistraw acrylic ribbon in assorted colors (either matte or brilliant finish); ruler; scissors; graph paper; permanent markers; needles.

General Instructions: Following measurements and patterns in the individual directions (below), mark and cut out shapes from the sheets of plastic mesh. If a measurement falls in the center of a mesh, continue to the next solid line. Trim all rough edges.

Cut a working strand of Swistraw about 60 inches long, thread it through the tapestry needle, and use it double. Begin at the lower left of the design chart for all patterns except for the cube design, which begins in the center.

On charts on page 39, each graph line represents a plastic filament, and each square a hole or mesh. Work straight bargello stitches, following charts for direction and length of stitches and colors.

Cylinder: From plastic mesh, cut two 4½-inch-wide strips; join by overlapping 4 meshes to make a strip 4½×18 inches. To work sides, follow general directions; work rows of flame stitch pattern across width (short side) of the mesh. Take each stitch over 5 meshes. In assembly, the needlepoint stitches are turned vertically.

Stitch needlepoint down length of 1 strip of canvas, leaving last inch unworked. Then join second strip by overlapping the 2 pieces 4 meshes and stitching through both layers of canvas. Continue stitching down the second strip to within 1 inch of the far end of the long strip. Use color order shown in photograph on page 30, or work in colors of your choice.

One inch from the end of the long strip, overlap the ends by 3 meshes and join the strip into a circle by stitching through both layers of canvas.

Complete the needlepoint, adjusting stitch length of last rows if necessary. Cut a 5½-inch-diameter circle from plastic mesh and attach to the cylinder by overcasting with matching Swistraw every 3 or 4 meshes.

Octagon: Mark and cut eight 6¾×3½-inch rectangles of mesh, according to the general directions.

continued

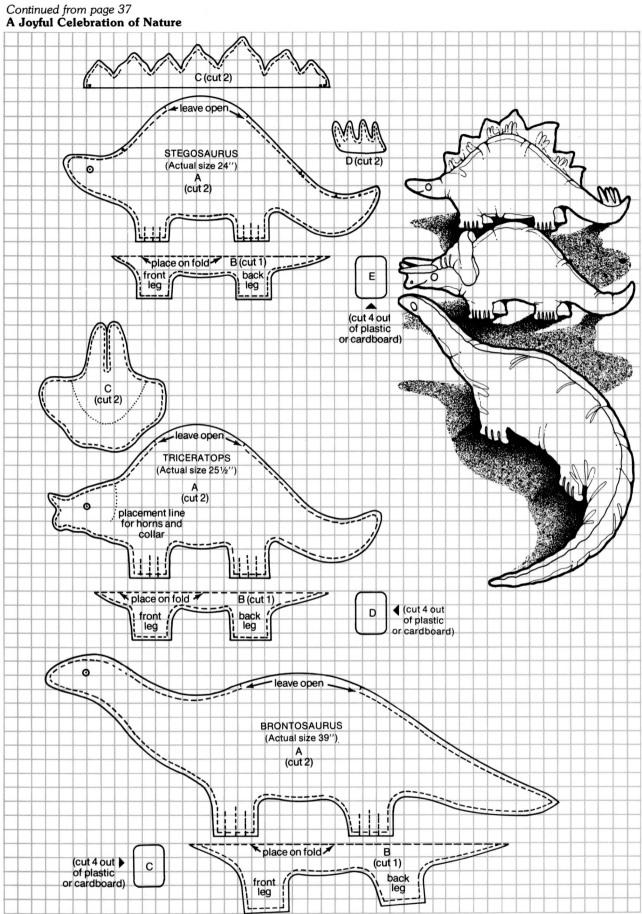

C (cut 2)

← leave open

STEGOSAURUS
(Actual size 24″)
A
(cut 2)

D (cut 2)

→ place on fold ←   B (cut 1)
front
leg

back
leg

E

▲
(cut 4 out
of plastic
or cardboard)

C
(cut 2)

← leave open

TRICERATOPS
(Actual size 25½″)
A
(cut 2)

placement line
for horns and
collar

→ place on fold ←   B (cut 1)
front
leg

back
leg

D

◄ (cut 4 out
of plastic
or cardboard)

← leave open →

BRONTOSAURUS
(Actual size 39″)
A
(cut 2)

(cut 4 out ►
of plastic
or cardboard)

C

← place on fold →   B
(cut 1)
front
leg

back
leg

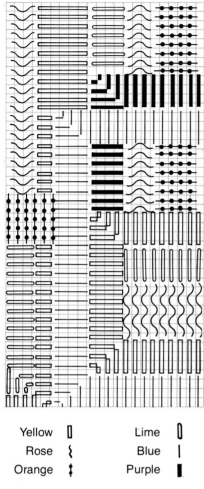

Yellow	0	Lime	0
Rose	{	Blue	|
Orange	‡	Purple	▮

Use the chart and color key (above) as a sample pattern. Complete this panel first, then work variations of color and pattern for each of the 7 additional panels. Study the color photograph on pages 30 and 31 to see how bars of color extend from one panel to next.

Take stitches over the edges of the plastic mesh at the top edges only; at the other edges, leave 1 line of plastic unstitched; it will be covered later when panels are joined. Join completed panels by overcasting along the side edges in matching colors.

To make a base pattern, draw an 8-sided figure, 3½ inches on a side; cut it from plastic mesh. Join it to sides by overcasting along bottom edges of sides in matching colors of Swistraw.

Cube: From sheets of plastic mesh, mark and cut 5 squares, each exactly 40 meshes square (approximately 6 inches on a side).

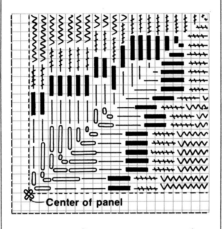

— Center of panel

Color 1	{	Color 4	|
Color 2	‡	Color 5	0
Color 3	▮		

Follow the general directions and the chart (above) to needlepoint each of the 4 sides. The chart represents the upper right-hand quarter of one side. Reverse and repeat the pattern for each quarter of the square.

Begin stitching in the center of the pattern by making a small cross-stitch at the center of the square and working outward. Each side of the square is made in a different combination of the same 5 colors by varying the order in which the colors are used. On all sides take stitches over the edge of the plastic mesh, leaving no mesh showing.

After completing all 4 sides, overcast the sides together on the reverse side of the edges at each corner. For the base, trim 1 line of plastic on each of the 2 adjacent edges of the fifth square, so base will fit easily between sides. Stitch sides to base at corners and in the center of each side.

REJOICE Banner
pages 30–31

Note: Finished size is 7×2½ feet.

Materials: 2½ yards of natural-colored drapery fabric or medium-weight muslin for the background; 2½ yards of white lining fabric; pieces of broadcloth in various colors and prints for vertical stripes and letters; 3 packages of 2-inch-wide red hem tape; fusible webbing; matching thread and embroidery floss; curtain rod.

Instructions: Enlarge the pattern (below) to size. Cut muslin background and matching lining pieces 32×84 inches. Pin vertical strips of broadcloth to the background, and machine- or hand-appliqué around the edges. Cut letters (averaging 12×24 inches) out of broadcloth and arrange on the background. Appliqué in place. Or, iron the letters on with fusible webbing and machine zigzag around the edges.

Sew piece of hem tape across the back of the lining to use as a casing. Sew lining to back of banner with ½-inch seam. Fold the hem tape around the edges and slip-stitch in place. Insert curtain rod or wood strip for hanging.

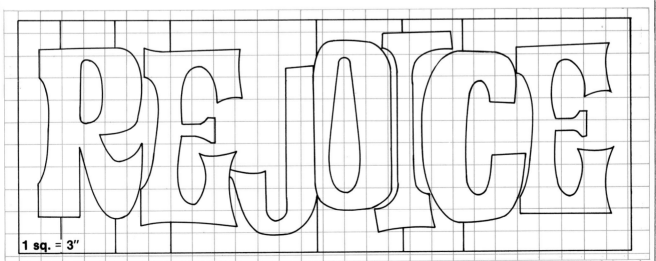

1 sq. = 3″

Traditional Family Cooking

For most Americans the holidays mean getting together with family and friends to share special foods and customs. All across the country families celebrate the season with their own style of food and fellowship. On the following pages we'll show you six meals you can serve to make your holiday gatherings special. Plus we've included a section of recipes for main dishes, salads, and vegetables so you can put together your own menus or fill out a menu you have already planned.

Start with the impressive menu shown at right. It's really a dozen or more meals all in one because you can mix and match each of the three main-dish choices with any of the side dishes. Pictured clockwise from left are Fruit-stuffed Rib Roast, Turkey with Squash Dressing, Cranberry-Glazed Ham, Mushroom-Rice Bake, Sweet Potato-Bacon Boats, Broccoli-Onion Deluxe, Asparagus Casserole, Cheddar-Cabbage Wedges, Sangria Salad *(center left)* and Frozen Fruitcake Salad *(center right)*. See index for recipes.

Christmas Meals

Mix-Match Dinner

Build a dinner by choosing one or more of the options in each category. (See photograph, pages 40–41.)

Turkey with Squash Dressing

or

Cranberry-Glazed Ham

or

Fruit-Stuffed Rib Roast

Sangria Salad

or

Frozen Fruitcake Salad

Cheddar-Cabbage Wedges

or

Broccoli-Onion Deluxe

or

Sweet Potato-Bacon Boats

or

Asparagus Casserole

or

Mushroom-Rice Bake
(See recipe, page 70)

Rolls * **Butter**

Pumpkin Pie
(See recipe, page 188)

Coffee * **Milk**

Sangria Salad

- 2 envelopes unflavored gelatin
- ½ cup sugar
- 1½ cups rosé wine
- 1 cup orange juice
- 2 tablespoons lemon juice
- 4 or 5 drops red food coloring (optional)
- 3 oranges, peeled and sectioned
- 1 large apple, cored and cut into chunks
- 1 cup red grapes, halved and seeded
  Lettuce leaves

In saucepan mix gelatin and sugar; stir in 1½ cups *water*. Cook and stir till gelatin dissolves. Remove from heat. Stir in wine, orange juice, lemon juice, and food coloring, if desired. Chill till partially set (consistency of egg white). Fold in fruits. Turn into a 6½-cup mold. (Or, arrange fruit in a decorative pattern by alternately adding and chilling the fruits and the gelatin mixture.) Chill till firm. Unmold on a lettuce-lined platter. Trim with *Frosted Grapes,* if desired. Makes 8 to 10 servings.

Frosted Grapes: Break ½ pound *red grapes* into small clusters. Dip into 1 beaten *egg white.* Drain; dip fruit into *sugar* to coat. Dry on rack 2 hours.

Frozen Fruitcake Salad

- 1 cup dairy sour cream
- ½ of 4½-ounce carton frozen whipped dessert topping, thawed
- ½ cup sugar
- 2 tablespoons lemon juice
- 1 teaspoon vanilla
- 1 15½-ounce can crushed pineapple, drained
- 2 medium bananas, diced
- ½ cup red candied cherries, sliced
- ½ cup green candied cherries, sliced
- ½ cup chopped walnuts
  Lettuce leaves

In mixing bowl blend together sour cream, dessert topping, sugar, lemon juice, and vanilla. Fold in fruits and nuts. Turn into 4½-cup ring mold. Freeze several hours or overnight. Unmold onto lettuce-lined plate. Garnish with additional candied cherries and lettuce, if desired. Let stand 10 minutes before serving. Makes 8 servings.

Turkey with Squash Dressing

- 1 10-ounce package corn bread mix
- ½ cup chopped onion
- ½ cup chopped celery
- 2 tablespoons butter *or* margarine
- 1 tablespoon all-purpose flour
- 1½ teaspoons salt
- ⅛ teaspoon pepper
- ½ cup milk
- 1 cup shredded American cheese (4 ounces)
- 3 slightly beaten eggs
- 2 10-ounce packages frozen crookneck squash, cooked and drained
- 1 12- to 14-pound turkey
  Salt
  Cooking oil

Prepare and bake corn bread mix according to package directions; cool on wire rack. Cut bread into ½- to ¾-inch cubes. Place in a bowl; let stand, lightly covered, overnight.

In a small saucepan cook onion and celery in butter or margarine till tender but not brown. Blend in the flour, the 1½ teaspoons salt, and pepper. Add the milk all at once. Cook and stir till mixture is thickened and bubbly. Add cheese; stir till melted. Add *half* of the hot mixture into eggs. Return egg mixture to remaining hot mixture in saucepan. In large bowl carefully fold squash and corn bread cubes into cheese mixture. Set aside.

Rinse turkey, pat dry with paper toweling. Sprinkle cavity with a little salt. Lightly spoon some of the dressing into the neck cavity. Pull the neck skin to back of bird and fasten securely with a small skewer. Lightly spoon remaining dressing into body cavity; do not pack. Tie legs together securely at tail. Twist wing tips under back of turkey. Place, breast side up, on a rack in a shallow roasting pan. Brush skin with cooking oil. Insert meat thermometer in center of inside thigh muscle, making sure the bulb does not touch bone. Roast, uncovered, in a 325° oven 4½ to 5½ hours or till meat thermometer registers 185°. Remove bird to serving platter. Let stand 15 minutes before carving. Garnish with parsley, if desired. Makes 12 to 14 servings.

Cranberry-Glazed Ham

1 8- to 10-pound fully cooked
    boneless smoked ham
½ cup chopped onion
4 teaspoons curry powder
¼ cup butter *or* margarine
1 16-ounce can whole
    cranberry sauce
2 tablespoons light corn syrup

Score ham, if desired. Place on a rack in a shallow roasting pan. Insert meat thermometer. Bake, uncovered, in a 325° oven 2 hours or till meat thermometer registers 140°.

Meanwhile, cook onion and curry powder in butter or margarine till onion is tender but not brown. Stir in cranberry sauce and corn syrup; heat through. Brush ham with glaze. Bake ham 20 minutes more. Keep glaze warm. Pass remaining glaze to serve over ham slices. Makes 16 servings.

Fruit-Stuffed Rib Roast

1 4-pound pork loin center rib
    roast, backbone loosened
1 20-ounce can sliced apples
1 pound ground pork
9 slices dry raisin bread, cut
    into ½-inch cubes (6 cups)
1 teaspoon ground cinnamon
½ teaspoon ground cardamom
¼ teaspoon ground allspice

Place roast, rib side down; cut pockets between rib bones. Season with salt and pepper. Drain apples reserving juice; finely chop apples. Add water to reserved juice to equal 1 cup liquid; set aside. In a skillet cook ground pork till browned; drain. Stir in bread cubes, cinnamon, cardamom, allspice, ¾ teaspoon *salt,* and dash *pepper.* Fold in chopped apple. Add reserved apple juice; toss to moisten. Spoon about ½ cup of the stuffing into each pocket of the roast. Spoon remaining stuffing into a 1-quart casserole. Refrigerate. Place roast on a rack in a shallow roasting pan. Insert meat thermometer, making sure bulb does not touch bone. Roast, uncovered, in a 325° oven 1½ hours. Cover loosely with foil to prevent stuffing from overbrowning. Roast 1 to 1½ hours more or till meat thermometer registers 170°. Bake stuffing in casserole, uncovered, with roast during the last 40 minutes of cooking. Transfer roast to serving platter. Garnish with spiced apples, if desired. Serves 8.

Cheddar-Cabbage Wedges

1 medium head cabbage, cut
    into 8 wedges
½ cup finely chopped green
    pepper
¼ cup finely chopped onion
¼ cup butter *or* margarine
¼ cup all-purpose flour
½ teaspoon salt
⅛ teaspoon pepper
2 cups milk
¾ cup shredded cheddar cheese
    (3 ounces)
½ cup mayonnaise
3 tablespoons chili sauce

In Dutch oven or large skillet cook cabbage wedges in a small amount of boiling salted water about 12 minutes or till tender. Drain well. Place wedges in a 13×9×2-inch baking dish.

In saucepan cook green pepper and onion in butter or margarine till tender but not brown. Blend in flour, salt, and pepper. Add milk all at once. Cook and stir till mixture thickens and bubbles. Pour over cabbage. Bake, uncovered, in 375° oven 20 minutes. Combine cheese, mayonnaise, and chili sauce. Spoon atop wedges. Bake 5 minutes more. Makes 8 servings.

Broccoli-Onion Deluxe

2 10-ounce packages frozen cut
    broccoli
2 cups frozen whole small
    onions
2 tablespoons butter *or*
    margarine
2 tablespoons all-purpose flour
¼ teaspoon salt
    Dash pepper
¾ cup milk
1 3-ounce package cream
    cheese, cut up
⅓ cup dry white wine
    Toasted sliced almonds

In saucepan cook broccoli and onions in boiling salted water about 10 minutes or till tender; drain.

In a saucepan melt the butter or margarine; blend in flour, salt, and pepper. Add milk all at once. Cook and stir till thickened and bubbly. Blend in cream cheese till smooth. Remove from heat; stir in wine. Fold in vegetables.

Turn into a 1½-quart casserole. Bake, uncovered, in a 350° oven 30 to 35 minutes. Sprinkle with almonds. Makes 8 servings.

Sweet Potato-Bacon Boats

6 to 8 medium sweet potatoes
1 cup shredded cheddar cheese
¼ cup butter *or* margarine,
    softened
1 teaspoon salt
6 slices bacon, crisp-cooked,
    drained, and crumbled

Scrub potatoes. Bake in a 350° oven 1 hour or till done. Cut a slice from the top of each potato; discard. Scoop out inside of potato bottoms, being careful not to break shell. Set shells aside.

In mixer bowl beat together scooped-out potatoes, ¾ *cup* of the cheese, butter or margarine, salt, and dash *pepper* with electric mixer till fluffy. Fold in ¾ of the crumbled bacon. Pile mixture into potato shells. Place in a shallow baking pan. Bake, uncovered, in a 350° oven 25 to 30 minutes. Top with remaining cheese and bacon during the last 5 minutes of baking. Makes 6 to 8 servings.

Asparagus Casserole

4 cups fresh mushrooms,
    halved
1 cup chopped onion
¼ cup butter *or* margarine
2 tablespoons all-purpose flour
1 teaspoon instant chicken
    bouillon granules
½ teaspoon salt
½ teaspoon ground nutmeg
1 cup milk
2 8-ounce packages frozen cut
    asparagus, cooked and
    drained
¼ cup chopped pimiento
1½ teaspoons lemon juice
¾ cup soft bread crumbs (1
    slice)
1 tablespoon butter, melted

In saucepan cook mushrooms and onions, covered, in the ¼ cup butter or margarine 10 minutes or till tender. Remove vegetables, leaving butter in skillet. Set vegetables aside. Blend flour, chicken bouillon granules, salt, nutmeg, and dash *pepper* into skillet. Add milk all at once. Cook and stir till bubbly. Stir in mushrooms and onion, cooked asparagus, pimiento, and lemon juice. Turn into a 1½-quart casserole. Combine crumbs and melted butter or margarine. Sprinkle atop. Bake, uncovered, in a 350° oven 35 to 40 minutes. Makes 8 to 10 servings.

Swiss Potatoes

5 tablespoons butter *or* margarine
2 tablespoons all-purpose flour
1½ teaspoons salt
½ teaspoon dry mustard
½ teaspoon worcestershire sauce
⅛ teaspoon pepper
3 cups milk
1 cup shredded Swiss cheese (4 ounces)
6 medium potatoes, peeled and thinly sliced (6 cups)
1 4-ounce jar sliced pimiento, chopped
¼ cup finely chopped onion
1½ cups soft bread crumbs

In saucepan melt *3 tablespoons* of the butter or margarine; blend in the flour, salt, mustard, worcestershire sauce, and pepper. Add milk all at once. Cook and stir till thickened and bubbly. Remove from heat. Add cheese; stir to melt. Stir in potatoes, pimiento, and onion. Turn into a 2½-quart casserole. Bake, covered, in a 350° oven 45 minutes. Melt remaining butter or margarine; toss with bread crumbs. Sprinkle over potatoes; bake, uncovered, 30 minutes more. Makes 6 servings.

Cranberry Relish

½ cup raisins
1 16-ounce package fresh cranberries
1½ cups sugar
2 oranges
1 grapefruit

In saucepan cover raisins with water; bring to boiling. Remove from heat; let stand 5 minutes. Drain. Put cranberries through a food grinder, using coarse blade. Stir in sugar. Peel, section, and dice oranges and grapefruit. Stir diced oranges, grapefruit, and raisins into cranberries. Chill overnight; stir occasionally till sugar dissolves. Makes ˜3 cups.

Celebrate Christmas in the English tradition by serving Beef with Yorkshire Pudding.

Boston Cream Pie

1 egg white
¾ cup granulated sugar
1 cup all-purpose flour
1½ teaspoons baking powder
½ teaspoon salt
½ cup milk
3 tablespoons cooking oil
1 egg yolk
1 teaspoon vanilla
Vanilla Cream Filling
Chocolate Glaze

Grease a 9×1½-inch round baking pan; line with waxed paper and grease again. With electric mixer beat egg white to soft peaks. Gradually add ¼ *cup* of the sugar, beating to very stiff and glossy peaks. In mixer bowl stir together flour, remaining sugar, baking powder, and salt. Blend in ¼ cup of the milk, oil, egg yolk, and vanilla. Beat 1 minute at medium speed of electric mixer; scrape bowl. Add remaining milk; beat 1 minute more. Gently fold in egg white. Turn batter into prepared pan. Bake in 350° oven 25 to 30 minutes. Cool 10 minutes; remove cake from pan. Cool on wire rack. When cake is cool, split into 2 layers. Fill with Vanilla Cream Filling. Spread Chocolate Glaze over cake; allow to flow down sides.

Vanilla Cream Filling: In saucepan combine ⅓ cup *sugar,* 2 tablespoons all-purpose *flour,* 1 tablespoon *cornstarch,* and ¼ teaspoon *salt.* Blend in 1⅓ cups *milk.* Cook and stir till thickened and bubbly. Beat 2 *eggs* slightly. Stir *half* of hot mixture into eggs; return to saucepan. Bring to boiling. Cook and stir 1 to 2 minutes more or till thick. Remove from heat; stir in 1 teaspoon *vanilla.* Cover surface with waxed paper; cool without stirring.

Chocolate Glaze: Melt one 1-ounce square *unsweetened chocolate* and 1 tablespoon *butter* over low heat; stir often. Remove from heat. Stir in ¾ cup sifted *powdered sugar* and ½ teaspoon *vanilla* till crumbly. Blend in 2 teaspoons *very hot water.* Beat in 3 to 4 teaspoons additional *hot water,* 1 teaspoon at a time, to make glaze of pouring consistency.

Beef Dinner

Beef with Yorkshire Pudding

Tossed Salad

with

French Dressing

Buttered Green Beans

Swiss Potatoes

Cranberry Relish

Boston Cream Pie

*Coffee * Milk*

Beef with Yorkshire Pudding

1 4-pound beef rib roast
Salt and Pepper

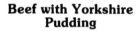

4 eggs
2 cups milk
2 cups all-purpose flour
1 teaspoon salt

Place roast, fat side up, in a shallow roasting pan. Season with salt and pepper. Insert meat thermometer, avoiding bone. Roast, uncovered, in a 325° oven about 2½ hours or till meat thermometer registers 140° for rare, 3 hours or 160° for medium, and 3¼ hours or 170° for well done. Remove meat to heated serving platter; keep warm. Reserve ¼ cup drippings. Increase oven to 400°.

In mixer bowl combine eggs, milk, flour, and salt. Beat with electric mixer 1½ minutes. Pour *half* of the reserved drippings into each of two 9×9×2-inch baking pans. Pour *half* the batter into each pan. Bake in 400° oven 30 minutes. Serve immediately with roast. Makes 8 servings.

Ham Dinner

Raspberry-Glazed Ham

Banana-Peach Salad
(See recipe, page 66)

Swiss Creamed Peas

Pineapple-Potato Boats

Wheat-Corn Muffins

Meringue-Chocolate Pie

Coffee * Milk

Pineapple-Potato Boats

3 medium baking potatoes
½ of a 5-ounce jar neufchatel
    cheese spread with
    pineapple
Milk

Scrub potatoes; prick with fork. Bake in 325° oven 1 to 1¼ hours. Cut potatoes in half lengthwise. Scoop out potatoes, reserving shells. Mash potatoes; blend in cheese spread and ¼ teaspoon *salt*. Beat in enough milk to make fluffy. Pile into shells. Place in a shallow baking pan. Bake in 325° oven 20 to 25 minutes. Sprinkle with *paprika*. Makes 6.

Wheat-Corn Muffins

1 cup whole wheat flour
1 cup cornmeal
4 teaspoons baking powder
2 beaten eggs
1⅓ cups milk
¼ cup honey
¼ cup cooking oil
¼ cup finely chopped onion
¼ cup shelled sunflower seeds

In a bowl stir together whole wheat flour, cornmeal, baking powder, and ½ teaspoon *salt*. In a separate bowl combine eggs, milk, honey, cooking oil, and onion. Add all at once to dry mixture. Stir just till moistened (batter will be very thin). Spoon into well-greased or paper-bake-cup-lined muffin pans, filling ⅔ full. Sprinkle with sunflower seed. Bake in a 400° oven 18 to 20 minutes. Makes about 1½ dozen.

Raspberry-Glazed Ham

1 4- to 5-pound fully cooked
    boneless smoked ham
¼ cup dry white wine
2 tablespoons lemon juice
2 teaspoons cornstarch
⅓ cup seedless red raspberry
    jam
1 tablespoon butter *or*
    margarine

Score ham in diamond pattern, if desired. Place on a rack in a shallow roasting pan. Insert meat thermometer. Bake, uncovered, in a 325° oven 1¾ hours or till meat thermometer registers 140°. Meanwhile, in small saucepan blend wine and lemon juice into cornstarch. Add about *half* of the jam. Cook and stir till thickened and bubbly. Stir in the remaining jam and butter or margarine. Heat and stir till butter is melted. Brush ham with raspberry glaze. Bake 10 minutes more. Spoon remaining glaze over ham. Transfer to heated serving platter; trim with watercress, if desired. Makes 6 to 8 servings.

Swiss Creamed Peas

3 cups frozen peas
1 cup sliced green onion
2 tablespoons butter
    or margarine
1 tablespoon all-purpose flour
1 cup whipping cream
½ teaspoon finely shredded
    lemon peel
¾ cup shredded Swiss cheese
    (3 ounces)

In a saucepan cook peas according to package directions. Meanwhile in a medium saucepan cook onion in butter till tender but not brown. Blend in the flour and ½ teaspoon *salt*. Add cream and lemon peel. Cook and stir till thickened and bubbly. Add cheese; cook and stir till cheese is melted. *Do not boil.* Drain peas. Add to sauce; stir to coat. Makes 6 servings.

Meringue-Chocolate Pie

Pastry Shell (see recipe
    below)
3 egg whites
½ teaspoon vinegar
¼ teaspoon ground cinnamon
½ cup sugar
1 6-ounce package (1 cup)
    semisweet chocolate
    pieces
3 egg yolks
1½ cups whipping cream
¼ cup sugar

Prepare and bake pastry; cool. In small mixer bowl combine egg whites, vinegar, and cinnamon. Beat with electric mixer to soft peaks. Gradually add the ½ cup sugar, beating to stiff peaks. Spread over the bottom and up the sides of the baked pastry shell. Bake in a 325° oven for 15 minutes. Remove from oven and cool on rack.

Meanwhile, melt chocolate in a saucepan over low heat; cool to room temperature. In a bowl beat together egg yolks and ¼ cup *water* till blended. Gradually stir in the melted and cooled chocolate. Spread ¼ cup of the chocolate mixture over the meringue. Chill 1 hour. Beat whipping cream and the ¼ cup sugar to soft peaks. Fold *half* of the whipped cream into the remaining chocolate mixture. Carefully spread over the chilled pie. Spread the remaining whipped cream in a 6-inch circle atop chocolate mixture. Refrigerate 4 hours or overnight. Top with chocolate curls, if desired.

Pastry Shell: In mixing bowl stir together 1¼ cups all-purpose *flour* and ½ teaspoon *salt*. Cut in ⅓ cup *shortening* till the size of small peas. Sprinkle 1 tablespoon *cold water* over part of mixture, gently toss with fork. Push to side of bowl. Repeat with 2 to 3 tablespoons more *cold water* till all is moistened. Form dough into ball. On a lightly floured surface roll dough to a 12-inch circle. Place in a 9-inch pie plate. Trim pastry to ½ inch beyond edge of pie plate; flute edge. Prick bottom and sides of shell with fork. Bake in 450° oven 10 to 12 minutes. Cool on wire rack. Makes 1 shell.

This delicious family dinner menu, planned so most of the work can be done ahead, comprises (clockwise from top right) Banana-Peach Salad (see recipe, page 66), Pineapple-Potato Boats, Swiss Creamed Peas, Wheat-Corn Muffins, Meringue-Chocolate Pie, and Raspberry-Glazed Ham.

Cornish Hen Dinner

(See recipes, pages 50-51)

Sherry Cooler

or

Ruby Spiced Toddy

Cock-a-Leekie Soup

Sausage-Stuffed Hens

Skewered Lamb

Cranberry Chutney

Wheat-Potato Bread

Strawberry Butter

Flummery

or

Brandy Snaps

Tea

Start this hearty Christmas dinner with Cock-a-Leekie Soup (back right), a combination of chicken, carrot, barley, and cream. Sausage-Stuffed Hens (front right) are filled with a walnut and fig stuffing. Cranberry Chutney (front center) is a relish containing cranberries, raisins, and candied ginger. Skewered Lamb (front left) features a kabob of marinated lamb cubes, onions, and green pepper squares topped off with a cherry tomato. For dessert serve Flummery (back left), a creamy custard laced with Drambuie. Other foods that complete the meal are Sherry Cooler (back center), a refreshing appetizer drink, and Wheat-Potato Bread (back center).

Ruby Spiced Toddy

1 32-ounce bottle cranberry
  juice cocktail (4 cups)
2 cups orange juice
1 cup unsweetened grapefruit
  juice
1 cup apple cider *or* juice
½ cup grenadine syrup
¼ teaspoon ground cloves
¼ teaspoon ground nutmeg
• • •
  Stick cinnamon

In a large saucepan combine cranberry juice cocktail, orange juice, grapefruit juice, apple cider or juice, grenadine syrup, cloves, and nutmeg. Heat mixture just to boiling.

To serve, pour hot cranberry-spice mixture into heat-proof glasses or mugs. Garnish each serving with a stick cinnamon stirrer. Serve warm. Makes 8 servings.

Cranberry Chutney

1 16-ounce package fresh
  cranberries
¾ cup packed brown sugar
½ cup light raisins
½ cup chopped celery
½ cup chopped apple
½ cup water
¼ cup coarsely chopped
  walnuts
2 tablespoons finely snipped
  candied ginger
2 tablespoons lemon juice
1 teaspoon onion salt
¼ teaspoon ground cloves

In a large saucepan combine cranberries, brown sugar, raisins, celery, apple, water, walnuts, ginger, lemon juice, onion salt, and cloves. Bring to boiling, stirring constantly. Simmer, uncovered, 15 minutes, stirring occasionally.

Store, covered, in the refrigerator. Serve chilled. Top with walnut half, if desired. Makes 3 cups.

Sherry Cooler

2 cups dry sherry
1 cup orange liqueur
½ cup brandy
• • •
  Ice (optional)
  Lemon-Lime carbonated
    beverage, chilled
  Orange slices (optional)
  Maraschino cherries
    (optional)

In a decanter combine dry sherry, orange liqueur, and brandy. Chill thoroughly. Divide sherry mixture among 8 cocktail glasses. Add ice, if desired. Fill each glass with about ½ cup of chilled lemon-lime carbonated beverage. Stir. Garnish with orange slices and cherries, if desired. Makes 8 servings.

Cock-a-Leekie Soup

1 2½- to 3-pound broiler-fryer
  chicken, cut up
4 cups water
½ cup finely chopped carrot
½ cup finely chopped celery
¼ cup finely chopped onion
2 sprigs parsley
2 teaspoons salt
¼ teaspoon white pepper
1 bay leaf
1½ cups thinly sliced leeks (½
  pound)
1 small potato, peeled and
  chopped (½ cup)
½ cup quick-cooking barley
2 cups light cream *or* milk

In a large kettle or Dutch oven combine chicken and water. Add carrot, celery, onion, parsley, salt, white pepper, and bay leaf. Cover; simmer 25 minutes or till chicken is tender. Remove chicken, bay leaf, and parsley from broth. Discard bay leaf and parsley. Cool chicken till it can be handled easily. Remove meat from bones; discard bones. Chop meat. Skim off excess fat from broth. Add leeks, potato, and barley to soup. Bring to boiling. Reduce heat; simmer, covered, 15 to 20 minutes. Blend in cream or milk and chicken. Heat through. Top with sliced leeks, if desired. Makes 8 servings.

Sausage-Stuffed Hens

1½ pounds mild bulk pork
  sausage
1½ cups chopped celery
3 cups snipped dried light figs
1½ cups chopped walnuts
1 tablespoon ground cinnamon
2 teaspoons salt
1½ teaspoons ground ginger
½ teaspoon ground nutmeg
½ teaspoon pepper
  Salt
• • •
8 1- to 1½-pound Cornish
  game hens
  Cooking oil
¼ cup orange juice
2 tablespoons butter *or*
  margarine, melted
  Parsley (optional)

In a skillet cook pork sausage and chopped celery till meat is browned and celery is tender. Drain off excess fat. Stir in snipped figs, walnuts, cinnamon, the 2 teaspoons salt, ginger, nutmeg, and pepper.

Rinse hens; pat dry with paper toweling. Season cavities of hens with salt. Stuff birds with sausage mixture; do not pack. For each bird tie legs securely to tail; twist wing tips under backs. Place hens, breast side up on a rack in a shallow roasting pan. Brush with cooking oil. Cover loosely with foil. Place remaining stuffing in a 12×7×2-inch baking dish. Cover with foil; refrigerate.

Roast hens in a 375° oven 30 minutes. In a bowl mix orange juice and butter or margarine. Uncover birds; baste with some of the orange juice mixture. Roast, uncovered, 1 hour more or till drumstick can be twisted easily, basting with orange juice mixture. Bake stuffing in baking dish, covered, with birds during last 45 minutes of cooking. Arrange stuffing from baking dish on a heated platter, place birds atop. Garnish with parsley, if desired. Makes 8 servings.

Skewered Lamb

½ cup burgundy
⅓ cup cooking oil
2 tablespoons finely snipped fresh mint *or* 1 teaspoon dried mint, crushed
1 teaspoon salt
½ teaspoon dried thyme, crushed
½ teaspoon dried basil, crushed
2 pounds boneless lamb, cut into 1-inch cubes
1 pound small whole onions, peeled
2 medium green peppers, cut into 1-inch squares
8 cherry tomatoes

In a bowl combine burgundy, cooking oil, mint, salt, thyme, and basil. Add lamb cubes. Cover; marinate 2 hours at room temperature or overnight in refrigerator. Drain meat, reserving marinade. Meanwhile, cook onions, uncovered, in boiling water 5 minutes till crisp-tender; drain.

On 8 skewers, alternate lamb cubes, green pepper squares, and onions. Broil 4 inches from heat 5 to 6 minutes, brushing occasionally with marinade; turn. Broil 5 to 6 minutes more; brush with marinade. Garnish each skewer with a cherry tomato. Makes 8 servings.

Strawberry Butter

1 10-ounce package frozen strawberries, thawed
1 cup butter *or* margarine, softened
1 cup sifted powdered sugar

In a blender container or food processor combine thawed strawberries, softened butter or margarine, and powdered sugar. Cover; blend at high speed till smooth and creamy. Stop blender or processor often enough to push mixture toward blades with a scraper. Makes 2½ cups butter.

Flummery

⅔ cup sugar
⅓ cup cornstarch
½ teaspoon salt
4 cups light cream
2 beaten egg yolks
2 teaspoons vanilla
½ cup Drambuie
8 fresh strawberries with hulls (optional)

In a saucepan combine sugar, cornstarch, and salt. Blend in cream. Cook and stir till mixture thickens and bubbles. Stir about *half* of the hot mixture into egg yolks; return to mixture in saucepan. Bring to boiling. Cook and stir 2 minutes more. Remove from heat; stir in vanilla. Pour into wine goblets. (To avoid breaking fine crystal, place a metal spoon in the goblet before pouring mixture.) Cover surfaces of dessert with clear plastic wrap. Chill 2 hours. To serve, top each serving with one tablespoon Drambuie. Top with strawberries, if desired. Serves 8.

Brandy Snaps

½ cup packed brown sugar
6 tablespoons butter *or* margarine, melted
¼ cup light molasses
1 tablespoon brandy
¾ cup all-purpose flour
½ teaspoon ground ginger
½ teaspoon ground nutmeg
⅛ teaspoon salt
   Whipped cream *or* frozen whipped dessert topping, thawed
   Candied ginger, chopped
   Brandy

In bowl combine brown sugar, melted butter or margarine, molasses, and the 1 tablespoon brandy; mix well. Stir together flour, ginger, nutmeg, and salt. Stir into butter mixture. Drop level teaspoonfuls 4 inches apart onto ungreased cookie sheet. Bake in 350° oven for 5 to 6 minutes. *(Bake only 3 at a time.)* Let cool *2 minutes* on cookie sheet; remove with wide spatula. *Immediately* roll each cookie to form a cone. (Reheat in oven for about 30 seconds if cookies harden before they are rolled.) Cool completely; store in airtight container. Just before serving, combine whipped cream and chopped candied ginger; flavor to taste with brandy. Use to fill cookies. Makes 60.

Wheat-Potato Bread

1 medium potato, peeled and finely chopped (¾ cup)
1½ cups buttermilk
• • •
2 packages active dry yeast
3 tablespoons sugar
2 tablespoons shortening
1 tablespoon salt
3 to 3½ cups all-purpose flour
2½ cups whole wheat flour
• • •
   Cornmeal
   Buttermilk

In a saucepan cook chopped potato in the 1½ cups buttermilk, uncovered, 15 minutes or till tender. (Milk will appear curdled.) Cool milk mixture to lukewarm (115° to 120°). Set aside ½ cup of the liquid. Mash potato in the remaining liquid; add *warm water* to make 2 cups potato mixture.

In large mixer bowl soften the yeast in the ½ cup reserved liquid. Add potato mixture, sugar, shortening, and salt; mix well. Stir in *2 cups* of the all-purpose flour. Beat at low speed of electric mixer for ½ minute, scraping sides of bowl constantly. Beat 3 minutes more at high speed. Cover; let rise in warm place till double (45 minutes). Stir dough down; add whole wheat flour and as much of the remaining all-purpose flour as you can stir in using a spoon. Turn out onto a lightly floured surface; knead in the remaining all-purpose flour to make a moderately stiff dough. Continue to knead dough till smooth and elastic (10 minutes). Shape into a ball. Place in a greased bowl, turning once to grease surface. Cover; let rise till double (35 minutes). Punch dough down; turn out onto lightly floured surface. Divide dough in half. Cover; let rest 10 minutes.

Shape each half into an 8-inch round loaf. Sprinkle a greased baking sheet with cornmeal. Place loaves on baking sheet. Cover; let rise till double. Brush tops lightly with buttermilk and dust with cornmeal. Bake in a 375° oven 30 to 35 minutes. Cool on a wire rack. Makes 2 loaves.

Pork Dinner

Apricot Crown Roast

Cucumber Ring
(See recipe, page 64)

Cauliflower Scallop
(See recipe, page 70)

Sweet Potato Soufflé

Regal Plum Pudding

with

Fluffy Hard Sauce

Demitasse

Sweet Potato Soufflé

1½ **pounds sweet potatoes**
 (about 2 large)
2 **tablespoons chopped onion**
¼ **cup butter *or* margarine**
¼ **cup all-purpose flour**
1 **teaspoon salt**
 Dash ground nutmeg
 Dash pepper
¾ **cup milk**
4 **well-beaten egg yolks**
4 **egg whites**

In a saucepan cook sweet potatoes in boiling water 30 to 40 minutes or till tender. Peel sweet potatoes; mash. Measure 2 cups, set aside.

In a saucepan cook onion in butter or margarine till tender but not brown. Blend in flour, salt, nutmeg, and pepper. Stir in milk. Cook and stir till mixture thickens and bubbles. Stir in mashed sweet potatoes; mix well. Add *half* of the hot mixture to egg yolks, stirring constantly. Return to remaining hot mixture; mix well. Set aside.

In large mixer bowl beat egg whites till stiff peaks form. Fold into potato mixture. Spoon into 1½-quart soufflé dish. Bake in a 350° oven about 45 minutes or till a knife inserted just off-center comes out clean. Makes 6 servings.

Regal Plum Pudding

4 **slices bread, torn into pieces**
1 **cup milk**
6 **ounces beef suet, ground**
1 **cup packed brown sugar**
2 **slightly beaten eggs**
¼ **cup orange juice**
1 **teaspoon vanilla**
2 **cups raisins**
1 **cup snipped pitted dates**
½ **cup diced mixed candied**
 fruits and peels
½ **cup chopped walnuts**
1 **cup all-purpose flour**
2 **teaspoons ground cinnamon**
1 **teaspoon ground cloves**
1 **teaspoon ground mace**
1 **teaspoon baking soda**
½ **teaspoon salt**
 Fluffy Hard Sauce (see
 recipe, below)

Soak bread in milk and beat to break up. Stir in ground suet, brown sugar, eggs, orange juice, and vanilla. In bowl combine raisins, dates, candied fruits and peels, and nuts. Stir together flour, cinnamon, cloves, mace, baking soda, and salt; add to the mixed fruits and mix well. Stir in bread-suet mixture. Pour into well-greased 2-quart mold (do not use ring mold or tube pan). Cover with foil and tightly tie foil on using string.

Place the mold on rack in deep kettle; add boiling water to the kettle to a depth of 1 inch. Cover and steam the pudding 3½ hours; add more boiling water if needed. Cool the pudding about 10 minutes before removing from the mold. Serve the pudding with Fluffy Hard Sauce. Makes 16 servings.

Fluffy Hard Sauce

2 **cups sifted powdered sugar**
½ **cup butter *or* margarine,**
 softened
1 **beaten egg yolk**
1 **teaspoon vanilla**
1 **egg white**

In mixer bowl cream together sugar and butter or margarine with electric mixer. Beat in egg yolk and vanilla. Set aside. Wash beaters. Beat egg white till stiff peaks form. Gently fold into butter mixture. Cover; chill. Makes 1¾ cups.

Apricot Crown Roast

1 **5½- to 6-pound pork rib**
 crown roast (12 to 16 ribs)
1 **tablespoon sugar**
1 **teaspoon instant chicken**
 bouillon granules
¾ **cup hot water**
¼ **cup snipped dried apricots**
4 **cups dry whole wheat bread**
 cubes (5½ slices)
1 **large apple, peeled, cored,**
 and chopped
½ **teaspoon finely shredded**
 orange peel
½ **teaspoon salt**
½ **teaspoon ground sage**
¼ **teaspoon ground cinnamon**
⅛ **teaspoon pepper**
½ **cup chopped celery**
¼ **cup chopped onion**
¼ **cup butter *or* margarine**
¼ **cup orange juice**
1 **tablespoon light corn syrup**
½ **teaspoon soy sauce**

Place roast, bone tips up, on rack in shallow roasting pan. Season with a little salt and pepper. Make a ball of aluminum foil and press into cavity to hold it open. Wrap bone tips with foil. Insert meat thermometer, making sure bulb does not touch bone. Roast, uncovered, in 325° oven 2½ hours.

Meanwhile, prepare stuffing. Dissolve sugar and bouillon granules in hot water; pour over apricots. Let stand 5 minutes. In large bowl combine bread cubes, apple, orange peel, salt, sage, cinnamon, and pepper. In saucepan cook celery and onion in butter or margarine till tender; add to bread mixture. Add apricot mixture; toss lightly to moisten. (If desired, add ¼ cup additional water for a moister stuffing.)

Remove all foil from roast. Pack stuffing lightly into center of roast, mounding high, do not pack. Combine orange juice, corn syrup, and soy sauce; spoon some over meat. Roast, uncovered, 45 to 60 minutes more or till thermometer registers 170°; baste occasionally with orange juice mixture. Carefully transfer to heated serving platter. Garnish with canned apricot halves, if desired. Slice between ribs to serve. Serves 12 to 16.

This spectacular entreé will add elegance to any holiday meal. Apricot Crown Roast features a stuffing of whole wheat bread, apple, and apricots, and is brushed with an orange juice and soy sauce glaze.

Lamb Dinner

Zippy Tomato Appetizer

Cauliflower Salad Bowl

Leg of Lamb Italian

with

Potato-Sausage Dressing

Green Beans Almond

Cherry Blossom Muffins
(See photograph, page 65)

Lane Cake

*Coffee * Milk*

Cherry Blossom Muffins
see photograph, page 65

¼ cup sugar
2 tablespoons all-purpose flour
½ teaspoon ground nutmeg
1 tablespoon butter *or* margarine
1 egg
⅔ cup orange juice
2 tablespoons sugar
2 tablespoons cooking oil
2 cups packaged biscuit mix
½ cup chopped pecans
½ cup cherry preserves

In small mixing bowl stir together the ¼ cup sugar, flour, and nutmeg. Cut in butter or margarine till mixture is crumbly. Set aside.

In a bowl combine egg, orange juice, the 2 tablespoons sugar, and cooking oil. Add biscuit mix; beat vigorously for 30 seconds. Stir in pecans. Fill greased or paper-bake-cup-lined muffin cups ⅓ *full* with batter. Top each with *2 teaspoons* cherry preserves. Cover with remaining batter till ⅔ full. Sprinkle with nutmeg mixture. Bake in a 400° oven 20 to 25 minutes. Makes 12.

Green Beans Almond

3 9-ounce packages French-style green beans (4½ cups)
¼ cup slivered almonds
¼ cup butter *or* margarine, melted
2 teaspoons lemon juice

In a large saucepan cook green beans according to package directions. Drain beans. In a saucepan cook almonds in melted butter or margarine till golden, stirring occasionally. Remove from heat; add lemon juice. Pour almond mixture over beans. Serves 8 to 10.

Leg of Lamb Italian

⅓ cup lemon juice
¼ cup cooking oil
1 tablespoon dried oregano, crushed
2 teaspoons chopped anchovies
1 teaspoon salt
1 teaspoon dry mustard
½ teaspoon garlic powder
1 5- to 6-pound lamb leg
¼ cup cold water
¼ cup all-purpose flour
10 canned pear halves (optional)
Strawberry jelly (optional)

For marinade, in a bowl combine lemon juice, cooking oil, oregano, anchovies, salt, mustard, and garlic powder. Place lamb in a large plastic bag; set in a deep bowl. Pour marinade over lamb in bag; close. Marinate in refrigerator overnight, pressing bag against meat occasionally. Drain, reserving marinade. Place meat, fat side up, on rack in shallow roasting pan. Insert meat thermometer, making sure it does not touch bone. Roast, uncovered, in 325° oven 3 to 3½ hours or till meat thermometer registers 175° to 180°. Baste occasionally with marinade.

Remove lamb to serving platter. Keep warm. Skim fat from pan drippings; pour drippings into measuring cup. Add enough of the reserved marinade to make 2¼ cups liquid. Blend the cold water into flour; stir into marinade mixture. Cook and stir till thickened and bubbly. If desired, arrange pear halves on platter with lamb. Fill pear hollows with strawberry jelly. Garnish with a twisted orange slice and parsley, if desired. Pass sauce with roast. Makes 8 to 10 servings.

Zippy Tomato Appetizer

1 10½-ounce can condensed beef broth
½ teaspoon dried marjoram, crushed

• • •

1 46-ounce can vegetable juice cocktail
2 tablespoons lemon juice
Dash garlic powder

• • •

Lemon slices (optional)

In a saucepan simmer beef broth and marjoram together 5 minutes; cool. Combine with vegetable juice cocktail, lemon juice, and garlic powder. Cover and chill.

Serve in a punch bowl. Float lemon slices atop, if desired. Makes 15 four-ounce servings.

Cauliflower Salad Bowl

1 small head cauliflower, broken into flowerets

• • •

½ large bermuda onion, sliced and separated into rings
½ cup sliced pimiento-stuffed olives
⅔ cup French salad dressing

• • •

1 small head iceberg lettuce, torn (4 cups)
½ cup crumbled blue cheese (2 ounces)
French dressing (optional)

Slice cauliflowerets. In a large salad bowl combine cauliflower slices, onion rings, and olives. Pour the ⅔ cup French dressing over. Toss to coat vegetables. Cover and refrigerate 30 minutes.

Just before serving, add iceberg lettuce and crumbled blue cheese; toss lightly. Pass extra French dressing, if desired. Makes 8 to 10 servings.

Leg of Lamb Italian *will win applause from all your hungry guests.*

Lane Cake

2¼ cups sugar
1½ cups butter *or* margarine
2 teaspoons vanilla
• • •
3⅓ cups sifted cake flour
4½ teaspoons baking powder
1½ teaspoons salt
1½ cups milk
8 egg whites
• • •
Lane Cake Filling (see recipe, left)
Fluffy White Frosting (see recipe, below)

In mixer bowl cream sugar and butter or margarine with electric mixer till light and fluffy. Add vanilla. Mix well.

In a bowl sift together flour, baking powder, and salt. Add to creamed mixture alternately with milk, beating after each addition. Set aside. Wash beaters. Beat egg whites till stiff peaks form. Fold into batter.

Pour batter into 3 greased and lightly floured 9×1½-inch round baking pans. Bake in a 375° oven 18 to 20 minutes. Cool 10 minutes; remove from pans. Cool thoroughly on wire rack. Spread *two* cake layers with half each‚ of the Lane Cake Filling. Stack layers filling side up. Top with remaining cake layer rounded side up. Frost with Fluffy White Frosting. Cover, refrigerate any leftover cake.

Potato-Sausage Dressing

1 pound bulk pork sausage
1 cup chopped onion
¾ cup finely chopped celery
1 teaspoon poultry seasoning
¼ teaspoon pepper
  Packaged instant mashed potatoes (enough for 8 servings)
2 eggs

In skillet cook sausage, onion, and celery till sausage is browned and vegetables are tender; drain. Stir in poultry seasoning and pepper. Prepare potatoes according to package directions, *except* reduce salt to ½ *teaspoon.* Beat in eggs. Stir potatoes into meat mixture. Turn into a 2-quart casserole. Bake, covered, in a 325° oven 30 minutes. Makes 6 cups dressing.

Lane Cake Filling

¾ cup sugar
6 tablespoons butter *or* margarine
3 tablespoons bourbon
2 tablespoons water
6 slightly beaten egg yolks
• • •
¾ cup finely chopped raisins
½ cup chopped pecans
⅓ cup flaked coconut
½ teaspoon vanilla

In saucepan combine sugar, butter or margarine, bourbon, and water. Bring just to boiling; stir to dissolve sugar and melt butter. Stir *half* of the hot mixture into egg yolks; return to hot mixture in saucepan. Cook till bubbly. Cook and stir about 3 minutes more or till thickened; remove from heat. Stir in raisins, pecans, coconut, and vanilla. Cover surface with clear plastic wrap. Chill thoroughly. Makes 2 cups.

Fluffy White Frosting

1 cup sugar
⅓ cup water
¼ teaspoon cream of tartar
  Dash salt
2 egg whites
1 teaspoon vanilla

In saucepan combine sugar, water, cream of tartar, and salt. Bring to boiling, stirring till sugar dissolves. Very slowly add sugar syrup to egg whites in mixer bowl, beating constantly with electric mixer about 7 minutes or till stiff peaks form. Beat in vanilla.

Recipes To Round Out the Meal

Roast Chicken or Turkey

To roast a chicken or turkey: Rinse bird and pat dry with paper toweling. Rub inside of cavity with *salt,* if desired. Do not stuff bird till just before cooking.

To stuff bird: Prepare any of the stuffing recipes on this page. Spoon some of the stuffing loosely into neck cavity; pull the neck skin to back of the bird and fasten securely with a skewer. Spoon remaining stuffing into the body cavity; do not pack. If opening has a band of skin across tail, tuck drumsticks under band. If band is not present, tie legs securely to tail. Twist wing tips under back.

For unstuffed bird: Place quartered *onions* and *celery* in body cavity, if desired.

Roasting directions: Place bird, breast side up, on rack in shallow roasting pan. Brush skin with *cooking oil.* To use meat thermometer, insert in center of inside thigh muscle, making sure bulb does not touch bone.

Roast in uncovered pan (unless otherwise specified) according to the chart on next page. When bird is two-thirds done, cut band of skin or string between legs so thighs will cook evenly. Continue roasting till bird is done. Meat thermometer should register 185°. Also, the thickest part of drumstick should feel very soft when pressed with fingers protected with paper toweling. The drumstick should move up and down and should twist easily in the socket. Remove bird from oven; cover loosely with foil to keep warm. Let stand 15 minutes before carving.

Holiday Rice Stuffing

1 cup grated carrot
½ cup chopped green onion
½ cup chopped parsley
2 tablespoons butter, melted
1 cup long grain rice
3 cups chicken broth

In saucepan cook and stir carrot, onion, and parsley in butter 10 minutes. Stir in rice; add chicken broth, ½ teaspoon *salt,* and dash *pepper.* Simmer, covered, 20 minutes or till rice is done. Use to stuff two 2½- to 3-pound roasting chickens. Makes about 5 cups stuffing.

Oyster-Corn Stuffing

4 cups soft bread cubes
2 cups corn bread stuffing mix
2 tablespoons chopped onion
1½ teaspoons ground sage
1 10-ounce can frozen oysters, thawed
¼ cup butter, melted

In large bowl mix bread cubes, stuffing mix, onion, sage, 1 teaspoon *salt,* and dash *pepper.* Drain oysters, saving ½ cup liquid. Chop oysters; add to bread mixture with reserved oyster liquid, butter, and ¼ cup *water.* Toss to mix. Use to stuff an 8-pound turkey (or two 3- to 4-pound roasting chickens), or bake, covered, in 2-quart casserole in 325° oven 35 minutes. Makes 6 cups.

Potato Dressing

¾ cup chopped onion
¼ cup chopped celery
¼ cup butter *or* margarine
2 medium potatoes, cooked and mashed (2 cups)
1½ cups soft bread crumbs
2 beaten eggs
2 tablespoons snipped parsley
¾ teaspoon salt
½ teaspoon dried marjoram, crushed
⅛ teaspoon pepper

In skillet cook onion and celery in butter till tender but not brown. Combine with remaining ingredients; mix thoroughly. Use to stuff a 4- to 5-pound roasting chicken, or bake, covered, in a 1-quart casserole in a 325° oven about 45 minutes. Makes 3 cups stuffing.

Grandma's Chestnut Stuffing

1 pound fresh chestnuts
1½ pounds ground beef
½ pound bulk pork sausage
1 cup chopped onion
1 cup chopped celery
3½ cups turkey *or* chicken broth
1 cup long grain rice
1 cup raisins
½ cup slivered almonds *or* pine nuts
2 tablespoons turkey *or* chicken drippings (optional)
1½ teaspoons salt
1 teaspoon ground cinnamon
¼ teaspoon pepper
2 beaten eggs

Cut a slash in chestnuts with a sharp knife. Roast on baking sheet in 450° oven for 5 to 6 minutes; cool. Peel and coarsely chop. In a 12-inch skillet cook ground beef, sausage, onion, and celery till meat is browned and vegetables are tender. Drain off fat. Add *3 cups* of the broth, chestnuts, uncooked rice, raisins, almonds or pine nuts, drippings, salt, cinnamon, and pepper. Cover; simmer for 30 minutes. Remove from heat. Combine remaining ½ cup broth and eggs; stir into meat-rice mixture. Use to stuff a 16- to 18-pound turkey, or bake, covered, in two 1½-quart casseroles in 325° oven for 30 to 35 minutes. Makes about 9 cups.

Old-Fashioned Bread Stuffing

½ cup chopped onion
½ cup butter *or* margarine
1 teaspoon poultry seasoning *or* ground sage
½ teaspoon salt
⅛ teaspoon pepper
8 cups dry bread cubes
1 cup chicken broth *or* water

Cook onion in butter or margarine till tender; add poultry seasoning or sage, salt, and pepper. Combine with bread cubes. Drizzle with broth or water; toss to mix well. Use to stuff a 10-pound turkey (or two 4- to 5-pound roasting chickens), or bake, covered, in a 2-quart casserole in 325° oven for 40 to 45 minutes. Makes 6 to 7 cups.

Serve roast chickens and Holiday Rice Stuffing *with orange shells and candied cranberries.*

POULTRY ROASTING CHART

Poultry	Ready-to-Cook Weight	Oven Temp.	Guide to Roasting Time	Special instructions
Chicken	1½-2 lbs.	400°	1-1¼ hrs.	Brush dry areas of skin occasionally with pan drippings. Cover chicken loosely with foil.
	2½-3 lbs.	375°	1¼-1½ hrs.	
	3½-4 lbs.	375°	1¾-2 hrs.	
	4½-5 lbs.	375°	2¼-2½ hrs.	
Turkey	6- 8 lbs.	325°	3½-4 hrs.	Cover bird loosely with foil. Press lightly at the end of drumsticks and neck; leave air space between bird and foil. Baste bird occasionally, if desired. Roast, uncovered, the last 45 minutes.
	8-12 lbs.	325°	4-4½ hrs.	
	12-16 lbs.	325°	4½-5½ hrs.	
	16-20 lbs.	325°	5½-6½ hrs.	
	20-24 lbs.	325°	6½-7½ hrs.	

Roasting directions: Rinse bird; pat dry with paper toweling. Season and stuff bird according to directions on page 56. Place bird, breast side up, on a rack in a shallow roasting pan. Brush skin with cooking oil. To use meat thermometer, insert in center of inside thigh muscle, making sure bulb does not touch bone. Roast in uncovered pan (unless specified) according to chart. When bird is two-thirds done, cut band of skin or string between legs so thighs will cook evenly. Continue roasting till bird is done. Meat thermometer should register 185°. Also, the thickest part of drumstick should feel very soft when pressed with fingers protected with paper toweling. The drumstick should move up and down and twist easily in the socket. Remove bird from oven; cover loosely with foil to keep warm. Let stand 15 minutes before carving.

Chicken Saltimbocca

3 whole large chicken breasts, skinned, boned, and halved lengthwise
6 thin slices boiled ham
6 slices process Swiss cheese
1 medium tomato, peeled, seeded, and chopped
Dried sage, crushed
⅓ cup fine dry bread crumbs
2 tablespoons grated parmesan cheese
2 tablespoons snipped parsley
¼ cup butter *or* margarine, melted

Place chicken, boned side up, between two pieces clear plastic wrap. Working out from the center, pound each lightly with meat mallet to 5½×5½ inches. Remove wrap. Place a ham slice and a cheese slice on each cutlet, cutting to fit within ¼ inch of edges. Top with some tomato; sprinkle lightly with sage. Fold in sides; roll up jelly-roll fashion, pressing to seal well. Combine crumbs, parmesan, and parsley. Dip chicken into butter, then roll in crumbs. Bake in shallow baking pan in 350° oven for 40 to 45 minutes. Remove to heated platter. Blend mixture remaining in pan till smooth; serve over chicken. Serves 6.

Chicken Breasts Amandine

¼ cup all-purpose flour
1½ teaspoons salt
½ teaspoon paprika
⅛ teaspoon pepper
3 tablespoons dry sherry
2 tablespoons butter *or* margarine, melted
2 whole large chicken breasts, halved lengthwise (2½ pounds)
⅓ to ½ cup sliced almonds

Combine flour, salt, paprika, and pepper. Combine sherry and butter. Coat chicken with flour mixture; then dip both sides into sherry mixture. Sprinkle both sides of chicken with nuts; pat firmly to stick. Place, skin side up, in a greased shallow baking pan. Bake, covered, in 375° oven for 20 minutes. Uncover; bake for 20 to 25 minutes more or till golden. Makes 4 servings.

Apple-Spiced Chicken Broil

1 2½- to 3-pound broiler-fryer chicken, quartered
Cooking oil
¼ cup apple jelly
1 tablespoon lemon juice
½ teaspoon ground allspice

Preheat broiler. Break joints of chicken; brush with oil. Season with a little salt and pepper. Place, skin side down, in broiler pan. Broil 5 to 6 inches from heat about 20 minutes or till lightly browned. Turn; broil for 15 to 20 minutes more or till tender.

Meanwhile, in small saucepan melt jelly over low heat. Stir in lemon juice and allspice. Brush chicken with *half* the glaze; broil 1 to 2 minutes more. Brush with remaining glaze before serving. Makes 4 servings.

Goose with Apple Stuffing

1 10- to 12-pound domestic goose
2 tablespoons butter
1½ cups chopped apple
¾ cup chopped onion
½ teaspoon instant chicken bouillon granules
4 cups soft bread cubes
1 cup raisins
½ cup chopped almonds
¼ cup snipped parsley
1 teaspoon dried marjoram, crushed

Finely chop goose liver. In small skillet cook liver in butter till tender. In a saucepan cover apple and onion with water; simmer, covered, till tender. Drain. Mix together ½ cup *boiling water* and bouillon granules till granules are dissolved. Mix apple mixture, liver, bouillon mixture, bread cubes, raisins, almonds, parsley, marjoram, 1 teaspoon *salt,* and ⅛ teaspoon *pepper.* Toss to combine. Rinse goose; pat dry with paper toweling. Pull neck skin to back; secure with a small skewer. Lightly spoon stuffing into goose cavity; do not pack. Tie legs to tail. Twist wing tips under bird. Place on a rack in a shallow roasting pan. Insert meat thermometer in center of inside thigh muscle, not touching bone. Roast, uncovered, in 375° oven 3¼ to 3¾ hours or till meat thermometer registers 185°. Makes 10 to 12 servings.

Pheasant with Wild Rice

½ cup chopped onion
¼ cup butter *or* margarine
2 cups water
⅔ cup wild rice, rinsed
1 teaspoon salt
1 6-ounce can sliced mushrooms, drained
½ teaspoon ground sage
2 1½- to 3-pound pheasants
6 to 8 slices bacon

In saucepan cook onion in butter or margarine till tender; add water, rice, and salt. Cover; cook 35 to 40 minutes or till rice is tender. Stir mushrooms and sage into rice. Rinse birds; pat dry with paper toweling. Season cavities with salt. Lightly spoon rice mixture into cavities; tie legs to tail. Twist wing tips under birds. Place birds, breast side up, on a rack in a shallow roasting pan. Place bacon over breasts. Roast, uncovered, in 350° oven for 1 to 2½ hours. Makes 6 to 8 servings.

Sausage-Stuffed Duckling

½ pound bulk pork sausage
4 cups dry bread cubes
1 cup chopped peeled apple
1 cup chopped celery
½ cup chopped onion
¼ cup snipped parsley
½ teaspoon dried thyme, crushed
½ teaspoon dried marjoram, crushed
1 4- to 5-pound domestic duckling

In skillet brown sausage; drain well. Transfer to bowl; stir in bread, apple, celery, onion, parsley, thyme, marjoram, ½ teaspoon *salt,* and dash *pepper.* Toss with 2 tablespoons *water.* Rinse bird; pat dry with paper toweling. Sprinkle cavity of duckling with salt; lightly spoon in sausage mixture, reserving any remaining. Tie legs to tail; twist wing tips under bird. Place, breast side up, on rack in a shallow roasting pan. Prick skin all over with a fork. Roast, uncovered, in 375° oven for 1½ to 2 hours or till tender. Spoon off fat as necessary. Place any reserved stuffing into a 1-quart casserole; sprinkle with 2 tablespoons *water.* Refrigerate. Cover; bake during last 30 minutes of roasting. Serve with duckling. Makes 4 servings.

Pork Chops with Anise-Corn Stuffing

1 medium green pepper, chopped (¾ cup)
1 medium onion, chopped (½ cup)
3 tablespoons butter *or* margarine
• • •
3 cups toasted bread cubes (see note below)
1 tablespoon snipped chives
½ teaspoon salt
¼ teaspoon aniseed, crushed
Dash pepper
1 8¾-ounce can whole kernel corn
• • •
12 thinly sliced pork chops
Salt
Pepper
Paprika

In a saucepan cook chopped green pepper and onion in butter or margarine till tender but not brown. Remove from heat.

Add toasted bread cubes, snipped chives, ½ teaspoon salt, aniseed, and dash pepper to onion mixture. Drain corn; reserve 3 tablespoons of the liquid. Stir corn and the reserved liquid into bread cube mixture; toss lightly to combine.

Season pork chops with a little of the salt and pepper. Spoon a generous ½ cup bread cube mixture atop 6 chops; top with remaining 6 chops. Place chop stacks into a shallow baking pan. Cover with foil. Bake in 325° oven about 1¼ hours or till done. (*Or,* place chops into a greased grill basket. Grill over medium coals 45 to 50 minutes or till done, carefully turning once.) Transfer to serving platter. Sprinkle with paprika. Makes 6 servings.

Note: For 3 cups toasted bread cubes, cut 6 slices of *bread* into cubes. Place into a shallow pan. Toast the cubes in a 350° oven 15 to 20 minutes or till browned, shaking pan occasionally to prevent burning.

Cherry-Almond Glazed Pork

1 3-pound boneless pork loin roast
Salt
Pepper
1 12-ounce jar cherry preserves
¼ cup red wine vinegar
2 tablespoons light corn syrup
¼ teaspoon salt
¼ teaspoon ground cinnamon
¼ teaspoon ground nutmeg
¼ teaspoon ground cloves
¼ cup slivered almonds, toasted

Rub pork roast with a little salt and pepper. Place the meat on a rack in a shallow roasting pan. Insert meat thermometer. Roast, uncovered, in 325° oven for 2 to 2½ hours. Meanwhile, in saucepan combine cherry preserves, red wine vinegar, corn syrup, salt, cinnamon, nutmeg, and cloves. Cook and stir the mixture till it boils; reduce the heat and simmer 2 minutes more. Add the almonds. Keep the sauce warm. Spoon some of the sauce over the pork roast to glaze. Continue cooking the roast or till meat thermometer registers 170°. Baste roast with sauce several times. Pass remaining sauce with roast. Makes 8 servings.

Noel Ham

1 5-pound fully-cooked boneless smoked ham
Whole cloves
1 16-ounce jar spiced crab apples *or* 1 14-ounce jar spiced apple rings
½ cup packed brown sugar

Score top of ham in a diamond pattern; stud with cloves. Place on a rack in a shallow roasting pan. Insert meat thermometer. Roast, uncovered, in a 325° oven for 1 hour.

Meanwhile drain apples, reserving syrup. In a saucepan stir apple syrup into sugar; bring to boiling. Reduce heat; simmer 2 minutes. Place apples around ham. Brush ham and fruit with sugar mixture. Continue roasting 30 minutes more or till meat thermometer registers 140°, basting ham and fruit often. Makes 14 servings.

Lamb with Curry Sauce

1 3- to 5-pound boneless lamb shoulder roast
1 medium onion, sliced and separated into rings
1 medium cooking apple, cored and chopped
1 tablespoon butter
4 teaspoons all-purpose flour
1 to 2 teaspoons curry powder
2 teaspoons instant chicken bouillon granules
1 teaspoon lemon juice
¼ cup light raisins
Hot cooked rice

Place meat on rack in shallow roasting pan; sprinkle with salt and pepper. Insert meat thermometer in thickest portion of meat. Roast in 325° oven for 2 to 3 hours or till thermometer registers 160°. Let stand 15 minutes. Remove strings or netting, and carve. Meanwhile, in saucepan cook onion and apple in butter till tender. Stir in flour, curry, and ⅛ teaspoon *pepper*. Add bouillon, lemon juice, and 1 cup *water*. Cook and stir till slightly thickened. Stir in raisins. Cover and simmer for 15 minutes, stirring occasionally. Serve with meat and rice. Serves 6 to 8.

Cranberry-Stuffed Lamb Chops

6 lamb shoulder chops, cut ¾ inch thick (2¼ pounds)
Cooking oil
2 cups whole cranberries, chopped
⅓ cup sugar
½ cup chopped celery
¼ cup chopped onion
½ cup butter *or* margarine
1 8-ounce package herb-seasoned stuffing mix
2 medium oranges, sectioned and chopped
½ cup chopped pecans

In skillet brown chops in oil 10 to 15 minutes. Remove from pan; drain fat. Combine cranberries and sugar; let stand a few minutes. Cook celery and onion in butter till tender. Remove from heat; stir in stuffing mix and 1 cup *water*. Mix well. Stir in cranberries, oranges, and pecans. Turn into 13×9×2-inch baking dish. Top with chops. Sprinkle with salt and pepper. Cover; bake in 350° oven for 45 minutes. Uncover; bake 15 minutes. Serves 6.

Mock Tournedos

1¼ to 1½-pound beef flank steak
½ cup cooking oil
¼ cup lemon juice
1 tablespoon grated onion
1 teaspoon coarsely ground pepper
  Potatoes Paille (see recipe, below)
4 slices bacon, partially cooked
  Herbed Hollandaise (see recipe, right)
1 9-ounce package frozen artichoke hearts

Score steak diagonally into diamonds; cut lengthwise into 4 strips. Combine oil, lemon juice, onion, and pepper in deep bowl. Add meat; stir to coat. Cover; refrigerate overnight, stirring occasionally. Prepare Potatoes Paille; keep warm. Preheat broiler. Drain meat. Roll strips jelly-roll fashion starting from narrow end to form rolls. Wrap a bacon slice around edge of each roll. Secure with string or a small skewer. Place meat on unheated rack in broiler pan. Broil meat 3 inches from heat 7 to 8 minutes *on each side* for medium rare. Remove string or skewer.

Meanwhile, make Herbed Hollandaise. Cook artichokes using package directions. Place steaks and artichokes on platter. Spoon some Herbed Hollandaise over steaks; pass remainder. Pass Potatoes Paille. Serves 4.

Potatoes Paille

3 medium baking potatoes, peeled
2 cups cooking oil

Shred potatoes using medium holes of grater. Rinse well in cold water and pat dry with paper toweling. In medium saucepan heat cooking oil to 360°. Place potatoes in a wire basket; fry in oil 5 to 7 minutes or till golden. Drain on paper toweling. Makes 4 servings.

Serve Mock Tournedos *for an elegant holiday dinner party. These marinated beef rolls are wrapped in bacon, topped with golden* Herbed Hollandaise Sauce, *and accompanied by crispy* Potatoes Paille.

Herbed Hollandaise Sauce

1 envelope hollandaise sauce mix
1¼ cups milk
2 tablespoons chopped green onion
½ teaspoon dried tarragon, crushed
¼ teaspoon dried chervil, crushed

In a saucepan prepare hollandaise sauce mix according to package directions *except* use the 1¼ cups milk in place of milk called for. Stir in green onion, tarragon, and chervil. Makes about 1¼ cups sauce.

Steak au Poivre

2 to 4 teaspoons whole black peppercorns
4 beef top loin steaks, cut 1 inch thick (about 2¼ pounds)
2 tablespoons butter *or* margarine
¼ cup chopped shallots *or* green onion
2 tablespoons butter *or* margarine
⅓ cup water
1 teaspoon instant beef bouillon granules
3 tablespoons brandy

Coarsely crack the peppercorns with mortar and pestle or with spoon in metal mixing bowl. Slash fat edge of steaks at 1-inch intervals; place 1 steak on waxed paper. Sprinkle with ¼ to ½ teaspoon of the cracked peppercorns; rub over meat and press in with heel of hand. Turn steak and repeat on other side. Repeat this procedure with the remaining three steaks.

In a 12-inch skillet melt the first 2 tablespoons butter or margarine. Cook steaks over medium-high heat to desired doneness, turning once. Allow 11 to 12 minutes total cooking time for medium doneness. Season steaks on both sides with a little salt. Transfer steaks to hot serving platter; keep hot.

In same skillet cook shallots in remaining 2 tablespoons butter 1 minute or till tender but not brown. Add water and bouillon granules; boil rapidly over high heat 1 minute, scraping up browned bits from pan. Stir in brandy; cook 1 minute more. Pour over steaks. Makes 4 servings.

Horseradish and Barley Stuffed Rib Roast

⅓ cup quick-cooking barley
¼ cup sliced green onion
¼ cup prepared horseradish
2 cloves garlic, minced
1 5- to 6-pound boneless beef rib roast

Cook barley according to package directions. Stir in green onion, horseradish, garlic, and ¼ teaspoon *salt*. Unroll roast; spread evenly with barley mixture. Reroll and tie securely. Place roast, fat side up, on rack in shallow roasting pan; sprinkle with a little salt and pepper. Insert meat thermometer. Roast in 325° oven for 2¾ to 3 hours for medium-rare or till thermometer registers 145°. Let roast stand about 15 minutes. Remove strings and carve. Makes 10 to 12 servings.

Corned Beef Platter

1 3- to 4-pound corned beef brisket
4 large sweet potatoes, peeled
6 to 8 boiling onions
1 20-ounce can pineapple chunks
2 tablespoons brown sugar
1 tablespoon cornstarch

Place meat into a Dutch oven, adding juices and spices from package, if desired. Add water to cover meat. Bring to boiling; reduce heat and simmer, covered, 2¼ hours or till nearly tender. Cut potatoes into 1-inch pieces; add with onions to Dutch oven. Cover; cook 20 minutes. Drain pineapple; reserving syrup. Add pineapple to pan; cook 10 minutes or till potatoes are tender. In small saucepan mix sugar and cornstarch; stir in reserved syrup. Cook and stir till bubbly. Arrange vegetables and pineapple around meat on a heated platter. Spoon glaze over. Makes 6 to 8 servings.

Cioppino Mediterranean

¼ cup chopped green pepper
2 tablespoons finely chopped onion
1 clove garlic, minced
1 tablespoon cooking oil
• • •
1 16-ounce can tomatoes, cut up
1 8-ounce can tomato sauce
½ cup dry red wine
3 tablespoons snipped parsley
½ teaspoon salt
¼ teaspoon dried oregano, crushed
¼ teaspoon dried basil, crushed
Dash pepper
• • •
1 pound fresh perch fillets or frozen perch fillets, thawed
1 7½-ounce can minced clams
1 4½-ounce can shrimp, drained

In a large saucepan cook chopped green pepper, onion, and garlic in cooking oil till vegetables are tender but not brown.

Add undrained tomatoes, tomato sauce, wine, parsley, salt, oregano, basil, and pepper to saucepan. Bring mixture to boiling. Reduce heat; cover and simmer 20 minutes.

Remove skin from perch fillets. Cut fillets into pieces, removing any bones. Add fish to mixture in saucepan; simmer 5 minutes. Add undrained clams and shrimp; continue simmering, covered, about 3 minutes more or till perch is tender. Serve in individual soup bowls. Makes 6 servings.

Cioppino Mediterranean *makes a hearty but very special Christmas Eve supper entrée. This meal-in-a-pot stew features perch, shrimp, and clams in a tangy green pepper, onion, tomato, and wine broth. Round out your meal with a crisp tossed salad, topped with your favorite bottled dressing, and crusty rolls or French bread with butter.*

Sole en Papillote

8 fresh sole fillets or frozen sole fillets, thawed
½ pound shelled shrimp, deveined
½ pound sliced fresh mushrooms
Salt
Pepper
Paprika
1 teaspoon lemon juice
White Sauce (see recipe, below)
½ cup snipped parsley

Wash fillets thoroughly; pat dry with paper toweling. Cut 8 pieces of foil, each about 14 × 14 inches. Place one fish fillet in the center of each foil square. Arrange shrimp and mushrooms over fillets. Sprinkle with salt, pepper, paprika, and lemon juice. Top each with about ¼ cup White Sauce; sprinkle with parsley. Fasten sides of foil together using a double fold to make a tight seal. Fold in ends of foil. (Packets may be refrigerated overnight, if desired.) Bake in a 400° oven 35 minutes. Serve in foil packets or place in au gratin dishes. Makes 8 servings.

Note: For "en papillote" version, instead of foil, cut two 14×6-inch ovals from brown paper or parchment for each fillet. Brush one side of paper ovals with cooking oil. Place fish and other ingredients on one piece oil side up; top with second piece of paper oil side down. Fold edges several times to seal. If folds tend to unwrap, secure with paper clips. Remove clips before serving. Do not prepare this variation in advance.

White Sauce

¼ cup butter or margarine, melted
¼ cup all-purpose flour
½ teaspoon salt
½ teaspoon seasoned salt
¼ teaspoon paprika
2 cups milk
1 teaspoon worcestershire sauce

In a saucepan combine butter or margarine, flour, salt, seasoned salt, and paprika. Mix milk and worcestershire sauce. Add to saucepan all at once. Cook and stir mixture till is thickened and bubbly. Makes about 2 cups.

Paella

¼ cup all-purpose flour
1 2½- to 3-pound broiler-fryer chicken, cut up
2 tablespoons olive oil or cooking oil
2½ cups chicken broth
2 medium onions, quartered
2 carrots, sliced (¾ cup)
⅔ cup regular rice
½ cup chopped celery with leaves
¼ cup chopped pimiento
1 clove garlic, minced
½ teaspoon dried oregano, crushed
¼ teaspoon ground saffron
12 ounces fresh or frozen shelled shrimp
12 small fresh clams in shells, washed
1 9-ounce package frozen artichoke hearts

Combine flour, 1 teaspoon *salt,* and dash *pepper* in a paper sack. Add chicken pieces a few at a time, shaking to coat.

In 4-quart Dutch oven brown chicken in hot oil about 15 minutes. Drain off fat. Add broth, onions, carrots, rice, celery, pimiento, garlic, oregano, saffron, and ½ teaspoon *salt.* Cover; simmer 30 minutes. Add shrimp, clams, and artichoke hearts. Simmer, covered, 15 to 20 minutes. Serves 6 to 8.

Trout Amandine

4 to six 8-ounce fresh or frozen pan-dressed trout
1 slightly beaten egg
¼ cup light cream or milk
¼ cup all-purpose flour
2 tablespoons cooking oil
2 tablespoons butter
¼ cup slivered almonds
¼ cup butter
2 tablespoons lemon juice

Thaw fish, if frozen; rinse and pat dry with paper toweling. Season with a little salt and pepper. Mix egg and cream. Dip trout in flour, then in egg mixture. In large skillet heat oil and the 2 tablespoons butter. Fry fish 8 to 10 minutes, turning once. Drain.

In another skillet cook almonds in melted butter till golden. Remove from heat; stir in lemon juice. Place fish on platter; pour almond mixture atop. Serve at once. Makes 4 to 6 servings.

Cucumber Ring

see menu, page 52

1 3-ounce package
  lemon-flavored gelatin
1 cup boiling water
¾ cup cold water
3 tablespoons lemon juice
• • •
1 cucumber, thinly sliced
2 tablespoons sugar
1 envelope unflavored gelatin
¾ teaspoon salt
¾ cup water
2 tablespoons lemon juice
1 8-ounce package cream
  cheese, cubed and
  softened
4 cucumbers
1 cup mayonnaise or salad
  dressing
¼ cup snipped parsley
3 tablespoons finely chopped
  onion
• • •
Lettuce
Cherry tomatoes (optional)

Dissolve lemon-flavored gelatin in boiling water; add the ¾ cup cold water and 3 tablespoons lemon juice. Pour into a deep 6½-cup ring mold. Chill till partially set (consistency of unbeaten egg white). Overlap the thinly sliced cucumber atop gelatin mixture in mold; press into gelatin. Chill till almost firm.

Meanwhile, in saucepan mix the sugar, unflavored gelatin, and salt. Add the ¾ cup water; stir over low heat till gelatin and sugar dissolve. Stir in the 2 tablespoons lemon juice. With rotary beater gradually beat hot gelatin mixture into softened cream cheese till mixture is smooth.

Peel and halve the 4 cucumbers lengthwise; scrape out seeds. Finely shred cucumbers (or grind using fine blade of food grinder). Drain; measure about 1½ cups. Stir shredded or ground cucumber, mayonnaise, parsley, and onion into cream cheese mixture. Pour over almost-firm gelatin mold. Chill till firm. Unmold onto lettuce-lined plate; garnish with cherry tomatoes, if desired. Makes 8 to 10 servings.

Cranberry-Whipped Cream Salad

1 8¼-ounce can crushed
  pineapple
1 3-ounce package
  raspberry-flavored gelatin
1 16-ounce can whole
  cranberry sauce
1 teaspoon finely shredded
  orange peel
1 11-ounce can mandarin
  orange sections, drained
1 cup whipping cream
• • •
Frosted Fruit

Drain pineapple; reserve syrup. Add boiling water to reserved syrup to make 1 cup. Dissolve gelatin in hot liquid. Stir in cranberry sauce and orange peel; chill till partially set (consistency of unbeaten egg white). Fold in orange sections and pineapple. Whip cream till soft peaks form; fold into fruit mixture. Pour into 6-cup mold. Chill till set. Unmold; garnish cranberry salad with Frosted Fruit. Makes 8 to 10 servings.

Frosted Fruit: Break 1 pound *green grapes* into small clusters. Dip grapes and ½ pound *cranberries* into beaten *egg white*. Drain; dip fruit in *sugar* to coat. Place fruit on rack to dry for 2 hours.

Spanish Vegetable Mold

1 6-ounce package
  lemon-flavored gelatin
1 12-ounce can (1½ cups)
  vegetable juice cocktail
¼ cup Italian salad dressing
3 tablespoons vinegar
1 8-ounce can red kidney beans
½ of a 15-ounce can (¾ cup)
  garbanzo beans
¾ cup tiny cauliflowerets
½ cup chopped, seeded tomato
½ cup chopped celery
⅓ cup chopped green pepper

In bowl dissolve gelatin in 1½ cups *boiling water*. Stir in vegetable juice cocktail, Italian salad dressing, and vinegar. Chill till partially set (consistency of unbeaten egg white). Drain the kidney beans and garbanzo beans. Fold beans, cauliflowerets, tomato, celery, and green pepper into gelatin mixture. Turn into a 6½-cup mold. Chill till firm. Unmold onto serving plate. Makes 10 to 12 servings.

Fruited Holiday Wreath

1 8-ounce package cream
  cheese, softened
¼ cup chopped walnuts
• • •
1 3-ounce package
  lime-flavored gelatin
2 cups boiling water
2½ cups cold water
½ cup chopped celery
1 envelope unflavored gelatin
1 6-ounce can frozen lemonade
  concentrate, thawed
¼ cup sugar
1 cup mayonnaise or salad
  dressing
1 16-ounce can fruit cocktail
1 3-ounce package
  cherry-flavored gelatin
½ cup whipping cream
Salad greens (optional)

Form cream cheese into 7 balls. Roll in walnuts; set cream cheese balls aside. Dissolve lime-flavored gelatin in *1 cup* of the boiling water, stir in *1 cup* of the cold water and the celery. Chill lime mixture till partially set (consistency of unbeaten egg white). Pour a little of the lime mixture into 8½-inch fluted tube pan or 9½-cup ring mold; chill till almost set. Carefully arrange cheese balls in mold. Slowly pour remaining lime gelatin over cheese balls being careful not to disturb arrangement; chill till just firm.

Soften unflavored gelatin in ½ cup of the cold water, stir over low heat till gelatin is dissolved. Add ½ cup lemonade concentrate, the sugar, and the remaining 1 cup cold water. Add ½ cup mayonnaise. Chill till second layer is partially set. Carefully pour over lime layer. Chill again till almost firm. Drain fruit cocktail; reserve syrup. Add enough water to syrup to make 1 cup. Dissolve cherry gelatin in remaining 1 cup boiling water; stir in syrup mixture. Chill till partially set. Fold in fruit cocktail; carefully pour over lemonade layer. Chill till firm. Unmold. Combine remaining mayonnaise and remaining lemon concentrate. Whip cream to soft peaks; fold into mayonnaise mixture. Serve with salad. Garnish with choice of greens, if desired. Makes 12 to 14 servings.

Brighten holiday meals with Cherry Blossom Muffins *(see recipe, page 54),* Cranberry-Whipped Cream Salad, *and* Fruited Holiday Wreath.

Orange-Apricot Freeze

**2 8-ounce cartons orange
      yogurt**
½ cup sugar
**1 17-ounce can unpeeled
      apricot halves, drained**
**⅓ cup coarsely chopped pecans
      Lettuce**

In mixing bowl stir together yogurt and sugar. Cut up apricots. Fold apricots and nuts into yogurt mixture. Spoon into 8 to 10 paper-bake-cup-lined muffin pans. Cover; freeze till firm. Peel off paper. Serve salads on lettuce-lined plates. Makes 8 to 10 servings.

Carrot-Pineapple Toss

½ cup raisins
**1 8¼-ounce can pineapple
      slices, drained**
**2 cups coarsely shredded
      carrot**
**½ cup mayonnaise *or* salad
      dressing**
**1 teaspoon lemon juice
      (optional)**

Place raisins in a bowl; cover with *boiling water.* Let stand 5 minutes. Drain well. Cut pineapple into small pieces; mix pineapple with shredded carrot and raisins. Cover; chill. Just before serving, blend in mayonnaise or salad dressing. Sprinkle with lemon juice, if desired. Makes 4 servings.

Yogurt-Pear Salad

**1 14-ounce can *or* jar
      mint-flavored pear halves**
**1 3-ounce package
      lime-flavored gelatin**
1 cup boiling water
1 8-ounce carton plain yogurt

Drain pears, reserving ½ *cup* of the syrup. Dissolve gelatin in boiling water; stir in reserved pear syrup. Chill till partially set (the consistency of unbeaten egg white). Beat in yogurt. Chop pear halves; fold into gelatin. Pour into a 9×5×3-inch loaf pan. Chill till firm. Cut into rectangles to serve. Serves 6.

65

Salad Nicoise

3 cups torn romaine
1 head bibb lettuce, torn (2 cups)
1 7-ounce can water-pack tuna, drained
1 10-ounce package frozen cut green beans, cooked, drained, and chilled
1 cup cherry tomatoes, halved
1 small green pepper, cut into rings
1 small onion, sliced and separated into rings
3 hard-cooked eggs, cut into wedges
1 medium potato, cooked, chilled, and sliced
½ cup pitted ripe olives
1 2-ounce can anchovy fillets, drained
¾ cup Vinaigrette Dressing (see recipe, below)

Line large platter with torn romaine and bibb lettuce. Break tuna into chunks; mound in center of torn greens. Arrange chilled green beans, tomatoes, green pepper, onion rings, egg wedges, potato, olives, and anchovy fillets atop the greens. Cover and chill. Just before serving, drizzle with Vinaigrette Dressing; toss. Makes 6 to 8 servings.

Vinaigrette Dressing

1 cup cooking oil
⅔ cup lemon juice
1 to 2 teaspoons sugar
1½ teaspoons salt
1½ teaspoons dry mustard
1½ teaspoons paprika
½ to 1 teaspoon dried oregano, crushed

In screw-top jar combine cooking oil, lemon juice, sugar, salt, mustard, paprika, and oregano. Cover and shake well to mix. Chill. Shake again just before serving. Store unused dressing in refrigerator up to one month. Makes about 1½ cups.

Banana-Peach Salad
see photograph, page 47

3½ cups cranberry juice cocktail
1 6-ounce package strawberry-flavored gelatin
1 16-ounce can peach slices, drained and coarsely chopped
1 large banana, sliced
½ cup chopped pitted whole dates
1 8-ounce package cream cheese, softened
¼ cup dairy sour cream
1 tablespoon lemon juice
Milk
Lettuce

In a saucepan heat *1½ cups* of the cranberry juice cocktail to boiling. Add to gelatin, stirring till gelatin is dissolved. Blend in remaining juice. Chill till partially set (consistency of unbeaten egg white). Fold in peaches, banana, and dates. Pour into a 6-cup mold. Chill till firm.

To make dressing, in small mixer bowl beat together cream cheese, sour cream, and lemon juice. Add enough milk (3 to 4 tablespoons) to achieve desired consistency. Cover; chill.

Before serving, unmold salad onto lettuce-lined platter. If desired, arrange sliced peaches around mold. Serve with cream cheese dressing. Serves 6.

Olive-Asparagus Salad

1 10-ounce package frozen asparagus spears
2 7¾-ounce cans artichoke hearts, drained and halved
Freshly ground pepper
⅓ cup olive oil *or* cooking oil
¼ cup lemon juice
1 clove garlic, halved
½ teaspoon salt
4 lettuce leaves
¼ cup sliced pitted ripe olives

Cook frozen asparagus according to package directions; drain. In mixing bowl combine cooked asparagus and drained artichoke hearts; sprinkle with the freshly ground pepper. Combine olive oil or cooking oil, lemon juice, garlic, and salt; pour over vegetables. Cover and chill several hours; toss once or twice. Drain and remove garlic. On individual serving plates, arrange vegetables on lettuce leaves; garnish with the sliced ripe olives. Makes 4 servings.

Christmas Eve Salad

1 fresh pineapple *or* 1 20-ounce can pineapple chunks
2 large oranges
2 medium bananas
1 large apple
3 medium beets, cooked, peeled, and sliced *or* 1 16-ounce can sliced beets, drained
1 jicama, peeled and sliced (optional)
1 stick sugar cane, peeled and chopped (optional)
Lettuce
½ cup peanuts
Pomegranate seeds
Mayonnaise *or* salad dressing
Milk

Remove crown of fresh pineapple. Peel pineapple and remove eyes; quarter and remove core. Cut pineapple into chunks. (Or, drain canned pineapple.)

Peel oranges; section over a bowl to catch juice. Peel and slice bananas. Core and slice apple. Toss apple and banana with orange sections and orange juice.

Drain fruits; arrange with pineapple chunks, sliced beets, jicama, and sugar cane on large lettuce-lined platter. Sprinkle with peanuts and pomegranate seeds. Thin mayonnaise or salad dressing using a little milk to make drizzling consistency. Pass with salad. Makes 6 to 8 servings.

Scandinavian Cucumbers

½ cup dairy sour cream
2 tablespoons snipped parsley
2 tablespoons tarragon vinegar
1 tablespoon sugar
1 tablespoon snipped chives
3 small cucumbers, thinly sliced (3 cups)

In a bowl stir together sour cream, parsley, tarragon vinegar, sugar, and chives. Gently fold in cucumbers. Cover and chill. Makes 6 servings.

Pineapple chunks, oranges, bananas, apples, beets, and pomegranate seeds make Christmas Eve Salad *truly festive.*

Waldorf Salad

- **4 medium apples, cored and chopped (3 cups)**
- **½ cup chopped celery**
- **½ cup red grapes, halved and seeded**
- **½ cup chopped walnuts**
  Romaine
- **½ cup mayonnaise *or* salad dressing**
- **1 tablespoon sugar**
- **½ teaspoon lemon juice**
- **½ cup whipping cream**

Combine apples, celery, grapes, and walnuts. Turn fruit mixture into a romaine-lined salad bowl; chill. Combine mayonnaise or salad dressing, sugar, and lemon juice. Whip cream till soft peaks form; fold into mayonnaise mixture. Spoon the dressing over the chilled apple mixture. Fold dressing into fruit mixture. Sprinkle lightly with nutmeg, if desired. Makes 6 servings.

24-Hour Vegetable Salad

- **1 head iceberg lettuce, torn**
  Sugar
- **6 hard-cooked eggs, sliced**
- **1 10-ounce package frozen peas thawed**
- **1 pound bacon, crisp-cooked, drained, and crumbled**
- **2 cups shredded Swiss cheese (8 ounces)**
- **1 cup mayonnaise *or* salad dressing**

In bottom of large bowl place *3 cups* of the lettuce; sprinkle with a little sugar, salt, and pepper. Layer eggs atop lettuce in bowl, standing some eggs on edge, if desired. Sprinkle generously with more salt. Next, layer in order: peas, remaining lettuce, bacon, and cheese. Spread mayonnaise or salad dressing over top, sealing to edge of bowl. Cover and refrigerate overnight. Toss. Makes 12 to 15 servings.

Frozen Lime-Mint Salad

- **1 29½-ounce can crushed pineapple**
- **1 3-ounce package lime-flavored gelatin**
- **1 6½-ounce package tiny marshmallows**
- **1 cup butter mints, crushed**
- **1 9-ounce container frozen whipped dessert topping, thawed**
  Lettuce

In large bowl combine *undrained* pineapple, *dry* lime gelatin, marshmallows, and crushed mints. Cover and refrigerate for several hours or till marshmallows soften and melt. Fold in dessert topping. Spoon mixture into 16 paper-bake-cup-lined muffin pans. Cover and freeze till firm. Peel off paper and serve on lettuce-lined plates. Makes 16.

Golden Carrot Bake

3 cups shredded carrot (1
    pound)
1½ cups water
⅔ cup long grain rice
½ teaspoon salt
    • • •
2 cups shredded American
    cheese (8 ounces)
1 cup milk
2 beaten eggs
2 tablespoons minced dried
    onion
¼ teaspoon pepper

In a saucepan combine carrot, water, rice, and salt. Bring to boiling; reduce heat and simmer, covered, 25 minutes. *Do not drain.* Stir in *1 ½ cups* of the shredded cheese, milk, eggs, onion, and pepper.

Turn into a 1½-quart casserole. Bake, uncovered, in a 350° oven about 1 hour. Top with the remaining ½ cup cheese. Return to oven about 2 minutes more to melt cheese. Makes 6 servings.

Green Bean Bake with Onion

2 9-ounce packages frozen
    or two 16-ounce cans
    French-style green beans
1 10¾-ounce can condensed
    cream of mushroom soup
2 tablespoons chopped
    pimiento
1 teaspoon lemon juice
    • • •
½ of a 3-ounce can French-fried
    onions

In saucepan cook frozen beans according to package directions; drain. (Or, drain canned beans.) Combine the beans, mushroom soup, pimiento, and lemon juice. Turn mixture into a 1-quart casserole. Bake, uncovered, in a 350° oven 35 minutes. Sprinkle with French-fried onions. Continue baking, uncovered, about 5 minutes more or till onions are heated through. Makes 6 servings.

Green Beans Supreme

2 9-ounce packages frozen
    French-style green beans
1 small onion, sliced
1 tablespoon snipped parsley
2 tablespoons butter *or*
    margarine
2 tablespoons all-purpose flour
½ teaspoon finely shredded
    lemon peel
½ teaspoon salt
    Dash pepper
½ cup milk
1 cup dairy sour cream
½ cup shredded American
    cheese (2 ounces)
¼ cup fine dry bread crumbs
1 tablespoon butter *or*
    margarine, melted

Cook green beans according to package directions. Drain. In a saucepan cook onion and parsley in the 2 tablespoons butter or margarine till onion is tender. Blend in flour, lemon peel, salt, and pepper. Add milk all at once. Cook and stir till mixture is thickened and bubbly. Stir in sour cream and cooked beans; heat till just bubbly. *Do not boil.*

Preheat broiler. Spoon mixture into a 1-quart casserole. Sprinkle with cheese. Toss bread crumbs with remaining melted butter or margarine. Sprinkle atop beans. Broil 4 to 5 inches from heat 1 to 2 minutes or till cheese melts and crumbs are browned. Makes 8 servings.

Baked Corn with Chive Sauce

2 12-ounce cans whole kernel
    corn, drained
1 4-ounce container whipped
    cream cheese with chives
¼ teaspoon salt
    Dash pepper

In a 1-quart casserole combine whole kernel corn, cream cheese with chives, salt, and pepper. Cover; bake in 325° oven about 45 minutes. Serve in sauce dishes. Makes 6 servings.

Scalloped Corn

1 beaten egg
1 cup milk
1 cup coarsely crushed saltine
    crackers (22 crackers)
¾ teaspoon salt
    Dash pepper
1 17-ounce can cream-style
    corn
¼ cup finely chopped onion
3 tablespoons chopped
    pimiento
1 tablespoon butter *or*
    margarine, melted

Combine egg, milk, ⅔ *cup* of the cracker crumbs, salt, and pepper. Stir in corn, onion, and pimiento; mix well. Turn into 1-quart casserole. Toss melted butter with the remaining ⅓ cup cracker crumbs; sprinkle atop corn mixture. Bake in 350° oven for 65 to 70 minutes. Makes 6 servings.

Sweet Potato and Cashew Bake

½ cup packed brown sugar
⅓ cup broken cashews
½ teaspoon salt
¼ teaspoon ground ginger
2 pounds sweet potatoes,
    cooked, peeled, and cut
    crosswise into thick pieces
    (5 or 6 medium)
1 8-ounce can peach slices,
    well drained
3 tablespoons butter *or*
    margarine

Combine brown sugar, cashews, salt, and ginger. In 10×6×2-inch baking dish layer *half* the sweet potatoes, *half* the peach slices, and *half* the brown sugar mixture. Repeat layers. Dot with butter or margarine. Bake, covered, in 350° oven for 30 minutes. Uncover and bake mixture about 10 minutes more. Spoon brown sugar syrup over potatoes before serving. Makes 6 to 8 servings.

Glazed sweet potatoes are enhanced by cashews and canned peach slices in golden Sweet Potato and Cashew Bake. Include this recipe in your Christmas day menu. It's sure to be a hit.

Mushroom-Rice Bake

see photograph, pages 40–41

2 cups water
1 cup long grain rice
1 teaspoon salt
2 cups fresh mushrooms, chopped (5 ounces)
¼ cup chopped onion
2 tablespoons butter *or* margarine
2 eggs
2 3-ounce packages cream cheese, softened
1 13-ounce can (1⅔ cups) evaporated milk
¼ cup snipped parsley
1 teaspoon salt

In 1-quart saucepan combine water, uncooked rice, and 1 teaspoon salt; bring to boiling. Cover; reduce heat and simmer, covered, for 20 minutes. In small skillet cook mushrooms and onion in butter or margarine till onion is tender but not brown. Beat together eggs and cream cheese till smooth. Blend in evaporated milk. Stir in parsley, the remaining salt, the rice, and the vegetables. Turn mixture into an ungreased 10×6×2-inch baking dish. Bake, uncovered, in 350° oven about 35 minutes or till knife inserted off-center comes out clean. Garnish with additional sliced mushrooms and sprigs of parsley, if desired. Makes 8 to 10 servings.

Colcannon

6 medium potatoes, peeled and quartered
4 cups shredded cabbage
1 cup chopped onion
¼ cup butter *or* margarine
½ to ¾ cup milk
1 teaspoon salt
⅛ teaspoon pepper
1 tablespoon snipped parsley

In a covered saucepan cook potatoes in boiling salted water to cover for 20 to 25 minutes; drain. Meanwhile, combine cabbage and onion. In a saucepan cook cabbage mixture in a small amount of boiling salted water for 15 minutes; drain. Mash potatoes using electric mixer. Beat in butter or margarine and as much milk as necessary to make fluffy. Add salt and pepper. Stir in cabbage and onion. Sprinkle with parsley. Makes 6 servings.

Potatoes and Eggs au Gratin

4 medium potatoes (1½ pounds)
¼ cup chopped onion
1 tablespoon butter *or* margarine
3 tablespoons all-purpose flour
1 cup dairy sour cream
¾ cup shredded American cheese (3 ounces)
½ cup milk
2 tablespoons snipped parsley
1 teaspoon salt
⅛ teaspoon paprika
⅛ teaspoon pepper
4 hard-cooked eggs, sliced
1 large tomato, peeled and cut into thin wedges
¾ cup soft bread crumbs (1 slice)
1 tablespoon butter *or* margarine, melted

In covered pan cook whole potatoes, in enough boiling salted water to cover, 20 to 25 minutes or till almost tender; drain. Peel and slice cooked potatoes (should have about 3 cups).

Meanwhile, in saucepan cook onion in 1 tablespoon butter or margarine till tender. Blend in flour. Stir in sour cream, shredded cheese, milk, parsley, salt, paprika, and pepper. Cook and stir over low heat till cheese melts. *Do not boil.* Combine sour cream mixture and sliced potatoes.

In 1½-quart casserole spread *half* the potato mixture. Top with egg slices and tomato wedges. Spoon remaining potato mixture atop. Toss bread crumbs with the melted butter; sprinkle atop. Bake in 350° oven for 45 to 50 minutes. Garnish with additional parsley, if desired. Makes 4 servings.

Harvard Beets

1 16-ounce can sliced beets
2 tablespoons sugar
2 teaspoons cornstarch
¼ teaspoon salt
¼ cup vinegar
2 tablespoons butter *or* margarine

Drain beets, reserving ½ cup liquid. In saucepan combine sugar, cornstarch, and salt. Stir in reserved beet liquid, the vinegar, and butter. Cook, stirring constantly, till mixture is thickened and bubbly. Stir in beets. Cook till heated through. Makes 4 servings.

Cauliflower Scallop

see menu, page 52

1 10¾-ounce can condensed cream of celery soup
½ cup milk
2 slightly beaten eggs
1 cup shredded cheddar cheese (4 ounces)
¾ cup soft bread crumbs (1 slice)
¼ cup snipped parsley
¼ cup chopped pimiento
1 tablespoon minced dried onion
2 10-ounce packages frozen cauliflower, cooked and drained

Combine soup, milk, and eggs; stir in *half* of the cheese, bread crumbs, parsley, pimiento, onion, ½ teaspoon *salt,* and dash *pepper.* Chop cauliflower; stir into soup mixture. Turn mixture into 10×6×2-inch baking dish. Bake in 350° oven for 35 minutes. Top with remaining cheese; bake 5 minutes more. Makes 6 to 8 servings.

Broccoli Soufflé

2 cups chopped broccoli *or* 1 10-ounce package frozen chopped broccoli
2 tablespoons butter *or* margarine
2 tablespoons all-purpose flour
½ teaspoon salt
½ cup milk
4 egg yolks
¼ cup grated parmesan cheese
4 egg whites

In covered saucepan cook fresh chopped broccoli in boiling water 8 to 10 minutes. (*Or,* cook frozen broccoli according to package directions.) Drain well. Chop any large pieces. In saucepan melt butter or margarine; blend in flour and salt. Add milk all at once. Cook and stir till bubbly; remove from heat. Beat egg yolks till thick and lemon-colored with electric mixer. Slowly stir *half* of the hot mixture into yolks; return to remaining hot mixture. Stir rapidly. Stir in cheese and broccoli. Wash beaters. Beat egg whites till stiff peaks form; fold into broccoli mixture. Turn into an *ungreased 1-quart* soufflé dish. Bake in 350° oven for 35 to 40 minutes or till a knife inserted off-center comes out clean. Serve at once. Makes 4 servings.

Baked Bean Quintet

6 slices bacon
1 cup chopped onion
1 clove garlic, minced
1 18-ounce jar baked beans in brown sugar sauce
1 17-ounce can lima beans, drained
1 16-ounce can dark red kidney beans, drained
1 16-ounce can butter beans, drained
1 15-ounce can garbanzo beans, drained
¾ cup catsup
¼ cup packed brown sugar
½ teaspoon dry mustard
¼ teaspoon pepper

In 12-inch skillet cook bacon till crisp; drain, reserving 2 tablespoons drippings. Crumble bacon and set aside. In same skillet cook onion and garlic in reserved drippings till onion is tender but not brown. Stir in crumbled bacon, baked beans in sauce, lima beans, kidney beans, butter beans, garbanzo beans, catsup, brown sugar, dry mustard, and pepper. Turn into a 2-quart casserole. Bake, covered, in a 375° oven 1 to 1¼ hours or till heated through. Makes 12 to 14 servings.

Rutabaga and Apple

1 medium rutabaga, peeled and cubed (1 pound)
1 medium apple, peeled, cored, and sliced
⅓ cup packed brown sugar
2 tablespoons butter or margarine
Salt

In covered saucepan cook rutabaga in a small amount of boiling salted water 20 minutes or till just tender; drain well. Place *half* the rutabaga and *half* the apple in a 1-quart casserole. Sprinkle with *half* the brown sugar; dot with *half* the butter. Sprinkle with some salt. Repeat layers. Bake, covered, in 350° oven for 30 minutes. Makes 4 to 6 servings.

Creole Peas

1 10-ounce package frozen peas *or* one 17-ounce can peas
¼ cup chopped onion
¼ cup chopped green pepper
2 tablespoons butter *or* margarine
1 8-ounce can tomatoes, cut up
½ teaspoon salt
Dash pepper
2 teaspoons cornstarch

In saucepan cook frozen peas according to package directions. Thoroughly drain the cooked or canned peas. In saucepan cook onion and green pepper in butter and margarine till tender but not brown. Drain tomatoes, reserving liquid. Add tomatoes to cooked onion. Stir in peas, salt, and pepper. Blend tomato liquid into cornstarch; stir into pea mixture. Cook and stir the mixture till thickened and bubbly. Makes 4 servings.

Scalloped Spinach

2 10-ounce packages frozen chopped spinach
¾ cup milk
¾ cup shredded American cheese (3 ounces)
3 beaten eggs
3 tablespoons chopped onion
½ teaspoon salt
Dash pepper
1 cup soft bread crumbs
1 tablespoon butter *or* margarine, melted

Cook spinach according to package directions; drain well. Mix with milk, *½ cup* of the cheese, eggs, onion, salt, and pepper. Turn into a greased 8×8×2-inch baking pan. Bake in a 350° oven for 25 minutes.

Combine crumbs, the remaining cheese, and butter or margarine; sprinkle atop spinach. Bake 10 to 15 minutes more or till a knife inserted just off-center comes out clean. Let stand 5 minutes before serving. Serves 6.

Hawaiian-Style Parsnips

2 pounds parsnips, peeled and sliced (about 10 medium)
• • •
2 tablespoons brown sugar
1 tablespoon cornstarch
¾ teaspoon salt
1 8¼-ounce can crushed pineapple
½ teaspoon finely shredded orange peel
½ cup orange juice
2 tablespoons butter *or* margarine

In a covered saucepan cook sliced parsnips in a small amount of boiling salted water for 15 to 20 minutes or till just tender; drain well.

In a large saucepan blend brown sugar, cornstarch, and salt; stir in *undrained* pineapple, orange peel, and orange juice. Cook and stir till thickened and bubbly. Add butter or margarine; stir till melted. Add parsnips to sauce. Cover and simmer 5 minutes more. Makes 6 to 8 servings.

Chilies Rellenos Bake

2 4-ounce cans green chili peppers (6 chili peppers)
6 ounces monterey jack cheese
4 beaten eggs
⅓ cup milk
½ cup all-purpose flour
½ teaspoon baking powder
½ teaspoon salt
½ cup shredded cheddar cheese (2 ounces)

Drain peppers; halve lengthwise and remove seeds. Cut monterey jack cheese into strips to fit inside peppers. Wrap each pepper around a strip of cheese; place in a greased 10×6×2-inch baking dish.

Combine eggs and milk; beat in flour, baking powder, and salt till smooth. Pour over peppers in baking dish. Sprinkle cheddar cheese atop. Bake in a 350° oven 30 minutes or till golden. Makes 6 servings.

An American Heritage Christmas

Traditional Stitchery Designs

A house aglow with the colors of Christmas, and brimful of beautiful, handcrafted treasures—that's what holiday memories are made of! Make this Christmas one to remember with a uniquely American celebration, using the favorite designs and techniques of generations of American needleworkers for ornaments, decorations, and gifts for family and friends.

The stars, garlands, wreaths, and other symbols of the holiday season in this section were all inspired by traditional American stitchery. Adapted from patterns cherished by the grandmothers of today's quilters and stitchers, these projects are sure to become heirlooms in your own family.

The calico bird and star ornaments on the tree, the quilts and pillows, the beautiful appliquéd skirt, and the fabric garland and treetop ornament all feature popular American quilt designs. The rose wreath gracing the mantel is a quickpoint version of an antique embroidery, and the tiny cross-stitched wreaths being embroidered are old favorites suitable for ornaments, sachets, or a table runner.

Instructions for all the projects shown in this section begin on page 82.

Traditional Stitchery Designs

Shining symbol of Christmas—the star also is a favorite motif of America's quilters. There are so many stars in a quilter's galaxy that it's a snap to find a whole constellation of patterns for the pillows (opposite) and the tree ornaments and wooden quilter's puzzle (below).

If you're looking for unique stocking stuffers, stitch plump little pincushions with the popular Dresden plate pattern (above).

The four patchwork pillows perched atop this heirloom sawtooth star quilt show just how varied star patterns can be. Here (clockwise from left) are the rising star, December star, blazing star, and variable star designs for novice and expert quilters alike.

The tiny, soft-sculpture ornaments (below and on pages 72–73) are four-, five-, six-, and eight-pointed stars. The wooden puzzle, made of scraps of pine, is shown here as a star, but the pieces combine into several different patchwork patterns.

Traditional Stitchery Designs

Say "Merry Christmas" to the rose fanciers on your list with a wreath of roses you've stitched yourself or a delicate necklace of blossoms. Wonderful roses grew wild over much of early America, admired and sought after for their beauty and fragrance. So it's not surprising that they found their way into our artistic and cultural heritage, to be "drawn" in fabric and thread by generations of needleworkers.

The petite cross-stitched wreaths (below) can embellish such needlework projects as ornaments and table runners. Filled with delicately scented dried blossoms, they make delightful sachets.

To stitch these wreaths, use several shades of pink and green pearl cotton embroidery thread worked into hardanger, Aida cloth, or even-weave linen. Although the ornaments will be about 2½ inches in diameter, their exact size

will be determined by the thread count of the fabric you choose.

Once the design is stitched, sew the wreath into a tiny pillow cover and tuck in a bit of fiberfill or potpourri. Finish with a ring of gold cord tacked over the seam and tied into a dainty bow.

For a runner or tablecloth, work the design along the edge of the fabric, alternating roses with plain green wreaths. Working a row or two of old-fashioned hemstitching as you turn up the hem on your embroidered cloth will enhance the heirloom look.

The rose blossom necklace (opposite) is made of air-dried clay. If you're a cake decorator used to crafting small flowers, you'll find these roses simple to make.

The rose wreath below and on page 73 is one to enjoy not only at Christmas but the year round as well. This quickpoint design is worked in wool rug yarns, padded lightly with quilt batting, and mounted in a wooden frame. Because of the large-mesh canvas, it works up quickly, and you use only two stitches—continental and basket-weave.

To stitch the wreath, begin with the blossoms and leaves and fill the background last. Working with the canvas in a frame will keep it from pulling out of shape and reduce the amount of blocking necessary when you're finished.

Traditional Stitchery Designs

A fabric wreath will last season after season, to grace a mantel or bid a warm welcome on your door. The custom of hanging a yuletide wreath originated in Europe and was brought to America by the early settlers. Although wreaths once were made chiefly of fresh fruits or fragrant greens, today we can choose from an abundance of additional materials. For an unusual wreath this Christmas, why not stitch the Christmas star (opposite) or the soft-sculpture holly wreath (above)? Both are beautiful expressions of the Christmas spirit.

The Christmas star wreath is pieced from five triangles of polka-dotted fabric sewn into a star and appliquéd onto a pretty print. Tiny red beads and rows of quilting stitches outline the design, and a fabric loop attached to the back makes it easy to hang.

To make the fabric "holly" wreath, you'll need to stitch and stuff about three dozen holly "leaves" in dainty green prints. Tack the leaves, with the tips of all the leaves pointing the same direction, to a foam wreath covered with fabric. Then add a bow and some red berries.

Traditional Stitchery Designs

Whether hung from the mantel or placed under the tree, the Christmas stocking is one of the oldest ways to "wrap" gifts. Bold letters and bright holly make the needlepoint stocking (right) an eye-catching package. This beautiful stocking is stitched in Persian yarns and backed with elegant green velveteen.

Granny-square devotees will like the crocheted stocking (opposite, above) that is so simple even a beginner can expertly do it.

If a country stocking is more your style, make the patchwork design (opposite, below).

For the needlepoint stocking, you'll need one-half yard of #10-count canvas, one-third yard of green velveteen, muslin for lining, and a yard of cording. For the colors and amounts of yarn required, see the chart on page 87.

To make the patchwork stocking, use the pattern on page 17, altering it to match the stocking in the photograph.

Directions for the granny square stocking are below, so you can refer to the photograph, if desired. Make this stocking with 3½-ounce skeins of Unger Roly Poly yarn in white (A), pink (B), red (C), and green (D), and a size H crochet hook. For a smaller stocking, use a size F hook.
Granny Square (make 10)

Rnd 1: With A, ch 4, sl st to form ring. Ch 3 (counts as 1st dc), make 11 dc in ring, join with sl st to top of ch-3—12 dc in ring.

Rnd 2: Change to B. Ch 3, dc in same st as joining,* ch 3 loosely, sk next dc, 2 dc in next dc. Repeat from * four times, ch 3 loosely, join with sl st to top of first ch-3. Fasten off yarn.

Rnd 3: Working on back side of motif, and in *front* loop of Rnd 2 only, attach C in top of left-hand dc of any 2-dc group, ch 2, make cluster stitch (* yarn over hook, insert hook through st, yarn over, draw hook back through; repeat from * three times, yarn over and draw through all seven loops on hook) in st of Rnd 1 between 2-dc group, sl st to center ch in ch-3 sp, sl st in next ch and front loops of next 2 dc. Repeat from * around, ch 1, turn to front side.

Rnd 4: Sc in front loop of 29 sts, join with sl st to ch-1—30 sc.

Rnd 5: Using D, ch 1; sc in joining, * sc in each of next 2 sts,

2 sc in next sts, repeat from * around, end with sc in last 2 dc—40 sc. Sl st to first ch, ch 1.

Rnd 6: Sc in each of next 2 sts, * hdc, dc, 5 tr, dc, hdc, sc in next 5 sts. Repeat from * around, ending with sc in each of last 2 sts, join to ch 1 with sl st.

Rnd 7: Using A, sc in each st, making 3 sc in corner tr. Tie off.

Heel and toe motifs. (Make 2 each.) Work first 5 rounds as for Granny Square. In Rnd 6, to make a rounded corner, substitute (sc, 2 sc in next st, sc, 2 sc in next st, sc) for (hdc, dc, 5 tr, dc, hdc) sequence. Reverse and alter position of corners as necessary.

Work Rnd 7 as for Granny Square. To assemble, hold right sides of each motif together; with A, sc through both loops of outer sc round. Follow photograph for position of squares.

Toe Shaping: Attach A in instep ch 3, sl st to front edge, dc in each of next 15 sts, (2 dc in next st, dc in each of next 2 sts) 6 times, dc in each of next 14 sts, hdc in each of next 4 sts, sc in each of next 5 sts. Fasten off. Attach D along front edge of stocking 1 st above joining of previous round, ch 1, sc in each dc around toe, changing to A and sc across width of central bottom square. Fasten off. Repeat on other side of stocking.

Gusset: Attach A at top of front edge of stocking, ch 3 (counts as first dc), dc in each st around, ending at top of back edge. (Do not work across cuff edge at this time.) Repeat on other side of stocking. To assemble stocking, hold right sides together and sc through both loops of gusset rnds.

Cuff: Rnd 1: Attach A at back edge, ch 3, dc in each st around top edge of stocking, making 2 dc in each post of gusset dc. Join to top of ch 3 with sl st.

Rnd 2: Using D, ch 1, sc in each st around, join to ch 1 with sl st.

Rnd 3: Change back to A, ch 3, dc in each st around, join to top of ch 3 with sl st. Repeat Rnd 3 once. Do not fasten off. For loop, ch 21, turn, sc in 2nd ch from hook and in each ch, join to stocking with sl st. Fasten off.

Instructions for An American Heritage Christmas: Traditional Stitchery Designs

The instructions that follow are for the ornaments, decorations, and gifts shown on pages 72-81. For directions for enlarging and transfering designs, see the glossary, pages 370–371.

Appliquéd Skirt
page 72

For a skirt like the one shown, use any floral garland pattern suitable for appliqué; quilt borders make excellent motifs. Appliqué the design in soft red and green fabrics around the bottom of a simple A-line or half-circle skirt. Make the skirt midcalf length and wear over a petticoat bordered with wide eyelet ruffling.

Soft Sculpture Garland and Treetop Ornament
pages 72-73

Note: Each swag measures 20 inches wide and 8 inches deep; each flower is 8 inches high and 11 inches wide.

Materials: Assorted red and white calico fabrics for flowers (⅔ yard of 44-inch fabric makes 5 flowers); green calico for swags (⅔ yard makes 3); batting; 8 inches of wire for ornament.

Instructions: Enlarge patterns (below); add ½-inch seam allowance except at fold lines. For each flower or swag, cut front and back and 1 piece of quilt batting.

With right sides together, place 1 fabric flower atop another; place batting on top. Stitch, leaving an opening. Turn, press, and slip-stitch opening. Quilt along dashed lines on pattern.

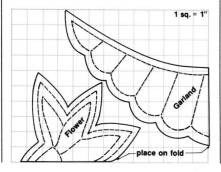

Repeat for each flower or swag. Hand-tack flowers and swags together in alternating sequence, and hang using small nails or double-faced tape.

For treetop ornament, stitch 2 quilted flowers together through the center (along fold line). Catch-stitch between halves of each flower to hold the 4 "petals" of the ornament at right angles to one another. To attach ornament, run flexible wire through center of ornament and twist around treetop.

Calico Bird Ornaments
page 73

Materials: Scraps of cotton calico fabric; embroidery floss; fiberfill.

Instructions: Enlarge the pattern (below) and cut 2 body pieces and 4 wing pieces for each bird, adding ¼-inch seam margins.

Stitch body front to back and wing fronts to backs, leaving an opening on each for turning. Turn and press.

Stuff body; slip-stitch the opening. Use 3 strands of floss to embroider the eye with satin stitches. Slip-stitch wing openings; pin wings onto body; slip-stitch. Add floss loop for hanging.

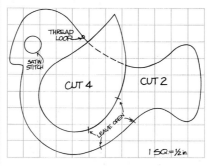

Calico Star Ornaments
page 73

Note: Each finished ornament is approximately 5 inches in diameter.

Materials: Scraps of cotton calico fabric; fiberfill; embroidery floss.

Instructions: Trace full-size patterns (right) onto cardboard or plastic templates. (Patterns include ¼-inch seam allowance.) Cut out the number

and variety of pattern pieces indicated on each pattern.

Pin and hand-stitch the star-point pieces together to form a back and a front for each star. Press all seams to one side.

Sew the star halves together, right sides facing; leave an opening for turning. Turn right side out, press, and stuff firmly. Slip-stitch the opening; add floss loop for hanging.

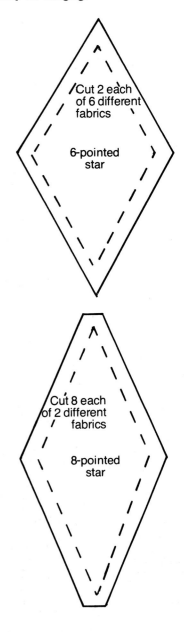

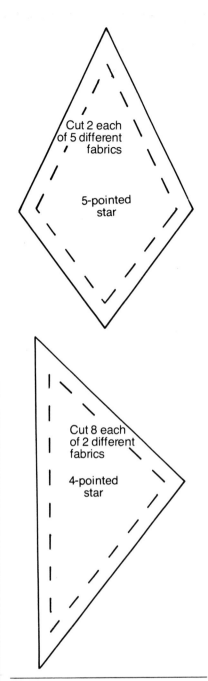

Cut 2 each of 5 different fabrics

5-pointed star

Cut 8 each of 2 different fabrics

4-pointed star

Star Pillows
page 74

Materials: *For each pillow:* 18-inch squares of quilt batting and cotton batiste; fiberfill or pillow form; quilting thread and needle; quilting frame or artists' stretcher strips. *For Rising Star:* ½ yard red and white polka dot fabric; scraps of six red prints; 1¾-inch-wide eyelet ruffle; single-fold red bias tape. *For Variable Star:* ½ yard each of dark green print (fabric *a*) and of white background print (*b*); ¼ yard each of solid green (*c*) and green-on-white print (for points of star—*d*). *For December Star:* ¼ yard each of 4 different green

prints for the star (colors 1, 2, 3, 4); ½ yard each of white fabric for background and of print for pillow back; 1⅔ yards each of cording and green bias tape to cover cord. *For Blazing Star:* ¼ yard each of 2 red prints for the inner star and of 2 green prints for the outer star; ¼ yard of white fabric; ½ yard of red cotton for border and back.

Rising Star

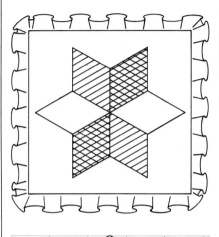

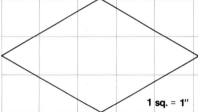

1 sq. = 1"

Variable Star

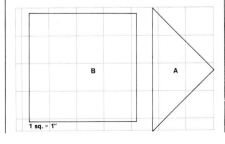

1 sq. = 1"

Blazing Star

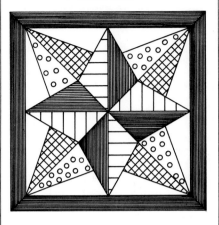

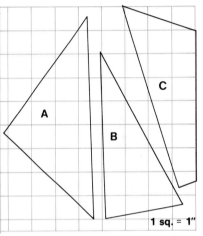

A

B

C

1 sq. = 1"

December Star

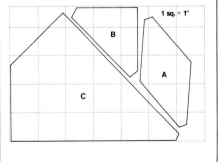

1 sq. = 1"

B

A

C

continued

Continued from page 83
Traditional Stitchery Designs

General Instructions: Enlarge pattern pieces on page 83; pieces include ¼-inch seam allowance. Cut out pieces according to directions below. Stitch pillow top, working from center outward; *except* for variable star piece squares with triangles and assemble top as for a 9-patch block.

Sandwich batting between completed top and cotton batiste; baste layers together and quilt. To finish, cut pillow back to match front. Stitch back to front, leaving one side open; turn and stuff. Slip-stitch opening closed.

● *Rising star*

Finished size is 14×14 inches, excluding ruffle. Cut 1 pattern piece from each of the 6 red prints. Assemble star and appliqué it to a 14-inch square of polka-dotted fabric.

Fold bias tape in half lengthwise; baste to seam line of top, raw edges even. Baste ruffle to seam line. Finish according to general directions.

● *Variable star*

Finished size is 15½×15½ inches. Cut 8 of piece A from fabric *d*, 4 of piece A from fabric *b*, and 4 of piece A from fabric *a*. Cut 4 of piece B from fabric *a*. Cut four 16½×1-inch strips from fabric *b* and four 16½×2-inch strips from fabric *c*. Cut pillow back from fabric *b*.

● *December star*

Finished size is 17 inches in diameter. Cut 56 diamonds (piece A)—8 of color #1 (center) and 16 each of colors 2, 3, and 4 (second, third, and fourth rows). Cut 8 of piece B and 8 of piece C from white fabric.

● *Blazing star*

Finished size is 16×16 inches. Cut 4 of pattern piece A from each of 2 red prints; cut 4 of piece B from each of 2 green prints; cut 8 of piece C from white. From red fabric, cut four 17×1¾-inch border strips and back.

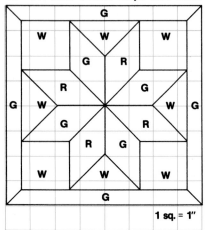

1 sq. = 1"

Quilter's Puzzle
page 75

Note: Finished size is 8x8 inches.

Materials: 7×7 inches of ¾-inch pine for the puzzle pieces; scraps of ½-inch pine for the frame; red, white, and green paint; nails; jigsaw.

Instructions: Enlarge pattern (below left). Center and trace star motif on the 7-inch square of wood; cut out pieces. Sand and paint pieces.

To make the box frame, cut a 7-inch square of ½-inch pine for the bottom. Nail 1-inch-wide strips ½-inch pine to each side of the base to form sides of the frame. Miter or butt corners, as desired. Sand and paint green.

Dresden Plate Pincushions
page 75

Note: Finished size is 4½ inches square.

Materials: Two 5-inch squares of muslin; scraps of 5 different cotton print fabrics; 6x6 inches of quilt batting; 6x6 inches of batiste; ⅔ yard cording; ⅔ yard bias tape; fiberfill.

Instructions: Cut template from the full-size pattern (below). (Pattern includes ⅛-inch seam allowance.) Cut 2 pattern pieces of each print (10 petals). Pin, baste, and stitch the 10 pieces into plate design. Turn outer and inner edges of "plate" under ⅛ inch; baste. Appliqué the design onto the center of 1 muslin square.

Sandwich batting between muslin top and batiste; baste and quilt. Trim any excess batting and backing.

Cover cording with bias tape and baste to top of pincushion. Stitch muslin back to front, right sides together. Turn, stuff, and slip-stitch the opening. Pincushions may be made into sachets.

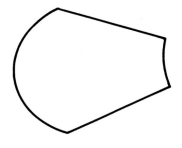

Rose Wreath Ornaments and Runner
page 76

Materials: Even-weave fabric (Aida cloth, hardanger, or linen); #5 pearl cotton in 4 shades of pink and 2 shades of green; gold wrapping cord for ornaments; tapestry needle; fiberfill.

Instructions: For ornaments, use only the floral wreath on the chart below, and work 1 complete wreath on each square of fabric. For runner, alternate the rose wreath and the smaller connecting wreath of green "leaves" all around the border of the runner. Work each floral wreath in 3 shades of pink and 1 of green, alternating the combination of colors on each wreath.

For ornaments, work a series of floral wreaths on fabric before cutting out pieces for ornaments. Cut backing to match front. With right sides together, stitch back to front ⅜ inch outside of the embroidered motif, leaving a small opening. Turn and press, stuff lightly, and slip-stitch the opening.

Whipstitch gold cord around edges of ornament; tie ends in a bow. Add a loop of clear nylon thread for hanging.

For runner, cut fabric 2 inches longer and wider than the desired size of the finished runner. (Before cutting fabric, stitch 1 complete motif to help you gauge the size of the finished runner.)

Begin in center of long side; work toward ends, completing the number of wreaths desired. For corner, turn pattern 90 degrees and connect green leaves to side of rose wreath at a 90-degree angle.

To finish, fold raw edges under ¼ inch. Press under an additional ¾ inch; hemstitch.

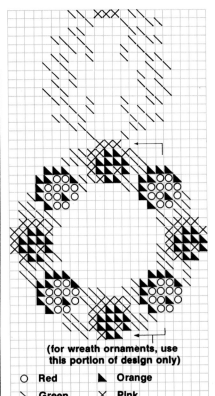

(for wreath ornaments, use this portion of design only)

○ Red   ◣ Orange
\ Green   ✕ Pink

Rose Blossom Necklace
page 76

Materials: Pendo Decorative Clay (available in craft and specialty shops) in the following colors: red, emerald, yellow ocher, white, and natural; florist wire and tape; silk or nylon cord.

Instructions: Mix colors first. Mix small amounts of red and white to desired shade of rose; add an equal portion of natural to extend color. For foliage, mix small amounts of emerald and yellow ocher; "extend" with natural. Set remainder of clay aside.

For each rose, shape a bud and attach it to the top of a folded-in-half strip of wire. Then build flower.

Attach 3 small petals to the bud, surrounded by 5 slightly larger, more open petals, to form an opening rose. Add additional petals if desired.

Make leaves from flat, leaf-shaped pieces of green Pendo and attach by smoothing lower edge of leaf to base of flower. Incise leaf "veins" using a small knife. Cover wire with florist tape and curl to make a loop through which the flower may be strung on cord. Allow finished flower to dry overnight, then seal with acrylic lacquer.

Cut silk or nylon cord to desired length, string flower, and add small green leaves to each end of the cord.

Quickpoint Rose Wreath
page 77

Note: Finished wreath is 23½ inches square, excluding the frame.

Materials: 26×26 inches of #5-count rug canvas; masking tape; tapestry needle; needlepoint frame or four 26-inch artist's stretchers; 23½×23½ inches of ⅜-inch plywood; quilt batting; frame; rug yarn in the colors and amounts noted on the pattern on page 86. (Color numbers refer to wool Pat rug yarn by Paternayan; similar yarns may be substituted.)

Instructions: Bind the edges of the canvas with tape; mount the canvas on a needlepoint frame or on artist's stretchers to minimize the need for blocking when needlepoint is finished.

Referring to chart on page 86, work the design in continental and basket-weave stitches. Fill the background until it is 23½ inches square.

Cut 2 layers of batting the exact size of the finished wreath. Center batting and canvas on plywood without cutting or turning the canvas; staple canvas to back of board. Insert finished wreath in frame of your choice. Add sawtooth hangers or picture-hanging wire.

Christmas Star Wreath
page 78

Materials: ⅔ yard flowered calico; ½ yard green and white polka-dotted fabric; four 23-inch squares of batting; 23×23 inches muslin; 150 red beads.

Instructions: Enlarge pattern (below). Cut two 22-inch circles from calico. With pencil, trace pentagon in *exact center* of both circles; cut out pentagon on one circle.

Cut triangles from polka-dotted fabric, adding ¼-inch seam margins. Turn under seam allowance on each side.

Mark center of short side of each triangle and each side of pentagon cut in circle. Matching center to center, pin triangles in place, lapping one corner over the next. Appliqué long sides only of triangles in place. Sew beads ⅜ inch from green star.

Sandwich one square of batting between wreath top and muslin; outline quilt around star in rows ¾ inch apart (see drawing below). After quilting, trim excess batting and backing.

Cut into corners of pentagon in second circle; trim excess fabric in center of pentagon ½ inch beyond marked line. Turn under raw edges to the line; baste.

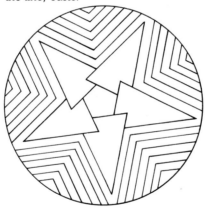

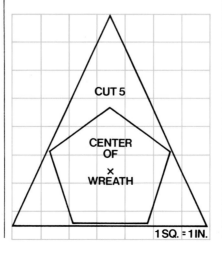

CUT 5

CENTER
OF
×
WREATH

1 SQ. = 1 IN.

With pentagons matched, stitch wreath front to back, right sides together, in a ½-inch seam around outside edge. Clip curves, turn, and insert 3 layers of batting cut to fit; slip-stitch center of wreath closed. Finish with a ribbon bow tacked to front.

Soft Sculpture Holly Wreath
page 79

Materials: ¼ yard red polka-dotted fabric; ⅔ yard green print fabric; 1 yard green polka-dotted fabric; 1½ pounds fiberfill; one 18-inch (diameter) plastic foam wreath (3 inches wide).

Instructions: Cut green polka-dotted fabric 8×58 inches and arrange around the foam wreath; slip-stitch closed, so fabric covers entire base.

Enlarge pattern (below); cut 23 leaf shapes from green polka-dotted fabric and 34 leaf shapes from green print fabric. Stitch and stuff 17 polka-dotted and 17 green print leaves.

Distribute leaves evenly around top of wreath base, alternating print and polka-dotted leaves and overlapping leaves slightly. Whipstitch each leaf to the base and to surrounding leaves.

To make berries, stuff twelve 2-inch circles of red polka-dotted fabric with fiberfill and gather edges closed. Tack berries in clusters to wreath. Add a red grosgrain ribbon bow.

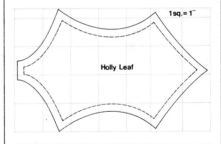

1 sq.= 1"

Holly Leaf

Patchwork Stocking
page 81

Materials: ⅜ yard red and green calico; ¼ yard green and white polka dot; ¼ yard red cotton; ⅜ yard muslin; 14×24-inch piece of muslin for back of quilted piece; 14×24-inch piece of quilt batting; red embroidery floss; alphabet stencils.

Instructions: Assemble the stocking, using the stocking pattern on page 17, except alter pattern to include heel and toe patches and curved top band.

Using alphabet stencils, with 2-inch letters as a guide, cut fabric for name. Appliqué name along top.

continued

Continued from page 85
Traditional Stitchery Designs

center

COLOR KEY

Symbol	Color		Symbol	Color
■	Dark red (15 yards)		◉	Dark green (15 yards)
◪	Medium dark red (15 yards)		▣	Medium dark green (15 yards)
⊠	Medium red (15 yards)		▭	Medium light green (15 yards)
⊡	Light red (15 yards)		⊞	Light green (15 yards)
⊙	Pink (15 yards)		☐	White (¾ pound)

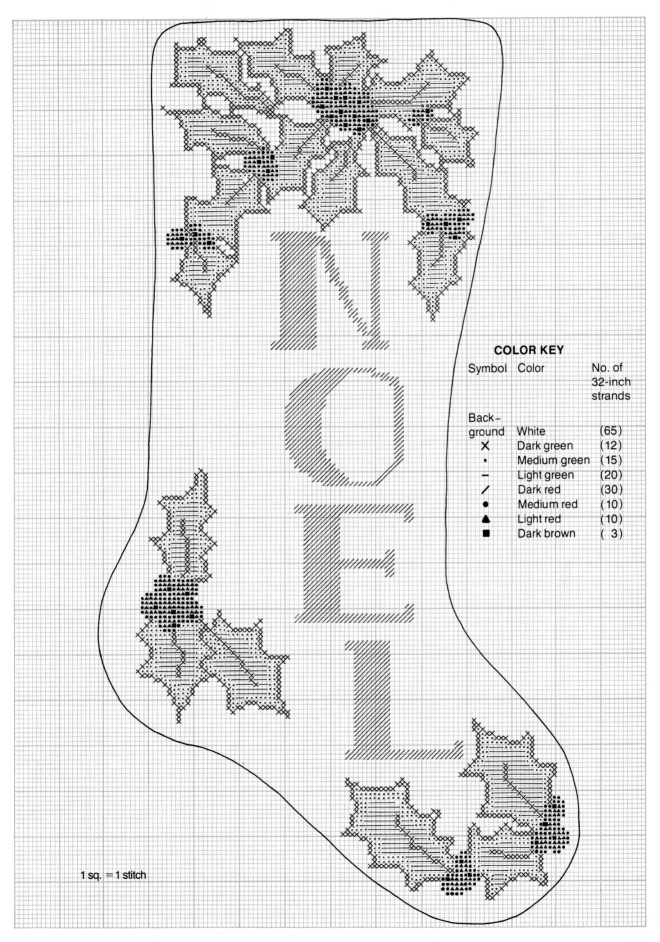

COLOR KEY

Symbol	Color	No. of 32-inch strands
Back-ground	White	(65)
X	Dark green	(12)
•	Medium green	(15)
—	Light green	(20)
/	Dark red	(30)
●	Medium red	(10)
▲	Light red	(10)
■	Dark brown	(3)

1 sq. = 1 stitch

An American Heritage Christmas

Homespun Quilts & Crafts

On the American frontier, winter was the time to stay home and make all manner of things. That was when bits of frugally saved fabric were stitched into quilts, and wood scraps were made into toys. Every day the simple materials of home and family were turned into treasures.

Now, generations from the hardy pioneers, we take pride in the heritage that has taught us the worth and beauty of handmade things. At Christmas, especially, we take pleasure in creating our own "homespuns"—gifts for children, holiday decorations, and all sorts of delightful treats.

All of the projects shown in this section can be made with inexpensive, easy-to-find materials. For example, you may have enough fabrics on hand for the dolls, wreaths, and tree trims shown here, or the schoolhouse block or log cabin quilt on the old Windsor chair—popular patterns that enabled creative and practical pioneer women to use every last inch of the dark and light fabrics they had stored in their baskets of scraps.

Instructions for projects begin on page 100.

Homespun Quilts & Crafts

Patchwork and appliqué are the time-honored craft techniques used to create this quaint farm scene (below). The clapboard siding on the house and barn are pieces of muslin sewn into tiny tucks and blindstitched to the background print. The trees, vines, and flowers are embroidered with floss after all the appliqué is complete. Fabric borders are used as matting for this "primitive" piece of needle art.

The old-fashioned doll is a copy of one in the Smithsonian. Made with yarn and fabric scraps, she wears a demure lace-doily shawl fastened with an antique button.

For imaginative package wraps, use printed paper tablecloths—they're inexpensive and large enough to cover even a bulky gift with one sheet.

The soft-sculpture Christmas candles on the tree (opposite) have all the charm but none of the hazard of real candles. This lovely tree also is trimmed with a choir of wooden angels adorned with calico, macrame snowflakes, and hardanger-embroidered ornaments in wooden rings. Instructions for the wooden and macrame ornaments are in this section; for directions for the embroidered ones, see page 212.

Homespun Quilts & Crafts

Since pioneer days the log cabin and the schoolhouse have been favorite quilt patterns. Here a variety of projects display these delightful and easy-to-stitch designs. In addition, there are pioneer dolls and a quilted and fabric-"woven" baby basket.

Schoolhouse patterns appear on the appliquéd quilt (below), tree decorations, fabric cards, and basket pincushions (opposite). Log cabin patterns were used for the sachet ornaments, quilted boxes, stocking, and picnic-basket lining.

Homespun Quilts & Crafts

From just a scrap of wood a country wood crafter could create not only practical things, such as kitchen spoons, but also fantastical toys and accessories. The primitive designs on such woodcrafts give them their special charm.

Birds, flowers, and geometric motifs turn unfinished boxes and cheese containers into stenciled beauties (below), if you use up-to-date materials and techniques. And you needn't be a master carver to create primitive toys (right). The crudity of these carvings is what makes them so appealing.

To make the boxes, daub clear shoe polish or a little paste wax over the stencil design to seal the raw wood. Then wipe the box with liquid fabric dye for a colorful, transparent stain.

Chunks of old, weathered pine or rough-cut lumber can be easily transformed into the delightful animals below.

Cut simple animals from wood, then use a coarse file for the rough shaping. Don't sand or file to perfection, though, or the primitive look will be lost.

For curly "wool" on the sheep and for other embellishments, use small chisels or linoleum cutters.

Homespun Quilts & Crafts

Homemade pies, cakes, cookies, and preserves of all kinds filled the larders in pioneer days. This Christmas treasure chest abounds with different kinds of homemade goods you can make by the batch for gifts and decorations.

With ribbons, muslin, and calico, you can make such projects as the decorative fabric bowls and the plump "preserve" pillows in this Christmas cupboard. Use the same materials to wrap your packages, make the star quilt, and fashion the sweet-as-cream country doll perched on the top shelf.

To make the wreath, use lacy trims gathered into rosettes and tacked into a plastic foam base. Finish with a cascade of ribbons.

For an unusual vest, weave small patches with a four-inch loom and strands of knitting worsted. Then piece the patches together into "fabric" and make the vest from a simple pattern.

Homespun Quilts & Crafts

A backdrop of winter sky, bare trees, and snow-covered meadows points up the coziness of this dining room filled with Christmas. The floor is warmed by a hand-made braided rug. A colorful star quilt rests on an old-time settle. The tree is bedecked with tiny dollhouse chairs and snowflakes macramed from waxed linen thread.

The braided rug (left) is a project for long winter nights. The braided place mats and napkin rings, however, are quick-to-makes. Home-dye your fabric to re-create these soft tones.

The needlepoint favors (below right) are stitched with naturally dyed yarns. You can achieve the same effect with purchased yarn in muted shades of blue and green or gold and brown. Stuff them with dried herbs or blossoms for pretty sachets. Or, use fiberfill for elegant pincushions.

Herb-scented candles rest in holders created from stairway turnings and wiped with liquid fabric dyes. To make them, cut unfinished decorative wooden spindles into sections 2 to 4 inches long. After trimming the base of each section so it stands firmly on the table, drill a hole in the top of each candlestick for the candle to rest in.

The fabric wreath (above right), the soft star on the Christmas tree, and several other decorations and gifts shown in this section are made from antique quilts with badly damaged or worn spots. Although the quilts were no longer usable as bed covers, some sections were still in good condition.

If you have such a quilt, you may wish to use it for these projects. If not, use fabric scraps to piece together a "mini-quilt," using our patterns as guides.

Then, from this newly pieced patchwork, cut out the pattern pieces for these projects.

To make the soft-sculpture star, draw a star pattern on an 11-inch-square piece of paper. Round the points and the angles between the points a bit to make sewing easier. And make the center of the star at least 5 or 6 inches across to allow room for a decorative lace doily.

Cut the star's front and back from a still-beautiful section of an old quilt or from a pieced patch-work square. Stitch and stuff the ornament, and then tack a doily to the front.

Trim the angles between the star points with bows tied from narrow grosgrain ribbon and sew tiny Christmas bells to the points. Fasten the star to the tree with a fabric loop sewn to the back.

Instructions for An American Heritage Christmas: Homespun Quilts & Crafts

The instructions below and on the following pages are for the ornaments, decorations, and gifts shown on pages 88-99. For directions for enlarging and transferring designs, see the glossary, pages 370–371.

Schoolhouse Block Wall Hanging
page 89

Note: Finished size is approximately 25 inches square.

Materials: ¾ yard blue broadcloth; ¼ yard each of 4 calico print fabrics; 25×25 inches quilt batting.

Instructions: Enlarge the schoolhouse pattern on page 104, using a scale of one square equals ⅜ inch. Divide the chimney in half, making 2 "bricks."

Cut pieces for the house from calico fabric, adding ¼-inch seam allowances. Turn under raw edges; baste.

Leaving a slim margin of background fabric between pieces, topstitch house pieces to a 10½-inch blue square. The base of the house should be 2¾ inches above the lower fabric edge.

Cut and stitch 6 rows of 1¼-inch-wide calico strips around the block in a log cabin design. (See photograph on page 89 for positioning.)

Cut blue backing. With right sides facing and batting on top, stitch front to back, leaving an opening. Turn, slip-stitch opening, and quilt.

Log Cabin Quilt
page 89

Note: Finished size is 76×88 inches.

Materials: Scraps of red fabric (centers); assorted print fabric scraps (strips); 1¼ yards of 44-inch-wide print fabric (borders); 3⅓ yards of broadcloth (back); quilt batting; cardboard scraps for pattern templates.

Instructions: Enlarge the pattern (right) and cut corresponding cardboard templates. (Number templates for easy reference.)

Cut the block's center from red fabric. Using assorted prints, cut strips 2, 3,

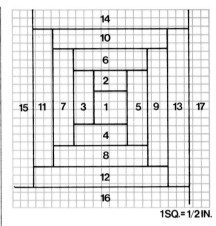

1SQ.= 1/2 IN.

10, and 11 from the same fabric; strips 4, 5, 12, and 13 from the same fabric; 6, 7, 14, and 15 from the same fabric; and 8, 9, 16, and 17 from the same fabric. (Add ¼-inch seam allowances to all pieces.)

Stitch pieces together in order (see pattern). Press seams to one side. Make 42 blocks.

To assemble the top, arrange blocks in a pattern (see photograph on page 89) and sew six blocks into a row. Make 7 rows; stitch rows together.

Piece backing fabric to size. Then, sandwich batting between backing and top, baste layers together, and quilt. Bind edges with remaining print fabric to make a 2-inch border.

Colonial Doll
page 90

Note: Finished size is 24 inches.

Materials: ¼ yard of muslin; 6×22 inches brown corduroy; ½ yard of brown broadcloth; 10×24 inches of print fabric (bloomers); ¾ yard of print fabric (arms, body, skirt); 16 inches of ¾-inch-wide lace; 20 inches of 1½-inch-wide lace; scrap of nylon fastening tape; rust, yellow, and brown yarn; green, orange, and brown embroidery floss; fiberfill; 8 inches of narrow elastic; 10- to 12-inch round or square lace doily; ¼×12-inch dowel.

Instructions: Enlarge patterns (at right), including ¼-inch seam allowance on all edges *except* on neck of bodice

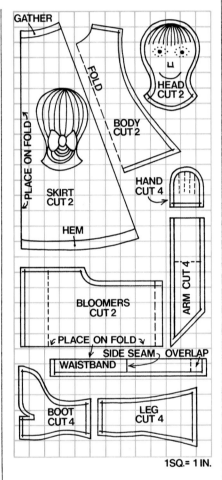

1SQ.= 1 IN.

and on wrists. Cut head, hands, and legs from muslin; bloomers from small piece of print fabric; arms, body, 2 skirt panels, and waistband from large piece of print; 2 skirt panels from broadcloth; and boots from corduroy.

Embroider green satin-stitch eyes with brown French knots around them. Backstitch the nose in brown and the mouth in orange.

Zigzag-stitch the body to the neck seam line and the wrist to the hand seam line. Sew boots to legs.

Stitch backs to fronts of legs, arms, and body, leaving one end open. Stuff legs and arms with fiberfill. Add yarn shoelaces to boots; stitch fingers and arm joints using brown floss.

Stuff the body and head piece; while adding stuffing, insert dowel into body to keep the head erect. (Trim dowel to fit.) Whipstitch the openings closed.

Sew arms and legs to body.

With rust-colored yarn, embroider the hair in rows of chain stitches ⅛ to ¼ inch apart. Satin-stitch a yellow hair bow to the back of the head, or add a bow tied with grosgrain ribbon. Trim neckline and wrists with ¾-inch-wide lace sewn over the seam line.

To make the skirt, alternately stitch together brown and print panels. Gather; stitch skirt to one long edge of band. Fold band over seam allowance, and whipstitch. Sew fastening tape to ends.

For bloomers, stitch front to back. Fold top down ½ inch to make casing. Stitch, then insert elastic. Sew 1½-inch-wide lace around legs. Using floss, gather each bloomer leg into a ruffle; tie ends of floss in a bow.

Make the doll's shawl from a doily folded in half. Sew a fancy button to one end of the shawl or fasten ends together with an old-fashioned pin.

Quilted Farm Scene Picture
page 90

Materials: 12×18 inches of green print fabric (ground); 4x18 inches of blue polka-dotted fabric (sky); ¾ yard of muslin (house, barn, fence, frame); assorted prints for remaining design details; embroidery floss in a variety of colors; quilt batting; embroidery needle; dressmaker's carbon; 20×24-inch purchased wooden frame.

Instructions: Enlarge the pattern (below). Trim one long edge of ground fabric to match hilltop, adding ¼-inch seam allowance. Turn under seam al-lowance; appliqué ground to sky to make the background. Transfer outlines of design to background (centered). Use outlines as placement guides for remaining motifs.

Cut a 15×20-inch piece of muslin for backing. Sandwich 3 layers of batting between backing and top, with top centered. Baste and quilt, spacing rows and stitches ½ inch apart.

Cut muslin fence rails, adding ¼-inch seam allowances; appliqué. Add fence posts; embroider roses.

For barn, cut muslin 2 inches wider than barn and 3 times longer. Tuck fabric into folds for a clapboard effect, turn under raw edges, and appliqué.

Appliqué roof and add tower by folding and sewing muslin to clapboard. Stitch round roof to tower, then embroider maroon weathervane.

For the house, fold and stitch 2 pieces of muslin into clapboard. Fold under raw edges and sew the two together at an angle (see photograph on page 90). Appliqué. Cut out remaining design details, adding seam allowances. Appliqué, then add embroidery.

To finish, cut 2-inch strips of floral print the length of the sides of the picture (about 12 inches). Turn under ½ inch; sew to sides with running stitches. Stitch 2-inch strips to top and bottom. Add a 6-inch border of muslin. Insert in frame.

Soft-Sculpture Candles
page 91

Materials: ¼ yard of 45-inch-wide, medium-weight, natural muslin (for 18 candles); assorted calico prints; yellow,

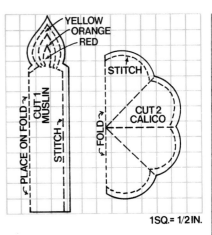

1SQ.= 1/2 IN.

orange, and red acrylic paints or embroidery floss; red embroidery floss; quilt batting; polyester fiberfill; small paintbrush or embroidery needle; light-gauge wire.

Instructions: Enlarge candle pattern (above); cut out pieces. Cut one base from quilt batting.

With right sides facing and quilt batting on top, sew base pieces (¼-inch seam); leave 2 inches open for turning. Turn and slip-stitch opening. Topstitch ⅛ inch from edges.

Following dotted lines on pattern, take ¼-inch tucks between each base scallop, stitching from outside edge to center. Alternate stitching on both sides so tucks face front and back.

Fold, right sides facing, and stitch candle, leaving end open; turn. Stitch two smaller flames inside large flame shape. Paint or embroider flame in red, orange, and yellow. Wrap red embroidery floss below flame; tie.

Stuff candle firmly with fiberfill; slip-stitch candle to base's center, turning raw edges under. Thread two 6-inch wires through bottom of base; twist ends together around branch.

Wooden Angel Ornaments
page 91

Materials: One 6×18-inch piece of ½-inch pine (for 6 ornaments); green, gold, copper, dark brown, aqua, light blue, light and dark pink, and white paint; gesso or white undercoat; sandpaper; scraps of calico fabric; iron-on interfacing; paintbrushes; white glue; gold cord, wire, or nylon thread.

Instructions: Enlarge pattern on page 102; trace onto pine. Cut out ornaments, drill hole in top, then sand and undercoat.

Paint both sides of ornaments. Feet and head are light pink; dress and wings are green, gold, copper, brown, or
continued

1SQ.= 1/2 IN.

Continued from page 101
Homespun Quilts & Crafts

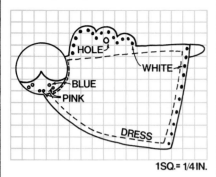

1 SQ.= 1/4 IN.

aqua; hair is gold, copper, or brown. Eyes are light blue dots; cheeks and mouth are dark pink dots. Paint white dots along wings and hem.

Iron interfacing to back of calico. Trace dress pattern onto interfacing, cut out, and glue in place. Add cord, wire, or thread hangers.

Macrame Snowflakes
page 91

Note: Finished size of snowflake A (at left in photograph), made with 3-ply waxed linen cord, is 3½ inches in diameter. Versions B (center) and C (at right) measure 4½ inches in diameter.

Materials: Twenty-four 24-inch lengths of 3-ply natural-colored waxed linen cord for each snowflake; ½-inch diameter metal rings; round and oval natural-colored wooden beads; T-pins; macrame board.

Instructions: You will use 5 different knots to work these snowflakes: lark's head knot, square knot, horizontal double half hitch, diagonal double half hitch, and half hitch sinnet. Diagrams of the knots are opposite.
● *Snowflake A*

To begin, fold 18 cords in half, and mount each one in a metal ring with a lark's head knot.

Insert a pin in macrame board and place the ring on it. Turn the ring as you work so that your knotting is in front of you at all times.

With any 4 cords, tie a square knot. With the adjacent 2 cords, tie a half hitch sinnet comprised of 6 knots. Repeat this knot sequence around.

Beneath any half hitch sinnet, divide the 2 cords into one facing right and one facing left. Using the right sinnet cord as a bearer cord, and the 2 closer cords from the adjacent square knot to the right as knotting cords, tie 2 diagonal double half hitch knots. (In a half hitch knot, the cord that remains stationary is the bearer cord, and the cords

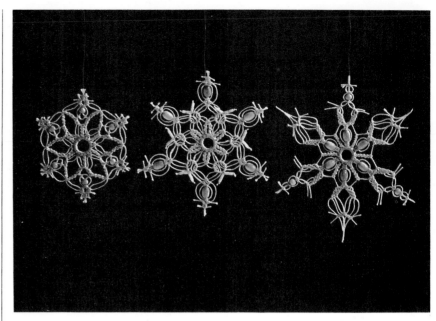

that are wrapped around it are the knotting cords.)

Do not pull the cords from the square knots tight—doing so will distort the symmetry of the snowflake and destroy the lacy effect.

Repeat, using the left sinnet cord and the 2 closer cords from the square knot to the left. Repeat around the ring until all sinnet cords have been tied.

This sequence of knots will form 6 inverted Y shapes around the ring. Each of the Y shapes will have 6 cords falling from it.

From the center of each Y shape, find the 2 center cords. Pull the left one to the left and the right one to the right. Tie 2 more rows of 2 diagonal double half hitch knots on these cords. You will have to use the bearer cords from previous rows to complete this, and all 3 rows of double half hitches should spread the Y outward. Repeat on each Y shape.

Using the bearer cord and the cord that tied the last half hitch knot, tie a half hitch sinnet comprised of 6 knots on each "leg" of the Y. Repeat on each Y shape around.

This, in effect, will lengthen each Y shape. Two cords remain the center of each Y shape.

Pull together the left leg of one Y and the right leg of the adjacent Y—there are 4 cords in your hand—and tie a square knot. Repeat around. The snowflake should have 6 "petals." Securely pin the point of each petal to the macrame board, stretching points so that the snowflake is symmetrical, but not so tightly that the snowflake warps when pins are removed. From now on turn the board as you work.

Attach 6 new cords between the petals. Tie double half hitch knots, and use the cords remaining in the Y shape as knotting cords and the new cords as bearer cords.

Then, hold the 2 knotting cords together and slide a wooden bead up them. Form a loose circle by bringing the ends of the new cord down around the bead, and anchor with a square knot. Leave a little slack in the new cord as you tie this knot so you won't crowd the bead. Repeat until all 6 new cords and beads have been tied in.

Separate the 4 cords beneath any bead into 2 groups. Gather together the left group with the 2 closer cords from the square knot at the tip of the petal to the left. With these 4 cords, tie 2 square knots, one above the other, as close to the bead as possible. Repeat this procedure with the right group of cords beneath the bead and the 2 closer cords from the square knot at the tip of the petal to the right.

As you draw the cords from the petal tips, leave plenty of slack so the snowflake will lie flat. Repeat this sequence beneath each bead. There are now 8 cords beneath each bead.

Gather together the center 4 cords from the 8-cord group beneath any bead. Tie 2 square knots, one above the other, with these 4 cords. Repeat under each bead.

When all knots are completed, remove snowflake from macrame board. Trim cords so they form a rough triangle, as shown in photograph.
● *Snowflake B*

Mount 18 cords in a metal ring as for Snowflake A. Start with any 2 cords, and tie a half hitch sinnet comprised of

6 knots. Take the adjacent 2 cords and repeat. Tie all 4 cords from both sinnets together with a square knot. Skip the next 2 cords and repeat the sinnet sequence over the next 4 cords. Repeat around until you have tied 6 sinnet "petals."

Pin all 6 points to the macrame board. Then, place one pin between the 2 cords between the petals. Tie in a new cord at these pins.

Using the 2 cords between the petals and the 2 closer cords from the square knots to the right and left, tie a row of double half hitch knots to the new cord to form the top of a circle. Bring the ends of the new cord around and tie double half hitch knots for the bottom half of the circle. Inside the circle, the cords should fall straight down. Complete the circle by tying a double half hitch knot with one end of the new cord to the other end of the same cord.

Slide 2 seed beads (or more, depending on their size) to the ends of the new cords. Secure with an overhand knot; trim and add a drop of white glue. Repeat new cord addition until all 6 circles have been formed.

Between any 2 circles, join the closer 3 cords from both circles on the right and left. You have a total of 6 cords. At a point where snowflake will lie flat, tie a square knot with the 4 center cords.

Divide the 6 cords below this square knot into 2 groups of 3 cords. In each 3-cord group, tie 2 square knots, one above the other, using only 1 cord as the filler. Tie another square knot with the center 4 cords. Repeat until you have tied this sequence between all 6 circles.

In any 6-cord group, slide an oval bead up the 2 center cords. Bring the 2 cords adjacent down and around in a loose oval shape; tie a square knot under the bead.

Bring the 2 remaining cords around loosely—you have 6 cords in a group again.

Divide cords into 2 groups of 3 cords; tie 2 square knots, one above the other as before. Then, tie a square knot with the 4 center cords as close to the rest of the knots as possible.

Remove the snowflake from the macrame board. Trim ends in a rough triangle shape as for snowflake A.

● *Snowflake C*

Mount 18 cords in metal ring. From any 2 cords, tie a half hitch sinnet comprised of 11 knots. With the adjacent 4 cords, tie 2 square knots, one above the other. Alternating these knots, repeat around ring.

Beneath any 2 square knots, find the center 2 cords in the 4-cord group.

Slide an oval bead up to the square knots. Bring the 2 outer cords around loosely, and anchor beneath bead with 2 square knots, one above the other. Repeat around. Pin snowflake out at 6 points.

*Attach a new cord by centering it under a group of square knots beneath any bead, and pinning it straight out left and right.

Tie a row of horizontal double half hitch knots to new cord using 4 cords from square knot as knotting cords.

Draw the closest cord from each of 2 adjacent half hitch sinnets to the new cord, pull taut to form even line, and tie with double half hitch knots to the new cord. This will form a rough hexagonal (6-sided) shape. There are now 6 cords knotted to the new cord.

Divide all 8 cords in half. Tie 3 rows of diagonal double half hitch knots, sloping out and downward from center of new cord.

Repeat the previous steps (from the *) around. At this point, you will treat the 6 points of the snowflake alternately to completion.

At any point, find the 4 center cords of an 8-cord group. Leaving about an inch of cord to fall free, tie a square knot with 4 cords. Draw over one cord from each adjacent sinnet, and tie 2 square knots, (using 3 cords) below this square knot. Draw remaining 2 cords over and tie 2 more square knots beneath last 2 knots using 3 cords per knot. These 5 knots will form a flattened, inverted V shape.

Trim 4 outer cords to ½ inch. Pull 4 center cords together forming a point; trim, and secure point with white glue. Repeat this step on *every other* 8-cord group.

In skipped 8-cord group, bring the bearer cords of the last row of diagonal double half hitch knots toward the center of the 8-cord group, and tie a row of diagonal double half hitch knots, sloping the cords down and toward the center of the 8-cord group. Find the center 4 cords of this group and tie a square knot at a point where the snowflake will lie flat. Do not pull thread too tightly or it will not lie flat.

Slide a small wooden bead up the 2 center cords; draw the 2 outer cords around loosely and anchor the bead with a square knot. Tie another square knot ¼ inch below the first one. Repeat on until all points are formed. Trim ends, leaving ⅜ inch.

Macrame snowflakes make lovely tree ornaments or gift-wrap trims. Knotted in heavy cord, they can be mounted on a wall or hung in a window.

continued

Lark's Head Knot

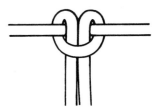

Square Knot

Horizontal Double Half Hitch

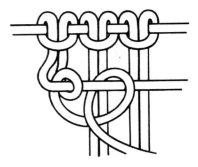

Diagonal Double Half Hitch

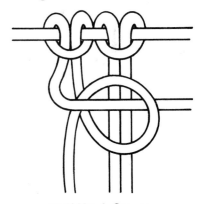

Half Hitch Sinnet

Continued from page 103
Homespun Quilts & Crafts

Baby Basket
page 92

Materials: Baby basket; 3½ yards of print fabric (lining); approximately 1½ yards of assorted print fabrics for weaving; 2-inch-thick foam pad (mattress); quilt batting; 20-inch zipper.

Instructions: To determine the length of the weaving strips, measure the basket's circumference. Cut and piece 3½-inch-wide strips to this length plus 12 inches. Fold the raw edges of the strips to the center, then fold the strips in half lengthwise. Weave the strips in and out of the basket, using a different color or print for each round. Sew the ends of the strips together from the inside, turning under raw edges. Also weave strips across the hood of the basket as shown in photograph.

Cut foam mattress to fit basket. Make a fitted cover from lining fabric, adding a zipper along the boxing strip. Or, make a loose pillowcase cover that can be removed easily.

Cut fabric for lining sides of basket, adding seam allowance. Turn edges under; tack to basket around bottom. Insert batting; stitch top of lining to top of side, turning in raw edges.

To line hood, measure inside of hood; cut lining fabric accordingly. Curve seams to match basket. Sew lining in place along bottom edge, place layer of batting beneath fabric and stitch around. Tack lining to basket.

Knitted Shoulder Wrap
page 92

Note: Instructions are for sizes 10 to 12. For a slightly larger size, use No. 10½ needles throughout. Knitting abbreviations are on page 371.

Materials: Lion Brand Pamela yarn, knitting worsted weight: 3 (4 oz.) skeins of eggshell, or a suitable substitute that will yield the gauge given below; No. 9 needles; 1 long, circular needle, No. 9, *or size needles to obtain gauge below;* markers; size G crochet hook.

Gauge: Pattern of 7 p sts plus 3 k sts equals 2½ inches.

Instructions: *Back:* Starting at back waistline, cast on 17 sts on a straight needle.

Row 1: K across. Starting with row 2, inc 1 st at beg of every row until further notice.

Row 2: P 2, k 3, p 7, k 3, p 2.
Row 3: K 2, p 3, k 7, p 3, k 3.

Row 4: P 3, k 3, p 7, k 3, p 3.
Row 5: P across.
Row 6: K 2, p 7, k 3, p 7, k 2.
Row 7: P 2, (k 7, p 3) twice.
Row 8: (K 3, p 7) twice: k 3.
Row 9: (P 3, k 7) twice: p 3, k 1.

These 9 rows form a pat of 2 "bands" of basket-weave sts across. Continue in pat, working groups of 7 p and 3 k sts (right side) in sequence. *Note:* Each "band" contains 4 rows. There is a single dividing row between "bands." Work dividing row alternately on right or wrong side. On right side, k across; on wrong side, p across. Also add sts in pat. Work until desired length, or until there are 25 "bands" of the basket-weave pat.

To divide for neck: Work across to center 17 sts. Place these sts on a holder; place sts for other shoulder on extra needle. (Sts on holder line up with 17 sts cast on at beg of work.)

Work in pat across first shoulder, without increasing or decreasing until there are 7 bands of basket-weave pat. Then continue in pat, decreasing 1 st at beg of every row at neck edge. Work until no sts are left. Put sts for other shoulder on proper needle and work to correspond to first shoulder.

Borders: With circular needle and right side of work facing you, pick up 140 sts along one long outer edge of piece. Do not join sts; work back and forth on circular needle. Work in garter st (k each row), inc 1 st at each end of every row until there are 6 ridges on right side. Bind off loosely.

Repeat border on opposite long, outer edge. Pick up 17 sts along narrow cast-on (starting) edge of piece. Work border without inc sts until there are 6 ridges on right side. Bind off loosely.

Starting at point of work, pick up 76 sts along inner edge of piece, place marker on needle, k across neck sts, place another marker on needle, pick up 76 sts along opposite inner edge of piece. Work garter st border, increasing 1 st at each end of every row. *AT SAME TIME,* work up to 2 sts before marker, dec 1 st, slip marker, dec 1 st, work up to 2 sts before next marker, dec 1 st, sl marker, dec 1 st. Repeat these decs for 3 rows in all. Continue until there are 6 ridges on right side of work. Bind off loosely. With yarn and large sewing needle, join ends of borders together.

Edging: With right side of work facing you, start at narrow cast-on edge of piece. Attach yarn at right corner. Ch 3, 3 dc in st where yarn was attached, *sk 2 sts, sc in next st, ch 3, 3 dc in st you just worked the sc in. Repeat from * across narrow edge and down long side to point.

Tie: Ch 50, sc in 2nd ch from hook and all across ch back to point. Work scallop edging all around neck edges to opposite point, make 2nd tie, then complete edging. Fasten off.

Steam press the finished piece under a damp cloth. Do not allow the weight of the iron to rest on the yarn.

Lacy Quilted Heart
page 92

Materials: 9×9 inches of quilt fabric; 9×9 inches of backing fabric; polyester fiberfill; 20 inches of 5-inch-wide ecru crocheted lace edging; 2½ yards of narrow grosgrain ribbon.

Instructions: Using an 8-inch square of paper, cut a heart-shaped pattern.

Adding ¼-inch seam allowance, cut a heart from an old quilt or from a new patchwork mini-quilt (see page 99). Cut the back to match the front.

Baste lace to front, matching raw edges, then stitch front to back (right sides facing) leaving an opening for turning. Turn, stuff, and slip-stitch closed. Sew 12 inches of ribbon to the top of the heart for a hanger. Tie ribbon bows to ends of hanging ribbon.

Schoolhouse Quilt
page 92

Note: Finished size is 50×56 inches.

Materials: 2⅛ yards of red calico for backing (yardages are for 44/45-inch-wide-fabric); 1⅔ yards of blue calico; ⅝ yard of red polka-dotted fabric; ⅔ yard of blue cotton; fabric scraps in assorted colors and prints; 6 yards of 2-inch-wide blue bias tape; embroidery floss; crib size polyester quilt batting; quilting thread.

Instructions: Enlarge the pattern (below) and cut out templates from cardboard or plastic lids for the separate pattern pieces. Add ¼-inch seam allowances. Cut pieces for 5 blocks from assorted fabric scraps. Pieces with the

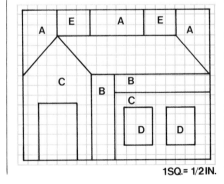

1SQ.= 1/2 IN.

same letter designation (A, B, C, etc.) should be cut from the same fabric within each block, *except* cut A pieces for all 5 blocks from blue fabric.

When cutting out pieces, keep in mind the relationship between dark and light fabrics within individual blocks. For example, you may wish to cut "windows" from light-colored fabrics and doors from darker ones.

Stitch pieces together into blocks, then appliqué each block to an 11×13-inch piece of blue fabric (add seam allowances). Cut four 11×13-inch pieces from blue calico.

Stitch 2-inch-wide polka-dotted border strips between blocks and rows, making 3 rows of 3 blocks each.

Finish the quilt top with a 4¾-inch-wide blue calico border around the outside edges (do *not* add seam allowances to this border).

Embroider design details, such as windowpanes, flowers, and curtains, using 2 strands of embroidery floss. Use the embroidery motifs characteristic of old-fashioned crazy quilts (feather stitching, etc.) or design your own motifs. Refer to the photograph on page 92 for stitch suggestions.

Cut and piece red calico for backing; also cut a piece of quilt batting the size of the quilt top. Baste all 3 layers together, quilt along the seam lines, and bind the edges of the quilt with wide bias tape.

Baby Ball
page 92

Materials: ¼ yard of solid-color fabric; ⅓ yard of print fabric; polyester fiberfill.

Instructions: Enlarge patterns (below), adding ¼-inch seam allowanc-

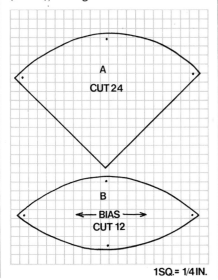

1 SQ.= ¼ IN.

es. Cut 24 pieces of A from print fabric and 12 pieces of B from plain fabric.

Stitch one A piece to each side of a B piece along curved edges. Sew A pieces together along straight sides, leaving an opening for turning. Turn, stuff, and whipstitch closed.

Make 12 wedge-shaped sections and join them together at the points of each triangle to form a ball.

Log Cabin Ornaments
page 93

Materials: Fabric scraps in assorted prints and colors; ½-inch-wide white lace; narrow ribbon; fiberfill.

Instructions: For each ornament, stitch a mini-quilt block in a modified log cabin design.

Start with a center block 1¼ inches square, add four ¾×2-inch strips around the center, and finish with four ¾×3½-inch strips. Add ¼-inch seam allowances to all dimensions before cutting. (Refer to the color photograph for the position of the strips around the central block.)

Cut backing to match front. Baste lace trim around the outside seam line, then stitch front to back, leaving an opening. Turn, stuff, and slip-stitch. Attach a ribbon loop for hanging.

Schoolhouse Ornaments
page 93

Materials: (for 9 ornaments) ¼ yard of 45-inch-wide blue cotton fabric; assorted print and calico cotton scraps; embroidery floss in assorted colors; embroidery needle; polyester fiberfill; fusible webbing; nylon thread.

Instructions: Enlarge the schoolhouse pattern (page 104), using a scale of 1 square equals ¼ inch. Next, referring to the photograph on page 92, adapt the pattern for ornaments—eliminate 1 chimney, draw a ⅛-inch border around the house (for background fabric), reposition windows, etc.

Using the new pattern, cut the front and back background pieces from blue fabric, adding ¼-inch seam allowances. Cut design details from assorted print and calico fabrics without adding seam allowances.

Iron small pieces to house front, using fusible webbing cut into shapes the same size as details. Trim the house with French knots, feather stitching, or other small embroidery stitches.

Sew front to back with right sides facing; leave an opening. Turn, stuff, and slip-stitch closed.

Pioneer Dolls
page 93

Materials: *For large doll*—⅓ yard of bleached linen (body); ⅓ yard of calico fabric (dress); scrap of ½-inch-wide lace; ½ skein nubby yarn (hair); brown and pink embroidery floss; polyester fiberfill.

For small doll—¼ yard of natural colored linen (body); ¼ yard of calico fabric (dress); 1 skein sport-weight yarn or linen thread (hair); red and black felt-tipped pens; polyester fiberfill; red embroidery floss.

Instructions: Enlarge patterns (below). Cut body pieces, adding ¼-inch seam margins.

With right sides facing, sew body pieces together, leaving armholes and bottom of body open. Turn and press.

With right sides facing, sew arms; leave ends open. Turn right side out, press, and stuff. Insert arms into openings on body and stitch, turning raw edges under. Stuff body firmly.

Repeat the above step to make legs (toes should point straight up). Insert tops of legs into body and stitch across, turning raw edges under.

Embroider brown eyes and pink cheeks and mouth on large doll using satin and outline stitches. For small doll, color features with felt pens.

Cut dresses from calico fabric; add ½-inch seam allowances. Hem skirt, *continued*

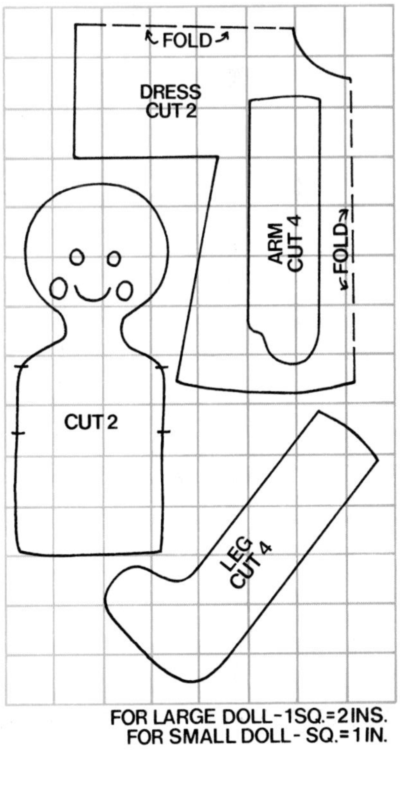

FOR LARGE DOLL–1 SQ.= 2 INS.
FOR SMALL DOLL– SQ.= 1 IN.

105

continued from page 105
Homespun Quilts & Crafts

sleeves, and the neckline. Add lace to neckline of large dress; gather with a strand of embroidery floss. For small doll, buttonhole-stitch around neckline; pull floss through loops to make a tie.

To make hair for large doll, spread ½ skein of yarn to make a 6×22-inch piece. Machine-stitch a "part" several times through yarn's center to hold strands together. Whipstitch hair to head along this part. Braid two pigtails; tie ends. Repeat for small doll, forming a 3×12-inch section.

Basket Pincushion
page 93

Materials: Woven round basket with a 12-inch opening; scraps of print fabric for appliqué; 16-inch square of blue print fabric for background; embroidery floss; ½ yard of muslin; sawdust or fiberfill for pincushion.

Instructions: Enlarge the pattern (below) and cut each pattern piece from a different fabric. Add ¼-inch seam allowances to all pieces. As you plan the pattern pieces, strive for a pleasing assortment of large- and small-scale prints. You also may wish to cut windows from light-colored fabric.

Turn under the seam allowance on all pieces and baste. Appliqué the ground piece to the background first; then add other pieces. Embroider the crossbars on the window in outline stitches and add a French-knot doorknob and other trims as desired.

Gather a large circle of muslin into a bag; pack tightly with sawdust or fiberfill. Whipstitch edges closed. Fit appliquéd piece over pincushion; whipstitch into place. Trim fabric edges; fit cushion into basket.

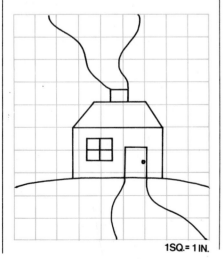

1 SQ. = 1 IN.

Lined Picnic Basket
page 93

Materials: Picnic basket; fabric scraps in assorted patterns and colors; sufficient fabric to face back of quilt; nylon fastening tape; staples.

Instructions: Measure the length, width, and depth of the basket top and base. On brown paper, draw a cross-shaped pattern for the lining with these dimensions.

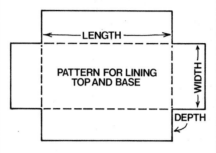

Divide the paper pattern into small squares and piece new quilt blocks to match the squares on the pattern diagram. Use assorted fabric scraps for the quilt blocks and a pattern of your own choosing. Assemble completed blocks to match patterns.

Cut facing fabric to match assembled quilt pieces. With right sides facing stitch quilt to lining, leaving an opening. Turn, press, and slip-stitch.

Fasten lining to basket with pieces of nylon fastening tape stapled to corners and sides of top and base. Stitch tape to back of basket lining; insert lining into basket.

Quilted Stocking
page 93

Materials: Old quilt or fabric scraps in assorted patterns and colors; ½ yard lining fabric; ½ yard of wide (5 to 8 inches) lace; grosgrain ribbon.

Instructions: Using the pattern on page 17, cut stocking front and back from an old quilt or from pieced quilt blocks. (The stocking shown is cut from a quilt pieced in the log cabin design. See page 99 before cutting an old quilt.) Add ½-inch seam allowances. Cut front and back lining to match top.

Stitch stocking front to back, right sides facing; leave top open. Clip curves and turn right side out.

Baste lace around the top, gathering it to fit the top of the stocking. Stitch lining front to back, insert in stocking, and whipstitch in place along the top, turning under raw edges. Add ribbon bows and hanger.

Quilted Boxes
page 93

Materials: Fabric scraps in assorted colors and prints; quilt batting; ¾ yard of lining fabric; heavy cardboard.

Instructions: For the large box, make each side by piecing four 6-inch-square quilt blocks (add ¼-inch seam allowances). Use the log cabin design (see page 100). Stitch the small blocks into a large block 12 inches square.

Cut backing fabric and 2 layers of batting to match front. With right sides facing and batting on top and bottom, stitch back to front along 3 sides, trim seams, and turn right side out. Insert a 12-inch-square of cardboard between layers of batting. Slip-stitch the opening, turning under raw edges. Make 6 sides. (Bottom may be plain fabric rather than pieced blocks.)

To assemble the box, slip-stitch 4 sides together. Slip-stitch bottom piece to sides. Sew top into place along one side only. Add an antique button clasp.

Quilt-Pattern Cards
page 93

Materials: White construction paper or purchased blank cards; scraps of cotton print fabric in a variety of patterns; fabric glue.

Instructions: Enlarge pattern on page 104, using a scale of 1 square equals ¼ inch. Cut all pieces from fabric. *Do not* add seam allowances.

Fold construction paper into cards. Position fabric pieces on the front of each card; glue into place.

Stenciled Wooden Boxes
page 94

Materials: Unfinished wooden containers (see note); precut stencils; #6 stencil brush; neutral shoe polish (in paste form); liquid dyes in scarlet, fuchsia; cocoa brown, evening blue, royal blue, kelly green, and tangerine; masking tape; turpentine; natural-bristle vegetable scrubbing brush; 1½-inch-wide paintbrush; non-waterbased polyurethane, shellac, or varnish; paper towels.

Instructions: (*Note:* Because the wax and dyes must soak into the wood, only porous raw wood is suitable for this project.)

Referring to photograph on page 94 for design ideas, tape stencil on wood.

Hold the stencil in place, dip end of brush into polish, and apply with daubing motion. Shoe polish has a waxy base and resists water-soluble dyes, so the natural color of the wood will show through each design.

After waxing, gently remove stencil; reposition for next design.

When all designs are stenciled, allow to dry until no wax comes off when you touch the polish.

Mix 2 parts dye to 1 part cold water. For darker colors, add more dye.

Wipe dye onto wood using a paper towel. (Don't worry about covering the stenciled areas—the shoe polish resists the dye.) The dyes are transparent so the wood grain shows through.

Remove beads of dye with a clean paper towel. Let dry.

Working in a well-ventilated area, pour a thin coat of turpentine over the wood; let it soak into the shoe polish for a few minutes. Scrub the stenciled areas with a vegetable brush until polish is removed. Wipe away turpentine with paper towels until wood feels dry. Dry thoroughly; apply a coating of non-water-based polyurethane, shellac, or varnish.

Primitive Wooden Animals
page 95

Materials: Pieces of old, weathered pine or rough-cut lumber for bodies and platforms; scraps of dowels for legs, old wooden checkers or slices of broom handle for wheels; paint; sponge or rag; scraps of leather, suede, and fabric for trim; coarse and fine wood files; glue; staples.

Instructions: Cut out simple animal shapes from lumber using a saber or band saw (refer to color photograph, page 95). If legs, made of dowels, are to be separate from body, drill holes in base of body.

Use a coarse wood file or rasp for the rough shaping of the animal. Then use a finer file to smooth the shape. Don't sand or file the animal to perfection, however, or the appealing primitive look will be lost.

Paint animals using a rag or sponge, wiping paint on lightly to let wood grain and roughness show through. Add facial details and trim.

For the large horse, cut and fringe leather pieces for the mane and tail. Cut small pieces for ears. Drill holes in wood and glue tail and ears in place. Staple mane down length of neck. Cut saddle and blanket from leather and fabric; glue into place.

For the tiger, paint white undercoat on body, then spray with orange and yellow paint. When the tiger is dry, add stripes, facial features, and mouth.

Make platforms for animals from planks or rough boards. Drill holes into top for legs of animals and into sides for wheels.

For wheels, use old wooden checkers or broom handle slices. Drill a hole into the wheel's center; insert dowel. Drill a small hole at end of dowel. Slip a wooden toothpick into hole; glue into place. Glue other dowel end to the platform.

Star Quilt
page 96

Note: Finished size is approximately 75×90 inches.

Materials: Assorted print fabrics equal to 6 yards of 44-inch-wide fabric (each star requires about 8×10 inches of fabric); scraps of solid-color fabric (centers); 8 yards of ecru polished cotton (diamonds and backing); quilt batting; 1½ yards of blue broadcloth (binding); cardboard or plastic lids.

Instructions: (*Note:* The quilt shown has 13 rows, each approximately 7 inches across at its widest point. To change the quilt size, alter the number of rows to change the width or the number of stars in each row to change the length. Adjust fabric requirements accordingly.)

Enlarge the pattern (below), reversing it as necessary to complete the design. Cut templates from cardboard or plastic lids for the star point, center, and diamond.

Add ¼-inch seam allowances. Cut pieces for 169 stars. Cut 2 lengths of backing fabric, each 44×96 inches; sew them together along one selvage. Trim to 78 inches wide. Cut diamonds from the remaining ecru fabric.

(*Before cutting all the pieces for the quilt it's a good idea to cut out and assemble a single star with 6 diamonds*

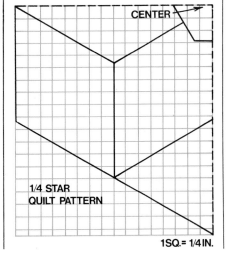

CENTER

1/4 STAR QUILT PATTERN

1 SQ.= 1/4 IN.

around it into a hexagonal block to check the accuracy of your pattern.)

Using ¼-inch seams, join star points as shown in the pattern (see photograph, page 96). Add the center hexagon, clipping corners. Press seams.

For each row, stitch 12 diamonds between 13 stars. Add one diamond to *one end only* of each row. Assemble 13 rows.

To assemble the top, lay rows side by side so the ends without diamonds face alternate directions. The stars will form diagonal rows across the quilt. Join rows by stitching diamonds between star points.

To assemble the quilt, sandwich batting between top and backing. Pin layers together, baste, and quilt. Trim batting and backing to match the front. Bind edges in blue.

Woven Checkerboard Vest
page 96

Materials: Small skeins of naturally dyed yarn (or sport-weight yarn in assorted colors); 4-inch square metal loom; simple vest pattern without darts; fabric for interlining, lining, and edging vest.

Instructions: Weave enough small squares to join together to form "fabric" to cover each pattern piece of the vest. Join squares together, following loom instructions. (The vest shown uses 48 squares.)

Cut all pattern pieces from interlining; baste each pattern shape to "fabric" of woven squares. Stay-stitch woven fabric to interlining to prevent raveling.

Cut out the pattern pieces to match interlining pieces. Assemble and line the vest following sewing directions with the pattern.

Country Girl Doll
page 97

Materials: One pair opaque long stockings; polyester fiberfill; 1 skein 2-ply angora yarn; red and brown embroidery floss; pink crayon; 2 black buttons; ½ yard each of white batiste, brown print, and blue print; 12-inch square of brown felt; 6 small buttons; embroidered, lace, and ribbon trims.

Instructions: Cut off one stocking 9½ inches below the top, ribbed edge. Stitch the bottom edge together; stuff to form body. (Doll's body is about 8 inches in circumference.) The ribbed top of the stocking becomes the doll's neck. Cut one stocking off 2 inches *continued*

Continued from page 107
Homespun Quilts & Crafts

beyond the bottom turning edge of the heel. Cut up the center front and center back of this section to make 2 pieces. Sew each of these pieces together, shaping the doll's foot beyond the heel-turning point. Turn legs right side out. Stuff legs and stitch to body.

Cut a section of stocking 9 inches long. Cut up the center back and front of this section. Sew the arm tubes, rounding one end of each tube to form hands. Turn right side out. Stuff, then slip-stitch arms to body.

Cut the heel of one stocking to form the face. The diagonal turning line of the heel should run from the side of the doll's face down the cheeks. Cut the stocking 3½ inches from the turning point of the heel (toward the toe) and 4½ inches from the point of the heel up the leg of the sock. Make slashes in the stocking; sew them together to give the head shape. Stuff.

After most of the stuffing is in place, take tucks at the back of the head to create the desired shape for the face. Sew to body.

Embroider mouth with red floss and eyebrows with brown floss. Make 2 French knots of brown thread for nostrils. Sew on 2 black buttons for eyes.

Cut strands of 2-ply Angora yarn about 24 inches long for hair. Center them across the doll's head; attach by stitching down the center line. Pull hair to each side; stitch to head at ear level, then braid. Shape braids atop the head and tack-stitch into place.

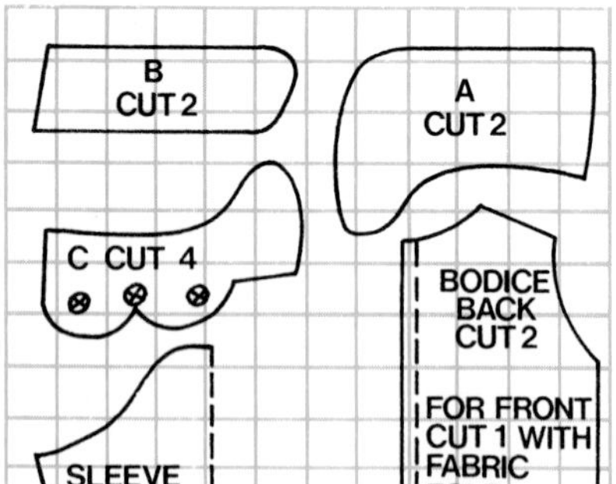

For pantaloons, cut pattern pieces (below left) from batiste. Sew the front and back seams using ¼-inch seam allowance. Sew the front and back together at the inseams, leaving the sides open. Sew eyelet trim to the bottom edge. Sew sides. Turn under ½ inch at the top edge to form casing for drawstring. Stitch; thread seam binding through the casing; tie.

For skirt, cut brown print 14×44 inches. Hem one long edge; gather other long edge. Measure doll's waist; cut 1½-inch-wide strip to size, plus 1½ inches. Stitch skirt to waistband in ¼-inch seam. Fold waistband over seam allowance and stitch, encasing raw edges. Sew snaps to ends of band.

For blouse, cut bodice and sleeves from batiste. Cut 8-inch piece of 2-inch-wide eyelet for collar and two 8-inch strips of 2-inch eyelet for sleeve trim. To assemble, sew bodice shoulder seams. Gather top edge of sleeve between notches. Sew sleeves to bodice. Turn under ¼ inch at lower edge of sleeve. Gather eyelet sleeve trim and sew to bottom of sleeve. Sew bodice side seams and sleeve seams.

Turn under ¼ inch at neck opening; sew on eyelet strip for collar. (When blouse is completed and on doll, fit collar to shape of neck. Take tucks at sides of collar for proper fit.) Narrowly hem center back edges of blouse. Add snaps along the edges.

For the pinafore, cut a blue print apron 12×22 inches; narrowly hem the sides and one long edge. Cut a bib 3×6 inches and fold it in half (3×3 inches), wrong sides together. Cut 2 shoulder straps, each 2×8¼ inches; fold under ¼ inch on the long sides of the shoulder straps; press. Fold each strap in half lengthwise. Pin straps to sides of bib, with raw edges of straps and bib even. Topstitch close to folded edge; continue stitching down the length of each strap to secure the edges.

Cut out 1½-inch-wide waistband for apron to fit doll's waist, plus 1½ inches. Gather top of apron to fit center 6 inches of waistband and stitch, using a ¼-inch seam.

Center the bib over the apron and stitch it to the opposite side of the waistband in a ¼-inch seam. Cut facing for waistband and stitch in place, encasing all raw edges. Tack lace trim to waistband and add snaps to ends of straps and ends of waistband.

For shoes, cut pattern pieces (left) from felt, making sure one is left and the other right. Place pattern piece C on A, lining up toes. Place B over A and C, lining up heels. Sew around, using ¼-inch seam. Leave top open. Turn

and join B and C by sewing 3 buttons on each shoe.

Fabric Bowls
page 97

Note: Directions are for a large bowl (14-inch-diameter). For small and medium sizes, adjust fabric and cording requirements. One yard of 44/45-inch fabric yields about 8 yards of bias strips.

Materials: 1¾ yards of muslin or cotton print fabric for large basket (see note); 12 yards of 1½-inch diameter cotton cable cord for large basket.

Instructions: Cut fabric into 4-inch-wide bias strips. Join strips into a continuous piece, using ¼-inch seams.

Stitch fabric around cording, right sides facing. Slide cording to end of fabric tube, leaving 4 inches *inside* the tube. Machine-stitch across short end of tube to anchor cording; turn fabric right side out over cording. Turn under raw edges at ends; blindstitch.

Starting at one end of cording, make a flat, circular coil about 10 inches in diameter for the bottom of the bowl. Whipstitch coils firmly together on the outside of the bowl.

To make the sides, position coils atop one another; whipstitch in place from the outside. To anchor, whipstitch the end of the cording firmly; turn the bowl right side out.

Soft-Sculpture Jam Jars
page 97

Materials: (for one jar) ⅓ yard of print fabric (jar); 12×12 inches of muslin (cover); 1 yard of ¼-inch-wide grosgrain ribbon; even-weave fabric and brown embroidery floss or pearl cotton (label); polyester fiberfill.

Instructions: The jar size will vary with size of fabric rectangle used.

one square = 1 stitch over 2 threads

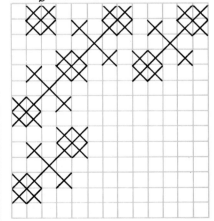

B CUT 2

A CUT 2

C CUT 4

BODICE BACK CUT 2

FOR FRONT CUT 1 WITH FABRIC FOLD ALONG DOTTED LINE

SLEEVE CUT 2

FOLD

PANTALOON CUT 4

1 SQ.= 1 IN.

Cut two 12×14-inch rectangles of print fabric, stitch together along long sides (¼-inch seam; right sides facing). Turn right side out and press.

Gather top of jar into a 2½×12-inch band of fabric to form rim. Top with a 3½-inch fabric circle. Stuff jar firmly with fiberfill; gather jar bottom into a 3½×6½-inch fabric oval for the base. Whipstitch base in place.

Cut a 12-inch muslin circle for the cover. Hem the circle's outer edge; place it over the jar's top. Gather the muslin snugly to the jar top rim; tack-stitch gathers into place. Conceal stitches with grosgrain ribbon.

Cut a square or rectangle of even-weave fabric for the label (size depends on size of jar), adding ¼-inch seam allowances. Work border design (below left) in brown cross-stitches around edge of label, then lightly write contents ("pickles," "jam," etc.) in pencil; work in stem stitches. Slip-stitch label to jar.

Lace Wreath
page 97

Materials: 12-inch plastic foam wreath; ¼ yard of muslin; 2 yards each of 6 different 2-inch-wide pre-ruffled lace edgings (crocheted, eyelet, etc.); 1 yard each of red polka-dotted, green, and yellow grosgrain ribbon; pins.

Instructions: Cut lace into thirty-six 12-inch lengths; gather each piece into a circular rosette. Tie off.

Wrap the wreath with a 2½-inch-wide strip of muslin; whipstitch the strips in place, overlapping edges.

Pin lace rosettes to circumference of wreath. Attach ribbon bows.

Treetop Star
page 98

Materials: 12-inch square from an old quilt, or sufficient fabric scraps to piece a 12-inch square; 12-inch square of backing fabric; polyester fiberfill; 4 yards of ¼-inch-wide red grosgrain ribbon; small lace doily; 5 small bells.

Instructions: Follow directions on page 99 for making a pattern. Adding ¼-inch seam allowances, cut star front from an old quilt or from a pieced patchwork square. Cut back to match front. With right sides facing, sew front to back, leaving an opening. Turn, stuff, and slip-stitch.

Appliqué a lace doily to the star front. Divide ribbon, fold into bows; tack bows between 4 star points. Add bells to the points. Add a thread loop to the star top for a hanger.

Wooden Candlesticks
page 98

Materials: Unfinished decorative wooden spindles (available in lumber and hardware stores); liquid fabric dyes; sandpaper; varnish.

Instructions: Using a saw, cut 2- to 4-inch-long sections from wooden spindles. Remove extra turnings from bottom of each piece but leave turnings at top of candlestick (see page 98).

Drill a hole in the top of each candlestick for the candle to rest in.

Stain wood using liquid dyes.

Braided Place Mats and Napkin Rings
pages 98-99

Materials: Three 2×320-inch fabric strips in 3 different colors (for each place mat); three 2×24-inch strips in three colors (for each ring).

Instructions: (*Note:* One yard of 44/45-inch-wide fabric yields about 22 yards of strips for braiding; 3 yards of fabric in 3 colors yield enough strips for 3 place mats and 3 napkin rings.)

To make braiding strips, cut and piece short lengths on the bias in ¼-inch seams.

Turn raw edges of each strip toward the middle. Fold strips in half.

Pin 3 strips together at one end; braid. Sew the braid at both ends so it doesn't unwind.

To make the place mat, coil braid into a circle measuring 14 inches in diameter. Join coils with small stitches.

To make napkin rings, coil the braid once, making a 1½-inch hole. Wrap braid into additional coils, joining the coils with small stitches.

Quilted Wreath
page 99

Materials: Old quilt, or sufficient fabrics to piece new patchwork fabric; ¾ yard of backing fabric; fiberfill; brown paper; 3 yards of 1½-inch-wide grosgrain ribbon; embroidery floss.

Instructions: On paper, draw a 25-inch circle with a 7-inch circle in the center to form wreath. Divide into 8 sections.

Using one section as a pattern and adding ½-inch seam allowances, cut 8 pieces from an old quilt for the wreath. Turn the pattern as you cut out the sections so the patchwork forms an interesting design around the wreath.

(In the wreath shown, each section has been turned so square patches ring the outer edge of the wreath. For additional design interest, you also may cut the pattern in half crosswise before cutting out wreath pieces; be sure to add seam allowances.)

Or, using a pattern of your own choosing, stitch 8 mini-patchwork quilts from which you can cut the sections for the wreath.

Stitch the 8 sections together into wreath shape. Cut backing fabric to match front, adding seam allowances.

With right sides facing, stitch wreath front to back around *outside* edge. Clip curves, turn, and stuff. Whipstitch front to back around inner circle.

Using embroidery floss, tie 8 knots through the wreath in centers of main seams. Add decorative ribbon bow.

To hang the wreath sew a ½×2 inch fabric tab to the upper back of the wreath, make a thread bar and buttonhole-stitch over the thread for strength, or tack a curtain ring to the back.

Needlepoint Sachet
page 99

Materials: 5-inch square of #14-count needlepoint canvas; 4 yards each of 5 shades of blue/green or gold/brown (or colors of your choice) 3-ply Persian wool yarn, or naturally dyed yarn; 5-inch square of matching backing fabric; #19 tapestry needle; polyester fiberfill or potpourri mixture.

Instructions: The pattern (below) represents 1 quadrant of the design.

Repeat it 3 more times.

Work the design in basket-weave, diamond eyelet, and cross-stitches, using 2 plies of yarn. Refer to the photograph on page 99 for colors.

Finish the canvas as a sachet or pincushion, using potpourri or fiberfill.

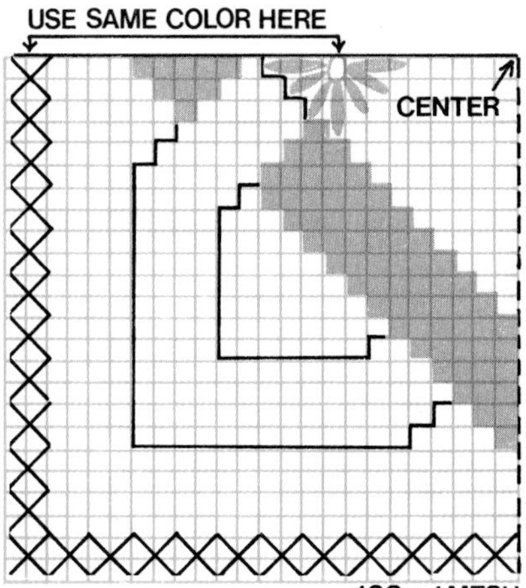

USE SAME COLOR HERE

CENTER

1 SQ.= 1 MESH

Christmas Gifts from Your Kitchen

If you are tired of racking your brain for new and different gift ideas for Christmas, try giving foods as gifts this year. Besides telling that special person that you really care, homemade food gifts are attractive, fun to make, and often cost less than gifts purchased in the store.

In this section you will find a selection of breads, coffee cakes, cookies, candies, homemade liqueurs, jellies, jams, pickles, relishes, drink mixes, and seasoning mixes that are perfect for even the hardest to please on your gift list.

Pictured (right) is a delicious assortment of holiday homemades. You won't believe how easy they are to make and how much fun they are to give. Clockwise from back left are Peanut Butter Granola, Fruited Rice Curry Mix, Buttermilk Dressing Mix, Bouquet Garni, Caesar-Seasoned Croutons, and Spiced Coffee Mix. (See page 112 for recipes.)

Along with the recipes we've also pictured a variety of ways you can wrap your food gifts. If you're looking for a more expensive gift, combine a utensil, such as a grater, wooden spoon, coffeepot, or cutting board, with your food gifts.

Peanut Butter Granola

see photograph, pages 110–111

1 cup raisins
⅔ cup creamy peanut butter
⅔ cup honey
½ teaspoon ground cinnamon
1 teaspoon vanilla
4 cups rolled oats
1 cup shelled peanuts
½ cup dried figs, snipped

Pour *boiling water* over raisins to cover; let stand 10 minutes. Drain. In saucepan combine peanut butter, honey, and cinnamon; heat through. Remove from heat; stir in vanilla. Place oats in large shallow roasting pan or 15x10x1-inch baking pan. Pour warm peanut butter mixture over oats and stir gently till mixture is coated; spread evenly in pan.

Bake in 300° oven for 35 to 40 minutes, stirring occasionally. Turn off oven; stir in raisins, nuts, and figs. Let dry in oven 1½ hours; stir occasionally. Store granola in airtight containers. Makes 8 cups.

Fruited Rice Curry Mix

see photograph, pages 110–111

1 cup long grain rice
¼ cup mixed dried fruits, chopped
¼ cup slivered almonds
2 tablespoons light raisins
1 tablespoon minced dried onion
2 teaspoons curry powder
2 teaspoons instant beef bouillon granules
½ teaspoon salt

In a bowl combine rice, dried fruits, almonds, raisins, onion, curry powder, beef bouillon, and salt. Package in airtight containers.

Directions to enclose with mix: To prepare rice, combine the mix with 2½ cups *water* and 2 tablespoons *butter* or *margarine* in a saucepan; cover tightly. Bring to boiling; reduce heat. Simmer 20 minutes. Do not lift cover. Makes 4 cups cooked rice.

Buttermilk Dressing Mix

see photograph, pages 110–111

1 cup dry buttermilk powder *or* nonfat dry milk powder
¼ cup sugar
4 teaspoons dried basil, crushed
4 teaspoons minced dried onion
2 teaspoons dry mustard
1 teaspoon garlic powder
1 teaspoon salt

In a bowl combine dry milk powder, sugar, basil, onion, mustard, garlic powder, and salt. Store in airtight containers. Makes about 1 cup mix.

Directions to enclose with mix: Combine ¼ *cup* of the Buttermilk Dressing Mix with ½ cup *water*. Blend into ¾ cup *mayonnaise* or *salad dressing*. Shake well before serving. Makes about 1½ cups dressing.

Bouquet Garni

see photograph, pages 110–111

1 tablespoon dried parsley
1 teaspoon dried basil
1 teaspoon dried rosemary
1 teaspoon dried oregano
2 bay leaves
6 whole peppercorns
1 clove garlic

Tie all ingredients together in a piece of cheesecloth. Add to stews and soups for seasoning. Makes 1.

Caesar-Seasoned Croutons

see photograph, pages 110–111

10 slices firm-textured white bread
¼ cup olive *or* cooking oil
¼ cup grated parmesan cheese
½ teaspoon garlic salt

Brush both sides of bread with olive or cooking oil; sprinkle with parmesan cheese and garlic salt. Cut into ½-inch cubes. Place in 15x10x1-inch baking pan. Bake in 300° oven for 30 minutes, stirring once. Cool. Store in airtight containers. Makes 4 cups.

Spiced Coffee Mix

see photograph, pages 110–111

1 cup regular grind coffee
8 whole allspice
8 whole cloves
8 inches stick cinnamon, broken
6 sugar cubes

In a bowl combine coffee, allspice, cloves, cinnamon, and sugar cubes. Store in airtight containers.

Directions to enclose with mix: To make coffee, place the Spiced Coffee Mix in a coffee percolator basket and brew with 6 cups *water*. Serves 8.

Hot Tea Mix

1 9-ounce jar (1¼ cups) orange-flavored breakfast drink powder
¾ cup iced tea mix with lemon and sugar
1 teaspoon ground cinnamon
½ teaspoon ground allspice
¼ teaspoon ground cloves

Combine all ingredients; mix well. Store in airtight containers. Makes 2 cups mix.

Directions to enclose with mix: For one serving, combine *2 tablespoons* of the Hot Tea Mix with 1 cup *boiling water* in a cup or mug.

Minty Chocolate Malt Mix

2 cups chocolate-flavored malted milk powder
½ cup white butter mints, chopped
3 cups nonfat dry milk powder
½ cup sweetened cocoa mix

In a covered blender container mix *1 cup* of the malted milk powder and mints. Blend about 1 minute or till mints are finely chopped. Turn into mixing bowl. Add remaining malted milk powder, nonfat dry milk powder, and cocoa mix. Stir well. Store in airtight containers. Makes 5¾ cups.

Directions to enclose with mix: For one serving, mix ¼ *cup* of the Minty Chocolate Malt Mix with ¾ cup *boiling water* in a cup. Stir to dissolve mixture.

Café au Lait Mix

1 6-ounce jar (1½ cups) instant
   non-dairy creamer
¼ cup packed brown sugar
¼ cup instant coffee crystals
   Dash salt

In a bowl combine non-dairy creamer, brown sugar, coffee crystals, and salt. Store in airtight containers. Makes 2 cups mix.

Directions to enclose with mix: For one serving, combine ¼ *cup* of the Café au Lait Mix with ⅔ cup *boiling water* in a cup or mug.

Orange Jupiter Mix

1¾ cups nonfat dry milk powder
1 9-ounce jar (1¼ cups)
   orange-flavored breakfast
   drink powder
½ cup sugar
2 teaspoons vanilla

In a bowl stir together nonfat dry milk powder, breakfast drink powder, and sugar. Blend in vanilla. Store in airtight containers. Makes about 4 cups mix.

Directions to enclose with mix: For *three servings,* place *1 cup* of the Orange Jupiter Mix and 1½ cups *cold water* in blender container. Cover; blend till smooth. Add 4 or 6 ice cubes, 1 cube at a time, blending till chopped after each addition.

For *one serving,* place ⅓ *cup* of the Jupiter Mix, ½ cup *cold water,* and 2 *ice cubes* into a blender container. Cover; blend for 30 to 45 seconds or till smooth.

Spiced Mocha Mix

2 cups sweetened cocoa mix
⅓ cup instant coffee crystals
1 teaspoon ground cinnamon

In a bowl combine cocoa mix, coffee crystals, and cinnamon. Stir thoroughly. Store in airtight containers. Makes 2¼ cups mix.

Directions to enclose with mix: For one serving, combine *3 tablespoons* of the Spiced Mocha Mix with ⅔ cup *boiling water* in a cup or mug.

Curried Corn Snacks

¼ cup butter *or* margarine
½ to 1 teaspoon curry powder
¼ teaspoon onion salt
⅛ teaspoon ground ginger
2 cups bite-size shredded corn
   squares
2 cups puffed corn cereal

In a large skillet melt butter. Blend in curry powder, onion salt, and ginger. Add corn squares and puffed cereal; toss to coat. Heat and stir 15 minutes over low heat. Cool; package in 1 cup portions. Makes 4 cups.

Spiced Mixed Nuts

1 slightly beaten egg white
1 teaspoon water
1 8-ounce jar (1⅔ cups) dry
   roasted peanuts
½ cup unblanched whole
   almonds
½ cup walnut halves
¾ cup sugar
1 tablespoon pumpkin pie
   spice
¾ teaspoon salt

Combine egg white and water. Add nuts; toss to coat. Combine sugar, pumpkin pie spice, and salt. Add to nuts; toss till all are well coated. Place in single layer on greased baking sheet. Bake in 300° oven for 20 to 25 minutes. Cool nuts on waxed paper. Break up large clusters. Makes 4½ cups.

Noodle-Cereal Snack

2 cups tiny pretzels
1 3-ounce can chow mein
   noodles
1 cup puffed corn cereal
¼ cup butter *or* margarine,
   melted
2 teaspoons worcestershire
   sauce
½ teaspoon onion salt
¼ teaspoon garlic powder

In a large bowl mix pretzels, noodles, and corn cereal. Combine butter, worcestershire, onion salt, and garlic powder; pour over pretzel mixture, stirring to coat. Spread in a baking pan. Heat in a 350° oven 5 minutes. Cool. Package in 1 cup portions. Makes 4 cups.

Seasoned Salt

1 cup pickling salt
2½ teaspoons paprika
2 teaspoons dry mustard
1½ teaspoons garlic powder
1½ teaspoons dried oregano,
   crushed
1 teaspoon dried thyme,
   crushed
1 teaspoon curry powder
½ teaspoon onion powder
¼ teaspoon dried dillweed

In a bowl combine salt, paprika, mustard, garlic powder, oregano, thyme, curry powder, onion powder, and dillweed. Mix thoroughly. Package in airtight containers. Seal. Makes 1 cup.

Make-Your-Own-Curry

¼ cup coriander seed
¼ cup ground turmeric
4 inches stick cinnamon,
   broken
1 tablespoon cumin seed
1 tablespoon cardamom pods,
   shelled (about 1 teaspoon
   seed)
1 teaspoon whole black pepper
1 teaspoon ground ginger
5 whole cloves
2 bay leaves

In a shallow baking pan combine coriander, turmeric, cinnamon, cumin seed, cardamom, pepper, ginger, cloves, and bay leaves. Bake in a 200° oven 25 minutes, stirring occasionally. Place in blender container. Cover; blend till well ground. Package in ¼-cup portions. Makes ¾ cup.

Poultry Seasoning

2 cups dried parsley
1 cup ground sage
½ cup dried rosemary, crushed
½ cup dried marjoram, crushed
3 tablespoons salt
1 tablespoon pepper
2 teaspoons onion powder
½ teaspoon ground ginger

In a bowl combine parsley, sage, rosemary, marjoram, salt, pepper, onion powder, and ginger. Pour into airtight containers. Seal. Before using shake mixture well. Makes 4 cups.

Lucia Buns

2 tablespoons hot water
⅛ teaspoon powdered saffron
3½ to 3¾ cups all-purpose flour
1 package active dry yeast
1 cup milk
½ cup sugar
6 tablespoons butter *or* margarine
1 teaspoon salt
1 egg
½ cup raisins, chopped
¼ cup chopped Brazil nuts

Pour hot water over saffron; set aside. Combine *2 cups* of the flour and the yeast. In saucepan heat together milk, sugar, butter or margarine, and salt till warm (115°), stirring constantly till butter almost melts. Add to dry mixture; add egg and saffron mixture. Beat at low speed of electric mixer for ½ minute, scraping sides of bowl constantly. Beat 3 minutes at high speed. Stir in raisins, nuts, and as much of the remaining flour as you can mix in using a spoon. On floured surface knead in remaining flour to make a moderately stiff dough. Continue kneading till smooth. Place in greased bowl, turning once to grease surface. Cover; let rise till double (1½ to 1¾ hours). Punch down dough; cover and let rest 10 minutes. Divide dough into 32 pieces. Roll each into a 10-inch rope. Lay 2 ropes side by side on greased baking sheet. Press centers of ropes to seal. Coil each of the 4 ends toward outside. Cover; let rise till double (30 to 45 minutes). Bake in 425° oven 8 to 10 minutes. Cool on wire rack. Makes 16.

Festively wrap an assortment of food gifts for Christmas including three different shapes of Christmas Tree Bread *(center),* Candy Tree *(top center; see recipe, page 122),* Chewy Popcorn Balls *wrapped in clear plastic wrap and decorated with a candy cane (top right and left; see recipe, page 121), and* Rolled Sugar Cookies *trimmed with decorative candies (extreme right; see recipe, page 121).*

Christmas Tree Bread

4 cups all-purpose flour
1 package active dry yeast
1 cup milk
½ cup shortening
¼ cup granulated sugar
1 teaspoon salt
2 eggs
2 cups sifted powdered sugar
1 teaspoon vanilla
   Milk

In large mixing bowl combine *1½ cups* of the flour with the yeast. In saucepan heat 1 cup milk, the shortening, granulated sugar, and salt just till warm (115° to 120°), stirring constantly till shortening almost melts. Add to dry mixture in mixing bowl; add eggs. Beat at low speed of electric mixer for ½ minute, scraping sides of bowl constantly. Beat 3 minutes at high speed. By hand, stir in as much of the remaining flour as you can mix in using a spoon to make a moderately stiff dough. Place in greased bowl; turn once to grease surface. Cover; let rise till double (about 1 hour). Punch down; cover. Let rest 10 minutes. On floured surface roll to a 15x10-inch rectangle. Cut dough into fifteen 1-inch-wide strips.

To shape tree at left in photograph (left): Lay a 10-inch strip of dough on greased baking sheet for trunk. For bottom branch, piece strips of dough to form a 15-inch strip. Fold in half. Seal ends; twist. Place on trunk. Repeat using 12-, 9-, and 6-inch strips.

To shape tree at center in photograph (left): Place a 10-inch strip of dough on greased baking sheet for trunk. Starting 1½ inches from base of trunk, place strips of dough—9, 8, 7, 6, 5, 4, and 3 inches long—on edges over trunk to form branches.

To shape tree at right in photograph (left): Lay a 10-inch strip of dough flat on greased baking sheet for trunk. Roll remaining pieces of dough to round slightly. Loop a 12-inch strip of dough atop trunk to form bottom branch. Repeat with 9- and 7-inch strips.

Let dough rise in warm place till double (about 1¼ hours). Bake in 400° oven for 12 to 15 minutes. Cool. Mix powdered sugar, vanilla, and enough milk to make of spreading consistency. Drizzle over trees. Garnish with candied cherries or gumdrops, if desired. Top each tree with a paper bow, if desired. Makes 3.

Cranberry Nut Bread

¾ cup sugar
½ cup butter *or* margarine, softened
1 egg
1 teaspoon finely shredded orange peel
2½ cups all-purpose flour
1 tablespoon baking powder
1 teaspoon salt
¾ cup chopped fresh *or* frozen cranberries
⅔ cup orange juice
⅓ cup milk
⅓ cup chopped almonds

In mixing bowl cream sugar and butter till fluffy. Beat in egg and orange peel. Stir together flour, baking powder, and salt. Combine cranberries, orange juice, and milk. Add alternately with dry ingredients to creamed mixture, mixing after each addition. Fold in nuts. Bake in 350° oven in a greased 8½x4½x2½-inch loaf pan about 60 minutes *or* bake in 2 greased 7½x3½x2-inch loaf pans for 45 to 50 minutes. Cool in pans for 10 minutes; remove from pans. Cool on wire rack. Makes 1 large or 2 small loaves.

Sherried Date and Nut Loaf

1 cup snipped pitted whole dates
⅔ cup dry sherry
1 tablespoon finely shredded orange peel
2 cups all-purpose flour
⅔ cup packed brown sugar
⅓ cup wheat germ
2 teaspoons baking powder
1 teaspoon salt
1 teaspoon ground nutmeg
¼ teaspoon baking soda
2 beaten eggs
⅓ cup milk
¼ cup cooking oil
¾ cup coarsely chopped walnuts

In small bowl combine dates, sherry, and orange peel; set aside. Stir together flour, sugar, wheat germ, baking powder, salt, nutmeg, and baking soda. Combine eggs, milk, oil, and date mixture. Add dry ingredients, stirring just till moistened. Fold in nuts. Turn into greased 8½x4½x2½-inch loaf pan. Bake in 350° oven for 50 to 55 minutes. Cool in pan for 10 minutes; remove loaf. Cool thoroughly on wire rack. Wrap and store overnight before slicing.

115

Clockwise from back: Cherry-Nut Fans, Lemon-Coconut Wreaths, Sour Cream and Chocolate Envelopes, *and* Date-Orange Pinwheels.

Basic Danish Dough

1 cup butter
⅓ cup all-purpose flour
• • •
3¾ to 4 cups all-purpose flour
2 packages active dry yeast
1¼ cups milk
¼ cup sugar
1 teaspoon salt
1 egg
½ teaspoon lemon extract
½ teaspoon almond extract

In mixer bowl cream butter with the ⅓ cup flour. On a baking sheet roll butter mixture between 2 sheets of waxed paper to a 12x6-inch rectangle. Chill thoroughly. In large mixer bowl combine *1½ cups* of the remaining flour with the yeast. In a saucepan heat milk, sugar, and salt just till warm (115° to 120°). Add to dry ingredients in mixer bowl; add egg, lemon extract, and almond extract. Beat at low speed of electric mixer for ½ minute, scraping sides of bowl constantly. Beat 3 minutes at high speed. Stir in as much of the remaining flour as you can mix in using a spoon. On a lightly floured surface knead in the remaining flour to make a moderately soft dough. Continue kneading till smooth and elastic (about 5 minutes). Cover; let rest 10 minutes.

On lightly floured surface roll dough to a 14-inch square. Place the chilled butter on one half of the dough. Fold over other half, sealing edges well with heel of hand. Roll dough to a 20x12-inch rectangle. Fold in thirds to make 3 layers. Stretch gently to even the corners. Cover, chill 30 minutes.

Repeat rolling and folding two more times; chill after each rolling. Divide dough in fourths. (Keep unused portions refrigerated.) Use one fourth to make each of Cherry-Nut Fans, Sour Cream and Chocolate Envelopes, Date-Orange Pinwheels, and Lemon-Coconut Wreaths.

Vanilla Icing

1½ cups sifted powdered sugar
2 tablespoons milk
½ teaspoon vanilla

In small mixing bowl combine powdered sugar, milk, and vanilla. Beat till icing is smooth.

Cherry-Nut Fans

2 tablespoons cherry preserves
2 tablespoons finely chopped
    pecans
1 tablespoon butter, softened
¼ recipe Basic Danish Dough
    (see recipe, page 116)
¼ recipe Vanilla Icing
    (see recipe, page 116)

Cut up large pieces of cherry preserves. Combine preserves, pecans, and butter. Roll dough on lightly floured surface to 10x8-inch rectangle. Cut in eight 4x2½-inch rectangles. Spoon 1½ teaspoons filling along center of each. Fold lengthwise. Moisten and press edges with fingers to seal. Place, seam side down, on ungreased baking sheet; curve slightly. Snip outer edge at 1-inch intervals. Press down lightly with fingers. Cover and let shaped dough rise in a warm place till almost double (25 to 30 minutes). Bake in 425° oven for 9 to 10 minutes. Cool pastries on wire rack; frost with Vanilla Icing. Makes 8.

Directions to enclose with pastries: Serve Cherry-Nut Fans warm or at room temperature.

Sour Cream and Chocolate Envelopes

1 ounce sweet baking
    chocolate, melted and
    cooled
2 tablespoons dairy sour cream
2 teaspoons sugar
¼ recipe Basic Danish Dough
    (see recipe, page 116)
¼ recipe Vanilla Icing
    (see recipe, page 116)

Combine cooled chocolate, sour cream, and sugar. Roll dough on lightly floured surface to 9-inch square. Cut into nine 3-inch squares. Place a spoonful chocolate filling in center of each square. Fold 2 opposite corners to center; moisten and press together firmly to seal. Place on ungreased baking sheet. Cover and let shaped dough rise in a warm place till almost double, (25 to 30 minutes). Bake in 425° oven for 9 to 10 minutes. Cool pastries on wire rack; frost with Vanilla Icing. Makes 9.

Directions to enclose with pastries: Serve Sour Cream and Chocolate Envelopes warm or at room temperature.

Date-Orange Pinwheels

⅓ cup finely chopped pitted
    whole dates
1 tablespoon sugar
½ teaspoon finely shredded
    orange peel
2 tablespoons orange juice
¼ teaspoon vanilla
¼ recipe Basic Danish Dough
    (see recipe, page 116)
¼ recipe Vanilla Icing
    (see recipe, page 116)

In saucepan combine dates, sugar, orange peel, juice, and dash *salt*. Bring to boiling; reduce heat. Cover and simmer 5 minutes, stirring once or twice. Cool. Stir in vanilla. Roll dough on lightly floured surface to 9-inch square. Spread with filling. Roll up jelly-roll fashion; moisten and press edge to seal. Slice into nine 1-inch-thick rolls. Place cut side down on ungreased baking sheet; press down lightly with fingers to form 2½-inch rounds. Cover, let rise in warm place till almost double (25 to 30 minutes). Bake in 425° oven 9 to 10 minutes. Cool on rack; frost with Vanilla Icing. Makes 9.

Directions to enclose with pastries: Serve warm or at room temperature.

Lemon-Coconut Wreaths

2 tablespoons butter, softened
1 tablespoon sugar
¼ cup toasted flaked coconut
¼ teaspoon finely shredded
    lemon peel
¼ recipe Basic Danish Dough
    (see recipe, page 116)
¼ recipe Vanilla Icing
    (see recipe, page 116)

Blend together butter and sugar. Add coconut and lemon peel; mix well. Roll dough on lightly floured surface to 12x9-inch rectangle. Spread with coconut filling. Carefully fold rectangle in half from long side to make a 9x6-inch piece. Cut dough into nine 6x1-inch strips. Twist each strip 3 or 4 times. Shape into circle; moisten and press ends together with fingers to seal. Place on ungreased baking sheet. Cover and let shaped dough rise in a warm place till almost double (25 to 30 minutes). Bake in 425° oven for 9 to 10 minutes. Let pastries cool on wire rack; frost with Vanilla Icing. Makes 9.

Directions to enclose with pastries: Serve warm or at room temperature.

Italian Panettone

2 packages active dry yeast
½ cup warm water (110°)
• • •
½ cup milk
½ cup honey
½ cup butter *or* margarine
1 teaspoon salt
5½ to 6 cups all-purpose flour
3 eggs
½ cup light raisins
½ cup currants
¼ cup chopped candied citron
2 to 3 teaspoons crushed
    aniseed
• • •
1 egg
1 tablespoon water

In a bowl soften yeast in the ½ cup warm water. In a large saucepan heat milk, honey, butter or margarine, and salt, stirring till butter almost melts; cool to lukewarm (110°). Stir in *2 cups* of the flour; beat well. Add softened yeast and the 3 eggs; beat well. Stir in raisins, currants, citron, and aniseed. Stir in as much of the remaining flour as you can mix in using a spoon. On a lightly floured surface knead in remaining flour to make a soft dough. Continue kneading till dough is smooth and elastic (8 to 10 minutes).

Shape dough into a ball. Place in a greased bowl, turning once to grease surface. Cover; let rise in warm place till double (about 1½ hours).

Punch down dough; divide in half. Cover; let rest 10 minutes. Shape into 2 round loaves; place on 2 greased baking sheets. Cut a cross ½ inch deep on the top of each loaf. Cover; let rise till double (about 45 minutes). Beat the remaining egg with the 1 tablespoon water; brush over tops of loaves. Bake in a 350° oven for 35 to 40 minutes. Remove from baking sheets to wire racks. Cool. Makes 2 loaves.

Directions to enclose with loaves: Butter toasted slices of the panettone and sprinkle with a mixture of sugar and cinnamon.

Coconut-Mint Cookies

2 cups sugar
1 cup butter *or* margarine
2 eggs
1 teaspoon vanilla
3 cups all-purpose flour
½ teaspoon salt
½ teaspoon baking soda
½ teaspoon cream of tartar
1 cup quick-cooking rolled oats
½ cup chopped pecans
1 3½-ounce can (1⅓ cups) flaked coconut
  Mint jelly

In large mixer bowl cream together sugar and butter or margarine. Beat in eggs and vanilla. Stir together flour, salt, baking soda, and cream of tartar; add to creamed mixture and blend well. Stir in oats and pecans. Cover and chill dough 2 to 3 hours. Shape into 1-inch balls; roll in coconut. Place on greased cookie sheet. Make an indentation in top of each cookie. Bake in 375° oven for 10 to 12 minutes. Remove cookies from cookie sheet and cool on wire rack. Fill each with about ¼ teaspoon mint jelly. Makes 6½ dozen.

Cinnamon Cereal Chewies

¾ cup packed brown sugar
¼ cup butter *or* margarine
½ cup dairy sour cream
½ teaspoon vanilla
1 cup quick-cooking rolled oats
¾ cup all-purpose flour
¼ cup wheat germ
½ teaspoon baking soda
½ teaspoon ground cinnamon
¼ teaspoon salt
24 maraschino cherries, halved

In mixer bowl cream together sugar and butter or margarine; beat in sour cream and vanilla. Stir together oats, flour, wheat germ, baking soda, cinnamon, and salt; stir into creamed mixture. Drop by rounded teaspoons onto greased cookie sheet. Press cherry half in top of each cookie. Bake in 375° oven for 10 to 12 minutes. Cool on cookie sheet 1 minute. Remove and cool on wire rack. Makes 4 dozen.

Almond Butter Cookies

1½ cups sugar
1 cup butter *or* margarine
1 8-ounce package cream cheese, softened
1 egg
1 teaspoon vanilla
½ teaspoon almond extract
3½ cups all-purpose flour
1 teaspoon baking powder
  Green food coloring
1 beaten egg white
  Green and red colored sugar
2 1-ounce squares semisweet chocolate melted and cooled
  Powdered Sugar Icing
  Milk
  Small multicolored decorative candies

In mixer bowl cream together 1½ cups sugar, the butter or margarine, and cream cheese till fluffy. Add egg, vanilla, and almond extract; beat smooth. Stir together flour and baking powder; stir into creamed mixture. Divide mixture in thirds. Chill one portion 1 to 1½ hours or till firm.

To second portion add food coloring. Force through cookie press onto an ungreased cookie sheet. Bake in 375° oven for 8 to 10 minutes. Remove to rack; cool. Brush with egg white; sprinkle with green sugar.

To third portion of dough blend in melted chocolate. Pinch off balls of dough about the size of a walnut. Roll to logs 2½ inches long. Bake on ungreased cookie sheet in 375° oven for 8 to 10 minutes. Remove to rack; cool. Prepare Powdered Sugar Icing. Set *three-fourths* of the icing aside. To remaining fourth of icing add enough milk to make of dipping consistency. Dip ends of chocolate cookies into icing, then into decorative candies.

Roll out chilled portion of dough on a lightly floured surface to ⅛ inch thickness. Cut into shapes with assorted cookie cutters. Bake on an ungreased cookie sheet in 375° oven for 8 to 10 minutes. Remove to rack; cool. Frost with remaining Powdered Sugar Icing; sprinkle with red sugar. Makes 8 dozen cookies.

Powdered Sugar Icing: Beat together 1 cup sifted *powdered sugar*, 1 tablespoon softened *butter* or *margarine*, and ⅛ teaspoon *almond extract*. Add 1 to 2 tablespoons *milk* or till icing is of spreading consistency.

Fruit and Spice Rounds

1 cup raisins
1 cup dried figs
1 cup pitted whole dates
½ cup walnuts
1½ cups sugar
1 cup butter *or* margarine
3 eggs
2 cups all-purpose flour
1 teaspoon baking soda
1 teaspoon salt
1 teaspoon ground cinnamon
¾ teaspoon ground cloves
½ teaspoon ground nutmeg
  Boiled Butter Icing

Using fine blade, put fruits and nuts through a food grinder.

In large mixer bowl cream together sugar and butter or margarine till light and fluffy. Add eggs; beat well. Stir together flour, baking soda, salt, and spices; gradually add to creamed mixture and mix well. Stir in ground fruit mixture. Cover and chill several hours or overnight. Divide dough in half. Roll out one portion on well-floured surface to ¼-inch thickness. Cut with floured 2½-inch round cookie cutter. Bake on greased cookie sheet in 375° oven for 10 to 12 minutes. Let cool on cookie sheet 2 to 3 minutes; remove to wire rack. Repeat with remaining half of dough. Cool cookies. Spread with Boiled Butter Icing. Makes 5 dozen cookies.

Boiled Butter Icing: In 1-quart saucepan mix 1 cup *sugar*, ½ cup *water*, and ¼ cup *butter* or *margarine*. Cover; bring to boiling. Uncover; continue cooking to soft ball stage (candy thermometer registers 238°). Cool to lukewarm (110°) without stirring. Add ½ teaspoon *vanilla*. Transfer to mixer bowl; beat with electric mixer about 6 minutes or till creamy.

> *Why not let home-baked cookies carry your holiday greetings?* Fruit and Spice Rounds *(bottom left), are a unique combination of raisins, figs, dates, and walnuts. You can make* Almond Butter Cookies *(top left), three different ways. Finally* Coconut-Mint Cookies *and* Cinnamon Cereal Chewies *(right), decorated with red and green, will brighten everyone's Christmas.*

Christmas Card Cookies

2 cups packed brown sugar
1½ cups butter *or* margarine, softened
1 egg
4 cups all-purpose flour
2 teaspoons ground cinnamon
1 teaspoon ground nutmeg
½ teaspoon ground cloves
¼ teaspoon baking soda
   Assorted colors decorator icing*

Cream sugar and butter; add egg. Beat till light and fluffy. Stir flour with spices and baking soda; add to creamed mixture. Mix well. Cover; chill till firm, about 2 hours.

For Giant Christmas Cards: For each cookie, roll ¾ cup of the dough to ¼-inch thickness directly on ungreased cookie sheet. Shape or cut into desired form—star, bell, circle, rectangle, or tree—keeping ¼ inch thick. Remove and reroll excess dough. Bake, one at a time in 350° oven about 12 minutes. Cool 10 minutes; remove to rack to cool more. Decorate as for Christmas cards, writing messages with decorator icing in desired colors. Let stand till icing is set before wrapping as gifts. Makes 6 Christmas cards.

For Cookie Cutouts: On floured surface, roll dough to ⅛-inch thickness. Cut into desired shapes with cookie cutters. Place on ungreased cookie sheet. Bake in a 350° oven for 8 to 10 minutes or till lightly browned. Cool 1 to 2 minutes on baking sheet; remove to wire rack. Cool completely. If desired, decorate with decorator icing. Makes about 6 dozen cookie cutouts.
*Note: Decorator icing is sold commercially in small and large tubes.

Rolled Sugar Cookies
see photograph, page 114

1 cup sugar
½ cup butter *or* margarine, softened
1 egg
¼ cup milk
½ teaspoon vanilla
2¼ cups all-purpose flour
2 teaspoons baking powder
½ teaspoon salt
½ teaspoon ground mace (optional)
   Small decorative candies (optional)

In mixer bowl cream together sugar and butter. Add egg, milk, and vanilla; beat well. Stir together flour, baking powder, salt, and mace, if desired. Blend into creamed mixture. Cover; chill 1 hour. Divide dough in half.

On lightly floured surface, roll each half to ⅛-inch thickness for thin cookies or ¼-inch thickness for thick cookies. Cut into desired shapes with cookie cutters. Place on an ungreased cookie sheet. Decorate with candies, if desired. Bake in a 375° oven 7 to 8 minutes for thin cookies or 10 to 12 minutes for thick cookies. Makes 4 to 4½ dozen thin or 3 dozen thick cookies.

Chewy Popcorn Balls
see photograph, page 114

5 quarts popped corn
2 cups sugar
1½ cups water
½ cup light corn syrup
1 teaspoon vinegar
½ teaspoon salt
1 teaspoon vanilla

Keep popcorn hot in a 300° to 350° oven. In a buttered saucepan combine sugar, water, corn syrup, vinegar, and salt. Cook and stir to hard-ball stage (or till candy thermometer registers 250°). Stir in vanilla. Slowly pour over hot popped corn. Stir just till mixed. Butter hands; shape into 3-inch balls. Wrap in clear plastic wrap. Makes 15.

Honey Macaroonies

1½ cups quick-cooking rolled oats
½ cup flaked coconut
½ cup chopped walnuts
½ cup all-purpose flour
¾ cup packed brown sugar
½ cup butter *or* margarine
2 tablespoons honey
36 red *or* green candied cherries

In large mixing bowl stir together rolled oats, flaked coconut, chopped walnuts, and flour; set aside. In saucepan combine brown sugar, butter or margarine, and honey; bring mixture to boiling, stirring frequently. Pour over oat mixture, blending well.

For each cookie, press one level tablespoonful mixture into greased 1¾-inch muffin pan. (For flatter, crisper cookie, place in 2-inch muffin pan.) Top each cookie with a candied cherry. Bake in 350° oven 15 to 20 minutes. Cool 10 minutes in pan; remove to rack. Cool thoroughly. Makes 3 dozen.

Rum-Coffee Cookies

1 cup packed brown sugar
½ cup butter *or* margarine
2 eggs
½ teaspoon rum extract
1 teaspoon instant coffee crystals
1 tablespoon boiling water
1½ cups all-purpose flour
1½ teaspoons baking powder
¼ teaspoon salt
1 cup finely chopped pecans

In mixer bowl cream together sugar and butter or margarine. Add eggs and rum extract; beat well. Dissolve coffee crystals in boiling water. Stir into creamed mixture. Stir together flour, baking powder, and salt. Stir into creamed mixture. Chill several hours.

Drop dough by teaspoons onto nuts; roll to coat. Place 2 inches apart on a greased cookie sheet. Bake in 350° oven 8 to 10 minutes. Transfer to wire rack; cool. Makes 4 dozen.

Honey Macaroonies are a delicious mixture of honey, oats, and coconut topped with red and green candied cherries and baked in small muffin pans. These sturdy cookies are perfect for packing in decorative boxes for Christmas giving.

121

Rum Balls

1 6-ounce package (1 cup)
   semisweet chocolate
   pieces
½ cup sugar
⅓ cup rum
3 tablespoons light corn syrup
2 cups crushed vanilla wafers
1 cup ground walnuts

In a saucepan melt chocolate pieces over low heat. Remove from heat. Stir in sugar, rum, and corn syrup. Fold in vanilla wafers and nuts. Shape mixture into 1-inch balls, using 2 teaspoons mixture for each. Roll in *sugar*. Store in an airtight container. Makes 4 dozen.

Lollipops

¾ cup sugar
½ cup light corn syrup
¼ cup butter *or* margarine
   Several drops desired food
   coloring
12 wooden skewers

In a buttered heavy 2-quart saucepan combine sugar, corn syrup, and butter or margarine. Cook and stir over medium heat till sugar dissolves and mixture boils. Continue cooking, *without stirring,* to soft-crack stage (candy thermometer registers 270°). Remove from heat. Stir in enough food coloring to achieve desired color. Arrange wooden skewers 4 inches apart on a buttered baking sheet. Drop hot syrup from the tip of a tablespoon over skewers to form 2- to 3-inch suckers. Cool. Wrap in clear plastic wrap. Makes 12.

Candy Tree
see photograph, page 114

1 12-inch plastic foam cone
   with 4½-inch base
   Red spray paint
3 pounds wrapped hard candies
   Steel dressmaker pins
   Red ribbon bow

Spray foam cone with paint. Dry. Trim ends of candy wrappers. Stick a pin through one end of each candy wrapper. Beginning at bottom and working in circles toward top of cone, attach candies, overlapping slightly. Top with red bow.

Seafoam Candy

2 cups packed dark brown
   sugar
¼ cup dark corn syrup
¼ cup water
2 egg whites
1 teaspoon vanilla
½ cup chopped walnuts
   (optional)

In a buttered heavy 2-quart saucepan combine sugar, corn syrup, and water. Cook, stirring constantly, till sugar dissolves and the mixture comes to boiling. Cook over medium heat *without stirring* to hard-ball stage (candy thermometer registers 260°). Remove from heat. In large mixer bowl *immediately* beat the 2 egg whites with electric mixer to stiff peaks. Gradually pour the hot syrup in a thin stream over beaten egg whites, beating constantly at high speed for 6 minutes. Add vanilla. Continue beating 10 minutes more or till the mixture forms soft peaks and begins to lose its gloss. Stir in nuts, if desired. Let stand 2 minutes. Drop by level teaspoons onto a buttered baking sheet. Bake in a 300° oven for 20 minutes. Makes 4½ dozen.

Creamy Pralines

2 cups sugar
¾ teaspoon baking soda
1 cup light cream
1½ tablespoons butter *or*
   margarine
2 cups pecan halves

In a heavy 3½-quart saucepan combine sugar and baking soda; mix well. Stir in cream. Bring to boiling over medium heat, stirring constantly. Reduce heat; cook and stir till mixture reaches soft-ball stage (candy thermometer registers 234°). Mixture will caramelize slightly. Remove from heat; add butter or margarine. Stir in pecans; beat 2 to 3 minutes or till thick. Drop mixture from a tablespoon onto waxed paper. If candy becomes too stiff to drop, add a tablespoon of *hot water*. Makes 30.

Caramel Fudge

¾ cup butter *or* margarine
2 cups packed brown sugar
½ cup evaporated milk
1 teaspoon vanilla
3 cups sifted powdered sugar
1 cup chopped walnuts

In a heavy 2-quart saucepan melt the butter or margarine. Add the brown sugar. Cook over low heat 2 minutes, stirring constantly. Add the evaporated milk and continue cooking and stirring till the mixture comes to boiling. Remove from heat. Cool till lukewarm (110°). Stir in vanilla. Gradually add the powdered sugar, beating vigorously till the mixture is a fudgelike consistency (it should take about 2 minutes). Stir in nuts. Spread the candy into a buttered 8x8x2-inch pan. Chill. Cut into squares. Makes 3 dozen pieces.

Apple-Peanut Butter Fudge

1 6-ounce package (1 cup)
   semisweet chocolate
   pieces
½ of a 7-, 9-, *or* 10-ounce jar
   marshmallow creme
½ cup peanut butter
1 teaspoon vanilla
2 cups sugar
⅔ cup apple juice

In a bowl combine chocolate, marshmallow creme, peanut butter, and vanilla. In a buttered heavy 2-quart saucepan combine sugar and apple juice. Cook and stir over medium heat till sugar dissolves and mixture boils. Continue cooking and stirring to soft-ball stage (candy thermometer registers 240°). Remove from heat; *quickly* add chocolate mixture. Stir just till mixture is blended. Pour into a buttered 9x9x2-inch baking pan. Cool; cut into squares. Makes 36.

Here is a sampling of candies that are all guaranteed to satisfy the sweet tooth of candy fans on your gift list. Choose from Rum Balls *(front left),* Caramel Fudge *(back left),* Lollipops *(back center),* Rocky Road *(back right; see recipe, page 186), and* Seafoam Candy *(front right).*

Peach Cordial

3 pounds fresh peaches, pitted
   and quartered
2½ cups sugar
4 strips of lemon peel, 2-inches
   long
4 inches stick cinnamon,
   broken
6 whole cloves
1 quart bourbon

In gallon screw-top jar combine peaches, sugar, lemon peel, and spices. Pour in bourbon; cover with lid. Invert jar daily till sugar is dissolved, about 4 days. Place in cool, dark place for at least 2 months. Strain through cheesecloth before serving. Makes 1½ quarts.

Plum Liqueur

3 pounds fresh purple plums,
   halved and pitted (7 cups)
4 cups sugar
1 quart gin

In gallon screw-top jar combine plums, sugar, and gin; cover with lid. Invert jar daily till sugar is dissolved, about 4 days. Place in cool, dark place for at least 2 months. Strain through cheesecloth before serving. Makes 2 quarts.

Blackberry Brandy

1 quart fresh blackberries
¾ cup sugar
¾ teaspoon whole allspice
12 whole cloves
2 cups brandy

In gallon screw-top jar combine blackberries, sugar, and spices. Pour in brandy; cover with lid. Invert jar daily till sugar is dissolved, about 4 days. Place in cool, dark place for at least 2 months. Strain through cheesecloth before serving. Makes about 3½ cups.

Create your own after-dinner drinks with Peach Cordial *(center and back right),* Plum Liqueur *(front left), and* Blackberry Brandy *(back left). For easy mixing, use screw-top jars for preparing the fruit mixture. Transfer the cordials to decorative decanters for gifts.*

Orange-Flavored Liqueur

4 medium oranges
   Water
2 cups sugar
2 cups vodka *or* rum

Squeeze juice from oranges; reserve peel from 1 orange. Scrape white membrane from reserved peel; cut peel into strips. Add water to juice to make 2 cups. In saucepan combine orange juice, orange peel, and sugar. Bring mixture to boiling; reduce heat and simmer over low heat for 5 minutes. Cool. Pour into ½-gallon screw-top jar. Stir in vodka or rum. Cover with lid. Let stand at room temperature for 3 to 4 weeks. Strain through cheesecloth before serving. Makes 5 cups.

Coffee-Flavored Liqueur

2 cups water
1½ cups granulated sugar
1½ cups packed brown sugar
⅓ cup instant coffee crystals
1 fifth (750 ml) vodka
2 teaspoons vanilla

In saucepan combine water, granulated sugar, and brown sugar. Simmer gently, uncovered, 10 minutes. Remove from heat. Stir in coffee crystals; cool. Pour mixture into 2-quart screw-top jar. Stir in vodka and vanilla; cover with lid. Let stand at room temperature for 2 weeks. Makes 5½ cups.

Cranberry Cordial

1 16-ounce package (4 cups)
   fresh cranberries
3 cups sugar
2 cups gin

Coarsely chop cranberries. Place into a ½-gallon screw-top jar or a crock. Add sugar and gin. Cover with lid or tightly with foil. Store in a cool place. If in jar, invert daily for 3 weeks; if in crock, stir gently daily. Transfer and store in tightly covered quart jars. Strain through cheesecloth before serving. Serve chilled. Makes 3¼ cups.

Apple Cordial

4 cups coarsely chopped apple
1 cup sugar
4 inches stick cinnamon,
   broken
2 cups brandy

In a large screw-top jar combine apple, sugar, and cinnamon. Pour brandy atop; mix well. Cover with lid. Invert jar daily till sugar is dissolved, about 4 days. Store in a cool, dark place 4 to 6 weeks. Strain through cheesecloth before serving. Makes 2½ cups.

Orange-Grapefruit Marmalade

3 large grapefruit
1 medium orange
1 medium lime
1½ cups water
¼ teaspoon baking soda
5 cups sugar
1 3-ounce foil pouch (½ of a
   6-ounce package) liquid
   fruit pectin

Remove peels from grapefruit, orange, and lime. Scrape off excess white. Cut peels into fine strips. In a saucepan combine the peels, water, and baking soda. Bring to boiling; cover. Simmer 20 minutes. Meanwhile remove white membrane from fruit. Section fruit, working over bowl to catch juices. Discard seeds.

In an 8- or 10-quart kettle or Dutch oven combine fruit sections, fruit juice, and undrained peel. Cover; simmer 10 minutes. Measure 3 cups cooked fruit mixture; add sugar. Mix well. Bring to full rolling boil; boil, uncovered, 1 minute. Remove mixture from heat; stir in liquid fruit pectin. Skim off foam with metal spoon. Skim and skim for 10 minutes. Pour into hot, sterilized half-pint jars or glasses. Seal the jars with metal lids and screw bands. Seal the glasses with paraffin or Snowdrift Paraffin (see recipe, page 126). Makes 6 half-pints.

Carrot-Raisin Honey

1 medium orange
1 large lemon
**2 cups shredded carrot
   (4 medium)**
2 cups water
¼ cup light raisins
5 cups sugar

Quarter orange and lemon. Remove seeds; thinly slice fruit with peel. In 8- to 10-quart kettle or Dutch oven combine orange and lemon slices, carrot, water, and raisins. Bring mixture to boiling. Reduce heat; simmer about 10 minutes or till carrot is tender. Stir in sugar. Bring to full rolling boil, stirring constantly. Continue cooking and stirring about 6 minutes or till mixture sheets from metal spoon. Remove from heat. Stir and skim off foam for 5 minutes. Pour into hot, sterilized half-pint jars or glasses. Seal the jars with metal lids and screwbands; seal the glasses with paraffin or Snowdrift Paraffin (see recipe, right). Makes 4 half-pints.

Fig-Lemon Jam

2½ pounds fresh figs (13 figs)
1 2x¼-inch strip lemon peel
½ cup light raisins
7½ cups sugar
½ cup lemon juice
**1 3-ounce foil pouch (½ of
   6-ounce package) liquid
   fruit pectin**

Wash figs; remove stem ends. Remove excess white membrane from lemon peel. Grind figs, lemon peel, and raisins through food grinder using coarse blade. Measure 4 cups fruit mixture into an 8- to 10-quart Dutch oven. Add sugar and lemon juice; mix well. Bring to full rolling boil, stirring constantly. Boil hard, uncovered, 1 minute; stir constantly. Remove from heat. Stir in fruit pectin. Skim off foam with a metal spoon. Pour into hot, sterilized half-pint jars or glasses. Seal the jars with metal lids and screwbands; seal the glasses with paraffin or Snowdrift Paraffin (see recipe, right). Makes 8 half-pints.

Snowdrift Paraffin

First Layer: Melt 2 blocks of *paraffin* over, but not touching, rapidly boiling water in an old double boiler. Using a wide-mouthed funnel, pour hot fruit mixture into sterilized glasses to within ¼-inch of top. Spoon a thin layer of melted paraffin over the surface of the jelly or jam to seal out air. (Make sure the layer is about 1/16 inch thick. Too thick a layer of paraffin will cause the jelly or jam to leak around the edges of the paraffin.) Hold the hot glasses, one at a time, with a pot holder and rotate them slowly so the paraffin will cling to the sides of the glasses. Prick any air bubbles. Let stand till paraffin hardens.
Second Layer: Melt 2 additional bars of *paraffin* in top of the double boiler over, but not touching, rapidly boiling water. Cool till paraffin becomes cloudy and starts to solidify. Quickly whip with electric mixer till foamy and slightly stiff. *Work fast.* (If paraffin solidifies, remelt and start again.) Spoon foamy paraffin over layer of hard paraffin. Cool till set. Covers 6 glasses.

Spiced Grape Jam

1½ pounds Concord grapes
1 cup water
**1 tablespoon finely shredded
   orange peel**
2¼ cups sugar
¼ teaspoon ground cinnamon
⅛ teaspoon ground cloves

Wash grapes; separate skins from pulp. Reserve skins. Cook pulp in 3-quart saucepan until soft; sieve to remove seeds from pulp.

Add water and orange peel to grape pulp; cook 10 minutes. Add grape skins, stirring constantly, bring to boiling. Add sugar, cinnamon, and cloves; cook over medium-low heat till thick. Pour into hot, sterilized half-pint jars or glasses. Seal the jars with metal lids and screwbands; seal the glasses with paraffin or Snowdrift Paraffin (see recipe, above). Makes 3 half-pints.

Honey-Orange Jelly

2 cups sauterne
**1 tablespoon finely shredded
   orange peel**
1 cup orange juice
2 tablespoons lemon juice
**1 1¾-ounce package powdered
   fruit pectin**
1½ cups sugar
**1 cup honey
   Snowdrift Paraffin (see
   recipe, left) *or* paraffin**

In large saucepan or Dutch oven mix sauterne, orange peel, orange juice, lemon juice, and fruit pectin. Bring to full rolling boil, stirring constantly. Stir in sugar and honey. Bring again to full rolling boil. Boil hard, uncovered, 1 minute, stirring constantly. Remove from heat. Quickly skim off foam using a metal spoon. Place a metal spoon into a hot, sterilized wine glass (to prevent glass from breaking). Quickly pour hot jelly into glass to ¼-inch from top. Remove spoon. Repeat with 5 more glasses. Top with Snowdrift Paraffin or paraffin. Makes 6 glasses.

Wine Jelly

3 cups sugar
2 cups any flavor wine
**1 3-ounce foil pouch (½ of a
   6-ounce package) liquid
   fruit pectin**
**Snowdrift Paraffin (see
   recipe, left) *or* paraffin**

Measure sugar and wine into top of double boiler; mix well. Place over, but do not let touch, rapidly boiling water. Stir 3 to 4 minutes or till sugar is dissolved. Remove from heat. At once stir in fruit pectin and mix well. Skim off foam, if necessary. Place a metal spoon in a hot, sterilized wine glass (to prevent glass from breaking). Quickly pour hot jelly into glass to within ¼ inch from top. Remove spoon. Repeat with 5 more glasses. Top with Snowdrift Paraffin or paraffin. Makes 6 glasses.

This selection of wine-flavored jellies is perfect for holiday gifts. Decorate each glass with Snowdrift Paraffin for a festive touch. Pictured clockwise from left are Honey-Orange Jelly and variations of Wine Jelly flavored with sherry, rosé, Concord grape wine, apple wine, strawberry wine, and burgundy.

Freezer Strawberry Jam

2 10-ounce packages frozen
  sliced strawberries
3½ cups sugar
1 3-ounce foil pouch (½ of
  6-ounce package) liquid
  fruit pectin

Thaw strawberries; put through food mill or mash. Stir in sugar; mix well. Let stand 20 minutes, stirring occasionally.

Add fruit pectin; stir 3 minutes. Ladle into clean freezer containers. Cover; let stand 24 hours at room temperature. Label and freeze. Store up to 1 year in the freezer. Jam will last up to 6 weeks in the refrigerator. Makes 5 half-pints.

Spicy Corn and Tomato Relish

½ cup sugar
2 tablespoons salt
1 tablespoon ground turmeric
2 17-ounce cans whole kernel
  corn, drained
1 16-ounce can tomatoes, cut
  up
2 cups chopped onion
2 cups chopped, peeled
  cucumber
2 cups chopped green pepper
1 cup chopped celery
1 cup vinegar
2 teaspoons mustard seed
¼ teaspoon dried hot red
  pepper, crushed
¼ cup cold water
2 tablespoons cornstarch

In 8- to 10-quart kettle or Dutch oven mix sugar, salt, and turmeric. Add corn, tomatoes, onion, cucumber, green pepper, celery, vinegar, mustard seed, and red pepper. Bring to boiling; reduce heat. Simmer, uncovered, 30 minutes, stirring occasionally. Stir cold water into cornstarch; blend well. Add to vegetables. Cook and stir about 3 minutes or till slightly thickened. Pack hot relish into hot, clean half-pint jars, leaving ½-inch headspace. Adjust lids. Process in boiling water bath 15 minutes. (Start timing after water returns to boiling.) Makes 8 half-pints.

Apple Marmalade

1 medium orange
6 medium apples, peeled,
  cored, and coarsely
  chopped (6 cups)
2 cups water
3 tablespoons lemon juice
5 cups sugar

Quarter unpeeled orange. Remove seeds. Thinly slice orange.

In an 8- to 10-quart kettle or Dutch oven combine orange slices, apples, water, and lemon juice. Bring mixture to boiling. Reduce heat; simmer about 10 minutes or till apples are tender. Add sugar. Bring to full rolling boil, stirring constantly. Continue cooking and stirring till thickened and clear (candy thermometer registers 220°). Remove from heat. Skim off foam with a metal spoon. Pour at once into hot, sterilized half-pint jars or glasses. Seal the jars with metal lids and screwbands; seal the glasses with paraffin or Snowdrift Paraffin (see recipe, page 126). Makes 6 half-pints.

Cranberry Jelly

3½ cups cranberry juice cocktail
1 1¾-ounce package powdered
  fruit pectin
4 cups sugar
• • •
¼ cup lemon juice

In 8- to 10-quart kettle or Dutch oven combine cranberry juice and pectin. Bring to full rolling boil. Stir in sugar. Bring again to full rolling boil, stirring constantly. Boil hard, uncovered, 1 minute, stirring constantly. Remove from heat. Stir in lemon juice.

Quickly skim off foam using a metal spoon. Pour at once into hot, sterilized half-pint jars or glasses. Seal the jars with metal lids and screwbands; seal the glasses with paraffin or Snowdrift Paraffin (see recipe, page 126). Makes 6 half-pints.

Cranberry-Orange Relish

2 16-ounce packages (8 cups)
  fresh cranberries
4 cups sugar
1½ cups water
2 teaspoons finely shredded
  orange peel
1½ cups orange juice
½ cup slivered almonds

In 6- to 8-quart kettle or Dutch oven mix cranberries, sugar, water, orange peel, and orange juice. Bring to boiling. Cook, uncovered, about 5 minutes or till cranberry skins pop, stirring once or twice. Stir in almonds. Remove from heat. Ladle hot relish into hot, clean half-pint jars, leaving ½-inch headspace. Adjust lids. Process in boiling water bath 10 minutes. (Start timing when water returns to boil.) Makes 8.

Carrot Chutney

4 pounds carrots, peeled and
  sliced (24 medium)
2 medium oranges
1 lemon
2½ cups sugar
1⅓ cups vinegar
2 tablespoons mixed pickling
  spices
1 cup flaked coconut
½ cup raisins
1 tablespoon grated gingerroot
½ teaspoon bottled hot pepper
  sauce

Cook carrots in boiling water to cover for 35 to 40 minutes. Drain; mash or put through food mill. Measure about 5 cups. Peel oranges and lemon. Reserve peel of *one* orange and *half* of the one lemon peel. Remove excess white membrane from reserved peels. Cut peels into very thin strips. Seed and thinly slice oranges and lemon.

In 6- to 8-quart kettle or Dutch oven mix sugar, vinegar, and peels. Place pickling spices in a piece of cheesecloth; tie securely. Add to kettle. Bring mixture to boiling; reduce heat. Cover; boil gently 5 minutes. Add carrots, orange and lemon slices, and remaining ingredients. Cook, uncovered, over medium heat about 30 minutes or till thickened; stir often. Remove spice bag; discard. Ladle into hot, clean half-pint jars; leave ½-inch headspace. Adjust lids. Process in boiling water bath 10 minutes. (Start timing when water returns to boil.) Makes 8 or 9 half-pints.

Beet-Apple Relish

6 cups cooked, peeled beets,
  cut up (4 pounds)
6 large apples, peeled, cored,
  and quartered
2 large onions, cut up
1½ cups sugar
1½ cups vinegar
½ cup water
4 inches stick cinnamon,
  broken
1 tablespoon salt

Using food grinder with coarse blade, grind beets, apples, and onions.

In large kettle or Dutch oven combine ground mixture, sugar, vinegar, water, cinnamon, and salt. Bring to boiling. Cover; simmer 20 minutes, stirring often. Remove cinnamon. Ladle hot relish into hot, clean half-pint jars; leave ½-inch headspace. Adjust lids. Process in boiling water bath 15 minutes. (Start timing when water returns to boiling.) Makes 11 half-pints.

Zucchini Relish

4 to 4½ pounds zucchini, cut
  up
2 medium onions, cut up
1 sweet red pepper, cut up
2 tablespoons salt
1½ cups sugar
1 cup vinegar
1 cup water
2 teaspoons celery seed
1 teaspoon ground turmeric
1 teaspoon ground nutmeg
⅛ teaspoon pepper

Using food grinder with coarse blade, grind zucchini, onions, and red pepper. Stir in salt. Cover; refrigerate overnight. Drain; rinse in cold water. Drain well.

In 4- to 5-quart kettle or Dutch oven combine zucchini mixture, sugar, vinegar, water, celery seed, turmeric, nutmeg, and pepper. Bring mixture to boiling. Cover; boil gently 10 minutes, stirring frequently. Ladle zucchini mixture into hot, clean pint jars, leaving ½-inch headspace. Adjust lids. Process in boiling water bath 15 minutes. (Start timing when water returns to boiling.) Makes 4 pints.

Curried Zucchini Pickles

24 medium zucchini (7 pounds)
¼ cup pickling salt
  Cold water
3 cups sugar
3 cups vinegar
⅓ cup mustard seed
4 teaspoons celery seed
1 tablespoon curry powder

Thoroughly wash zucchini and cut into 3-inch sticks or ¼-inch slices. Sprinkle with pickling salt. Add cold water to cover. Let stand 3 hours. Drain; rinse with cold water. Drain well.

In 10-quart kettle or Dutch oven combine sugar, vinegar, mustard seed, celery seed, and curry. Bring to boiling. Add the zucchini. Cook for 5 minutes or till heated through *(do not boil)*. Pack zucchini in hot, clean pint jars; leave ½-inch headspace. Pour hot liquid over zucchini; leave ½-inch headspace. Adjust lids. Process in boiling water bath 10 minutes. (Start timing when water returns to boiling.) Makes 9 pints.

Pineapple Pickles

2 medium pineapples
2 cups packed brown sugar
2 cups water
1 cup vinegar
2 tablespoons whole cloves
3 inches stick cinnamon,
  broken

Peel pineapples; core. Cut into 1-inch cubes or spears. In kettle or Dutch oven mix sugar, water, and vinegar. Tie spices in cheesecloth; add to mixture. Bring to boiling; boil 5 to 8 minutes. Add pineapple. Cover; simmer 5 minutes. Remove spice bag; discard. Pack hot pineapple into hot, clean half-pint jars; leave ½-inch headspace.

Pour hot syrup over fruit; leave ½-inch headspace. Adjust lids. Process in boiling water bath 15 minutes. (Start timing when water returns to boiling.) Makes 6 half-pints.

Rum-Cinnamon Syrup

1½ cups water
8 inches stick cinnamon,
  broken
3 cups light corn syrup
1½ cups packed brown sugar
¼ teaspoon rum extract
• • •
6 pieces stick cinnamon (each
  2 to 3 inches long)

In saucepan combine water and broken stick cinnamon. Simmer, covered, for 15 minutes. Add corn syrup and brown sugar. Cook and stir till sugar is dissolved; bring to boiling. Stir in rum extract. Strain out cinnamon. Pour hot syrup into hot, clean half-pint jars; leave ½-inch headspace. Add one piece of stick cinnamon to each jar. Adjust lids. Process in boiling water bath 10 minutes. (Start timing when water returns to boiling.) Makes 6 half-pints.

Homemade Horseradish Mustard

2 vegetable bouillon cubes
1½ cups hot water
• • •
4 teaspoons cornstarch
4 teaspoons sugar
4 teaspoons dry mustard
2 teaspoons ground turmeric
¼ cup white wine vinegar
4 teaspoons prepared
  horseradish
• • •
2 slightly beaten egg yolks

Dissolve bouillon in hot water. In saucepan blend cornstarch, sugar, mustard, and turmeric. Stir in vinegar and horseradish. Slowly blend in bouillon. Cook and stir over low heat till thickened and bubbly. Stir a moderate amount into egg yolks. Return to saucepan. Cook and stir 1 minute. Pack in ½-cup containers. Refrigerate. Makes 1½ cups.

Directions to enclose with mustard: Store mustard, covered, in refrigerator.

An Old-World Christmas

A Festival of Folk Art

We Americans are profoundly lucky. Not only do we have a magnificent folk tradition native to our own soil, but also we've fallen heir to a vast treasure of folk art brought to our shores from other countries by many waves of new citizens. Why not celebrate the joy of Christmas by filling your holiday home with the vibrant colors, dynamic designs, and natural beauty of the people's art?

The wonderful thing about a festival of folk art displayed at Christmastime is that each year you can add the special items you've collected on your travels or made yourself. Throughout this section you'll find an international assortment of ornaments, decorations, and gifts to choose from.

For example, many cultures contributed to this richly laden Christmas tree. Toys from the Slavic countries, dolls from Southern Europe, and baskets from China mix comfortably with a collection of ornaments from Latin America and the Scandinavian countries. In addition, there are jewel-toned eggs from the Ukraine scattered about the tree. Traditionally, these eggs are batiked with wax and dyed, but they also can be more simply decorated with felt-tipped marking pens.

Instructions for all the projects shown in this section begin on page 138.

A Festival of Folk Art

From the world to you—here is a great gathering of folk art for your Christmas tree! To these ornaments, alive with the joyful spontaneity of many diverse peoples, you can add your own skill, zest, spirit, and imagination.

All these ornaments are easy to reproduce using ordinary materials such as tin can lids, clay, bread dough, and yarn.

A Festival of Folk Art

The folk art of many lands abounds with simple but beautiful representations of motifs from nature. These delightfully stylized animals and flowers often are worked in wood, yarn, and other commonplace materials.

To the people of Poland, the animals of farm and forest have special appeal, and often are woven into the fabric of their art. The majestic Christmas reindeer standing as quiet sentinels on the holiday buffet (right) are crude wooden sculptures in this folk style.

To make a reindeer, cut scraps of pine or fir to the sizes specified in the diagram on page 140. Saw the body pieces roughly into shape. Round sharp corners with a wood rasp and whittle the head, neck, legs, tail, and ear pegs with a knife. Then sand each piece with coarse sandpaper.

Drill ⅜-inch holes in the side pieces for the legs and in the rear of the middle section for the tail. Drill ⅛-inch holes in the head for the ears and twig antlers.

Glue all the body sections together with wood glue, wrapping the joints with masking tape until they are dry. Next, strip the bark from some dried twigs and glue them into the head. Finish by sanding the entire piece smooth and applying a coat of linseed oil.

One of the best-known forms of native American folk art is the lively peasant painting of the Pennsylvania Germans. The tree of life (opposite) borrows its quaint, primitive design and bold coloration from this rich tradition. A project for the entire family, the tree is "painted" by gluing rug yarn onto plywood.

To make the tree of life, transfer the pattern (page 140) to a two-by-three-foot piece of ¼-inch plywood. Outline the design and all four edges of the plywood with a bead of white glue (the kind that dries transparent). Press heavy black rug yarn into the strip of glue while it is still tacky.

To fill in the background, work in areas four to five inches in size. First coat an area with glue. Then, starting at the outside edges and working inward, press white yarn into the glue, keeping the strands close together. Work swirls in the corners and other, smaller shapes between the branches, as shown in the photograph.

"Color" the tree, birds, and flowers in the same way that you worked the background, using an assortment of brightly colored rug yarns. A toothpick comes in handy for pushing yarn into tight spots, so that all the plywood is covered.

134

A Festival of Folk Art

The "flowering" of folk art can be seen in the wreath, créche, and stockings on these pages. The cornhusk blossoms tucked into the wreath (opposite) have been handcrafted for generations in the mountains of North Carolina, and the familiar hearts and flowers motifs on the créche figures and the stockings recall the vitality of old-world needlework.

Ordinary cornhusks can be crafted into beautiful flowers if they're soaked in a glycerin and water solution first to make them pliable. Make some flowers with natural-colored husks and others with husks that have been tinted with red and orange fabric dyes. Wire the finished flowers into a 10-inch straw wreath trimmed with baby's breath and dried ferns.

The crèche figures (above right) are embroidered in samplerlike stitches so even a novice can work these designs to perfection. Use natural linen for the figures and work the motifs in red and green crewel wools. For perfect cross-stitches, tack needlepoint canvas in place over the fabric, work the cross-stitches, and then gently pull away the threads of the canvas. Stuff the completed figures using birdseed, and gather small pieces of lace into halos.

Christmas stockings come in so many different sizes, shapes, colors, and patterns that it's a wonder Santa hasn't become confused over the years. If you'd like to add your own exciting element of surprise this Christmas, make folk art stockings like those at right.

The embroidery patterns here were inspired by the sampler wrapping shown on the packages below the stockings. The designs were enlarged and worked on coarse linen.

Instructions for an
Old-World Christmas:
A Festival of Folk Art

The instructions below and on the following pages are for the ornaments, decorations, and gifts shown on pages 130–137. For directions for enlarging and transferring designs, see the glossary, pages 370–371.

"Mexican" Tin-Can-Top Ornaments
page 132

Materials: Assortment of tin can tops; rough sandpaper; indelible felt marking pens in various colors; paper towels; ½-inch round mirrors (available in craft stores); white glue; gold metallic thread; hammer and nail.

Instructions: Lightly sand edges of can tops (discard all tops with jagged or bent edges).

Using felt pens, color can tops with light, bright colors (red, orange, yellow). Use indented rings on tops as guides. (*Note:* Because electric lights reflect off metal, daylight is best for this project and is easiest on the eyes.)

When entire can top is covered, use darker colors (blue, purple, green, black) to draw narrow bands on lighter areas. Add lines of fringes, scallops, petals, polka dots, etc. (refer to photograph for design ideas). Fine-tip markers are helpful here, but corners of fat-tip pens will do quite well.

"Erase" errors by coloring over mistakes with a light felt pen and immediately blotting with paper towel. Wipe pen tip on towel to remove darker ink. Use this technique also to add light accents to dark areas of design.

When both sides of top have been decorated, lay top on thick magazine and drive tip of nail through one edge. Thread with a 5-inch piece of gold thread; tie ends to make a hanger.

Glue small round mirrors to centers of designs on both sides of can tops.

Mexican Yarn/Clay Figures
page 132

Note: Finished ornaments measure approximately 2 to 3 inches long; because of their weight, they are most suitable for lower or inside branches of the tree, or for hanging on wreaths.

Materials: 2-ply acrylic yarn in assorted colors; oven-hardening modeling compound; wire for hanging; clay tool or small stick for hollowing out forms; stick glue; pointed tool (such as a cuticle stick).

Instructions: Shape clay into *simple* animal forms, balls, stars, etc. Avoid complex shapes. (See the color photograph on page 132 for ideas.)

Hollow out center of each form; patch hole with clay. Insert a small loop of wire in center top of each ornament.

Bake ornaments in medium oven, according to package directions. Cool.

Apply glue to small area of ornament. Work strands of yarn into patterns (flowers, stripes, etc.) in sticky area, pressing strands into glue and wrapping yarn tightly in the desired design. Cover the rest of the ornament in the same way, using a pointed tool to press glue and strands into place in tight spots.

Ecuadorian Bread Ornaments
page 132

Materials: 18 slices white bread with crusts removed; large bottle white glue; cold cream; tube acrylic paints in assorted colors; plastic sandwich bags; clay tools or other utensils for shaping dough (garlic press and scissors are useful); waxed paper; acrylic spray.

Instructions: Crumble bread into bowl with 9 ounces of glue. Rub cold cream on your hands, then mix and knead the bread and glue until the mixture no longer feels sticky.

Divide dough into 8 balls; place in separate bags. Keep bags closed when you're not using the dough.

Color 7 balls different colors by kneading a teaspoon of acrylic paint into each one; leave one its natural color. (Wash hands between colors.)

Shape basic background form out of untinted dough on sheet of waxed paper (so figure will not stick).

Brush basic figure with mixture of ½ glue and ½ water, then add layers of other design elements that you have

rolled, pressed, squeezed, pinched, or cut from pieces of colored dough (see photograph for ideas). Mash added shapes in an inconspicuous spot to secure them to base figure. Although clay seems to stick easily, it's a good idea to brush finished figure with the glue-and-water mixture.

Poke small hole with pointed tool in top of each ornament for hanging.

Ornaments will dry in about 24 hours, then they may be sprayed with clear acrylic for added protection.

Note: Air dries the dough, so keep plastic bags closed at all times. Unused dough, if covered, may be kept in the refrigerator for several weeks.

Mexican Mirror Ornaments
page 132

Materials: Cardboard scraps, spool or floral wire; dime-store mirrors; white glue; pointed stick (such as cuticle stick); roll of 2-inch self-adhering aluminum foil tape; felt-tip markers; scissors; art knife; cotton swabs.

Instructions: Enlarge the patterns (right) and transfer them to scraps of cardboard. Cut out base shape (frame) and all design units (small circles to be glued to oval frame, small diamonds for large diamond frame, etc.). Cut out centers of each frame.

Trace scroll and flower patterns on frame and design units, using enough pressure on the pencil or cuticle stick to indent pattern into cardboard. Glue all design units to frames.

Tape is not wide enough to cover entire frame, so plan how you're going to cut and apply it. Cut tape strips ½ inch longer than actual measurement. Remove backing and apply tape.

Gently smooth down tape; press it into the indented patterns with a cotton tip swab. Butt additional strips into place; smooth down until the entire frame is covered. Press excess tape to the back of the frame, slashing edges where necessary to make tape lie flat.

Make loop of floral wire for hanging; attach to back of ornament with strip of tape. Place mirror on back of frame; secure in place by applying tape over

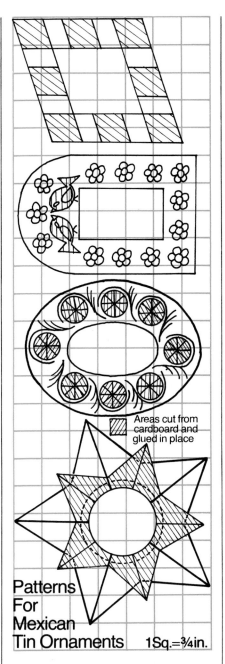

Areas cut from cardboard and glued in place

Patterns For Mexican Tin Ornaments

1 Sq. = ¾ in.

entire back of frame and mirror. (*Note:* Triangular mirrors were purchased at craft store and glued directly on foil-wrapped frame with contact cement.)

Color raised designs on front of frame with felt-tip pens.

Pysanky Eggs
page 132

Traditional Pysanky eggs are decorated by using a time-consuming, but rewarding, batiking technique. An easier, but equally effective, decorating method is to draw traditional designs on eggs with colored marking pens. Instructions for both methods follow.

Materials: Eggs; ice pick or needle; nylon thread; clear acrylic (optional).

Traditional method: Food coloring or permanent craft dyes in assorted colors; 2x2-inch copper foil; 6-inch, ¼-inch-diameter dowel; lightweight wire; candle; beeswax; vinegar; paper towels; aluminum foil.

Simplified method: Permanent felt-tip markers in assorted colors; fine-point black marker.

Instructions: Make a small hole in one end of an egg with an ice pick or needle. At other end, make a slightly larger hole, puncturing the yolk and membrane. Gently blow the egg through the shell. Wash and dry the shell, then set it in an egg cup or other holder so it doesn't break.

Decorate eggs by using the traditional or shortcut method described below and on the next page. After eggs are dry, make hangers. For each egg, cut nylon thread, double it, and push the folded end through both holes in the egg so there's a loop at the top. Tie knots at base of egg so thread is secure and won't slip through the egg.

Traditional method: Decorate traditional Pysanky eggs by alternately drawing designs on eggs with wax and dipping them in successively darker dyes. Before you begin, make a stylus for the wax. Cut half circle of copper foil; roll into cone with small hole at

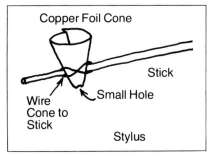

Copper Foil Cone

Stick

Small Hole

Wire Cone to Stick

Stylus

bottom. Wire cone to dowel so point extends below the stick, as in diagram.

Prepare craft dyes according to package instructions, or dilute food dyes with a few drops of vinegar. For dipping, pour dyes into small cups.

Grate pieces of beeswax into copper cone; heat cone over candle until beeswax starts to melt near point of cone. (Handle wax carefully near flame; it's flammable.) Melted wax will be charred.

If the wax is too hot, it will be runny and difficult to draw with. Wipe the tip of the cone occasionally with paper toweling to keep it clean.

With melted wax, which flows from the stylus tip, draw a design on the egg.
continued

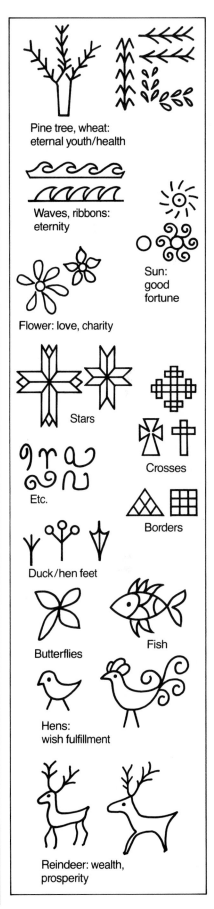

Pine tree, wheat: eternal youth/health

Waves, ribbons: eternity

Sun: good fortune

Flower: love, charity

Stars

Crosses

Etc.

Borders

Duck/hen feet

Butterflies

Fish

Hens: wish fulfillment

Reindeer: wealth, prosperity

Continued from page 139
A Festival of Folk Art

For design suggestions, see the photograph on page 132, the motifs on page 139, and the drawings of the eggs on this page.

Use motifs singly or in combinations. Simple zigzag-line borders accent bands of traditional motifs on some eggs. On others a single large motif is made by combining several small ones.

If you dye eggs only one color, designs will be white. By dyeing eggs several colors (such as yellow, red, and black) and waxing between dyeings, motifs will be multicolored.

Place waxed egg in wire egg dipper (the kind that comes in Easter egg-dye packages—or make one from wire); submerge it in dye bath.

Let the color deepen to about 2 shades darker than you want the finished color to be; the color lightens as the egg dries. Then remove the eggs from the dye and allow them to dry.

After all dyeing is completed, place waxed and dyed eggs on a cookie sheet covered with foil in a 250-degree oven for about 20 seconds, just until the wax begins to melt. *Watch the eggs closely because wax is flammable.*

Remove eggs from the oven and wipe off wax with paper towels. Coat with clear acrylic, if desired.

Create multicolored designs by using more than one color dye. Draw the first set of designs on the egg with wax. Submerge the egg in the lightest color dye (yellow, for example). Remove the egg from the dye and dry it carefully, without removing any wax.

Eggs must be thoroughly dry before rewaxing or wax won't stick.

Draw more designs on the egg and dip it into a darker color dye (perhaps red). The second set of designs will remain yellow. Finally, draw a third set of designs on the egg and dip it into a final, dark dye, such as black. The third set will be red, while unwaxed areas of the egg will be black.

· Remove the wax. On the egg you'll have white, yellow, and red designs (traditional Ukrainian colors for Pysanky eggs) etched on black eggs.

Simplified method: Following general instructions, remove yolks and membranes from the eggs. Carefully wash and dry the shells.

Decorate eggs by marking off sections and filling them with bright bands of color. Add designs with a fine-point permanent black pen.

Protect the finish on the eggs by coating them with clear acrylic, if desired, and make hangers for each.

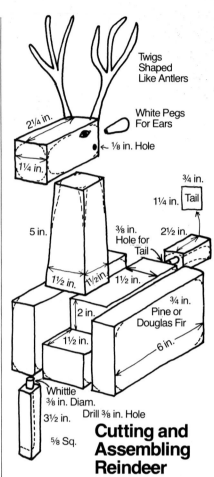

Cutting and Assembling Reindeer

Tree of Life Yarn Painting
page 135

For yarn painting, use diagram below; directions for the project are on page 134.

Tree of Life Pattern   1 Sq. = 3½ in.

Wooden Deer
page 134

To make the reindeer use the diagram (above right) and the instructions on page 134.

Cornhusk Flower Wreath
page 136

Materials: Two 2-ounce packages of natural corn husks (for 10 to 14 flowers); 26-gauge wire (for tying petals); 19-gauge wire (for stems); florist's tape; fabric dye in scarlet and deep orange; glycerin; 10-inch straw wreath form; dried baby's breath and ferns; needle-nose pliers.

Instructions: Soak husks in solution of 2 teaspoons glycerin per quart of hot water for 5 minutes.

Into 4 cups boiling water mix 1½ teaspoons scarlet fabric dye. Dye 7 husks for each red flower you want to make. Completely submerge flowers so they will color evenly.

When desired color is reached (about 5 minutes) remove husks from dye, rinse, and return to bowl containing water/glycerin solution (keep dyed husks separate from undyed husks).

All subsequent steps must be done while husks are wet and pliable, so spread newspapers over work surface.

Cut 8-inch length of #19 wire and bend over the last ½ inch to double thickness using pliers. For the flower center, cut a 2x3-inch strip of husk (with grain running across width of strip). Fold the husk lengthwise, insert folded tip of wire into one end of folded husk, and wrap husk tightly around stem wire. Secure with a twist of #26 wire.

Using pattern (right) cut cardboard template for flower petals. Using template, cut 18 petals (grain of husk should run lengthwise). You should be able to cut 2 to 3 petals from each husk.

Following guide on petal pattern, fasten first petal to flower center (1½ inches of petal should protrude above center) with 2 turns of #26 wire. Secure second and third petals to flower with one turn of wire each. Finished center should form even whorl of 3 petals.

Secure remaining 15 petals of blossom to center, taking full advantage of petal length (see guideline on pattern). Position first body petal between any 2 center petals and secure with twist of wire. Space all successive petals evenly around and down the stem wire.

When all petals are in place, secure with additional twists of wire, then wrap from base of flower down stem with florist's tape.

For wreath, make 5 natural-colored flowers, 3 red flowers, and 2 orange ones. Insert flowers into straw wreath (refer to photograph for positioning). Add sprigs of baby's breath and dried fern. The finished wreath will be about 12 inches in diameter.

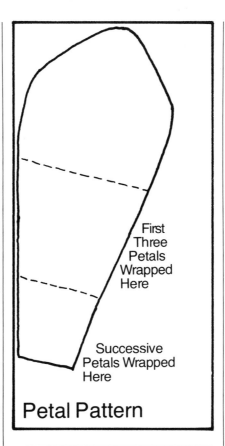

First Three Petals Wrapped Here

Successive Petals Wrapped Here

Petal Pattern

Embroidered Crèche Figures
page 137

Materials: ⅜ yard off-white linen or other coarsely woven fabric; small skeins red and green Persian yarn; 6-inch square of cardboard; embroidery hoop; ⅔ yard of 1½-inch-wide crocheted lace; white glue; dressmaker's carbon paper or hot transfer pencil; scraps of #5-count Penelope canvas; 5-pound bag birdseed; quilt batting.

Instructions: Enlarge the patterns (right and on page 142) and transfer the figure *outlines only* to the wrong side of the fabric using dressmaker's carbon or a hot transfer pencil. Do not cut out pattern pieces. Place the pieces far enough from the selvages that you'll be able to use an embroidery hoop easily. Allow for ⅜-inch seam margins around each of the pieces.

Trace inside details of each figure on the right side of the fabric.

Embroider each figure according to the pattern. Use satin stitches on heart, flowers, and leaves; stem stitches on hands and flower stems. Edge Mary's robe with a line of chain stitches and a row of French knots; Joseph's robe has 2 rows of chain stitches separated by flowers worked in detached chain. (Refer to color photograph).

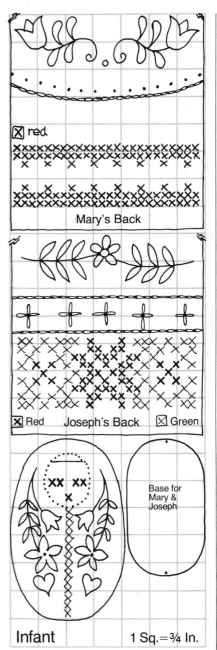

⊠ red

Mary's Back

⊠ Red   Joseph's Back   ⊠ Green

Base for Mary & Joseph

Infant   1 Sq. = ¾ In.

Features and base of both figures are worked in cross-stitches. Use scraps of needlepoint canvas as guide for cross-stitches. Pin canvas in position and work stitches over canvas threads. When you've finished, moisten the canvas; gently pull out threads.

Cut out each piece, leaving ⅜-inch seam allowance around all figures. Using infant shape as pattern, cut another oval of fabric for back.

To assemble the figures, pin appropriate fronts and backs together, right sides facing. Stitch along marked outline of each seam, leaving bottom of Mary and Joseph open; leave a 2-inch opening on the infant for turning.

continued

Continued from page 141
A Festival of Folk Art

X Red

Mary   1 Sq. = ¾ In.

Clip curves and turn each form right side out. Press bottom edges inward.

Using pattern, cut 2 pieces of cardboard for the bases of the large figures. Place cardboard on fabric and trace around edges. Cut fabric bases out, adding a ⅜-inch seam allowance.

Center cardboard bases on fabric bases and glue the pieces together. Clip curved edges of fabric; fold edges in and glue fabric to cardboard.

Place seams of figures at dots on base; hand-sew edges of figures around base, leaving a 2-inch opening.

Insert funnel into openings and fill each figure as full of birdseed as possible. Sew bottom openings closed on Mary and Joseph. Finish stuffing infant with batting, then close by hand.

Stand Mary and Joseph upright and carefully open the seams at the tops of the heads. Stuff figures tightly with batting; then close by hand.

Gather 8-inches of crocheted lace into halo. Tack halos to heads.

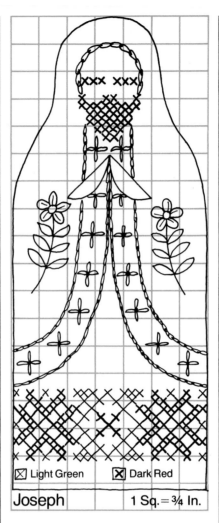

⊠ Light Green   ⊠ Dark Red

Joseph   1 Sq. = ¾ In.

Folk Art Stockings
page 137

Materials: (for each stocking) ½ yard natural linen or linenlike fabric; ½ yard muslin for lining; 2¼ yards of cable cord; 2¼ yards of 1½-inch red grosgrain ribbon; 6 inches of ¾-inch red grosgrain ribbon; small skeins of 3-ply Persian yarn (2 red, 2 green); hot transfer pencil or dressmaker's carbon paper; embroidery hoop; crewel needle; tissue paper.

Instructions: Enlarge the stocking and cuff patterns (right), and transfer them to fabric using a hot transfer pencil or dressmaker's carbon paper. Lightly sketch centering lines (dotted lines on pattern) on fabric with regular pencil. Add ½-inch seam allowances. Do not cut out shapes yet.

Select design motif, enlarge and transfer to stocking. Slip fabric into hoop and embroider center motif, cuff, and toe designs, following pattern. Cut out embroidered pieces (leaving ½-inch seam allowance around each piece).

Cover cable cord with wide grosgrain ribbon and baste covered cord along seam line on front of stocking to within 3 inches of top of either side.

With right sides together, stitch stocking front to back, leaving top open. Turn and press.

Using full stocking pattern, cut 2 pieces muslin for lining. Sew lining pieces together (½-inch seams), leaving top open. Clip curves, trim seams, but do not turn. Slip lining inside stocking; baste lining to stocking around top.

Baste cording along side seams of front cuff. With right sides facing, stitch cuff front and back. Stitch narrow hem in non-embroidered cuff edge.

Baste cording along top (embroidered) seam edge of cuff. With right sides together, slip cuff over stocking; line up seams; stitch around top. Trim seams, turn cuff to inside, and press. Fold finished cuff over stocking. Add grosgrain ribbon loop for hanging.

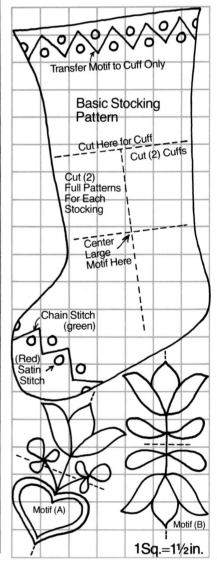

Transfer Motif to Cuff Only

Basic Stocking Pattern

Cut Here for Cuff

Cut (2) Cuffs

Cut (2) Full Patterns For Each Stocking

Center Large Motif Here

Chain Stitch (green)

(Red) Satin Stitch

Motif (A)

Motif (B)

1 Sq.=1½ in.

Embroidery Tips, Tools, and Techniques

To start you off successfully toward many years' enjoyment of your Christmas projects, here are some stitchery tips to use for the stockings and crèche figures in this section as well as for other embroidered decorations and gifts shown in this book.

Fabrics

Unusual fabrics can make your stitchery exciting, but the most commonly used fabrics for traditional embroidery such as the folk art stockings in this section or the rose-patterned tablecloth in the next section are even-weave cottons or linens and other fabrics with a fairly smooth texture and a regular weave.

An even-weave fabric is one with the same number of horizontal and vertical threads per inch, as shown.

Even-weave Fabric

The advantage of stitching on even-weave fabric is that embroidery stitches will be uniform in size, which is an important consideration for cross-stitch and other counted-thread techniques. Aida cloth and hardanger fabric are among the most widely available and popular even-weave fabrics because the threads (and spaces between them) are easy to see and count. Each can be purchased with a specific thread count, such as 11 or 22 threads per inch.

For counted-thread embroidery (including cross-stitching) on fabric so closely woven that counting threads is difficult, use needlepoint canvas. Select a mono canvas of the appropriate size and thread count, baste it securely to the embroidery fabric, and stitch over the meshes of the canvas, using them as a guide for the accurate placement of stitches. When the embroidery is finished, remove the basting stitches, dampen the canvas, and carefully remove the threads of the canvas, one strand at a time, from beneath the embroidery stitches.

Whatever fabric you decide upon for your embroidery, choose a high-quality fabric that is firm enough to support the threads and stitches you intend to use and one that is sturdy enough to wear well. If you intend to launder the object you're making, preshrink the fabric before you begin, using the same water temperature and soap or detergent you expect to use on the finished project.

Yarns and threads

Many yarns and threads are available for stitchery. Use wool yarns for crewelwork and embroidery floss and pearl cotton for traditional stitchery. For special effects, try rayon, silk, and metallic threads.

Choose good-quality threads that are colorfast. If necessary, preshrink them by soaking the skeins or strands in cool water. Dry the thread thoroughly before you begin stitching.

Cut wool yarns into pieces about 18 inches long for embroidery. Longer threads will look worn and tired from being pulled through the fabric. Pearl cotton and floss can be cut into longer lengths, but silk threads generally should be cut into shorter lengths.

Yarns and threads have a lengthwise "grain" just as fabrics do, and are slightly smoother in one direction (with the grain). Thread the needle so you stitch with the grain; the thread will be attractive looking longer.

Do not be afraid to use brightly colored yarns and threads. Colors will not be as bright on the fabric as they are in the skeins.

Store your stitchery materials in a plastic bag to keep them clean.

Needles

Keep both blunt and sharp needles on hand for embroidery. Blunt-end tapestry needles are used for counted-thread work and surface stitchery when the needle is worked into the spaces between threads or does not otherwise enter the fabric.

Use sharp needles for regular embroidery. Be sure the eye of the needle is large enough for the thread to slide through it easily without breaking. If crewel needles are too small, use chenille needles, which have larger eyes and sharper points.

Embroidery hoops and frames

Many stitchers like to use a hoop or frame for their embroidery. Stretch the fabric in a large hoop, lace it into a needlepoint frame, or tack it to artist's stretcher strips assembled into a frame.

When the hoop or frame is propped against a table or mounted on a floor stand, both hands will be free for embroidery. Stitch with one hand above the fabric and the other beneath, working the needle with a stabbing motion straight through the fabric from front to back or back to front.

The advantage in using a frame is that the embroidery will go faster than when you stitch with the in-and-out motion of regular sewing. The fabric is less apt to become soiled by excessive handling. And the tension on the thread will be uniform, reducing both the amount of distortion in the fabric and the need for blocking when the embroidery is finished.

Other small tools

Among the small pieces of equipment stitchers find helpful are embroidery scissors with sharp, narrow points, such as stork scissors. They're handy for snipping out mistakes.

A flexible leather thimble is useful to protect your fingers.

Yarn caddies are useful for keeping all the yarn for a project together but tangle free. Commercial caddies are widely available, or you can make one at home. Divide yarns for each project by color and sandwich them between 2 layers of fabric cut into a strip. Baste together the layers between the strands of yarn, making a pocket for each. When you need a thread, pull it from the pocket. Remaining threads stay clean in their pockets.

Blocking

To block a finished piece of embroidery, steam press lightly on the wrong side over a thickly padded ironing board. Pin fabric to the board, if necessary, and use a damp cloth between the fabric and the iron. If colors might run, insert a dry cloth between stitchery and damp cloth.

143

An Old-World Christmas

An Album of Heirloom Patterns

If you cherish old-fashioned things, you'll feel right at home in this gracious living room. Pewter pots and candlesticks, Jacobean floral motifs, crisp blue and white trims, embroidered linens, and handmade lace are all heirlooms, beloved of our grandmothers and their grandmothers, too, for their elegance, charm, and appealing warmth.

Everything in this inviting Christmas room is rich with the aura of yesteryear. The ornaments, decorations, and gifts were inspired by the treasured possessions of our English and Dutch ancestors and by the designs, colors, materials, and techniques used by artisans to craft the objects these settlers loved. And all are handmade, including the painted ornaments, the marbelized gift paper, the crewel-embroidered stockings, the needlepoint welcome rug, the candlesticks, the Della Robbia wreath, and the elegant hobbyhorse.

In the dining room (shown again on page 150), beautifully stitched tablecloths, lovely flowers, and a cluster of candles on the sideboard preserve the look of the past.

Directions for all the projects shown in this section begin on page 153.

An Album of Heirloom Patterns

Crisp blue and white really sparkle in a Christmas outfit and on a holiday table (below). The appliqué-and-patchwork vest and skirt are a delightful blend of quaint and trendy with their old-fashioned fabrics and splashy floral motifs. An array of pretty ribbons arranged atop a pleasing print makes the table covering.

The beautiful Christmas tree ball (right) is a one-of-a-kind ornament made from air-dried clay.

The quick-to-stitch cloth (opposite) requires only a 45-inch square of blue print fabric and seven 45-inch lengths of patterned ribbons in a variety of colors and widths.

Arrange the ribbons symmetrically on the cloth so four ribbons run horizontally and the remaining three run vertically, as shown in the photograph. Pin and stitch the ribbons to the cloth, then turn up a half-inch hem all around.

Stockings are not only hung with care, they're also made with care so they can be proudly displayed Christmas after Christmas. The crewel-embroidered one (above) is stitched with wool yarn on linen. Like the picture frame, the stocking features an old-time china and embroidery pattern.

Use the embroidered frame for an old-fashioned photograph, a mirror, or dried flowers.

Three shades of copen blue wool are used for the Christmas stocking and picture frame. The designs, adapted from Jacobean floral motifs, are worked in the stitches of traditional crewel embroidery. All the satin-stitched areas have been under-stitched first to give the final stitching a firm, rich look. Additional padding behind the fabric adds to the luxurious appearance of these projects.

An Album of Heirloom Patterns

Each of these Christmas tree ornaments (above) is a handmade art object you'll be proud to hang on your tree or to give as a delightful Christmas remembrance. The antique delft designs painted on the ornaments come down to us from the 16th century when porcelain makers in Europe adapted patterns from Oriental motifs.

The "porcelain" wreath (opposite) is a frankly fake rendition of the traditional Della Robbia wreath of fruits and nuts. Named for a 15th century Italian sculptor, Della Robbia wreaths were popular in colonial Williamsburg and all along the middle- and southern-Atlantic seaboard where fruit was plentiful even in winter.

148

The ornaments (opposite) are made with glass Christmas tree balls that are mirror-finished silver on the inside and clear glass on the outside. A coating of gesso on the outside of each ornament enables the paint used for the designs to adhere to the glass. Floral motifs are added with artists' oil paints. For the delicate tints on these ornaments, use three shades of blue mixed with white or black. A final coating of varnish—and careful handling—will protect your beautiful handwork for years.

The attractive Della Robbia wreath (above) is not exactly the porcelain heirloom it purports to be. This inexpensive version of an old-fashioned wreath is made of plastic fruit from the dime store. To make the wreath, gather an assortment of oranges, apples, lemons, bananas, and pears. Paint each piece pristine white, then attach it to a plywood and wire base. Tuck white-painted leaves in and around the fruit to fill out the wreath, and trim it with a tailored ribbon bow.

In your grandmother's day, a holiday table would be spread not only with delicacies from her kitchen but with treasured needlework from her linen closet. Why

not stitch your own heirloom linen and lace like this embroidered tablecloth and crocheted edging?

The porcelainlike blue blossoms on the table are fresh flowers that

have been preserved so they can be used in bouquet after bouquet. To make the tiny packages, wrap small boxes in dollhouse wallpaper and tie them with dainty bows.

An Album of Heirloom Patterns

An amateur alchemist can change simple wooden spindles into "pewter" candlesticks (right) simply by painting on the "patina" with a silvery paint. The designs on the dime-store crocks were borrowed from classic blue-and-white delft patterns.

Instructions for the porcelainized flowers, the filet-crochet rose-pattern edging, and the candlesticks are given below.

To make the porcelainized flowers, you'll need a half pint each of white and blue China Magic ceramic coating, and a small can of China Magic clear glaze, which you can find at most craft and hobby stores. Then gather a selection of *fresh* flowers (such as carnations or roses), some florist's wire and tape, small artist's paintbrushes, an electric skillet, and a block of plastic foam.

Begin by removing the leaves and stems from several of the flowers. Insert florist's wire into the base of each blossom and wrap the wire stems with florist's tape.

Gently heat an opened can of white China Magic in an electric skillet filled with water. Following the manufacturer's directions, brush a thin coat of white China Magic on each petal of the flower. Coat all sides of all the petals with one application.

Insert the florist-wire stems into the foam block and allow the flowers to dry for about an hour. Then apply a second thin coat of blue China Magic that also has been warmed in the skillet. Allow the flowers to dry overnight. When they are completely dry, apply a thin coat of clear glaze.

The filet-crochet, rose-pattern edging beneath the tablecloth (opposite) is about 10 inches wide when finished. To make it, use a #11 steel crochet hook and J&P

Coats size 20 white, mercerized crochet cotton.

The gauge is: 5 spaces equal 1 inch; 5 rows equal 1 inch.

A charted pattern for the rose motif is on page 157. Begin with the instructions below, and refer to the chart as necessary. Crochet abbreviations are on page 371.

Starting at the narrow edge, make a ch 9 inches long (15 ch to 1 inch).

Row 1: Starting at A on the chart, dc in 4th ch from hook—starting bl made; ch 2, skip 2 ch, dc in next ch—sp made; make 4 more sps; dc in next 3 ch—another bl made; make 6 more bls, 11 sps, 1 bl, 1 sp, 1 bl, 4 sps, 1 bl, 1 sp, 1 bl, 2 sps, 1 bl, dc in next 3 ch—end bl made at shaped edge. Cut off any remaining chain. Ch 8, turn.

Row 2: Dc in 4th ch from hook and in next 4 ch, dc in next dc—2 bls dc increased at beg of row; making bls over bls (and working in back loop only of each dc), make 1 bl, 4 sps, 1 bl, 6 sps, 2 bls, 9 sps, 2 bls, 2 sps, 1 bl, 1 sp, 1 bl, 2 sps, 2 bls, 3 sps; dc in next ch—1 ending bl made. Ch 3, turn.

Next 12 rows: Following the chart, work from B to C.

Following Row: Follow 15th row to within last 2 bls of previous row; do not work over last 2 bls—2 bls decreased. Ch 3, turn. Continue to follow chart to D.

Repeat from A to D until the edging is the desired length. Then press the border and hand appliqué it to the edge of a tablecloth.

To make the candlesticks (above) select an assortment of carved banister spindles, wooden furniture legs, and other wood turnings from the lumber store. You'll also need: wooden curtain rings and rod ends; scraps of pine from which to cut square and circular bases; candle holder inserts; fast-drying glue; finishing nails; a can of silver, rub-on pewter finish; and an electric drill.

Cut and combine various shapes, sizes, and heights of wood turnings, using the photograph (above) as a guide. Add wooden circles or squares as bases, and glue wooden curtain rings on tops.

Drill ⅞-inch holes for the candle holders, holding the candlestick in a vise, if necessary. Then glue all the sections together, or drill holes and secure the pieces with finishing nails. Mount the candle holder inserts in the holes.

Seal the wood with silver acrylic paint, then sand the wood and seal it again. Finally, apply pewter finish with your fingers and buff.

An Album of Heirloom Patterns

In every family photo album, there are pictures everybody loves. Now, by combining your sewing ability and a little chemical know-how, you can transform those pictures into unique portrait pillows like the ones below or beautiful fabric pictures like the one on page 147. The process is somewhat complex, but not difficult with the hints on page 158.

For your own hearth, or as a special gift, needlepoint this lovely 27x42-inch throw rug with an heirloom border pattern. Or, use the rug as a wall hanging, as shown on page 145.

You'll find a list of the materials required for the rug and a charted diagram of the pattern on pages 158 and 159. Instructions for stitching the rug follow.

To make the rug, first bind the edges of the canvas with masking tape to prevent raveling. Locate the center horizontal and vertical threads of canvas and mark them with a waterproof pen.

The charted pattern on page 159 represents the upper-left quadrant of the rug's border design. Copy the entire rug pattern onto a piece of graph paper, flopping the pattern as necessary to reproduce the stitch sequence for each quarter of the design.

Begin the rug by centering the "Welcome" letters on the canvas and working them in dark blue continental stitches. Next, work the inner dark blue border and the outer two blue borders. Fill in the background around the letters with white basket-weave stitches. Work the floral design around the border as shown on the chart, then fill the white background between the two outer blue borders.

After all the stitching is completed, block the rug. Whip-stitch rug binding to the unworked canvas, turn the edges back, and hand-tack the binding to the back of the rug. Or, staple the rug to a frame made of 1x2-inch lumber, add eye hooks and picture wire, and hang it in place.

Instructions for an Old-World Christmas: An Album of Heirloom Patterns

The instructions below and on the following pages are for the ornaments, decorations, and gifts shown on pages 144–152. For directions for enlarging and transferring designs, see the glossary, pages 370–371.

Marbelized Wrapping Paper
page 144

Materials: White craft paper; small can royal blue enamel oil paint; turpentine or paint thinner; large waterproof container (roasting pan, shallow bucket, old wading pool); newspapers:

Instructions: Fill large container with water. Drop 3 dots of blue oil paint or a narrow, 3-inch-long strip of oil paint on top of water. (Oil-based paint should float on water but if the paint is too heavy and sinks, mix it with a little thinner in a glass jar, before applying to water.)

Swirl the paint with a pencil so it forms an interesting design, and quickly but gently lay the more absorbent side of the paper *on top of the water.* Make sure paper is flat but doesn't sink.

Remove paper from water, allowing excess water to drip off. Lay paper face up on newspapers to dry overnight. When it's dry, lightly press back of paper with warm iron.

Start with fresh paint after 2 or 3 pieces of paper have been painted. Drag newspaper over top of water to remove paint residue that has settled on it before adding more paint.

Elegant Hobbyhorse
page 144

Materials: ½ yard white velveteen; 1 skein bright blue yarn; scraps of 2 different blue print fabrics for appliqués; black and blue embroidery floss; small gold bells; ⅔ yard of white tassel trim; scraps of blue and brown felt; 3 yards each of blue and white satin ribbon; 3-foot length of 1-inch dowel; round wooden drawer pull; wood stain or paint; fiberfill.

Instructions: Enlarge the pattern (above right).

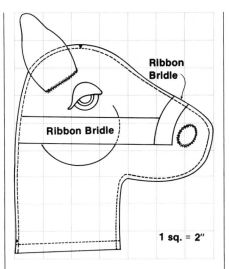

Fold white fabric in half, and cut 2 horse's head pattern pieces. Transfer all placement markings to the wrong side of the fabric. Also cut 2 ears from white fabric (adding ¼-inch seam allowances) and 2 matching ears from blue print fabric for ear linings.

Machine- or hand-appliqué all pieces to each side of the horse's head and embroider details.

With right sides together, stitch the horse's head; turn and press. Turn up a ⅝-inch hem at the base of the head to make a casing for a gathering cord. Run cord through casing. Stuff horse's nose firmly with fiberfill.

Finish the dowel with wood stain or paint and let dry. Cushion the top of the dowel with a wad of batting, insert dowel into horse's head and nail through fabric into top of dowel. Stuff carefully around dowel and the remainder of horse's head. Draw casing closed.

Stitch and stuff ears, and appliqué them in place with tiny cross-stitches. Add double set of ribbon reins to horse's nose and slip-stitch into place.

For mane, divide a skein of yarn into 8-foot lengths. Take half of the lengths in one hand and tie loose knots in the bundle of yarn every 12 inches. Stitch the knots close together along back seam of horse and up to forehead (forming loops of yarn). Trim excess at nape of neck and over forehead.

Finish the raw end of the dowel with a stained wooden doorknob; attach the doorknob with a dowel screw.

Appliquéd Vest And Skirt
page 146

Materials: One-size-fits-all vest is completely lined and requires ½ yard each of 2 contrasting fabrics, ¼ yard each of 3 additional prints, plus ¼ yard of plain off-white fabric, and a scrap of plain blue fabric.

Skirt is made from McCall's pattern 5248; adapt appliqué to suit any A-line

continued

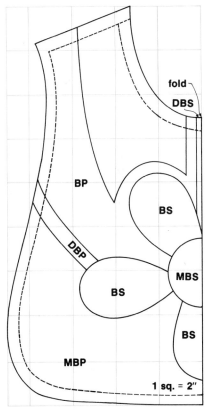

Vest Color Key
DBS—dark blue solid
BS—beige solid
MBS—medium blue solid
DBP—dark blue print
BP—beige print
MBP—medium blue print

skirt. (Consult pattern package for required yardage for basic skirt.) Appliquéd flowers require an additional ¼ yard of each of the fabrics listed for the vest above.

Instructions: For vest, enlarge the pattern on page 153 to size and transfer it to brown paper. This is the master pattern.

Place the pattern on the fold of the fabric, and cut 2 complete fronts and 2 backs from contrasting fabrics. (For the back pieces, alter the neckline so it is about 2 inches higher at the center back to ensure a smooth fit across the upper back of the vest.)

From the master pattern, trace the pattern pieces for the appliqués (for front of vest only) and cut each piece from appropriate fabric (add ¼-inch seam allowances to all appliqué pieces).

Press under seam allowances and hand- or machine-appliqué all pieces on front of vest. Assemble front and lining; assemble back piece and lining; join lined front and lined back of vest together at shoulder seams. Topstitch ¼ inch inside all edges and around the neck of the vest.

Make four ¼-inch wide, 15-inch long ties from blue print fabric and attach 2 ties to each side of the front and back of the vest, just under the arms.

For matching appliquéd skirt, first assemble skirt according to pattern directions. (Cut each panel of the skirt from a different fabric.) Then enlarge

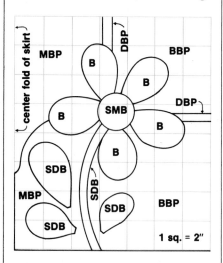

Skirt Color Key
MBP—medium blue print
B—beige
BBP—beige/blue print
DBP—dark blue print
SDB—solid dark blue
SMB—solid medium blue

appliqué pattern (below) and cut 2 of each appliqué piece (adding ¼-inch seam allowances to all pattern pieces). Press under seam allowances and hand- or machine-stitch all appliqué pieces to the bottom of the skirt.

Pendo Christmas Ball
page 146

Materials: Plastic foam balls; white glue; white and natural colored Pendo Decorative Clay, plus Pendo in other colors of your choice for ribbons and flowers (or, substitute another air-drying clay of similar quality); hairpins; brayer; acrylic sealant.

Instructions: Mix one part white and one part natural Pendo or other air-drying clay. Leave the mixture slightly marbleized. For a tinted base color, marbelize the white/natural mixture with the color of your choice.

Using a brayer or rolling pin, roll a piece of this base color into a thin slab. Cover the surface of a plastic foam ball with a thin layer of white glue and allow to dry. Press the slab of base color onto the foam ball. Repeat until ball is completely covered.

Smooth the pieces together, then smooth entire surface of ball using a little water and your fingers. Touch hairpin with white glue and insert into ball for hanging. Allow ball to dry thoroughly.

Shape tiny flowers and thin strips of ribbon out of various shades of Pendo and gently affix to top of the ball. When entire ball is finished and dry, seal with acrylic spray.

Crewel-Embroidered
Picture Frame
page 147

Materials: 21x26 inches white linen; 3-ply Persian wool in light, medium, and dark copen blue; embroidery hoop and crewel needle; 17x22 inches ⅛-inch plywood for frame; tracing paper; transfer pencil; quilt batting; tape or staples.

Instructions: Enlarge the pattern (above right) to size; pattern represents one quarter of total design. Transfer motifs to remaining 3 quadrants of frame, extending small flower motif up sides and across top and bottom.

Baste fabric along edges of frame as indicated on pattern.

Embroider design as indicated on color and stitch guide, using one strand of yarn throughout. When embroidery is finished, block fabric.

Cut out oval on plywood to correspond to oval on pattern. Pad wood with 2 to 4 layers quilt batting and stretch embroidered fabric over batting, aligning basted lines with frame edges. Clip curves on oval so fabric fits smoothly. Tape or staple fabric to back of picture frame.

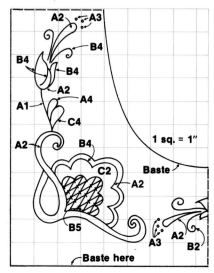

Color and Stitch Key
A—dark copen blue
B—medium copen blue
C—light copen blue
1—chain stitch
2—satin stitch
3—French knot
4—laid work
5—stem stitch

Crewel-Embroidered
Stockings
page 147

Materials: *(for each stocking)* ½ yard each white linen, lining fabric and polyester fleece (padding); 1½ yards cable cord; ¼ yard copen blue cotton; Persian yarn in dark, medium, and light copen blue; transfer pencil.

Instructions: Enlarge pattern on page 155. Trace outlines with black marking pen, then transfer design to linen by taping pattern to a window, taping linen over the pattern, and tracing outlines with pencil.

Using one strand of yarn, embroider the design, following color and stitch key for the crewel picture frame.

Cut out embroidered stocking shape and a matching shape for stocking back (add seam allowances). Baste front and back to padding. Cover cording with blue fabric and baste along seam line of front. Sew padded stocking front to padded back, right sides together, except at top. Turn, press.

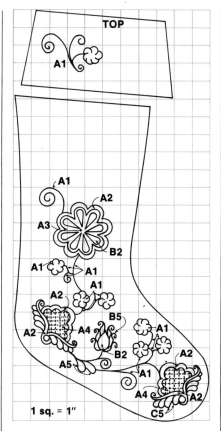

1 sq. = 1"

Sew lining front to back. Press but do not turn. Insert lining in stocking, wrong sides facing.

Baste padding to front and back cuff. With right sides facing, stitch front and back cuff together at sides. Baste covered cording along lower seam line.

Stitch front and back cuff lining together at sides. Sew lining to cuff along corded edge. Turn, press. Baste lining and cuff together at top.

Sew cuff top to stocking top but don't include lining in seam. Trim seam, press down. Slip-stitch lining over seam allowance. From blue fabric, make a narrow hanging loop. Sew to upper back corner.

Painted Delft Ornaments
page 148

Materials: Glass Christmas tree balls in various sizes (mirror-finish silver on the inside, plain glass on the outside); wooden dowels to fit inside ornaments (¼ and ⅛ inch); plastic foam blocks; two ⅝-inch lettering brushes and three sable brushes (#5, #1, and #0); gesso; oil paints in the following colors; cobalt, ultramarine, phthalocyanine blue, titanium white, and mars black; high-gloss urethane varnish; high-gloss off-white enamel; rubbing alcohol; tissue paper; soft rags, paint thinner; water and soap.

Instructions: First make a rack of dowels on which to paint and dry your ornaments. Cut several ¼-inch dowels into 9-inch lengths and jam dowels into plastic foam block.

Remove the metal caps from a group of ornaments and set the caps aside. Clean each ornament thoroughly with rubbing alcohol and a soft rag, then dry the ornaments with tissue paper and place each one on a dowel. Make sure that ornaments are cleaned and dried *thoroughly* before beginning to paint.

Mix a solution of 50 percent gesso and 50 percent water—distilled water is desirable—and apply even coats of the mixture to each ornament. Using one of the ⅝-inch lettering brushes, make smooth, even strokes once around the stem of the ornament and then, using as few vertical strokes as possible, cover the entire ornament. This base coat dries rapidly and the ornament should be ready for detail painting in about one hour. If desired, sand gesso lightly.

Mix small amounts of phthalocyanine, cobalt, and ultramarine with titanium white, and use this clear blue color to paint on the basic outlines of the floral design (refer to full-scale patterns for varisized ornaments on page 156). Then use medium blue (same mixture as above, only a little more of the ultramarine blue) to add depth and details to the designs. Finally, the dark blue (phthalocyanine and mars black) is used for final detailing and definition of the design.

For all 3 stages of painting, use the #5 brush for large areas of color and a #1 or #0 for details and fine lines. Paint should be applied as thinly and evenly as possible.

Use the second ⅝-inch brush to apply 2 coats of varnish when paint is dry. Brush, varnish, ornament, and work area must be absolutely dust-free. Both coats of varnish should be applied sparingly and brushed on smoothly. Second coat should be applied only after first coat is completely dry. (If drips appear in the first coat of varnish, they may be carefully sanded away with #500 wet and dry sandpaper.)

Dip metal ornament caps in white paint; string on the ⅛-inch dowels to dry. Tops should dry in about 24 hours, and may then be placed on dry ornaments for the finished product.

Della Robbia Wreath
page 149

Note: Finished size is approximately 25 inches in diameter.

Materials: Plastic fruit—16 lemons, 16 oranges, 16 apples, 8 large pears, 8 small pears, 8 bananas, 36 leaves; 25-inch-diameter plywood circle with 15-inch circle cut out in the center; 18-inch wire wreath; high-gloss white enamel; gesso; acetone; fine-grade steel wool; florist wire; white florist tape.

Instructions: Paint plywood and wire wreaths with gesso; dry thoroughly. Then paint a coat of white enamel on the gesso; dry thoroughly again.

Position the wire wreath atop the plywood wreath, matching centers, and lightly trace around the wire wreath with a pencil. Drill 4 holes along this line, spacing the holes evenly. Wire the 2 wreaths together by threading florist wire through each hole.

Also, drill 2 holes 1 inch inside the outer edge of the plywood wreath. Thread the holes with strong wire for hanging the finished wreath.

Pour a small amount of acetone into a container. Dip steel wool into the acetone and rub the entire surface of each fruit so the gesso and enamel will adhere. Add wire stems to the fruit.

Paint the fruit using one coat of gesso and hang from clothesline to dry; then paint with enamel and hang to dry. Wrap wire stems with white floral tape. Arrange fruit on wire wreath and attach with wire stems. Clean leaves with acetone and paint them with gesso and enamel the same as for fruit. Wire leaves to wreath around fruit.

Note: Painted fruit is fragile and will flake easily, so handle it with care.

Embroidered Tablecloth
page 150

Materials: Purchased even-weave tablecloth or even-weave linen yardage of desired length; thread to match fabric; #5 pearl cotton in light, medium, and dark blue; embroidery needle; embroidery hoop or frame; graph paper (optional).

Instructions: The rose motif (page 157) and openwork border are embroidered once in the center of each side of the tablecloth shown. The pattern may be worked on any size square or rectangular tablecloth or runner, and repeated as often as you wish.

The tablecloth is worked on #36-count even-weave linen; each motif measures approximately 3¼x13 inches. A fabric with a different count (number of threads per inch) will yield a rose of a different size. For example, on #22-count hardanger cloth, the motif will be about 1½ times larger than on #36-count fabric.

continued

Continued from page 155
An Album of Heirloom Patterns

Design for a
3½-to-4-inch
diameter
ornament

Design for a
large
flower
crock

Design for a
small flower
crock

Design for a
2-inch-diameter
ornament

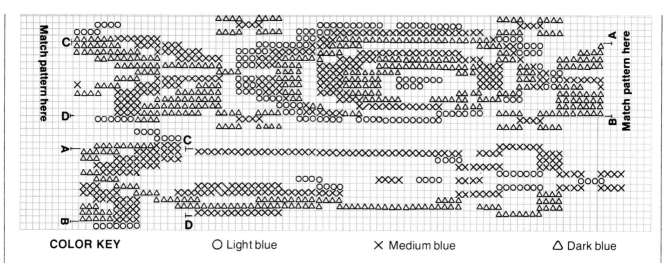

Before plotting out the design for the cloth, you may wish to embroider one complete motif, either with or without the drawn thread border, on a scrap of the fabric you intend to use for your tablecloth. This way, you will be able to determine exactly what size the motif will be on the fabric you have chosen.

The graphed pattern (above) represents the center rose motif and the oblong extension to one side of it. For a complete pattern, reverse the oblong motif, match it to the center at the points indicated, and repeat it on the other side of the rose.

The proportions of the pattern as shown on the graph are deceiving. Each square on the graph actually represents a long, thin straight stitch, even though we have used squares to indicate each stitch in order to include color indications for the pattern. If you find working from a colored graph easier, transfer the design to graph paper using colored pencils.

Embroider the entire design in straight stitches. (If you are unfamiliar with this stitch, see page 374.) Work each stitch over 7 threads of fabric and leave 2 threads between each stitch. Except in the top row of stitches, the top of each stitch is worked into the same space as the bottom of the stitch in the row above.

To work the rose motif once in the center of each side of the tablecloth, begin by finding the exact center of each side of the cloth. Mark it with a tailor's tack about 5 inches above the raw edge. Then stitch the rose, starting in the center. After finishing the rose, work the drawn thread box and border according to the directions that follow.

For the drawn thread work, first plan for the ends of the box to fall about ¾ inch beyond the ends of the rose motif, with the sides about ⅝ inch above and below the sides of the motif.

Start drawn thread work on long sides of cloth. From the fabric, withdraw about 6 threads that run parallel to the hem. (This makes the drawn area about ¼ inch wide if your fabric is #36-count linen. On fabric with a different count, simply withdraw as many threads as necessary to make a channel about ¼ inch wide.) Then with thread the same weight and color as the threads in your fabric, hemstitch the remaining (vertical) threads in groups of four.

Bind both edges of the drawn area, creating a "ladder" of threads around the rose motif.

Find the center of the short sides of the box; withdraw an additional 6 threads to make the border that extends around the cloth to join the boxes. In corners of the drawn area, where warp and weft threads are both withdrawn, work buttonhole stitches to stabilize edges of fabric and prevent raveling.

Finish the cloth with a double row of decorative hemstitching. Or simply turn up the raw edge ¼ inch, then turn it up again; press and blindstitch for a plain, tailored hem.

Filet-Crochet Rose-Pattern Edging
page 150

Use the pattern (below) for the tablecloth edging. Materials required and how-to instructions are on page 151.

continued

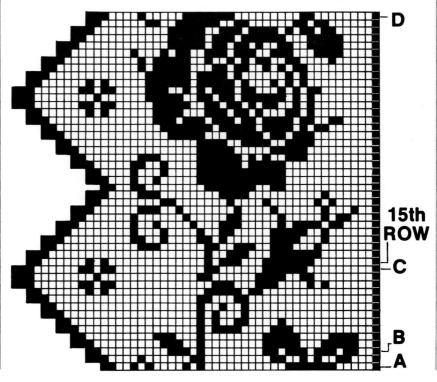

Continued from page 157
An Album of Heirloom Patterns

Painted Delft Flower Crocks
page 151

Materials: White and off-white ceramic crocks in various shapes and sizes; acrylic or oil paints in colors listed for delft ornaments (page 155); good-quality paintbrushes in various sizes.

Instructions: Refer to patterns on page 156 for suggested delft designs or select floral motifs of your own. Use all or a portion of any design, depending on the size and shape of your crock. Trace the outlines of the design on the crock, using a soft pencil or light-colored carbon paper.

Mix colors as described for delft ornaments (page 155) and paint crocks.

Acrylic paints are waterproof when dry. Decorated crocks may be cleaned by sponging them gently, but scrubbing or soaking will cause the paint to peel. For greater protection, give the entire crock a coat of clear polyurethane.

Portrait Pillows
page 152

Important Note: The fabric portraits on each of our pillows are made by a process called cyanotype printing. The process itself is fairly simple, but requires the use of *dangerous chemicals that must be handled with care and kept out of the reach of children.*

We suggest that you read through the entire set of instructions at least once before beginning the project.

Materials: For each different fabric print you will need a Kodalith (or high-contrast) negative made from a sharp, good-quality photograph (old or new, color or black and white, any size). Each negative can be used over and over again for making more than one fabric print of the same picture.

You also will need *ferric ammonium citrate* and *potassium ferricyanide* chemicals in crystal form. These chemicals may be ordered through photography supply houses. Or, use a paint-on-emulsion designed for photosensitizing fabric; follow manufacturer's directions.

Additional materials: Red light bulb; glass or plastic bowls; brown glass jars; plastic spoons; white, untreated 100 percent cotton fabric; soft paintbrush; 9x12-inch squares of regular window glass; rubber gloves; assorted blue, printed fabrics and pillow forms in sizes needed for pillows.

Instructions: *Begin this project in the evening, before a sunny day. Mix the chemicals and paint the fabric in the evening, so fabric can dry overnight.*

Before you begin, you will need one high-contrast Kodalith negative for each image you want to print. These can be made from any photograph through many photo studios and print shops.

Large Kodalith negatives are not inexpensive, but the negative may be used over again in the cyanotype process. (For example, you could print enough squares for a picture quilt.) Ordinary negatives may be used, but a Kodalith negative, which eliminates grays and strengthens black and white contrasts, gives better results.

A 9x12-inch negative is a good size for a framed picture or pillow portrait. For smaller negatives, put 2 to 4 photographs on one 9x12-inch negative.

The chemicals used in this process are sensitive to light, and you must work with them in the dark. Cover the windows and replace the light bulb in your work area with a red bulb (available at photo supply stores), which will not damage chemicals. Wear rubber gloves to protect your hands.

Dissolve 1 ounce of ferric ammonium citrate in ½ cup water. Store remaining crystals in a clearly marked brown glass bottle. Next, mix ½ ounce of potassium ferricyanide with ½ cup water, using a plastic spoon; stir the mixture until the chemical is dissolved. Store the second chemical in the same way as the first. Carefully mix the 2 dissolved chemicals together in a glass bowl.

Chemicals begin to lose their effectiveness soon after dissolving, so fabric painting should be done immediately. For best results, print fabric within 6 to 12 hours after chemicals are mixed.

Cut white cotton fabric to size. Using a soft brush, paint the chemical solution on 2 or 3 pieces of fabric at a time. Use about 4 tablespoons of chemical per piece of fabric.

Wet a paintbrush with water before beginning, then cover each piece of fabric with smooth, even strokes (avoid wrinkling the cloth). Hang the pieces up to dry on a clothes hanger in a dark closet; mark the side that has been painted. As the chemicals dry, the fabric turns chartreuse.

When fabric is *thoroughly* dry, press it with a barely warm iron on *unpainted* side. Next, place fabric in a sandwich arrangement of glass, fabric (painted side up), then the clean negative with the emulsion (dull) side down, centered on the straight grain of the fabric. Finally, place a second piece of glass atop the negative, making sure glass is clean, free of fingerprints, and in good contact with the negative.

Expose the entire package outside in direct sunlight on a dry surface. When fabric has turned dark blue, almost black, the print has been properly exposed. Exposure time depends on amount of available sunlight: from 10 to 30 minutes should be sufficient. Don't attempt to do cyanotyping on a cloudy day or with artificial light.

When printing several different negatives on fabric, keep a list of the exact time each has been exposed. Although circumstances may be the same, different negatives may vary in results; some will make consistently lighter prints.

After prints have been exposed, rinse fabric in lukewarm water until every trace of the chartreuse color has gone (3 to 10 minutes). Dry the fabric indoors, on a flat surface.

Prints are hand or machine washable (delicate cycle and mild soap). However, cyanotype print is sensitive to light and will fade in time. This can be slowed considerably by rinsing the set print in a solution of *potassium dichromate* (an inexpensive chemical available through photo supply houses).

To retard fading, mix one teaspoon of *potassium dichromate* in one quart of water in a glass bowl. After rinsing out the print following the first bath of chemicals, dip fresh print into the *potassium dichromate* solution. In a few seconds blue will darken somewhat. Rinse this chemical out, and lay the print on a towel to dry. The color will be somewhat intensified and the print will be much more resistant to fading.

To make cyanotype prints into portrait pillows, stitch each print behind a blue print fabric mat cut with a square, rectangular, or oval opening. Then border this with a fabric frame in a contrasting print. (Refer to the photograph on page 152 for ideas if necessary.) Pad or quilt pillow tops as desired, back with a piece of matching fabric, and stuff.

Quick Point Welcome Rug
page 152

Note: For instructions, see page 152.

Materials: 1⅓ yards of 36-inch-wide #5 interlock rug canvas; Paterna 100 percent wool rug yarn (or equivalent rug yarn) in the following amounts and colors: 250 yards white, 200 yards dark blue, 50 yards medium blue, 50 yards light blue; tapestry needle; masking tape; waterproof pen; graph paper; 4 yards of 4-inch-wide rug binding or a 42x27-inch wooden frame.

(Actual dimensions of rug are 42 x 27 inches, worked on five-squares-per-inch interlock canvas. Pattern is ¼ of border.)

↘ Dark blue
○ Medium blue
■ Light blue

center of
side border

center of
top border →

An Old-World Christmas

A Legacy of Elegance

Colorful, elegant, and sumptuous in every detail—that's a Victorian Christmas! The delicate lace ornaments (opposite), embroidered satin angel (below), and other projects in this section are all a heritage from that magnificently romantic era. Directions for all the projects begin on page 170.

A Legacy of Elegance

Soft and lovely is the manner of this old-fashioned Christmas Eve scene (below). Firelight falls gently on a tree brimming with a choir of satin angels and silken ornaments lightly frosted with antique lace. Tiny personal treasures tied on in gold bring back memories of Christmases past.

Satin and lace cloak this holiday table, and beneath the tree are gift boxes made of satin, silk, and snippets of lace. Such boxes are worthy of being given as gifts all by themselves—or make truly elegant "wraps" for special presents.

Enchanting angelic ornaments (below and on page 161) are tiny soft sculptures made of bridal satin. Quilting gives gentle contours to the wings. Piquant faces are embroidered in silky floss.

Lovers of lace will be delighted with the ornaments (opposite). Here's a way to use those precious bits and pieces you've been snipping and saving. Attach them to plastic foam balls that have been swathed in Swistraw for elegant and gleaming decorations.

Directions for angels and lace ornaments are included here.

To make the angels, you'll need eggshell satin or cotton sateen, brown and yellow permanent marking pens, embroidery floss, narrow velvet ribbon, lace edging, miniature floral appliqués, and bits of pillow stuffing.

Enlarge the pattern on page 170 and cut a double thickness of fabric for each angel. With the right sides facing, stitch the front and back together, leaving the chin open. Clip the curves, trim the seam to 1/8 inch, turn, and press the angel.

Using a light pencil or white dressmaker's carbon paper, trace quilting lines and facial features onto the front of the angel.

Lightly pad each wing with pillow stuffing, and machine-quilt the wings and the outline of the hair. Next, lightly stuff the top of the head, and quilt the hairline (around the face). Add a little more stuffing to the face and whip-stitch the neck seam closed.

Color the hair yellow or brown with a permanent marking pen.

Embroider the eyes, eyelashes, cheeks, and mouth, using two strands of floss. Gather lace into a collar and tack beneath the chin.

Fold half a yard of 1/4-inch-wide velvet ribbon in half. About three inches below the fold, tack the ribbon to the middle of the angel's hair. Tie the ends into a bow and tack it in place. Trim the ends of the ribbon, and add a tiny embroidered floral appliqué to the middle of the bow.

The lace ornaments (right) can be made in a variety of sizes. Each ornament is covered with two layers of Swistraw: a thin, matte underlayer and a heavier, satin outer layer. The chart below tells you how many balls you'll be able to wrap with a 24-yard skein.

	Number of matte under-layers per skein:	Number of satin outer layers per skein:
3-inch balls	8	3
4-inch balls	4	2
5-inch balls	3	1

To make the ornaments, gather an assortment of plastic foam balls, some white glue, pins, scraps of old lace, Swistraw ribbon, scraps of felt or flannel, and dental floss or nylon fishing line.

Begin by soaking the matte and satin straw in water. Squeeze out the excess water, but be careful not to unravel the skeins.

Hold the ornament in your left hand, using your left thumb to hold one end of the matte straw tightly next to the ball.

Hold the straw with the fingers of your right hand about three inches from the ball. Using light tension, draw the right thumb along the straw, flattening and smoothing the straw as you pull. Wrap smooth straw once around the ball, crossing it over the end to secure it in place.

Picture a north and south pole on the ball; each time you wrap the straw around the sphere, cross over these points. Don't use pins to hold the straw in place because wet straw will break.

Wrap the ball evenly, overlapping each row of straw until the ball is covered. Then cut the straw at a crossover point and glue it down. If the straw breaks, cut it back to a crossover point, glue, and begin again.

Wrap the balls with an outer layer of satin straw using the same procedure. Let the balls dry overnight, or until the straw becomes opaque and feels dry.

Before adding lace, determine whether your lace pieces will look better as borders or medallions.

For borders, repeat patterns frequently work best. Lay the lace around the ball and pin it in place, clipping the edges so the lace fits smoothly. Unpin half of the lace strip, dab glue on the back of the lace, and repin it to the ball. Then unpin, glue, and repin the remainder of the lace. Let the glue dry, then remove any pinholes or spilled glue by scrubbing the area lightly with a clean, damp piece of felt or flannel.

For medallions, cut motifs free from the lace and glue them to the balls, securing them with pins until the glue is dry.

Thread dental floss or fishing line through the tops of the balls to form loops for hanging.

A Legacy of Elegance

These doll folk (opposite) look as if they came from a Dickens' novel. Each is a delightful turn-of-the-century character with a distinctive personality.

Embellish the designs with acrylic paints for a sophisticated set of Christmasy dolls. Or, use crayons, felt pens, and a smidgen of embroidery to enrich their costumes and highlight their delicate features.

After decorating, stitch the dolls with care and stuff them ever so slightly. (You may wish to tuck in a bit of delicately scented potpourri.) Then they're ready to bestow as gifts or to hang on your tree.

The Tiffanylike stained-glass masterpiece (below) is an angel worthy of adoration. Although not a quick-and-easy project, it isn't impossible for the inexperienced craftsman. Copper foil was used to join the sections of glass. This requires skill and the use of a soldering iron; but it is much easier than the traditional method of making stained glass.

If you don't dream of making stained glass, then consider using the angel pattern for a fabric or other appropriate adaptation.

The angel is approximately 32 inches from halo to hem and 29 inches from sleeve to wing tip.

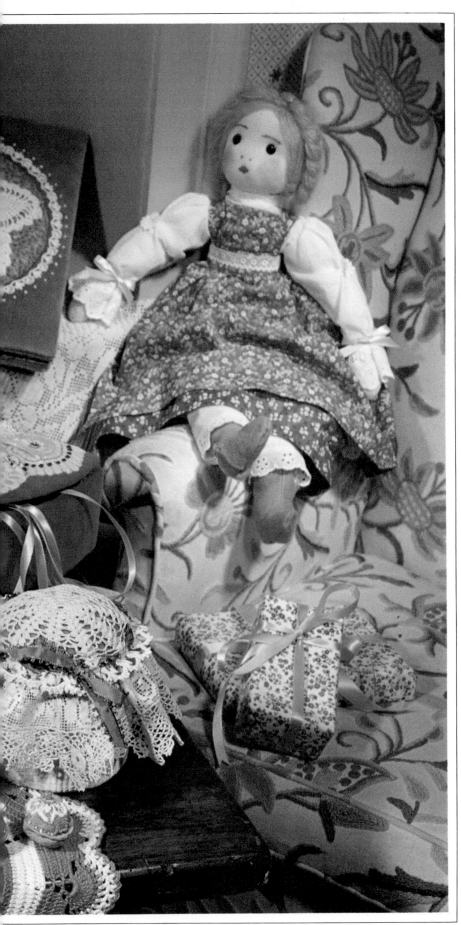

A Legacy of Elegance

In Victorian days, beautiful hand-made laces were prized posses-sions. They still are, so they've been used sparingly to enhance such simple projects as photo-graph albums, boxes, pincushions, and a picture frame. Just the tini-est bit of lace turns these ordinar-ies into treasures you can give with pride to anyone on your Christmas list.

Use handmade or purchased laces to make any of the projects shown here. If you have old doilies, for example, now's the perfect time to stitch them on a quilted box or a puffy pincushion. Even the small-est lace medallion can be put to good use atop an emery-filled pincushion (for sharpening pins and needles) tucked into half a walnut shell.

Seed pearls, beads, antique but-tons, and beautiful ribbons adorn the lace, adding to the look of yesteryear.

To make a large pincushion, cut a circle of velvet or velveteen and wrap it around a handful of stuff-ing. Appliqué a lace doily on top of the velvet puff, then stitch the puff into an old-fashioned basket or atop the lid of a woven box. Embellish with beads and bows to your heart's content.

Each of the boxes is constructed from scratch, using pieces of card-board for a base. First craft an outer box of lustrous satin, soft velvet, or plush corduroy. For the inner box use a contrasting fabric, such as one of the tiny floral prints that were used to line the insides of Victorian travelers' trunks. Cover the outer box with lace, add French knots and other em-broidered accents, and finish with antique buttons or golden tassels for clasps.

167

A Legacy of Elegance

Remember how much fun it was helping your grandmother get ready for Christmas dinner? The grown-ups prepared the turkey; the little children tore up the bread for the stuffing; and, when you were old enough to be "careful," you polished the silver until it gleamed, shined the crystal until it sparkled, and set out the family's very best china. And just before dinner, you smoothed the cloth over the table, laid all the places, and set the flowers you'd so neatly arranged into the middle of the table—to much fanfare and applause from the family for your very own contribution to this special meal.

It's just as much fun now as it was then to set an elegant table. If you don't have your grandmother's heirloom lace cloth, you can make one that's every bit as appealing from ribbons and pieces of eyelet. And graceful needlepoint flowers will transform even a simple bouquet into a charming reminder of days gone by.

The beautiful lace tablecloth shown here is really a piece of patchwork. It's assembled from a variety of white fabric and lace scraps, pretty embroidered ribbons, and ungathered crocheted edgings. To make one like it, cut rectangles in assorted sizes as large or as small as your scraps permit. Lay them out on the floor in a pleasing arrangement of lacy patterns, add ribbons and edgings between the rectangles, and stitch everything together. Finish with a lace ruffle along the hem.

The needlepoint flowers are about 6 and 10 inches across— just the right size for a spectacular display on your holiday table. To make them, use the instructions that follow. A list of the materials you'll need and charted patterns for both large and small blossoms are on page 175.

Begin by cutting ten 4x7-inch pieces of needlepoint canvas for petals for two small flowers and five 5x8-inch pieces of canvas for the petals for a large flower.

Work each petal in basket-weave stitches, following the color key with the patterns. Substitute shades of lavender for the pink if you wish. Use full, three-ply strands of yarn throughout. Work the outer edges of each petal first, then fill the center vein with magenta or deep purple, and stitch the remainder of the petal.

After finishing a petal, cut around the needlepoint, leaving ½ inch of unworked canvas. Carefully fold under the canvas edges and steam press.

Cut copper wire 14 inches long for small petals and 17 inches long for large petals. Bend the wire to fit the outer edge of each petal and slip it beneath the folded edges. Using matching yarn, anchor the wire in place with closely spaced overcast stitches.

To make the facing for each petal, lay the petal on the bias of the backing fabric and cut out the facing, adding a quarter-inch seam allowance. Slip-stitch the facing to the needlepoint, turning in the seam allowance. Complete five petals for each flower.

For the flower centers, cut one yard of bead wire. Tie a knot three inches from one end and string beads on the wire to within four inches of the end. Knot the wire again three inches from the end, leaving one inch free between the beads and the knot.

Loop the wire into eight circles. Anchor the circles together at the bottom with a few twists of the wire ends.

To assemble each flower, grasp five petals in one hand placing the ends pointing down. Arrange them so they fan out gracefully, as shown in the photograph. Insert the free ends of the beaded cluster into the center, and anchor them by twisting the wires together. Wrap additional wire around the bottom of the petals, then cover the wire with florist's tape. Shape the petals by gently bending the wires in them.

Instructions for an Old-World Christmas: A Legacy of Elegance

The instructions below and on the following pages are for the ornaments, decorations, and gifts shown on pages 160–169. For directions for enlarging and transferring designs, see the glossary, pages 370–371.

Satin Angel Ornaments
page 161

To make these ornaments, use the pattern below. Materials needed and how-to instructions are on page 163.

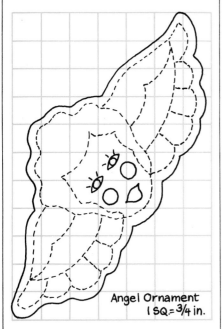

Angel Ornament
1 SQ.=³⁄₄ in.

Old-Fashioned Dolls
page 164

Note: This collection of dolls comprises 4 adults and 6 children. When finished, adult dolls are about 7½ inches tall; juveniles are about 6 inches tall.

Materials: 1½ yards closely woven white fabric; brown, fine-tip permanent marking pen; fiberfill; acrylic paints in assorted colors; embroidery floss; dressmaker's carbon paper.

Instructions: Enlarge patterns (right and on following 2 pages). Transfer back and front of each design onto fabric using dressmaker's carbon. Trace outlines with a fine-tipped, dark brown permanent marking pen.

The simple brown outlines of the figures look charming on plain white or natural-colored fabric. However, if you decide to color the dolls, they should be decorated *before* they are cut out and assembled. Suggestions for decorating dolls follow.

Paint: Use acrylic paints or paints especially formulated for working on fabric. Paints should be thinned (with water) to the consistency of light cream.

continued

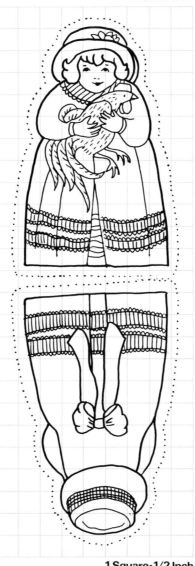

1 Square=1/2 Inch

1 Square=1/2 Inch

Continued from page 171
A Legacy of Elegance

1 Square=1/2 Inch

Lay fabric on newspaper; paint larger areas of color first (coats, gowns, et cetera). Use just a light wash of color so that outlines and details show through. Rinse brushes frequently and thoroughly. When paint is completely dry, carefully press dolls on the wrong side to set colors. The dolls now may be stitched and stuffed.

Crayons: Color dolls carefully, being sure not to leave stray flecks of crayon on the fabric. Then lay fabric face up on several layers of paper towels. Cover with additional layers of toweling; iron at high setting to remove excess wax and set colors. Change paper towels and repeat if necessary.

Permanent fabric markers: Select waterproof markers that do not bleed on the fabric. Use a very light touch because markers tend to yield deep, vibrant colors that might overwhelm the finer details of the designs. Press completed fabric on wrong side to set color.

Embroidery: Embroidery may be added to the plain background fabric or used in combination with a colored background. Using single strands of embroidery floss, work outline, satin, and chain stitches and French knots to accent facial features and other details, such as flowers, bows, buttons, hats, trim on skirts and jackets. (For diagrams of embroidery stitches, see page 374.)

To assemble dolls: Cut out front and back at least ¼ inch beyond outlines. With right sides facing, pin and baste front and back, matching up the solid outlines. Stitch so that stitches fall *between* solid and dotted outlines. Follow curves and details closely. Leave the base of each figure open for turning. Clip corners and curves, trim seams, turn, and press. Stuff lightly with fiberfill. Do not overstuff because that will distort features and clothing details. To finish, turn the doll's base under and slip-stitch the opening.

Stained-Glass Angel
page 165

Materials: 36x30-inch piece of illustration board and typing paper for patterns; soldering flux; 2 pounds wire solder; household cleaner or solvent for cleaning flux; 1 roll of ½-inch copper foil tape; black patina or copper sulfate solution for darkening solder; sandpaper; 13 feet jack chain (from hardware store); heavy fishing leader for hanging.

Glass: 2½ feet blue opalescent, 1½ feet amber opalescent, 1 foot brown, ½ foot pale amber, 1 foot royal blue, 1 foot medium blue, 1 foot clear; scraps of yellow, yellow-orange, red-orange, and bright red for halo; scraps of light and dark green for leaves.

Tools: Soldering iron, safety glasses, breaking pliers, glass cutter, putty knife, paper-cutting scissors.

Note: Tools and materials are available at craft or stained-glass stores.

Instructions: Enlarge design (below) to size and transfer pattern to large piece of illustration board. Number all pieces. This is your master pattern. Trace each individual pattern piece onto typing paper. Cut out all paper pattern pieces and number according to master pattern. See color key.

Color Key: 1—Blue Opalescent. 2—Royal Blue. 3—Medium Blue. 4—Pale Amber. 5—Amber Opalescent. 6—Brown. 7—Yellow. 8—Yellow Orange. 9—Red Orange. 10—Bright Red. 11—Dark Green. 12—Light Green. 13—Clear.

Arrange pattern pieces on glass; score around pieces using glass cutter.

Break short, straight cuts using your fingers or lay on a table edge and snap (wear safety glasses while working). Use ball on cutter to tap under curved scores. A good continuous score is essential—practice on scrap glass.

Use breaking pliers to snap off small pieces or trim uneven cuts. Fit each piece on illustration-board pattern to make sure it's the right size. Avoid gaps; if necessary recut glass.

Copper foil tape (a thin strip of adhesive-backed copper) makes the joining of glass pieces easy. Center a strip of tape on edge of cut glass pattern piece, then bend over extra tape to form a U channel around glass edge. Use putty knife to smooth tape down tight against glass. Lay all taped pieces back on master pattern.

Paint liquid soldering flux (a weak acid) on the copper strips to clean for soldering. Use solid wire solder (no rosin or acid core) and a soldering iron to tack pieces together at corners.

Next, flow solder over all the exposed copper. Carefully turn the angel over and repeat the soldering procedure on the other side.

Solder chain around the entire edge of the angel to reinforce the piece and facilitate hanging.

Clean the glass with household cleaner. Apply black patina liquid to all soldered edges to darken them. Repeat if not dark enough. Clean with detergent again.

Hang the finished angel using clear fishing line from points on the halo, wing, and hem of dress.

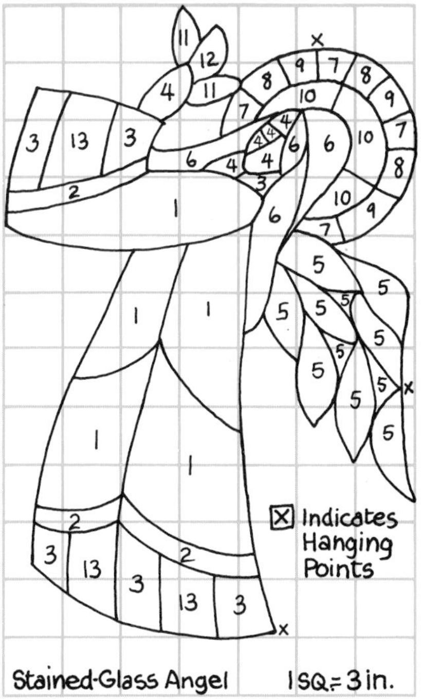

Lace Boxes
pages 166 and 167

Materials: Sufficient cardboard for inside and outside of box (*Note:* Use thin, stiff cardboard; matt board and corrugated board are too heavy for small boxes); polyester quilt batting; satin, velveteen, or other fabric for outside of box; lining fabric; buttonhole thread to match fabrics; double-sided carpet tape (sticky on both sides); white cloth tape or masking tape; laces, beads, ribbons, mirrors and other trims.

General Instructions: Using the patterns on page 174, cut cardboard shapes for the sides, top, and bottom of the box you wish to make. Cut 2 pieces of each shape—one for the outer box and one for the inner box (lining). Trim ⅛ inch off all sides of the pieces for the inner box; set aside.

Cut fabric to match cardboard pieces, plus a 1-inch margin all around.

Individual sections of the box may be embellished before pieces are assembled or after outer box is complete. Boxes shown are decorated with antique laces, beads, buttons, ribbons, and decorative embroidery stitches.

To cover the sides of the box, tape quilt batting to one side of the cardboard with carpet tape. Trim batting to match cardboard. Cover batting with fabric, folding fabric edges around cardboard; tape securely in place with white cloth tape. Corners must be flat. Repeat for all sides of outer box.

Whipstitch the sides of the box to the base, working from the wrong side of the box. Whipstitch sides together, again working from the wrong side—the inside—of the box.

Use second set of cardboard pattern pieces to construct sides and base of inner box, according to directions above. (If your box will have dividers, see below.) If lining fabric is heavy, you may need to trim more than ⅛ inch from the edges of the cardboard pieces for the inner box. Whipstitch the sides of the lining box to the lining base.

Dividers for boxes are held in place by slots. Cut cardboard lining patterns wherever needed along the sides and bottom. Trim ⅛ inch off each side of slot before covering cardboard.

To cover dividers, cut cardboard as wide as needed but twice as long. (For example, for a 3-inch square divider, cut cardboard 3x6 inches.) Fold divider in half; trim ⅛ inch from sides and ¼ inch from bottom. Unfold divider; and cover according to directions above.

Next, apply carpet tape to half of the wrong side (inside) and refold. Whipstitch sides together.

To assemble the box, lay carpet tape on the inside base of the outer box. Set the lining box into the outside box, pressing bases firmly together. Blindstitch lining to outside box around upper rim. Insert dividers and catch-stitch to upper rim of box.

Cover the lid of the box according to directions above. Lids may be left unattached, as in the white box; or they may be hinged to the box by blindstitching to the rim along one side as in the small green box, or by including a fabric hinge as part of the design, as in the fan-shaped box.

To prevent the lid from falling back too far, crochet a chain-stitch retainer and attach one end to the lid and the other to the side of the box.

To make a decorative fastener for the box, use buttons or beads and a small ribbon or crocheted loop. Add small tassels if desired.

● *House Box*

For the outer box, cut along sides and base, using the diagram on page 174. Cut 2 short sides, 2x3 inches, and 2 lids, 2¾x3 inches.

For the lining box, cut 2 long sides and base in half on the line (see pattern). Cut 2 short sides and 2 lids. Trim ⅛ inch from all pieces.

Cut a divider 3x6 inches. Cover and fold to 3x3 inches, following general instructions.

Cover outer box with green velveteen and lining box and divider with floral print fabric. Assemble box according to general instructions.

Tack antique lace to sides and lids of box, accent with French knots, and add antique buttons to lids for handles. Hinge lids to short sides by slip-stitching; add crocheted retainers to prevent them from falling all the way back when the box is opened.

continued

Stained-Glass Angel   1 SQ.= 3 in.

☒ Indicates Hanging Points

Continued from page 173
A Legacy of Elegance

● *Fan-Shaped Box*

For the outside box, cut top and base in overall fan shape. For sides, cut 1 piece 3x17 inches (outside curve), 2 pieces each 3x4½ inches, and 1 back 3x3½ inches. Cut hinge pieces as shown on the patterns at right.

For the lining box, cut 1 overall shape for the top. For the base, cut 1 of #1 on pattern, 2 of #2, and 2 of #3. For the sides, cut four 3x4¼-inch pieces for the outside curve, two 2¾x3-inch pieces for the sides, two 1¾x3-inch pieces for sides, and one 3x3½-inch piece for the back. Trim ⅛ inch from all sides.

For dividers, cut four 2x6-inch pieces (for center, around #1), two 3¾x6-inch pieces, and one 4¼x6-inch piece. Score pieces with a blunt table knife and a ruler before folding to measure 3 inches high. When pieces are folded, trim sides ⅛ inch and bottom ¼ inch.

Using rust velveteen for the outer box, and a brown and rust calico for lining, cover pieces and assemble box according to general directions.

To make the hinge, tape hinge pieces together from A to B. Turn pieces over and tape again on the other side. Trim excess tape, then bend the pieces several times to develop some give in the tape. Cover cardboard using fabric only (omit batting). For lining, use hinge lining only (see pattern), attaching it after the hinge is covered with outer fabric. Slip-stitch hinge to back and top of box.

Embellish box with lace, beads, and buttons. For a clasp, make a ribbon loop for top, to slip over button attached to the front. Tie tassels to center

of loop. Finish with crocheted retaining cords attached to the top and sides.

● *Eight-Sided Box*

For outer box, cut top and bottom to match pattern. For sides, cut 2 pieces 4⅛x4¼ inches (front, back), 4 pieces 2½x4⅛ inches (corners), and 2 pieces 2¾x4⅛ inches (ends). On side pieces, mark a point 1½ inches from one end along the 4⅛-inch side. Slide cardboard over a table edge, making a slight curve at the marked point.

For lining box, cut top and bottom to match pattern. Sides of box are straight. Cut 2 pieces 3½x4¼ inches (front and back), 4 pieces 2x3½ inches (corners), and 2 pieces 2½x3½ inches (ends). Trim ⅛ from all sides of each piece.

Assemble the box; embellish with 4-inch-wide lace sewn to sides of box. Make ball feet for the bottom of the box

by gathering six 3-inch circles. Tuck stuffing into the center of each circle, pull threads taut and tie off. Tack feet to box as shown on pattern.

For the center medallion on the top, cut cardboard as indicated on pattern and cover with batting. Then cut a 3x16-inch strip of fabric; gather along both sides. Hold fabric around cardboard, pulling gathers until inside hole is about 1 inch in diameter. Tie off gathers and glue a 2-inch oval picture frame or piece of antique jewelry over the gathers. Add French knots and beads around edge of frame.

Blindstitch the covered medallion to the lid and embellish the seam using lace, French knots, and ribbon.

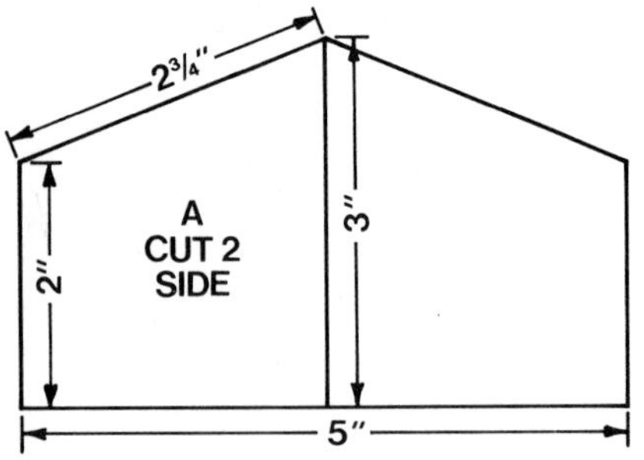

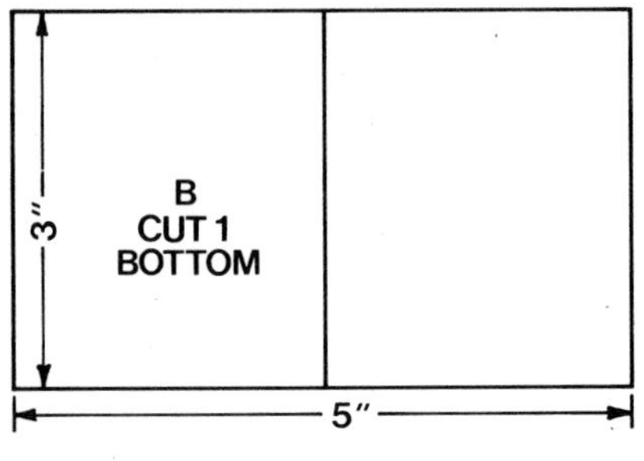

Lace Frame
page 166

Materials: 8x10-inch oval picture frame; soft cardboard; quilt batting; muslin; cover fabric (striped or checked fabrics work best); double-sided carpet tape; lace; cord trim; ribbon.

Instructions: To pad the frame, trace around the inside and outside of the frame onto cardboard. Cut out cardboard; cover one side with several layers of batting. Use tape to secure the batting to the cardboard.

Trace outlines of frame onto muslin, cut out, allowing 1½-inch margins on inside and outside. Lay muslin on table, placing frame (right side up), cardboard, and batting on top. Wrap muslin over frame and batting. Stitch edges of muslin together around top of frame.

Using your hands, mold cardboard down over the edges of the frame to soften the edges. Mark center of top,

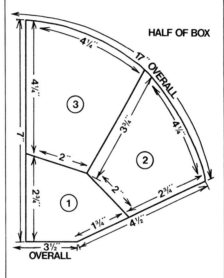

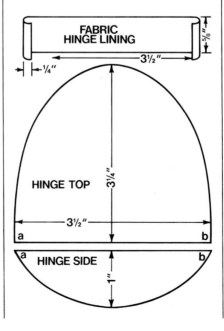

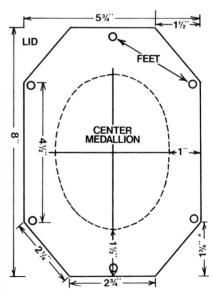

bottom, and sides of frame. Smooth muslin over back of frame.

Cut decorative fabric so it is twice as long as frame's outside circumference and wide enough to cover top and sides; add 1 inch to width. Mark the strip in quarters; gather long edges.

Snug gathering fabric around frame, matching quarter-marks on fabric to marks at center of top, bottom, and sides of frame. Adjust gathers evenly. Turn under raw edges so fabric does not cover back of frame; stitch fabric to muslin cover on frame back. Make sure no extra bulk covers screw holes.

To finish, cut lace and cording for inside of frame. Glue lace to inside or outside of glass, and cording to outside of glass. Add a ribbon bow.

Lace Photo Album
page 166

Materials: Lace medallion or doily; purchased scrapbook (the kind with eyelets visible on the front); thin, stiff cardboard; cover fabric; lining fabric; carpet tape; white cloth tape; quilt batting; assorted beads, ribbon, lace edging, and embroidery threads.

Instructions: Remove cord, eyelets, and pages from the photo album. Set aside. Cut cardboard to fit front and back album covers, making sure it doesn't overlap score line or hinge on cover. Cut batting to match cardboard; attach to one side of each piece with carpet tape. Set cardboard for back cover aside.

Cut cover fabric so it is 1 inch larger than padded cardboard. Lay front cover fabric face down; center batting-covered cardboard over it. Tape fabric to back of cardboard, ensuring corners are flat. Repeat for back cover.

Cut a cardboard circle, oval, or square slightly larger than lace medallion. Cut cover fabric 3 inches larger than cardboard medallion. Cover cardboard with batting cut to size; cover cardboard and batting with fabric. If cardboard is square, tape raw edges of fabric to back. If it is circular or oval, gather raw edges to fit; tape in place.

Blindstitch lace medallion to top of covered cardboard. Accent with trims, using the color photo as a guide. Blindstitch medallion to padded front piece; embellish with additional trims.

To assemble book covers, cut cover fabric to size (plus 1 inch all around) for front and back, allowing extra fabric on hinged side to fold over eyelets and past hinge. Tape fabric in place.

Place padded front in position and blindstitch in place around the edge.

Repeat for back covers. Assemble the album by punching holes through the fabric (using an ice pick) where existing holes are in the album and by replacing eyelets and cording after setting the pages back into the book.

Basket Pincushions
page 166

Materials: Small purchased basket with or without a lid (4 to 6 inches in diameter); 20x20 inches of velveteen, corduroy, or other fabric; 6- to 8-inch lace doily; fiberfill; cardboard; assorted ribbons, beads, lace edging, and other trims.

Instructions: For a pincushion in a basket, measure across the basket top, down the side, across the bottom, and up the opposite side; add 2 inches. Cut a fabric circle to this measurement. For a pincushion atop the lid of a basket, cut a fabric circle twice the basket's diameter.

Gather the circle's edge, tuck stuffing into the fabric, and draw the fabric up into a ball. Tie off.

Cut a circle of cardboard the same size as the basket bottom (if the pincushion will be inserted into the basket). For a pincushion on a lid, cut cardboard slightly smaller than lid. Cut fabric to cover cardboard, adding a ½-inch margin all around. Cover cardboard with fabric, gathering the fabric edge around the cardboard with small running stitches. Tie off. Slipstitch cardboard base to pincushion, covering the bottom hole.

Push pincushion into basket; tack through the basket to secure. Or, stitch pincushion to the lid of the basket.

Embellish with a lace doily blindstitched atop the pincushion ball. Accent the ball edge with trims.

Walnut Emery Pincushions
page 166

Materials: Half of a walnut shell; clean, refined sand or other emery mixture; 2¾-inch circles of muslin and velveteen; assorted laces and seed beads; beading needle; white glue; sandpaper.

Instructions: To prepare the walnut shell, sand sharp edges smooth; sand shell bottom flat so it will stand.

Gather edge of muslin circle, fill with 1 teaspoon sand or emery mixture; pull gathers snug. Whipstitch edges together. Gather edge of velveteen circle around muslin ball; whipstitch edges together. Squeeze glue into walnut shell. Set fabric ball into shell; let dry.

Sew seed beads around rim. Embellish with tiny lace appliques.

Needlepoint Flowers
page 169

Materials: 1 yard #10-count penelope canvas (for 1 large and 2 small flowers); 1 skein 3-ply Persian yarn in the following colors: dark, medium, and light pink and magenta (or 4 shades of purple), and white; ¾ yard backing fabric; small pearl or silver beads; copper bead wire; green florist's tape; 6½ yards medium-gauge wire; needle.

Instructions: Make the flowers using the petal patterns below and the directions on page 168.

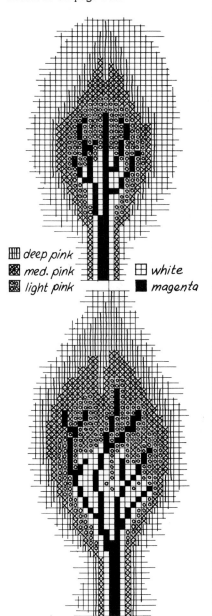

⊞ deep pink
▨ med. pink
▩ light pink
⊞ white
■ magenta

Holiday Sweets from Around the World

When the frost is on the windowsill and a cold bite is in the air, it's time to start baking for the holidays. If you enjoy making sweets for Christmas, you'll love this section of the book. You'll find a wide variety of Christmas goodies from around the world, as well as some of the traditional American favorites—everything from yeast breads, coffee cakes, and quick breads to doughnuts, cookies, candies, pies, fruitcakes, and homemade pastries.

Here's a sample of what's to come—pictured clockwise from back left are: Mexican Three Kings' Ring, *crowned with a powdered sugar icing and candied pineapple poinsettias;* Miniature Eggnog Coffee Cakes, *baked in fluted cupcake pans;* German Stollen, *shown in the traditional foldover shape,* Scandinavian Julekaga, *baked in round loaves topped with an icing lattice; and* Christmas Braid, *studded with Brazil nuts and raisins. (See recipes, pages 178–179.)*

Breads

Miniature Eggnog Coffee Cakes

see photograph, pages 176–177

1⅓ cups granulated sugar
½ cup butter *or* margarine, softened
2 eggs
3 cups all-purpose flour
1 tablespoon baking powder
2 cups eggnog
1 cup chopped mixed candied fruits and peels
1½ cups sifted powdered sugar
¼ teaspoon ground nutmeg
¼ teaspoon ground cinnamon
Eggnog
Candied red cherry halves

In mixing bowl cream together granulated sugar and butter or margarine. Beat in eggs. Stir together flour and baking powder. Stir into creamed mixture alternately with the 2 cups eggnog. Fold in fruits and peels. Fill greased and floured 2½-inch fluted cupcake pans or 2¾-inch muffin pans two-thirds full with batter. Keep remaining batter refrigerated till ready to bake. Bake in a 325° oven 30 minutes. Remove from pans; cool on wire rack. Repeat with remaining batter. In a bowl combine powdered sugar, nutmeg, and cinnamon. Add enough eggnog to make of drizzling consistency. Drizzle frosting over cooled cakes. Top with cherry halves. Makes 24 to 28 cakes.

German Stollen

see photograph, pages 176–177

¾ cup raisins
½ cup chopped mixed candied fruits and peels
¼ cup currants
¼ cup rum
4½ to 4¾ cups all-purpose flour
2 packages active dry yeast
1 cup milk
½ cup butter *or* margarine
¼ cup sugar
2 eggs
2 tablespoons finely shredded orange peel
1 tablespoon finely shredded lemon peel
½ teaspoon almond extract
½ cup chopped almonds
Rum Icing

Soak raisins, mixed fruits, and currants in rum. Meanwhile, in large mixing bowl combine *1½ cups* of the flour and the yeast. Heat milk, butter or margarine, sugar, and 1 teaspoon *salt* just till warm (115° to 120°), stirring constantly till butter almost melts. Add to dry mixture in mixing bowl. Add eggs, orange and lemon peels, and almond extract. Beat at low speed of electric mixer for ½ minute, scraping sides of bowl constantly. Beat 3 minutes at high speed. By hand, stir in fruit-rum mixture, chopped almonds, and enough of the remaining flour as you can mix in using a spoon.

Turn out onto a lightly floured surface; knead in remaining flour to make a soft dough. Continue kneading till smooth and elastic (8 to 10 minutes). Shape into a ball. Place in greased bowl, turning once to grease surface. Cover; let rise in warm place till double (1 to 1¼ hours). Punch down; divide in half. Cover; let rest 10 minutes.

Roll *one half* to a 12x8-inch oval. Fold long side of oval to within ½-inch of opposite side; seal edge. Place on greased baking sheet. Repeat with remaining dough.

Cover; let rise till double (30 to 45 minutes). Bake in 375° oven 15 to 20 minutes. Transfer to wire rack. Cool slightly. While stollens are still warm, frost with Rum Icing. Garnish with toasted slivered almonds, if desired. Makes 2.

Rum Icing: In a small mixing bowl combine 1 cup sifted *powdered sugar* and enough *rum* or *milk* to make frosting of drizzling consistency.

Three Kings' Ring

see photograph, pages 176–177

2½ to 2¾ cups all-purpose flour
1 package active dry yeast
⅔ cup milk
¼ cup butter *or* margarine
¼ cup granulated sugar
½ teaspoon salt
2 eggs
¼ teaspoon ground cinnamon
½ cup chopped walnuts
½ cup chopped mixed candied fruits and peels
2 teaspoons finely shredded orange peel
½ teaspoon finely shredded lemon peel
Light cream *or* milk
1 cup sifted powdered sugar
Candied red, green, and yellow pineapple
Walnut halves

In large mixing bowl combine *1½ cups* of the flour and the yeast. In a saucepan heat milk, butter or margarine, granulated sugar, and salt just till warm (115° to 120°), stirring constantly till butter almost melts. Add milk mixture to dry mixture in mixing bowl; add eggs and cinnamon. Beat at low speed of electric mixer for ½ minute, scraping side of bowl constantly. Beat 3 minutes at high speed. By hand, stir in chopped walnuts, the ½ cup candied fruits and peels, orange peel, lemon peel, and enough of the remaining flour as you can mix in using a spoon. Turn out on well-floured surface. Knead in remaining flour to make a stiff dough. Continue kneading till dough is smooth and elastic (6 to 8 minutes).

Place dough in lightly greased bowl, turning once to grease surface. Cover; let rise till double (about 1½ hours). On lightly floured surface roll dough into a 26-inch rope. Carefully seal ends together to form a ring. Place on greased baking sheet. Cover; let dough rise till almost double (40 to 50 minutes). Bake in 375° oven for 10 minutes. Cover with foil; continue baking about 10 minutes more. Cool on wire rack. In bowl add enough light cream to sifted powdered sugar to make of drizzling consistency. Frost cooled coffee cake. Decorate ring with "poinsettias" made out of candied pineapple pieces. Place a walnut half in the center of each poinsettia. Makes 1 coffee cake.

Scandinavian Julekaga

see photograph, pages 176–177

8 to 8¼ cups all-purpose
    flour
2 packages active dry yeast
2 teaspoons ground cardamom
3 cups milk
½ cup butter *or* margarine
½ cup granulated sugar
2 teaspoons salt
½ cup raisins
½ cup currants
½ cup chopped candied citron
½ cup chopped candied red
    cherries
½ cup chopped candied green
    cherries
2 cups sifted powdered sugar
    Milk

In large mixing bowl combine *3½ cups* of the flour, the yeast, and ground cardamom. In saucepan heat together 3 cups milk, butter or margarine, granulated sugar, and salt just till warm (115° to 120°), stirring constantly till butter almost melts. Add milk mixture to dry mixture in mixing bowl. Beat at low speed of electric mixer for ½ minute, scraping sides of bowl constantly. Beat 3 minutes at high speed. By hand, stir in raisins, currants, candied citron, red and green candied cherries, and enough of the remaining flour as you can mix in using a spoon.

Turn out on a lightly floured surface; knead in remaining flour to make a moderately stiff dough. Continue kneading till smooth and elastic (8 to 10 minutes). Shape dough into a ball. Place dough in lightly greased bowl, turning once to grease surface. Cover; let rise in warm place till double (about 1 hour). Punch down dough. Cover. Let rest 10 minutes. Turn out on light floured surface. Divide dough into 3 portions. Shape each portion into a round loaf and place each in a greased 8-inch round baking pan. Cover loaves and let rise till double (45 minutes).

Bake in a 375° oven for 30 minutes. Cover with foil; bake about 10 minutes more or till done. Remove loaves from pans to a wire rack; cool.

In a small mixing bowl combine powdered sugar and enough milk to make of piping consistency. Using a pastry tube and tip, pipe icing into a diamond-shaped lattice atop each loaf. *Or* add enough milk to make frosting of drizzling consistency and drizzle over loaves. Makes 3.

Christmas Braid

see photograph, pages 176–177

5 to 5½ cups all-purpose
    flour
1 package active dry yeast
2 cups milk
½ cup sugar
6 tablespoons butter *or*
    margarine
1 teaspoon salt
1 egg
1 cup raisins
1 cup finely chopped mixed
    candied fruits and peels
½ cup chopped Brazil nuts
1 egg yolk
1 tablespoon water

In large mixing bowl combine *3 cups* of the flour and the yeast. In saucepan heat together milk, sugar, butter or margarine, and salt just till warm (115° to 120°), stirring constantly till butter almost melts. Add to dry mixture in mixing bowl; add egg. Beat at low speed of electric mixer for ½ minute, scraping sides of bowl constantly. Beat 3 minutes at high speed. Stir in raisins, candied fruits and peels, Brazil nuts, and enough of the remaining flour as you can mix in using a spoon.

Turn out on a floured surface; knead in remaining flour to make a moderately stiff dough. Continue kneading till smooth and elastic (8 to 10 minutes). Place in greased bowl, turning once to grease surface. Cover; let rise in warm place till double (about 1½ hours).

Divide dough in thirds. Then divide each third in three portions. Roll each portion into a 15-inch rope. Place 3 ropes on a greased baking sheet. Braid. Repeat with remaining ropes, forming 3 braids. Cover and let rise in warm place till double (about 30 to 40 minutes).

Combine egg yolk and the 1 tablespoon water; brush some of the mixture over braids. Bake in a 350° oven 10 minutes. Brush with more egg yolk mixture. Bake 10 minutes more. Cover with foil; continue baking 5 minutes more. Transfer to wire rack; cool. Makes 3.

Austrian Kugelhof

½ cup raisins
¼ cup hot water
¾ cup milk
1 13¾-ounce package hot roll
    mix
2 beaten eggs
¼ cup butter, melted
¼ cup sugar
1 teaspoon finely shredded
    lemon peel
½ teaspoon ground mace
½ cup chopped walnuts
1 tablespoon butter, melted
3 tablespoons fine dry bread
    crumbs

Soak raisins in hot water; let stand till raisins are plump. Drain; set aside. Heat milk just till warm (115° to 120°); add yeast from hot roll mix. Stir till yeast is dissolved. Combine eggs, ¼ cup butter, sugar, lemon peel, mace, and yeast mixture. Add flour from mix; beat by hand till smooth. Stir in raisins and chopped walnuts. Cover; let rise in warm place till double (1½ to 2 hours).

Meanwhile brush an 8-cup fluted tube pan or kugelhof mold with the 1 tablespoon melted butter. Sprinkle bottom and sides of mold with fine, dry bread crumbs. Stir down batter. Carefully spoon batter into mold; cover. Let batter rise till almost double (50 to 60 minutes). Bake in 350° oven for 25 to 30 minutes. Cool in pan for 10 minutes. Remove. Cool on rack. Makes 1.

Raspberry Braid

1 3-ounce package cream
    cheese
¼ cup butter *or* margarine
2 cups packaged biscuit mix
⅓ cup milk
½ cup raspberry preserves
    Rum Icing (see recipe, page
    178)

In a bowl cut cream cheese and butter or margarine into biscuit mix till crumbly. Blend in milk. Turn out on lightly floured surface. Knead 8 to 10 strokes. On waxed paper, roll dough to a 12x8-inch rectangle. Turn onto greased baking sheet; remove waxed paper. Spread preserves down center of dough. Make 2½-inch cuts at 1-inch intervals on long sides. Fold strips over filling. Bake in 425° oven 12 to 15 minutes. Cool slightly. Drizzle warm coffee cake with Rum Icing. Makes 1.

Ukranian Christmas Doughnuts

4½ cups all-purpose flour
2 packages active dry yeast
1 cup milk
¼ cup shortening
⅓ cup sugar
1 teaspoon salt
1 teaspoon vanilla
2 eggs
3 egg yolks
1 12-ounce can prune cake and pastry filling
Cooking oil for deep-fat frying
Vanilla Glaze

In large mixer bowl combine *2 cups* of the flour and the yeast. In saucepan heat the milk, shortening, sugar, and salt just till warm (115° to 120°), stirring till shortening almost melts. Add vanilla. Add to dry ingredients in mixer bowl. Add eggs and egg yolks. Beat at low speed of electric mixer ½ minute, scraping sides of bowl constantly. Beat 3 minutes at high speed. Stir in as much of the remaining flour as you can mix in using a spoon. On a lightly floured surface knead in the remaining flour to make a moderately stiff dough. Continue kneading till smooth and satiny (4 to 5 minutes). Place in a greased bowl, turning once to grease surface. Cover and let rise till double (about 1¼ hours). Punch down. Let rest 10 minutes. Roll dough ⅛ inch thick. Using floured 2½-inch round cookie cutter, cut out 48 circles.

Place *1 teaspoon* prune filling on *half* of the circles; top with remaining circles. Moisten edges with water and press edges firmly to seal. Cover. Let rise on a floured surface till double. Fry in deep hot oil (375°) 1 to 1½ minutes on each side or till golden. Drain on paper toweling. When cool, frost with Vanilla Glaze. Makes 24 doughnuts.

Vanilla Glaze: In a bowl combine 2 cups sifted *powdered sugar,* ¼ cup *milk,* and 1 teaspoon *vanilla.*

Nothing symbolizes the holidays more than warm baked goods straight from the kitchen—especially doughnuts. Serve Ukranian Christmas Doughnuts (left), sugar-coated Dutch Oliebollen (front right), or muffinlike Cranberry-Orange Rumbas (back right), and you'll find the snackers at your house coming back for seconds.

Dutch Oliebollen

3¼ cups all-purpose flour
2 packages active dry yeast
1 cup milk
¼ cup shortening
⅓ cup sugar
1 teaspoon salt
1 teaspoon vanilla
2 eggs
3 egg yolks
½ cup raisins
½ cup chopped mixed candied fruits and peels
Cooking oil for deep-fat frying
½ cup sugar
1 teaspoon ground cinnamon

In large mixer bowl combine *2 cups* of the flour and the yeast. In small saucepan heat milk, shortening, the ⅓ cup sugar, and the salt just till warm (115° to 120°), stirring occasionally till shortening almost melts. Stir in vanilla. Add milk mixture, eggs, and egg yolks to dry ingredients in mixer bowl. Beat at low speed on electric mixer for ½ minute, scraping sides of bowl constantly. Beat 3 minutes at high speed.

Stir in remaining flour, raisins, and candied fruits and peels. Cover; let rise till double (about 30 minutes). Drop from tablespoon into deep hot oil (375°); fry about 3 minutes, turning to brown all sides. Drain on paper toweling. While oliebollen are still warm, coat with mixture of the ½ cup sugar and the cinnamon. Makes 36.

Cranberry-Orange Rumbas

1 egg
1 cup cranberry-orange relish
⅓ cup milk
¼ teaspoon rum flavoring
1 14-ounce package apple-cinnamon muffin mix

In medium bowl beat egg; stir in relish, milk, and rum flavoring. Add muffin mix, stirring with fork just till moistened. Fill greased or paper-lined muffin cups ⅔ full. Bake in 400° oven for 20 to 25 minutes or till done. Serve warm. Makes 12 muffins.

Spicy Spud Doughnuts

4 cups all-purpose flour
2 tablespoons baking powder
1 teaspoon salt
½ teaspoon ground cloves
½ teaspoon ground cinnamon
3 beaten eggs
1 cup packed brown sugar
1½ cups mashed cooked potatoes
2 tablespoons shortening, melted
1 5⅓-ounce can (⅔ cup) evaporated milk
Cooking oil for deep-fat frying

In a bowl stir together flour, baking powder, salt, cloves, and cinnamon. Beat eggs and sugar till thick. Stir in cooled potatoes, the 2 tablespoons shortening, and the evaporated milk. Gradually add dry ingredients to egg mixture, stirring till combined. Chill at least 3 hours.

On well-floured surface roll dough, half at a time, to ⅜-inch thickness. Cut with floured doughnut cutter; chill 15 minutes. Fry in deep hot oil (365°) for 1 to 1½ minutes per side, turning once. Drain on paper toweling. Makes 36 doughnuts.

Apple Fritter Rings

1 cup all-purpose flour
2 tablespoons sugar
1 teaspoon baking powder
1 beaten egg
⅔ cup milk
1 teaspoon cooking oil
Cooking oil for deep-fat frying
4 large tart cooking apples, peeled, cored, and cut into ½-inch thick rings
¼ cup sugar
½ teaspoon ground cinnamon

In mixing bowl stir together flour, the 2 tablespoons sugar, baking powder, and dash *salt.* Mix egg, milk, and the 1 teaspoon cooking oil. Add egg mixture all at once to dry ingredients, stirring just till blended.

Heat 1 inch cooking oil to 375° in a skillet that is at least 2 inches deep. Dip apple slices in batter one at a time. Fry in hot oil about 1½ minutes per side or till brown. Drain on paper toweling. Combine remaining sugar and cinnamon. Sprinkle warm fritters with sugar mixture. Serve at once. Makes 16.

Cookies & Candies

German Brown Sugar Spritz

Holiday Pineapple Filling
1 cup butter *or* margarine,
   softened
½ cup packed brown sugar
1 egg
1 teaspoon vanilla
2⅔ cups all-purpose flour
1 teaspoon baking powder

Prepare Holiday Pineapple Filling; cool. Cream together butter and brown sugar; beat in egg and vanilla. Stir together flour and baking powder; add gradually to creamed mixture, mixing till smooth. Do not chill.

Place *half* of dough into cookie press (see note below). Using ribbon plate, press dough in ten 10-inch strips on ungreased cookie sheets. Using star plate and remaining dough, press lengthwise rows of dough on top of each strip, making a rim along both edges. Spoon red or green Holiday Pineapple Filling between rims atop ribbon strips. Bake cookies in 400° oven for 8 to 10 minutes. While cookies are hot, cut strips into 1¼-inch diagonals. Cool. Makes 6½ dozen.

Holiday Pineapple Filling: In saucepan stir together one 29½-ounce can *crushed pineapple,* drained, and 1 cup *granulated sugar;* bring to boiling. Simmer 30 to 35 minutes or till mixture is very thick, stirring often. Divide filling in half. Using a few drops *food coloring,* tint half the filling *red* and the other half *green.* Cool.

Note: Or, omit filling and force all of dough through a cookie press on ungreased cookie sheet into desired shapes. Shake *ground almonds* with a few drops *red* or *green food coloring* in screw-top jar; sprinkle over cookies. Bake in 400° oven 8 minutes. Cool on rack. Makes about 5 dozen.

Finnish Chestnut Fingers

¾ cup butter *or* margarine,
   softened
¼ cup sugar
1 egg yolk
½ cup chestnut purée *or* canned
   chestnuts, drained and
   puréed
¼ teaspoon vanilla
1 cup all-purpose flour
¼ teaspoon salt
¼ teaspoon ground cinnamon
1 slightly beaten egg white
   Sugar
½ cup semisweet chocolate
   pieces, melted

In mixer bowl cream butter and ¼ cup sugar; add egg yolk. Beat till light and fluffy. Beat in chestnut purée and vanilla. Stir together flour, salt, and cinnamon; stir into creamed mixture.

Using a scant tablespoon dough for each cookie, roll into 2½-inch fingers. Dip one side of each finger in egg white, then in sugar. Place sugar side up on greased cookie sheet. Bake in 350° oven about 20 minutes. Remove from sheet; cool on rack. Dip one end of each cookie in chocolate; place on waxed paper till set. Makes 2½ dozen.

Norwegian Berlinerkranser

1 cup butter *or* margarine,
   softened
½ cup sifted powdered sugar
1 hard-cooked egg yolk, sieved
1 egg yolk
1 teaspoon vanilla
2¼ cups all-purpose flour
1 slightly beaten egg white
   Sugar cubes, crushed

In bowl cream together butter or margarine and powdered sugar. Add hard-cooked egg yolk, raw egg yolk, and vanilla. Stir in flour. Cover and chill.

Work with a small amount of dough at a time; keep remainder chilled. Roll walnut-size pieces of dough to 6-inch ropes, about ½ inch in diameter. Shape into a wreath, overlapping about 1 inch from ends. Place on ungreased cookie sheet. Brush with egg white; sprinkle with crushed sugar. Bake in a 350° oven 12 minutes. Makes 3½ dozen.

Chewy Noels

2 tablespoons butter *or*
   margarine
1 cup packed brown sugar
1 cup chopped nuts
⅓ cup all-purpose flour
⅛ teaspoon baking soda
⅛ teaspoon salt
2 beaten eggs
1 teaspoon vanilla
   Sifted powdered sugar
1 tube green decorator icing
   (optional)

In 9x9x2-inch baking pan melt butter or margarine. In a bowl stir together brown sugar, nuts, flour, baking soda, and salt. Stir in eggs and vanilla. Carefully pour over butter in pan; *do not stir.* Bake in 350° oven for 20 to 25 minutes. Sift powdered sugar over top. Place waxed paper under a wire rack; immediately invert pan onto rack. Cool. Dust again with powdered sugar. Cut into bars. Write "Noel" on each bar using decorator icing, if desired. Makes 24.

Santa's Whiskers

1 cup butter *or* margarine,
   softened
1 cup sugar
2 tablespoons milk
1 teaspoon vanilla *or* rum
   flavoring
2½ cups all-purpose flour
¾ cup finely chopped red *or*
   green candied cherries
½ cup finely chopped pecans
¾ cup flaked coconut

In mixing bowl cream together butter or margarine and sugar; blend in milk and vanilla or rum flavoring. Stir in flour, cherries, and pecans. Form dough into two 8-inch rolls. Roll in flaked coconut. Wrap in clear plastic wrap; chill well.

Cut into ¼-inch slices. Place on an ungreased cookie sheet. Bake in 375° oven about 12 minutes or till golden. Makes about 5 dozen.

Choose your Christmas cookies from some of Europe's favorites: wreath-shaped Norwegian Berlinerkranser *(left),* Finnish Chestnut Fingers *(top right), and* German Brown Sugar Spritz *(bottom right).*

Greek Kourabiedes

see photograph, page 195

1 cup butter *or* margarine
½ cup sifted powdered sugar
1 egg yolk
2 tablespoons brandy
½ teaspoon vanilla
⅓ cup finely chopped almonds
2¼ cups all-purpose flour
½ teaspoon baking powder
Sifted powdered sugar

In mixer bowl cream together the butter and the ½ cup powdered sugar. Add the egg yolk, brandy, and vanilla; mix well. Stir in the almonds. Stir together the flour and baking powder. Blend into the sugar mixture. Wrap and chill the dough 30 minutes. Form dough into 1-inch balls or ovals. Place on an ungreased baking sheet. Bake in a 325° oven 20 to 25 minutes or till a light sand color. Cool on a wire rack. Roll in additional powdered sugar. Makes 3½ to 4 dozen.

Norwegian Krumkake

3 eggs
½ cup sugar
½ cup butter, melted
    and cooled
1 teaspoon vanilla
½ cup all-purpose flour

With rotary beater beat eggs with sugar till thoroughly mixed. Blend in butter and vanilla. Beat in flour till smooth.

Heat krumkake iron on medium-high heat. Make one cookie at a time. For 6-inch iron drop about ½ tablespoon batter on hot, ungreased iron; close gently (do not squeeze). Bake over medium-high heat 15 to 20 seconds or till a light golden brown. Turn iron over; bake 15 to 20 seconds more. Loosen with knife and remove with spatula. Immediately shape around a wooden or metal roller. Reheat iron; repeat baking and shaping with remaining batter. Makes about 2 dozen.

Norwegian Stags' Antlers

¾ cup sugar
½ cup butter *or* margarine,
    softened
2 egg yolks
1 egg
¼ cup milk
½ teaspoon ground cardamom
2¼ cups all-purpose flour
½ cup cornstarch
1 teaspoon baking soda
½ teaspoon salt
Sugar

In mixing bowl cream together the ¾ cup sugar and butter or margarine. Beat in egg yolks and egg. Add milk and cardamom; mix well. Stir together flour, cornstarch, baking soda, and salt. Add to creamed mixture; blend well. Cover; and chill.

Divide dough in half. On lightly floured surface, roll each portion to a 12x6-inch rectangle. Cut each into thirty-six 2x1-inch strips. Place on ungreased cookie sheet. Make a slit ¾ inch from each edge of cookie, cutting a little more than halfway through. Curve cookie so slits open. Sprinkle with additional sugar. Repeat with remaining strips. Bake in 350° oven 12 to 15 minutes. Cool on rack. Store in airtight container. Makes 6 dozen.

German Pfeffernuesse

⅓ cup dark corn syrup
¼ cup granulated sugar
¼ cup honey
¼ cup shortening
1 beaten egg
2¼ cups all-purpose flour
½ teaspoon baking soda
¼ teaspoon ground cloves
¼ teaspoon ground allspice
¼ teaspoon ground cinnamon
Sifted powdered sugar

In saucepan combine corn syrup, granulated sugar, honey, and shortening. Cook and stir till shortening and sugar melt. Cool. Stir in egg. Stir together flour, baking soda, and the spices. Add to honey mixture; mix well. Form into balls using a level tablespoon of dough for each. Place on a greased cookie sheet. Bake in 375° oven about 10 minutes. Cool on wire rack. Sift powdered sugar over cookies. Makes 4 to 4½ dozen.

Dutch Letterbanket

1 8-ounce can (1 cup) almond
    paste
1 egg
¼ cup sugar
• • •
3 cups all-purpose flour
¾ teaspoon salt
1½ cups butter *or* margarine
½ to ⅔ cup ice water
• • •
1 egg yolk
1 tablespoon water

For filling, in a bowl combine almond paste, the egg, and sugar; mix well. Cover filling; chill well while preparing dough.

Stir together flour and salt. Cut in butter or margarine till mixture resembles coarse crumbs. Add ice water, a tablespoon at a time, till dough is moistened. Shape dough into a ball; cover. Let stand 30 minutes for easier rolling.

Divide dough in thirds. On lightly floured surface roll one part to a 12x6-inch rectangle. Cut in half lengthwise, forming two 12x3-inch strips. For each strip, roll 3 *tablespoons* of the almond filling to an 11-inch log on a very lightly floured surface. Place one log in center of each strip. Moisten edges of dough with a small amount of water. Fold dough over filling; seal side seam and ends. Place long rolls on an ungreased cookie sheet.

Roll each of the remaining parts of dough to an 8-inch square. Cut each square into four 8x2-inch strips. For each strip, roll about 1 *tablespoon* of the filling to an 8-inch log. Place a log on each strip; moisten and seal as for long rolls. Shape into desired letters. Place on ungreased cookie sheets.

Combine the egg yolk and the 1 tablespoon water; brush on letters and long rolls. Bake in 375° oven 30 to 35 minutes for letters and 40 to 45 minutes for long rolls. Cool. Cut long rolls into 1-inch pieces. Makes 8 individual letters and 24 (1-inch) pieces.

184

Italian Crostoli

2 tablespoons butter *or* margarine
1½ cups all-purpose flour
3 eggs
2 tablespoons granulated sugar
½ teaspoon almond extract
½ teaspoon orange extract
⅛ teaspoon salt
Cooking oil for deep-fat frying
Sifted powdered sugar

In small mixing bowl cut butter into flour till mixture resembles the size of small peas. Combine eggs, granulated sugar, almond extract, orange extract, and salt. Stir into flour mixture. Turn out onto a floured surface; knead till smooth. Cover; let rest 30 minutes.

Divide the dough in half. Roll each half to a 12x6-inch rectangle. Cut each rectangle into sixteen 6x¾-inch strips. Carefully tie strips into knots. Fry a few at a time in deep hot oil (375°) about 3 minutes or till golden, turning once. Drain on paper toweling. Cool; sprinkle with powdered sugar. Makes 32.

Candy Cane Cookies

¾ cup butter *or* margarine, softened
¾ cup sugar
1 egg
½ teaspoon vanilla
½ teaspoon peppermint extract
2 cups all-purpose flour
½ teaspoon salt
¼ teaspoon baking powder
⅓ cup flaked coconut
1 teaspoon red food coloring

In bowl cream together butter or margarine and sugar. Beat in egg, vanilla, and peppermint extract. Stir together flour, salt, and baking powder. Stir into creamed mixture. Divide dough in half. Stir coconut into one portion; blend food coloring into the second portion. Cover each one and chill 30 minutes.

Divide each dough into 30 balls; keep half of each dough chillled till ready to use. Roll each ball into a 5-inch rope. For each cookie, pinch together one end of a red rope and one end of a white rope; twist ropes together. Pinch together remaining ends. Place on an ungreased cookie sheet. Curve to form a cane. Repeat with remaining balls. Bake in a 375° oven about 10 minutes. Transfer to a wire rack. Cool. Makes 30.

Festive Tassies

½ cup butter, softened
1 3-ounce package cream cheese, softened
1 cup all-purpose flour
Almond *or* Fruit Filling (see recipes, below)

Blend butter and cheese. Stir in flour. Cover; chill 1 hour. On lightly floured surface roll dough ⅛-inch thick. Cut in 3-inch rounds with a scalloped cookie cutter. Pat into 1¾-inch muffin pans. (Or, divide dough into 24 balls; press balls against sides and bottom of muffin cups.) Fill with desired filling. Bake according to filling directions. Makes 24.

Almond Filling

¼ cup raspberry preserves
Festive Tassies (see recipe, above)
½ cup sugar
¼ cup almond paste (2 ounces)
2 egg yolks
3 tablespoons all-purpose flour
2 tablespoons light cream
1 tablespoon orange juice

Spoon ½ *teaspoon* of the preserves into each *unbaked* tassie shell. Combine sugar and almond paste. Add egg yolks, one at a time, beating well after each. Blend in flour, cream, and orange juice. Spoon a rounded teaspoon of filling atop preserves in each shell. Bake in 400° oven 15 minutes. Cool in pans before removing. Makes 24.

Fruit Filling

1 egg
¼ cup granulated sugar
¼ cup packed brown sugar
½ cup chopped walnuts
½ cup chopped candied cherries
½ cup raisins, chopped
1 teaspoon grated lemon peel
3 tablespoons lemon juice
Festive Tassies (see recipe, above)

Beat egg; gradually beat in sugars and ⅛ teaspoon *salt*. Stir in nuts, cherries, raisins, lemon peel, and lemon juice. Divide filling among *unbaked* tassie shells. Bake in 375° oven 25 minutes. Cool before removing. Makes 24.

Holiday Divinity

2½ cups sugar
½ cup light corn syrup
½ cup water
¼ teaspoon salt
2 egg whites
1 teaspoon vanilla
1 cup chopped walnuts
¼ cup chopped candied cherries
¼ cup chopped candied pineapple

In a heavy 2-quart saucepan combine sugar, corn syrup, water, and salt. Cook and stir till sugar is dissolved. Continue cooking *without stirring* to hard-ball stage (candy thermometer registers 260°). Meanwhile, beat egg whites with an electric mixer till stiff but not dry. Gradually pour syrup over the egg whites, beating constantly at high speed of mixer. Add vanilla and beat 4 to 5 minutes till candy holds its shape. Fold in walnuts, candied cherries, and candied pineapple. Quickly drop from a teaspoon onto waxed paper. Makes 48.

Brown Sugar Peanut Brittle

1 cup granulated sugar
1 cup packed brown sugar
1 cup light corn syrup
½ cup water
Dash salt
¼ cup butter *or* margarine
2 cups raw peanuts
1 teaspoon baking soda

Butter two 15½x10½x1-inch baking pans or two baking sheets. Butter a heavy 3-quart saucepan. In saucepan combine sugars, corn syrup, water, and salt. Cook and stir till sugars dissolve. When syrup boils, blend in butter or margarine. Cook *without stirring* till mixture reaches thread stage (candy thermometer registers 230°). Cook and stir till candy reaches soft-crack stage (candy thermometer registers 280°). Stir in peanuts. Stir constantly till hard-crack stage (candy thermometer registers 300°). Remove from heat. Quickly stir in baking soda; mix well. Pour onto buttered pans. As candy cools, stretch it by lifting and pulling with two forks from edges to make candy thinner. Break into pieces when cool. Makes 2 pounds.

Slovakian Nut Candy

1 cup sugar
1 cup finely chopped pecans
1 teaspoon vanilla

In 10-inch skillet heat and stir sugar over low heat till melted and golden brown. Stir in pecans, vanilla, and ⅛ teaspoon *salt*. Pour immediately on buttered baking sheet. Roll using buttered rolling pin to 8x8-inch square. Cut into diamonds. Makes ½ pound.

Molasses Taffy

2 cups sugar
1 cup ight molasses
2 teaspoons vinegar
2 tablespoons butter
½ teaspoon baking soda

Butter a heavy 3-quart saucepan. In it combine sugar, molasses, and ¼ cup *water*. Heat slowly, stirring till sugar dissolves. Bring to boiling; add vinegar. Cook to soft-crack stage (candy thermometer registers 270°).

Remove from heat; add butter. Sift in baking soda; stir to mix. Pour into buttered 15½x10½x1-inch pan. Use spatula to turn edges toward center. Cool till comfortable to handle.

Butter hands. Gather taffy into a ball; pull with fingertips. When light tan color and hard to pull, cut in fourths. Pull each piece into a long strand ½ inch thick. With buttered scissors, quickly snip into bite-size pieces. Wrap in clear plastic wrap. Makes 1½ pounds.

Glazed Cashew Clusters

2 cups cashew nuts
2 cups sugar
1 cup water
¼ teaspoon cream of tartar
1 teaspoon vanilla

Spread cashews on a baking sheet. Toast in a 350° oven till golden brown.

In saucepan cook and stir sugar, water, and cream of tartar till sugar dissolves. Bring to boiling; boil to hard-crack stage (candy thermometer registers 300°). Remove from heat; stir in toasted nuts and vanilla. Set pan in hot water to keep candy soft. Drop by tablespoons onto a greased baking sheet. Cool. Makes 1 pound.

Healthful Fudge

1 cup honey
1 cup peanut butter
1 cup carob powder
• • •
1 cup shelled sunflower seed
½ cup toasted sesame seed
½ cup flaked coconut
½ cup chopped walnuts
½ cup raisins

In large saucepan heat honey and peanut butter, stirring constantly just till smooth. Remove from heat; stir in carob powder. Mix well.

Stir in sunflower seed, sesame seed, coconut, walnuts, and raisins. Press into a buttered 8x8x2-inch pan. Chill, covered, several hours or overnight. Cut into 1-inch squares. Store in refrigerator. Makes 2½ pounds fudge.

Rocky Road

1 12-ounce package (2 cups) semisweet chocolate pieces
1 14-ounce can *sweetened condensed* milk
2 tablespoons butter *or* margarine
• • •
1 10½-ounce package (5½ cups) tiny marshmallows
1 8-ounce jar (1⅔ cups) unsalted roasted peanuts

In a saucepan combine chocolate pieces, sweetened condensed milk, and butter or margarine. Heat over low heat till chocolate is melted; remove from heat. In a large bowl combine marshmallows and peanuts. Fold in chocolate mixture. Spread in a 13x9x2-inch pan whose sides and bottom have been lined with waxed paper. Chill 2 hours or till firm. Remove from pan; peel off waxed paper. Cut into 1-inch squares with a wet knife. Wrap pieces in plastic wrap. Makes 8 dozen.

Jingle Popcorn Balls

3 quarts popped corn
2 cups snipped gumdrops
1 cup snipped pitted dates
1 cup light corn syrup
½ cup honey
1½ teaspoons vinegar
¾ teaspoon salt
1 tablespoon butter *or* margarine
1½ teaspoons vanilla

In large bowl combine popped corn, gumdrops, and dates. In heavy saucepan combine corn syrup, honey, vinegar, and salt. Bring to boiling. Cook over medium heat to hard-ball stage (candy thermometer registers 260°). Add butter or margarine and vanilla, stirring till butter is melted. Pour over popcorn mixture, stirring to coat. Form into 2-inch balls. Makes 30.

Filbert Fancies

1 cup shelled unblanched filberts
1 beaten egg
2 cups sifted powdered sugar
3 tablespoons butter *or* margarine, softened
1 teaspoon vanilla
Dash salt
2 1-ounce squares unsweetened chocolate, melted and cooled
4 cups tiny marshmallows
1 cup shredded coconut

Coarsely chop filberts; spread on a baking sheet. Toast in 350° oven about 10 minutes or till golden brown. Cool. Beat together egg, powdered sugar, butter or margarine, vanilla, and salt till very light and fluffy. Add cooled chocolate. Fold in marshmallows and nuts. Drop from a teaspoon into a bowl of coconut; roll evenly to coat. Place on waxed paper-lined baking sheets. Let stand till set. Makes 48.

Brighten your holidays with this assortment of candies. Pictured clockwise from top left are: Jingle Popcorn Balls, Filbert Fancies, Healthful Fudge, Rocky Road, and Slovakian Nut Candy.

Desserts

Pecan Pie

**Pastry for Single-Crust Pie
(see recipe, right)**
3 **eggs**
⅔ **cup sugar**
Dash salt
1 **cup dark corn syrup**
⅓ **cup butter or margarine,
melted**
1 **cup pecan halves**

Prepare and roll out pastry. Line a 9-inch pie plate. Trim pastry to ½ inch beyond edge of pie plate. Flute edge; do not prick pastry.

For filling, in mixing bowl beat eggs slightly with rotary beater or fork. Add sugar and salt, stirring till dissolved. Stir in dark corn syrup and melted butter or margarine; mix well. Stir in the pecan halves. Place pie shell on oven rack; pour filling into the pastry-lined pie plate. To prevent overbrowning, cover edge of pie with foil. Bake in 350° oven for 25 minutes. Remove foil; bake about 25 minutes more or till knife inserted off-center comes out clean. Cool thoroughly on rack before serving. Cover; chill to store.

Cranberry-Pecan Pie: Prepare the pastry shell as above. Prepare the egg-corn syrup filling. Stir in 1 cup coarsely chopped *fresh cranberries* and pecans. Bake as above.

Orange-Pecan Pie: Prepare the pastry shell as above. Prepare the egg-corn syrup filling. Stir in ½ teaspoon of finely shredded *orange peel,* ½ cup finely chopped *orange,* and the pecan halves. Bake as directed above.

Eggnog-Custard Tarts

**Pastry for Double-Crust Pie
(see recipe, right)**
4 **eggs**
3 **cups canned or dairy eggnog**
½ **cup sugar**
2 **tablespoons light rum**
1 **teaspoon vanilla**
Ground nutmeg

Prepare and roll out pastry. Roll *half* of the pastry at a time to ⅛-inch thickness. Cut each half into three 6½- or 7-inch circles. Line 4½-inch tart pans with pastry. Flute edge high; do not prick pastry. Bake in 450° oven 5 minutes. Cool on rack.

In mixing bowl beat eggs slightly with rotary beater or fork. Stir in the eggnog, sugar, light rum, vanilla, and ¼ teaspoon *salt;* mix well. Place tart pans on baking sheet. Place sheet on oven rack; pour some filling into each partially baked tart shell. Sprinkle each tart with a little nutmeg. Bake in 350° oven about 40 minutes or till knife inserted off-center comes out clean. Cool on rack. Cover; chill to store. Makes 6 tarts.

Pumpkin Pie

**Pastry for Single-Crust Pie
(see recipe, right)**
1 **16-ounce can pumpkin**
¾ **cup sugar**
1 **teaspoon ground cinnamon**
½ **teaspoon salt**
½ **teaspoon ground ginger**
½ **teaspoon ground nutmeg**
3 **eggs**
1 **5⅓-ounce can (⅔ cup)
evaporated milk**
½ **cup milk**

Prepare and roll out pastry. Line a 9-inch pie plate. Trim pastry to ½ inch beyond edge of pie plate. Flute edge high; do not prick pastry. In large mixing bowl combine pumpkin, sugar, cinnamon, salt, ginger, and nutmeg. Add eggs; lightly beat eggs into pumpkin mixture. Add the evaporated milk and milk; mix well. Place pie shell on oven rack; pour mixture into the pastry-lined pie plate. To prevent overbrowning, cover edge of pie with foil. Bake in 375° oven for 25 minutes. Remove foil; bake for 25 to 30 minutes more or till knife inserted off-center comes out clean. Cool on rack. Garnish with dollops of whipped cream, if desired. Cover, chill to store.

Pecan Tassies

**Festive Tassie dough (see
recipe, page 185)**
1 **beaten egg**
¾ **cup packed brown sugar**
1 **tablespoon butter or
margarine, softened**
1 **teaspoon vanilla**
Dash salt
½ **cup coarsely chopped pecans**

Prepare Festive Tassie dough and press into muffin pans as directed.

In small mixing bowl stir together egg, brown sugar, butter or margarine, vanilla, and salt just till smooth. Spoon about *1 teaspoon* of the chopped pecans into each pastry-lined muffin cup. Fill each with egg mixture. Bake in 325° oven about 25 minutes or till filling is set. Cool; remove from pans. Cover; chill to store. Makes 24.

Pastry for Double-Crust Pie

2 **cups all-purpose flour**
1 **teaspoon salt**
⅔ **cup shortening or lard**
6 **to 7 tablespoons cold water**

In medium mixing bowl stir together flour and salt. Cut in shortening or lard till pieces are the size of small peas. Sprinkle *1 tablespoon* of water over part of mixture, gently toss with a fork. Push to side of bowl. Repeat till all is moistened. Form dough into 2 balls.

Pastry for Single-Crust Pie: Prepare as above *except* use: 1¼ cups all-purpose *flour,* ½ teaspoon *salt,* ⅓ cup *shortening* or *lard,* and 3 to 4 tablespoons *cold water.* Form dough into 1 ball.

> *Pies and tarts just seem to go with Christmas. Choose from Cranberry-Pecan Pie (top), Pecan Tassies (center), or Eggnog-Custard Tarts (bottom). They're sure to please all your guests.*

Homemade Mincemeat Pie

1 pound beef stew meat
4 pounds cooking apples, peeled, cored, and quartered (9 cups)
4 ounces suet
2½ cups sugar
2½ cups water
1 15-ounce package raisins
2 cups dried currants (9 ounces)
1 teaspoon finely shredded orange peel
1 cup orange juice
½ cup diced mixed candied fruits and peels
1 teaspoon finely shredded lemon peel
¼ cup lemon juice
1 teaspoon salt
½ teaspoon ground nutmeg
¼ teaspoon ground mace
Pastry for Double-Crust Pie (see recipe, page 188)
Milk
Brandy Hard Sauce

In large saucepan combine beef stew meat and enough water to cover. Cover and simmer for 2 hours or till tender. Drain; cool. Using coarse blade of food grinder, grind cooked beef, apples, and suet. In large kettle combine sugar, the 2½ cups water, raisins, currants, orange peel, orange juice, mixed candied fruits and peels, lemon peel, lemon juice, salt, nutmeg, and mace; stir in the ground meat-apple mixture. Cover and simmer 45 minutes; stir mixture frequently.

Prepare and roll out pastry. Line a 9-inch pie plate with *half* of the pastry. Trim pastry to edge of pie plate. Fill pastry-lined pie plate with *4 cups* of the meat mixture. (Freeze remaining mincemeat in 4-cup portions.*) Cut slits in top crust (or cut a design in pastry with a small cookie cutter). Place pastry atop filling. Seal and flute edge. Brush with a little milk. To prevent overbrowning, cover edge of pie with foil. Bake in 375° oven for 20 minutes. Remove foil; bake about 15 minutes more or till crust is golden. Cool on rack before serving. Serve with Brandy Hard Sauce. Cover; chill to store.

Brandy Hard Sauce: Thoroughly cream together 2 cups sifted *powdered sugar,* ½ cup softened *butter* or *margarine,* and 1 teaspoon *brandy.* Stir in 1 beaten *egg yolk;* fold in 1 stiff-beaten *egg white.* Chill.

Note: This recipe makes enough mincemeat for 3 pies.

Lemon Chess Pie

Pastry for Single-Crust Pie (see recipe, page 188)
5 eggs
1½ cups sugar
1 cup light cream *or* milk
¼ cup butter, melted
1 teaspoon finely shredded lemon peel
2 tablespoons lemon juice
1 tablespoon all-purpose flour
1 tablespoon yellow cornmeal
1½ teaspoons vanilla

Prepare and roll out pastry. Line a 9-inch pie plate. Trim pastry to ½ inch beyond edge of pie plate. Flute edge; do not prick pastry. Bake in 450° oven for 5 minutes. Cool on rack.

For filling, beat eggs till well blended. Stir in sugar, cream or milk, butter, lemon peel, lemon juice, flour, cornmeal, and vanilla. Mix well.

Place pie shell on oven rack. Pour filling into the partially baked pastry shell. To prevent overbrowning, cover edge of pie with foil. Bake in 350° oven 20 minutes. Remove foil; bake 20 to 25 minutes more or till knife inserted off-center comes out clean. Cool pie on rack. Cover; chill to store.

French Silk Pie

Pastry for Single-Crust Pie (see recipe, page 188)
1 cup sugar
¾ cup butter (*not* margarine)*
3 squares (3 ounces) unsweetened chocolate, melted and cooled
1½ teaspoons vanilla
3 eggs

Prepare and roll out pastry. Line a 9-inch pie plate. Trim pastry to ½ inch beyond edge of pie plate. Flute edge; prick bottom and sides of pastry with tines of a fork. Bake in 450° oven for 10 to 12 minutes. Cool on wire rack.

In small mixer bowl cream sugar and butter about 4 minutes or till light. Blend in cooled chocolate and vanilla. Add eggs, one at a time, beating on medium speed of electric mixer for 2 minutes after each addition, scraping sides of bowl constantly. Turn into baked pastry shell. Chill overnight. Cover and chill to store.

Note: Some brands of margarine produce a non-fluffy, sticky filling. We recommend using only butter.

High Citrus Pie

Pastry for Single-Crust Pie (see recipe, page 188)
⅔ cup sugar
1 envelope unflavored gelatin
¼ teaspoon salt
½ teaspoon finely shredded lemon peel (set aside)
½ cup lemon juice
1 teaspoon finely shredded orange peel (set aside)
¼ cup orange juice
¼ cup water
5 slightly beaten egg yolks
5 egg whites
⅓ cup sugar

Prepare and roll out pastry. Line a 9-inch pie plate. Trim to ½ inch beyond edge. Flute edge; prick pastry. Bake in 450° oven for 10 to 12 minutes or till golden. Cool on wire rack.

In saucepan combine ⅔ cup sugar, gelatin, and salt. Stir in lemon juice, orange juice, water, and egg yolks. Cook and stir just till mixture thickens slightly. Remove from heat; stir in lemon and orange peels. Chill till consistency of corn syrup, stirring occasionally. Immediately beat egg whites to soft peaks. Gradually add ⅓ cup sugar, beating to stiff peaks. When gelatin is partially set (the consistency of unbeaten egg whites), fold in stiff-beaten egg whites. Chill till mixture mounds when spooned. Turn into baked pastry shell. Chill several hours or overnight till set. If desired, top with orange slices. Cover and chill to store.

Stained-Glass Fruitcakes
see photograph, page 192

2 cups walnut halves
2 cups pecan halves
1½ cups candied pineapple, cut up
1½ cups light raisins
1⅓ cups pitted whole dates
¾ cup whole red candied cherries
¾ cup whole green candied cherries
1 14-ounce can (1¼ cups) *sweetened condensed* milk

In large bowl combine walnuts, pecans, candied pineapple, raisins, dates, and cherries. Stir in condensed milk. Mix thoroughly. Pack firmly into buttered 1¾-inch muffin pans. Bake in 275° oven 25 minutes. Cool. Makes 80.

Dark Fruitcake

3 cups all-purpose flour
2 teaspoons baking powder
2 teaspoons ground cinnamon
1 teaspoon salt
½ teaspoon ground nutmeg
½ teaspoon ground allspice
½ teaspoon ground cloves
• • •
1 16-ounce package (2½ cups) diced mixed candied fruits and peels
1 15-ounce package (3 cups) raisins
1 8-ounce package (1½ cups) whole candied red cherries
1 8-ounce package (1⅓ cups) pitted whole dates, snipped
1 cup slivered almonds
1 cup pecan halves
½ cup candied pineapple, chopped
• • •
4 eggs
1¾ cups packed brown sugar
1 cup orange juice
¾ cup butter *or* margarine, melted and cooled
¼ cup light molasses

In a bowl stir together flour, baking powder, cinnamon, salt, nutmeg, allspice, and cloves. Add fruits and peels, raisins, cherries, dates, almonds, pecans, and pineapple; mix till well coated. Beat eggs till foamy. Gradually add brown sugar. Add orange juice, butter or margarine, and molasses; beat till blended. Stir the egg mixture into fruit mixture.

Grease one 6×3×2-inch loaf pan, one 8×4×2-inch loaf pan, and one 10×3½×2½-inch loaf pan. Line bottom and sides of pans with brown paper; grease paper. Turn batter into pans, filling each about ¾ full.

Bake in 300° oven 1½ hours for 6×3×2-inch pan and 2 hours for two other pans or till cakes test done. Cover all pans with foil after 1 hour of baking. Cool on wire rack; remove from pans. Wrap in wine-, brandy-, or fruit juice-moistened cheesecloth. Overwrap with foil. Store in refrigerator. Remoisten cheesecloth as needed if cakes are stored over 1 week. Makes 3 loaves.

Banana Fruitcake
see photograph, page 192

1 16-ounce package (3 cups) pitted prunes
1 8-ounce package (1½ cups) dried apricots
1 15-ounce package (3 cups) raisins
1 16-ounce package (2 cups) diced mixed candied fruits and peels
1 8-ounce package (1⅓ cups) chopped pitted dates
½ cup brandy
2 cups packed brown sugar
1½ cups butter *or* margarine, softened
6 eggs
3 cups all-purpose flour
2 teaspoons salt
1 tablespoon ground cinnamon
1 teaspoon ground nutmeg
1 teaspoon ground allspice
2 large ripe bananas, mashed
2 cups walnut halves
½ cup brandy
Brandy

Cut prunes and apricots into quarters. In bowl combine prunes, apricots, raisins, candied fruits and peels, and dates. Pour ½ cup brandy over fruit. Cover; let stand overnight.

In large mixer bowl cream brown sugar and butter or margarine till fluffy. Add eggs, one at a time; beat well after each. Stir together flour, salt, and spices. Add flour mixture alternately with banana to butter mixture. Stir in nuts and fruit mixture. Divide the 15 cups batter into any of the following very well-greased loaf pans:

size of pan	cups of batter	baking time (hours)
9×5×3-inch	4	3
7½×3½×2-inch	3	2
4½×2½×1½-inch	2	2

Bake in 250° oven for time indicated above or till golden. Cool in pans 10 minutes; remove from pans. Cool on rack. Pour ½ cup brandy over tops of cakes. Wrap in brandy-soaked cheesecloth; overwrap with foil. Store in refrigerator. Occasionally add additional brandy to soak cakes.

Fruited Cupcakes
see photograph, page 192

1½ cups finely diced mixed candied fruits and peels
⅔ cup light raisins
¼ cup pitted whole dates, snipped
1 cup all-purpose flour
¾ teaspoon baking powder
½ teaspoon salt
½ cup shortening
½ cup sugar
½ teaspoon vanilla
3 eggs
⅓ cup unsweetened pineapple juice
• • •
¼ cup sugar
¼ cup unsweetened pineapple juice
1 tablespoon rum
1 teaspoon lemon juice
• • •
Candied cherries, candied pineapple pieces *or* walnut halves (optional)

In a bowl combine mixed candied fruits and peels, raisins, and dates.

In a bowl stir together flour, baking powder, and salt.

In large mixer bowl thoroughly cream together shortening, the ½ cup sugar, and vanilla. Add eggs, one at a time, beating well after each. Add dry ingredients to creamed mixture alternately with the ⅓ cup pineapple juice, beating well after each addition. Stir in fruit mixture.

Fill 36 well-greased 2-inch muffin cups almost to top. Place a pan of water on bottom rack of oven. Place muffin cups on top rack. Bake in 350° oven 25 to 30 minutes. Remove cupcakes from pans to wire rack; cool. When cupcakes are cool, prick holes in the top of each using a long-tined fork.

In a small saucepan combine the ¼ cup sugar, ¼ cup pineapple juice, rum, and lemon juice; bring to boiling. Brush *half* of the hot mixture over cupcakes. When glaze is set, decorate with candied fruits or nuts, if desired. Bring remaining rum mixture to boiling and brush over cupcakes. Cool. Makes 36.

191

Champagne Fruitcake

2 cups chopped pecans
1¼ cups chopped slivered
    almonds
1 8-ounce package (1¼ cups)
    pitted whole dates,
    snipped
1 cup candied cherries,
    chopped (8 ounces)
½ cup raisins
¼ cup diced candied orange
    peel
¼ cup diced candied lemon
    peel
¼ cup diced candied citron
½ cup butter, softened
½ cup sugar
4 eggs
2 tablespoons dark rum
2 tablespoons brandy
1 cup all-purpose flour
½ teaspoon ground nutmeg
½ teaspoon ground cinnamon
½ teaspoon ground mace
¼ teaspoon ground cloves
1½ cups champagne *or* white
    wine
½ cup brandy
¼ cup strawberry syrup

In a large bowl combine nuts, dates, fruits, and peels. In small mixer bowl cream together butter and sugar till light. Beat in eggs, one at a time, beating well after each. Beat in rum and the 2 tablespoons brandy.

Stir together flour and spices. Add to creamed mixture; mix well. Stir batter into fruit mixture. Turn into a greased 9-inch spring-form pan. Bake in 250° oven 2½ to 2¾ hours. Cool in pan 30 minutes. Remove from pan; cool.

In a jar combine champagne or wine, the ½ cup brandy, and strawberry syrup. Brush all over cake. Wrap in several layers of cheesecloth moistened with more of the champagne mixture. Overwrap in foil. Refrigerate remaining champagne mixture, covered. Refrigerate cake for 4 to 6 weeks. Soak cheesecloth with reserved champagne mixture every few days for the first 10 days. Then remoisten at 1-week intervals, rewrapping in foil each time.

Make fruitcakes, such as those pictured at left, early so they will have time to age. Try Dundee Cake (top left), Champagne Fruitcake (top right), Banana Fruitcake (center), Fruited Cupcakes (bottom right), and Stained-Glass Fruitcakes (bottom left). (See recipes this page and on pages 190-191.)

Dundee Cake

¾ cup butter *or* margarine
¾ cup sugar
3 eggs
2¼ cups all-purpose flour
1 teaspoon baking powder
¾ cup milk
1 cup raisins
½ cup currants
½ cup chopped blanched
    almonds
¼ cup diced mixed candied
    fruits and peels
¼ cup candied cherries,
    quartered
    Blanched whole almonds

In large mixer bowl cream butter and sugar till light. Add eggs and beat till fluffy. Mix flour, baking powder, and ¼ teaspoon *salt;* add to creamed mixture alternately with milk, beating after each addition. Fold in next 5 ingredients.

Turn into greased and floured 8-inch spring-form pan. Arrange whole almonds atop batter. Bake in 325° oven for 1¼ hours or till done. Cool 10 minutes in pan. Remove sides from pan. Cool. Wrap in *brandy*-soaked cheesecloth, then in foil. Refrigerate.

Brandy Nut Cake

3 cups chopped walnuts
1½ cups maraschino cherries,
    halved
1 cup light raisins
½ cup dark raisins
¾ cup all-purpose flour
¾ cup sugar
½ teaspoon baking powder
½ teaspoon salt
3 eggs
2 tablespoons apricot brandy
½ cup apricot brandy

In a bowl combine nuts, cherries, and raisins. Stir together flour, sugar, baking powder, and salt. Add to nut mixture, tossing to coat well. Beat eggs till frothy; add the 2 tablespoons brandy. Pour egg mixture over nut mixture; mix well. Pour into a greased and floured 9×5×3-inch loaf pan. Bake in 300° oven 1¾ hours. Cool cake in pan; remove. Moisten several layers of cheesecloth with ¼ *cup* of the remaining brandy. Wrap cake; then overwrap in foil. Refrigerate 2 to 3 days. Remoisten cheesecloth with remaining brandy. Rewrap and refrigerate cake.

French Buche de Noel

4 egg yolks
½ cup granulated sugar
½ teaspoon vanilla
4 egg whites
½ cup granulated sugar
1 cup sifted cake flour
½ teaspoon baking powder
    Powdered sugar
2 tablespoons rum
    Chocolate-Rum Filling (see
    recipe, below)

Beat egg yolks with electric mixer till thick and lemon-colored. Gradually add the first ½ cup granulated sugar, beating constantly. Stir in vanilla. Wash beaters. Beat egg whites till soft peaks form. Gradually add the second ½ cup granulated sugar till stiff peaks form. Fold in yolk mixture. Sift together flour, baking powder, and ¼ teaspoon *salt;* fold into egg mixture. Spoon into greased and floured 15½×10½×1-inch baking pan. Bake in 375° oven 10 to 12 minutes. Promptly loosen edges; turn out onto towel sprinkled with powdered sugar. Sprinkle cake with rum. From long side roll cake and towel together; cool. Unroll cake; spread with *half* the Chocolate-Rum Filling. Reroll. Diagonally cut 4-inch piece from roll. Place cut edge of piece against longer roll on serving plate. Frost with remaining Chocolate-Rum Filling; mark with tines of fork to resemble bark.

Chocolate-Rum Filling

1½ squares (1½ ounces)
    unsweetened chocolate
⅔ cup sugar
⅓ cup boiling water
2 egg yolks
½ cup butter, softened
1 tablespoon rum
1 teaspoon instant coffee
    crystals

In a saucepan melt chocolate; cool completely. In a second small saucepan heat sugar and water to boiling; attach candy thermometer to pan. Cook mixture to soft-ball stage (candy thermometer registers 240°). In small mixer bowl beat egg yolks with electric mixer till thick and lemon-colored. Very gradually add hot syrup, beating constantly. Continue beating till mixture is completely cool. Beat in butter, *1 tablespoon at a time.* Add chocolate, rum, and coffee. Beat till thick.

Greek Baklava

16 ounces frozen filo dough (21
    16×12-inch sheets)
• • •
1½ cups butter, melted
  4 cups finely chopped walnuts
  3 cups finely chopped pecans
  ¾ cup sugar
  1 tablespoon ground cinnamon
• • •
  2 cups sugar
  1 cup water
  2 tablespoons honey
  2 tablespoons lemon juice
  4 inches stick cinnamon

Thaw frozen filo dough at room temperature for 2 hours. Cut 16×12-inch sheets in half crosswise. (If filo is a different size, cut to fit pan.) Cover with a slightly damp towel.

Lightly butter the bottom of a 13×9×2-inch baking pan. Layer *nine* of the half sheets of filo in the pan, brushing each sheet with some of the melted butter or margarine. Mix the walnuts, pecans, the ¾ cup sugar, and ground cinnamon. Sprinkle about *1 cup* of the nut mixture over the filo in the pan. Drizzle with some of the melted butter. Top with *four* more half sheets of the filo, brushing each with more of the melted butter. Repeat the nut-and-4-half-sheet-filo layers *five* times more. Sprinkle with the remaining nut mixture. Drizzle with some of the melted butter. Top with the remaining *nine* half sheets of filo, brushing each with some of the remaining melted butter.

Cut into diamond-shaped pieces or squares, cutting to but not through the bottom layer. Bake in a 325° oven for 60 minutes. Finish cutting diamonds or squares; cool thoroughly.

Meanwhile, in a saucepan combine the 2 cups sugar, the water, honey, lemon juice, and stick cinnamon. Boil gently, uncovered, for 15 minutes. Remove from heat. Remove cinnamon. Stir till blended. Pour warm syrup over cooled pastry. Cool completely. Garnish each diamond with a whole clove, if desired. Makes 4½ dozen pieces.

Greek Melamakarona

⅓ cup cooking oil
½ cup butter, softened
⅓ cup sugar
1 tablespoon orange juice
1 teaspoon baking powder
½ teaspoon baking soda
1¾ to 2 cups all-purpose flour
¾ cup sugar
⅓ cup honey
⅓ cup finely chopped walnuts

In mixer bowl beat cooking oil into butter till blended. Beat in the ⅓ cup sugar. Add orange juice, baking powder, and baking soda; mix well. With mixer add enough of the flour, a little at a time, to make a medium-soft dough. Shape dough into 2-inch ovals and place on an ungreased baking sheet. Bake in 350° oven 20 to 25 minutes or till golden. Cool pastries on rack.

Meanwhile, in a saucepan combine the ¾ cup sugar, honey, and ½ cup *water*. Bring to boiling. Boil gently, uncovered, 5 minutes. Dip cooled pastries into the warm syrup. Sprinkle immediately with nuts. Dry on wire rack. Makes 2½ to 3 dozen.

Greek Koulourakia

½ cup butter
¼ cup shortening
½ cup sugar
2 beaten eggs
1 teaspoon vanilla
3 cups all-purpose flour
2 teaspoons baking powder
½ teaspoon baking soda
¼ teaspoon salt
¼ teaspoon ground cinnamon
¼ teaspoon ground nutmeg
½ cup whipping cream
  Sesame seed

In mixer bowl cream together butter, shortening, and sugar. Add one of the eggs and vanilla; beat well. Stir together flour, baking powder, baking soda, salt, cinnamon, and nutmeg. Add to creamed mixture alternately with whipping cream; beat well after each addition. Cover; chill 1 hour. On a floured surface, using 1 tablespoon dough for each pastry, roll dough into 6-inch lengths. Shape into wreaths, pressing to seal ends. Place on a greased cookie sheet. Mix remaining egg and 1 teaspoon *water*. Brush pastries; top with sesame seed. Bake in 325° oven 20 minutes. Cool. Makes 3½ to 4 dozen.

Greek Diples

5 egg yolks
1 egg
¼ cup butter, melted and
    cooled
1 teaspoon finely shredded
    orange peel
¼ cup orange juice
2 tablespoons brandy
1 tablespoon lemon juice
2½ to 3 cups all-purpose flour
1 teaspoon baking powder
  Cooking oil for deep-fat
    frying
• • •
1 cup honey
2 tablespoons water
  Ground cinnamon
¾ cup ground walnuts

In small mixer bowl beat egg yolks and egg at high speed on electric mixer about 4 minutes or till thick and lemon-colored. Stir in butter, orange peel, orange juice, brandy, and lemon juice. Stir together *2 cups* of the flour and the baking powder. Stir into egg mixture.

Stir in as much of the remaining flour as you can mix in using a spoon. On a lightly floured surface knead in remaining flour to make a moderately stiff dough. Continue kneading till dough is smooth and elastic (about 5 to 8 minutes). Divide dough into quarters. Cover; let rest 10 minutes.

Roll each quarter to a 16-inch square. If dough is difficult to roll, cover and let rest a few minutes more. Cut dough into 4-inch squares. Drop one square into deep hot oil (360°). Slip dough between tines of a long-tined fork and quickly twist dough into a roll, using a second fork to guide the dough. Continue cooking till roll is browned, turning once. Transfer to paper toweling; remove fork. Repeat with remaining dough squares. Store in a covered container.

Just before serving, combine honey and water in a saucepan. Heat just till warm. Dip the desired number of rolls, one at a time, in syrup. Sprinkle with cinnamon and walnuts. Makes 64.

Part of the Greek Christmas tradition are special holiday pastries, a sampling shown here. Pictured on the platter in the foreground are Greek Kourabiedes (center; see recipe, page 184), Greek Baklava (middle), and Greek Melamakarona (outside edge). On the plates in back are Greek Koulourakia (left) and Greek Diples (right).

A Child's Fantasy Christmas

Fresh and Fanciful Trims

Do you love to get down on the floor with your children and shake the packages under the tree? Do you listen with them for the sound of reindeer on the roof? If so, then you know what a magical holiday Christmas is—for kids of all ages!

In this section are all sorts of fanciful, child-pleasing decorations to make your Christmas delightfully merry. For starters, here is a country Christmas, with a tree full of whimsical animals, a gift-box banner big enough to thrill any child, and some prim and proper apple-head dolls to preside over all the holiday hoopla.

Directions for all projects begin on page 206.

Fresh and Fanciful Trims

Crisp and fresh as country air, these down-on-the-farm trims will delight youngsters and oldsters alike. The big-box banner (below) is wrapped with ribbons and bows in perky prints. Fantasy farmyard ornaments bedeck the Christmas tree. And the country-patchwork stockings (opposite) feature motifs tailored to tickle the fancy of each owner.

Big bright bows are all the added decorations you'll need if you trim your tree with the plump stuffed hens and other animals shown here. From small scraps of colorful felt, you can make a whole bunch of ducks swimming in water, mama pigs and piglets, or barns bursting with hay.

Give your Christmas tree critters some whimsical touches if you want to see little eyes light up. The felt goat wouldn't be the same without the weed in his mouth.

And a few flowers make any fleecy ram all the more lovable.

These ornaments make terrific toys for all the tiny-tot farmers at your homestead because each is padded with a bit of stuffing.

Hugs and kisses will be your reward when you present one of these stockings to your young fisherman, horse fancier, gardener, or candy lover. Or, using these for inspiration, design a motif to suit your youngster's own special interests or talents.

Fresh and Fanciful Trims

It's Christmas—and anything is possible. You can ice your Christmas tree with delicately colored snowflake ornaments made from cake frosting, or create other fanciful confections even the sugar plum fairy would find irresistible.

Everything in this delectable Christmas extravaganza is something you can do in your own home sweet home. If you can make a pillow, why not create one in the yummiest satins to look like an ice cream cone or a giant gingerbread boy as a delightful and unexpected present? Or make the entire bakeshop assortment, including an elegant wedding cake, a supreme cupcake, and a luscious eclair, to display during the holidays for everyone to enjoy.

Use pretty printed dress-weight satins for the cupcake and the ice cream cone, and luscious bridal satins for the wedding cake, cupcake frosting, and mounds of ice cream in the cone. Embroidered ribbons, bits of lace, and swags of soft, velvet tubing trim the three-tiered cake.

The wall hanging (left) depicts "Home Sweet Home" as sweetly as we've ever seen it. This beautiful banner is stitched in satins and trimmed in lace. You may hand- or machine-stitch the letters and then trapunto them so they look soft and puffy. The rosettes on the banner are readymade ones stitched on by hand.

Carry your confectionery Christmas to completion with pastel package wraps and candy-colored satin or moire ribbons. Trim extra-special presents with tiny nosegays or silk flowers tucked into the bows.

201

Fresh and Fanciful Trims

Sugary ornaments, a candy wreath, stockings as pretty as a freshly frosted cake, and a lovable gingerbread doll can make this Christmas a sweet, sentimental time for your family. To create these delightful projects, all you need are ordinary materials and a little time.

Even a novice cake decorator will find ornaments like the one at right delightfully fun and simple to make. And the candy nosegay wreath (below) is a Christmas specialty that is so easy to make you'll probably end up designing a few as gifts for your sweetest friends and neighbors. Directions for the frosting snowflakes and candy wreath follow.

The satin stockings (opposite) come in different sizes for each member of the family. The small white satin bootee, delicately trimmed, is the perfect cache for an infant's first Christmas. Larger stockings are just right for an older brother or sister and proud parents and grandparents.

If you've been making confectionery pillows such as the gingerbread boy or those shown on pages 200 and 201, a few scraps of the leftover fabric and small bits and pieces of lace and ribbon are all you'll need for these elegant stockings.

Make your gingerbread boy in soft brown taffeta, frost with white satin cord, add big sugary-looking buttons, and maybe your creation will get a great big kiss from an enchanted child too. All the confectionery pillows also make great gifts for such devoted pillow fanciers as teen-agers and college students.

For the snowflake ornaments, use: one cup of confectioner's sugar; one egg white; one-eighth teaspoon cream of tartar; red, yellow, green, and blue food coloring; silver cake decorating beads; waxed paper; and small plastic bags or a pastry bag.

In a small bowl, beat the first three ingredients until the mixture is very thick. For white snowflakes, spoon one-third of the frosting into a plastic bag or a pastry bag. For pastel snowflakes, add a few drops of food coloring to the frosting. If you plan to make edible ornaments, you may wish to add flavored extract to the mixture.

Squeeze the frosting into one corner of the bag. Then snip off the tip of the corner. (The size of the hole in the bag determines the thickness of the snowflake.)

Enlarge the snowflake design on page 209. Place the pattern beneath a 4-inch square of waxed paper, and squeeze the frosting onto the paper, following the design lines. Accent the ornaments with silver cake beads as shown in the photograph.

Let the snowflakes harden overnight. Then, gently remove the waxed-paper backing. Attach a loop of thread to each snowflake so you can hang them on the tree.

For a candy wreath, you'll need: about 60 pieces of paper-wrapped saltwater taffy, or any twist-wrapped candy; ten six-inch paper doilies; a 12-inch plastic foam wreath (the ring should be one and one-half inches wide); a yard of pink moire ribbon (1½ inches wide); a yard each of picot-edged narrow ribbon in pink, purple, and green; some T-pins; and some heavy-duty straight pins.

Begin by covering the wreath with the moire ribbon, and securing it with straight pins. Gather the center of each paper doily, twist the doily slightly to ruffle it, and secure the doilies to the ring using T-pins. Next, using straight pins, attach six pieces of candy on each doily in a cluster. Tie a large bow using all three strands of ribbon, attach it to the wreath with pins, and ENJOY.

Fresh and Fanciful Trims

Everything nice—that's the Christmas wish of children everywhere. And what could be nicer than sweet dreams in a room dressed for Christmas in delicate laces, dainty bows, and old-fashioned colors, patterns, and projects?

When your child wakes on Christmas morning to special presents like the ones shown here, every minute you've spent will be worth the time and effort. The yo-yo quilt and the stocking (on the windowsill) are not only pretty, but child's play to sew. Each yo-yo is made from a circle of fabric gathered into a puff. Stitch the puffs together into a lightweight coverlet or join them into "fabric" for the Christmas stocking.

You'll need a little more expertise to stitch the appliquéd parlor pillow (next to the stocking) and the tea cozy and dolls on the table. Hand quilting, touches of embroidery, and a lace ruffle make the parlor-scene pillow a special gift indeed. For the charming tea-party hostess and her guests, use diminutive prints, scraps of broadcloth, and snippets of lace machine-stitched to a muslin background.

Snowy hardanger-embroidered ornaments in wooden rings and tiny soft-sculpture bows trim this very feminine tree. These bows are stuffed with batting, but they also could be filled with potpourri and used as sachets or pretty package trims.

Tiny packages are a child's delight. Those on the tea table are matchboxes and other small containers wrapped in doll-house wallpapers and topped with miniature bows.

Instructions for a Child's Fantasy Christmas Fresh and Fanciful Trims

The instructions below and on the following pages are for the ornaments, decorations, and gifts shown on pages 196–205. For directions for enlarging and transferring designs, see the glossary, pages 370–371.

Apple Head Dolls
page 196

Materials: 3 Golden Delicious apples; apple peeler; lemon juice; sharp knife; coat hangers; thin wire; cotton batting; gauze; white glue; peppercorns or small beads; white yarn for hair; fabric scraps for clothing.

Instructions: *For heads,* gently peel apple completely; use apple peeler if available. Dip peeled apple in lemon juice to prevent discoloration.

Lightly mark a triangle in center of apple using point of knife. This will be the nose. Slice away bits of apple from around the sides and bottom of the nose to make it protrude.

Make a cut ½ inch beneath nose for mouth, and cut out 2 wedges for eyes. Cut light lines in forehead for wrinkles. Dip apple in lemon juice again.

Dry apples either by hanging them in a warm place for 3 weeks or by setting oven on "warm" and leaving apples inside with door ajar for 24 hours.

For hands, dry 2 apple slices in oven 1 hour; cut hands with scissors.

For body frame, bend a 15-inch piece of coat hanger wire into inverted V shape, making neck, body, and legs of figure. With thin wire, secure a 7-inch piece of coat hanger wire (arms) ½ inch below point of V (neck).

Wrap a 3-inch-wide strip of cotton batting around midsection of frame, forming upper torso. Overwrap batting with gauze; hold layers of fabric together with a few stitches. Wrap and overwrap arms and legs in same manner.

Push apple head into place on bent neck wire. Secure with white glue. Glue 2 small beads or peppercorns in place for eyes. Glue strands of yarn to top of head for hair. Gently push hands onto ends of arm wire; glue.

To clothe, lay doll on fabric and trace shape to obtain basic shirt, dress or pants pattern. Allow for ¾-inch seam allowances and neck, arm, and leg openings. Dress doll, then make tucks, darts, gathers, and hems by hand until clothes fit as you desire. Add lace trim, apron, and bonnet to lady; purchase straw hat for gentleman. Glasses are strips of wire, bent to shape with pliers.

Barnyard Animal Ornaments
page 199

Note: Colors and types of fabric or other adornments needed for this project depend on the animals you choose to make. See photographs for ideas.

Materials: Scraps of felt in assorted colors; scraps of fuzzy, shiny, or other novelty fabrics; white glue or fusible webbing; fiberfill; beads for eyes, feathers, straw, et cetera; fishline or plastic thread for hanging; dressmaker's carbon paper.

General Instructions: Patterns and construction tips for individual animals follow this section.

Using dressmaker's carbon and a pencil, trace animal shapes and features onto desired fabrics and cut out.

Glue, stitch, or iron fabric features such as eyes, mouth, ears, spots, et cetera onto basic animal shapes.

Pin back and front animal shapes together, right sides out. Topstitch outside of shape, following dotted lines on pattern. Leave 1½ inches open for stuffing. Stuff the animals lightly; stitch openings closed.

Topstitch lines for legs where applicable. Attach any non-fabric adornments, such as beads or feathers.

For hanging the animals, make loops of fishline and attach.

● *Duck*

Stitch the wing and back to the front piece before sewing the front and back together. (See placement indicated by dotted lines on pattern.) Cut small ovals of felt and glue on for eyes.

After body is stitched and stuffed, lay the completed duck on piece A. Lay piece B atop the duck and piece C atop B. Pin all layers together, then stitch them together at the base.

● *Goat*

Glue the horn and ear in place before stuffing. Stitch leg lines *after* the body has been stuffed.

● *Pig*

Stitch the tail to the pig after the body is stuffed. Tails and eyes on piglets are embroidered. Glue little pigs in place last.

● *Chicken*

After the chicken and nest are stuffed, lay the chicken on the nest, insert the eggs (see photograph), and glue or hand-tack eggs in place.

● *Cow*

Cut scraps of brown felt or fur to match spot outlines on body, or place spots at random. Leave an opening for

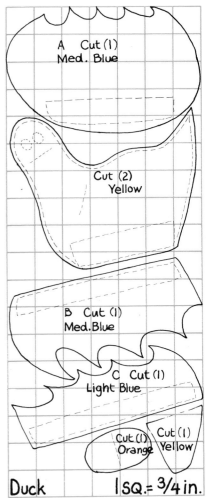

A Cut (1) Med. Blue

Cut (2) Yellow

B Cut (1) Med. Blue

C Cut (1) Light Blue

Cut (1) Orange Cut (1) Yellow

Duck   1 SQ. = ¾ in.

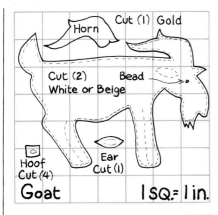

Horn Cut (1) Gold

Cut (2) Bead
White or Beige

Hoof
Cut (4)

Ear
Cut (1)

Goat 1 SQ.= 1 in.

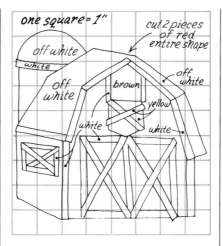

one square = 1"

cut 2 pieces
of red
entire shape

off white
white
off
white
brown
off
white
yellow
white
white

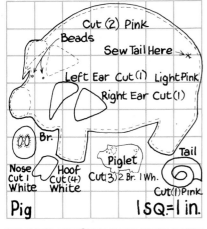

Cut (2) Pink
Beads
Sew Tail Here

Left Ear Cut (1) Light Pink
Right Ear Cut (1)

Br.

Piglet
Cut (3) 2 Br. 1 Wh.

Tail
Cut (1) Pink

Nose
Cut 1
White

Hoof
Cut (4)
White

Pig 1 SQ.= 1 in.

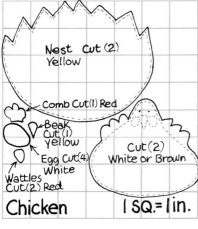

Nest Cut (2)
Yellow

Comb Cut (1) Red

Beak
Cut (1)
Yellow

Egg Cut (4)
White

Cut (2)
White or Brown

Wattles
Cut (2) Red

Chicken 1 SQ.= 1 in.

(Spot)

Beads

Cut (2) White

Br.

Udder Cut (1)
Pink

Spot

Nose
Cut (1) Pink

Spot

Hoof
Cut (4)
Flesh

L. Ear
Cut (1)
White
Pink Lining

R. Ear
Cut (1)
Brown

Horns
Cut (1) ea.
Flesh

Cow 1 SQ.= 1¼ in.

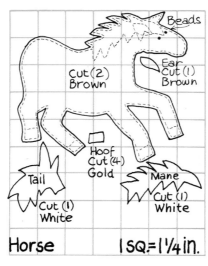

Beads

Cut (2)
Brown

Ear
Cut (1)
Brown

Hoof
Cut (4)
Gold

Tail

Cut (1)
White

Mane
Cut (1)
White

Horse 1 SQ.= 1¼ in.

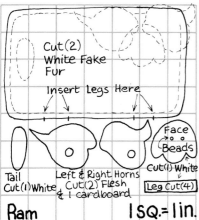

Cut (2)
White Fake
Fur

Insert Legs Here

Tail
Cut (1) White

Left & Right Horns
Cut (2) Flesh
& 1 cardboard

Face
Beads

Cut (1) White

Leg Cut (4)

Ram 1 SQ.= 1 in.

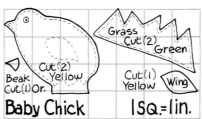

Grass
Cut (2)
Green

Beak
Cut (1) Or.

Cut (2)
Yellow

Cut (1)
Yellow

Wing

Baby Chick 1 SQ.= 1 in.

inserting the udder when you stitch the cow together; stitch leg lines after the body of the cow has been stuffed.

● *Ram*

Make body of ram of white fake fur, stitched with right sides together and turned right side out. Leave opening for insertion of legs. Mount horns on cardboard for added stability. *Note:* To make a sheep, cut ram body pattern slightly smaller; omit horns.

● *Horse*

Follow the general instructions.

● *Baby Chick*

Stitch and stuff chick first. Insert completed chick between 2 pieces of felt "grass"; stitch on lines indicated.

Patchwork Package Banner
page 198

Materials: 3 yards of 45-inch-wide blue sailcloth; 1½ yards each of 5 printed fabrics for ribbons and bows; thread to match fabrics; 1 package of ¼-inch-wide black bias tape; yardstick; rod for hanging.

Instructions: Cut blue fabric into two 1½-yard lengths; sew them together along the selvage. Press seam open, then spread out fabric, right side up.

Sketch the outlines of the package, using a yardstick to make straight lines. Use the diagram below as a guide. At the top, leave a 6-inch flap to be folded under.

Cut out box shape. Turn all edges under ½ inch, then ½ inch again so there are no raw edges. Pin, then stitch.

continued

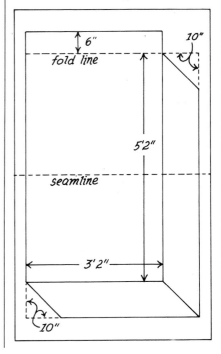

6"
fold line
10"
5'2"
seamline
3'2"
10"

Continued from page 207
Fresh and Fanciful Trims

Piece printed fabric into ribbons 4 yards long. Make 2 ribbons 4 inches wide and one each 5, 6, and 7 inches wide. Set aside remaining printed fabric for bows. Fold long edges of ribbons under ½ inch. Pin and press edges.

Arrange ribbons inside main rectangle, using a horizontal and vertical strip of each fabric. Don't do the sides yet. Alternate wide and narrow ribbons, and weave ribbon strips over and under each other, using the photograph as a guide. Leave ½ inch of extra fabric at edges of package top and sides; trim remaining ribbon. Pin ribbons in place.

Finish sides by turning long edges of remaining ribbons under an additional ¼ inch. Pin ribbons to side of package, slanting ribbons to match angled sides. Stitch all ribbons in place.

Pin black seam binding along the lines marking the edges of the package top. Be sure to run seam binding between ribbons, as shown, rather than over them.

For each bow, cut 2 fabric strips 45 inches long and twice the width of the ribbon. Add 1 inch seam allowance. Stitch with right sides together, leaving ends open; turn. Tie strips into bows; tack in place.

Tack all loose ends of ribbons at edges of banner under ½ inch. Turn top margin to back; stitch to make a slot for hanging rod. Trim rod to width of slot, insert, and hang.

Country Patchwork Stockings
page 199

Materials: Medium-weight natural canvas (or similar substitute); scraps of calico prints; ½ yard red cotton (names); fabric adhesive or fusible webbing; fiberfill; ½ yard muslin.

Instructions: Enlarge patterns and cut out pattern pieces. Using the alphabet (right), cut names, overlapping the letters.

Glue or fuse pattern pieces to stocking front. Zigzag stitch around edges of each pattern piece, as shown.

For cuffs, cut twenty 2½-inch squares of calicos. Using ¼-inch seam, sew 2 rows of 10 squares. Cut a muslin lining the same size as the cuff. With right sides facing, sew lining to cuff along one long edge. Open both pieces so they're flat, with right side facing up. Fold in half across width, right sides together; sew sides. Turn cuff over lining.

Sew together front and back stocking; start and stop 2 inches from top.

Clip seam margin 2 inches from top. Turn stocking. With wrong sides together, stitch top 2 inches on both sides.

Pin long, unsewn edges of cuff to top of stocking. Right side of cuff should be inside stocking, facing wrong side of stocking. Sew a ¼-inch seam; fold cuff down over top. Stitch narrow muslin loop to upper edge for hanging.

Stitch and stuff horseshoe, candy canes, fish, and flower. Attach to stockings. Trim horseshoe, horse's neck, and candy canes with red ribbon. Tie yarn to a twig for a fishing pole.

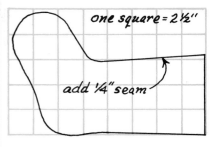

"Home Sweet Home" Banner
page 200

Note: Finished size is 24x36 inches.

Materials: 28x40 inches white velveteen; ½ yard blue satin; 7 yards lace and ribbon trim (1 inch wide); 6 large (2½ inch) and 2 small (1½ inch) flower appliqués; 3 small butterfly appliqués (hand embroidery may be substituted); 1 yard each muslin and quilt batting; fiberfill; 1 pair each 24-inch and 36-inch artist's stretcher strips; fabric glue.

Instructions: Enlarge the pattern (right) for use as a master pattern. Trace letters onto tissue paper, adding ⅜-inch seam allowances. Cut letters from blue satin.

Turn under seam allowance on letters. Appliqué to velveteen; allow 2 inches all around for framing.

For trapunto quilting, cut small slits through background fabric; lightly pad

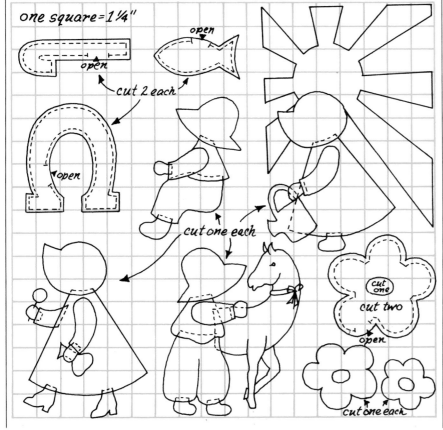

each letter with fiberfill. Whipstitch openings closed.

Position flowers and butterflies onto backing; glue or hand-tack in place.

Assemble stretcher strips. Stretch a layer of muslin, then a layer of quilt batting over the frame; staple in place. Stretch fabric banner tightly over the padded frame; staple to back. Trim excess fabric and batting.

Hand-tack or glue a row of lace and ribbon edging along the top edges of the wall hanging. Add a second row of edging 1 inch inside the first. Add wire or loops for hanging, if desired.

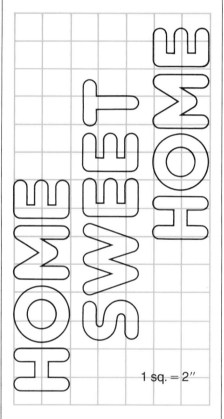

1 sq. = 2"

Snowflake Frosting Ornaments
pages 200 and 202

For ornaments, see pattern (above right) and instructions (on page 203).

Five Confectionery Pillows
page 201

General Instructions: (Materials lists and directions for individual pillows follow.) Enlarge and transfer patterns to tissue paper; add ¾-inch seam allowance to each pattern piece.

Cut out patterns in both satin pillow fabric and muslin. (Exceptions are gingerbread boy and eclair base, which

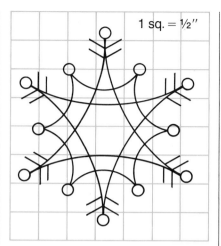

1 sq. = ½"

need no muslin.) Baste satin and muslin shapes together.

For cupcake, ice cream cone, and wedding cake, pin patterns directly over front satin pieces. Add decorative stitching by machine sewing directly over tissue onto fabric. Tear away tissue.

Where required, add trims and piping to pillow fronts. Sew pieces together to complete fronts. (Pillow backs have no decorative stitching or trims.)

To trapunto-quilt fronts, cut a slit in the muslin backing (not the satin) and gently stuff between satin and muslin. Whipstitch openings.

Stitch pillow front to back with right sides together. Leave an opening for turning. Clip curves, turn, and stuff. Slip-stitch opening.

● *Ice Cream Cone Pillow*

Materials: ½ yard light pink satin (ice cream); ⅜ yard printed satin (cone); 1 yard muslin; pink and burgundy thread; 2⅔ yard cable cord; fiberfill.

Instructions: To quilt, use pink thread to zigzag-stitch along dotted lines on pink satin. Use burgundy thread to topstitch cone.

For the pillow front and back, cover 11 inches of cord with printed satin; baste cord along upper cone edge and around corner (as shown on pattern). Cover remaining cord in pink. On the front, baste cord along seam line completely around the pink fabric except for the part sewn to the cone by the printed cord. On back, baste cord along seam line where pink fabric will meet printed fabric in finished pillow.

Stitch upper and lower front together. Clip curves; stuff. Sew front to back, right sides together. To turn and stuff, leave seam open between upper and lower back pieces.

● *Cupcake Pillow*

Materials: ½ yard light pink satin (icing); ½ yard printed satin (base); 1

yard muslin; 2⅓ yards ¼-inch cable cord; medium pink and burgundy thread; fiberfill.

Instructions: Using pink thread, zigzag-stitch the upper front; using burgundy thread, topstitch the lower front.

Cover cable cord with remaining pink satin. On pillow front, baste cording around pink fabric on seam line. On back, baste cording along top of printed fabric base where pink will meet printed satin (on finished pillow).

With the right sides together, sew upper to lower pillow front. Clip the curves. Quilt the front according to the general instructions.

With right sides together, join upper and lower pieces of pillow back for 2 inches at each side. Clip curves. Leave rest of seam open for turning. Stitch pillow front to back; complete the pillow according to general instructions.

● *Wedding Cake Pillow*

Materials: ⅞ yard white delustered bridal satin; ⅞ yard muslin; 1⅓ yards white lace (1½-inches wide); 2½ yards ⅞-inch-wide white lace; 3 yards white velvet cording; white thread; fiberfill; tissue paper.

Instructions: Follow general instructions up to and including adding decorative topstitching by machine. Use heavy white thread.

Baste velvet cord at seam line on upper left side of first cake layer. Measure along 9 inches of cord; baste cord in the center of the topstitching line on cake's top layer. Measure 9 inches of cord; baste it to seam line at upper right side. On second and third layers, velvet loops should be 11 inches long. On second layer, baste cord to seam line at layer's top and again ⅓ and ⅔ of

continued

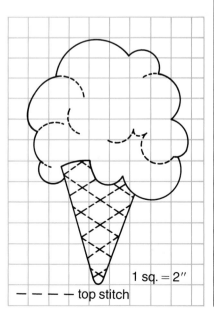

1 sq. = 2"

– – – – top stitch

Continued from page 209
Fresh and Fanciful Trims

distance across topstitching and at right seam line. On third layer, baste cord on seam line at layer's top and again ¼, ½, and ¾ of distance across topstitching and at right seam line.

Sew wide lace directly over topstitching at base of first and second layers, turning raw edges under.

Sew narrow lace along topstitching at top of first, second, and third layers, catching in basted velvet cord.

Baste narrow lace over seam line of pillow top and sides that correspond to top of each cake layer.

With right sides together, stitch base to pillow front; clip curves. Sew wide lace over seam.

Trapunto quilt only the sides of each cake layer, stuffing them lightly. Do not quilt tops of layers. Complete the pillow according to general instructions.
● *Gingerbread Boy Pillow*

Materials: ¾ yard medium brown taffeta; 2 yards white satin or nylon macrame cord; 4 yellow buttons (¾ inch); 2 white buttons (¾ inch); 1 white button (½ inch) for nose; polyester fiberfill; tissue paper.

Instructions: Using general instructions (page 209), enlarge and cut out pattern pieces.

Hand-sew white cord to pillow front along guidelines. Add buttons. Omit quilting and complete according to general instructions.
● *Chocolate Eclair Pillow*

Materials: ⅔ yard beige taffeta; 1 yard dark brown satin; 1 yard muslin; 5 yards cable cord; polyester fiberfill; tissue paper.

Instructions: For eclair base, cut beige taffeta to 32x20 inches. Cut a 6-inch square from each corner.

Sew adjoining 6-inch flaps together in a narrow seam. Cut an 8x20-inch

piece of beige taffeta for a top; stitch this to the base along one long side. Stuff the base; slip-stitch the opening.

Using general instructions, enlarge and cut out pattern pieces and baste satin and lining fabric together.

Cover cable cord with brown satin; baste along seam lines of both brown satin pieces (A, B). Gather curved edges of satin where indicated on pattern B before adding cord. Clip curves.

Sew smaller satin piece A to center of larger one (B) by hand or machine.

Quilt both satin pieces according to the general instructions. To finish, pin brown satin "icing" over beige taffeta base; slip-stitch in place.

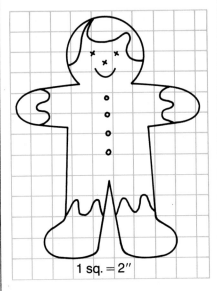

1 sq. = 2"

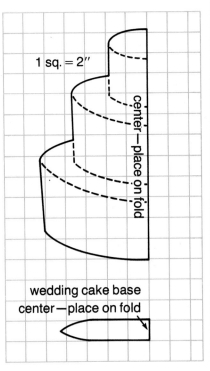

1 sq. = 2"

wedding cake base
center—place on fold

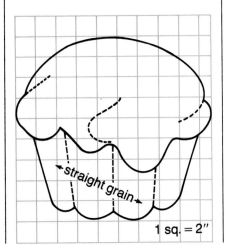

←straight grain→

1 sq. = 2"

Family Satin Stockings
page 203

General Instructions: (*Note:* Materials lists and instructions for individual stockings follow.) Pattern (right) is for 4 stockings: Child's stocking measures 18 inches long from top to toe (unstitched); father's stocking measures 23½ inches; mother's is 22 inches; and baby's is 10½ inches.

Enlarge the patterns; add ⅝-inch seam allowance. Cut 2 stocking shapes from the satin fabric.

Add trims (see specific directions for each stocking); stitch cuff back to stocking back, cuff front to stocking front with right sides together.

Sew stocking back to front, leaving top open. Clip curves, trim seams.

To form lining, cut out the stocking's shape to the fold line *only,* adding seam allowance. Sew lining back to front; insert lining into stocking.

Fold cuff down inside stocking; slip-stitch lower cuff edge to lining top.
● *Father's Stocking*

Materials: 24x28-inch piece of blue satin; 6x22-inch piece of printed crepe-back satin; 24-inch square of white lining fabric; 20-inch length of 1½-inch-wide maroon satin ribbon.

Instructions: To trim, fold satin ribbon in half lengthwise and baste in place along the stocking top with folded edge extending ⅜ inch beyond seam allowance. Stitch stocking to cuff, trim seams, and turn cuff down.

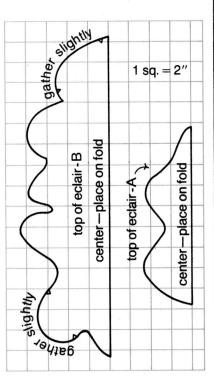

gather slightly

1 sq. = 2"

top of eclair-B
center—place on fold

top of eclair-A

center—place on fold

gather slightly

• *Mother's Stocking*
Materials: 22x25-inch piece of pink satin; 6x20-inch piece of printed or crepe-back satin; 22-inch square of white lining fabric; 18-inch length of ¾-inch-wide lace edging for trim.

Instructions: To trim, baste lace edging along the top of the stocking. Stitch the cuff to the stocking, trim seam, and turn cuff down.

• *Child's Stocking*
Materials: 22x20-inch piece of printed satin; 6x18-inch piece of aqua satin; 18x20-inch piece of white lining fabric; 1⅜ yards of ½-inch-wide crocheted white edging.

Instructions: Center the trim directly over the seam line for the stocking top; baste. Half the edging will show on the finished stocking.

On the cuff, stitch 2 rows of trim close together with the lower edge of the first row 1 inch inside the seam line. Finish the stocking according to the general instructions.

• *Baby's Stocking*
Materials: 18-inch square of white satin; 10x16-inch piece of white lining fabric; 1¼ yards of ½-inch-wide decorative ribbon and lace edging for trim.

Instructions: To trim, remove the lace from the ribbon and baste the lace only along the seam line (gather lace slightly).

On the cuff, stitch the trim with lace attached to one side of the ribbon, 1 inch inside the seam line.

To finish, see general instructions.

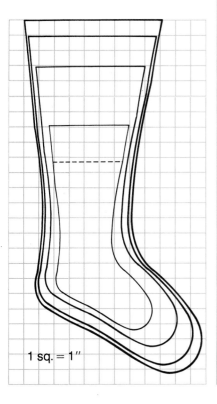

1 sq. = 1"

Yo-Yo Quilt
page 204

Note: Finished size is approximately 76x87 inches; the quilt contains about 3,000 yo-yos.

Materials: Cotton or cotton-blend fabrics in assorted colors and prints (see note below); thread.

Instructions: (*Note:* To reduce the cost of your quilt and take advantage of materials on hand, make yo-yos from old clothes, sewing remnants, or other scrap basket fabrics. You'll need the equivalent of 21½ yards of fabric.)

If you use new material, plan to cut about 140 yo-yos from 1 yard of 44/45-inch-wide fabric.

Make a template from cardboard or a plastic lid; cut as many 3¼-inch-diameter circles from fabric as desired.

To make each yo-yo, turn under raw edges of circle ⅛ inch; run a line of basting/gathering stitches along the edge, using strong thread. Pull gathering thread to draw edges into the center; tie off thread in a double knot. Flatten fabric into a 1½-inch circle.

To assemble the quilt, arrange yo-yos side by side in rows, in any pattern of light and dark shades desired. The quilt shown has simulated blocks about 7½ inches square. Two adjacent sides of most blocks are marked with an L-shaped arrangement of yo-yos all made from the same fabric (see photograph).

Slip-stitch each yo-yo to adjoining yo-yos where they touch. Yo-yos may be first slip-stitched together into blocks (before entire quilt is assembled) to make final assembly easier.

Yo-Yo Stocking
page 204

Materials: Assorted fabric scraps in 5 different prints (we used shades of pink and blue, taking leftover fabric from bow ornaments); ½ yard 36-inch-wide light blue fabric; 1½ yards 2-inch-wide white eyelet edging; 3 yards 1½-inch-wide pink satin ribbon.

Instructions: Using directions for the yo-yo quilt, make about 64 yo-yos for each stocking. Assemble yo-yos into stocking shape, using patterns (below left) as a guide.

Enlarge stocking pattern (below left); cut 2 stockings from blue fabric, adding ½-inch seam allowances. Tack yo-yos to the front of one piece.

Baste eyelet edging around the stocking and sew stocking front to back. Trim seams, turn right side out, and attach pink ribbon bows to corners.

Hearth Scene Pillow
page 204

Note: Finished size is approximately 16x21 inches.

Materials: 1 yard of muslin 8½x18 inches of striped floral print (wallpaper); 5½x18 inches of floral print (floor); 8x20 inches of floral print (narrow border); assorted scraps of print fabrics for design details; three 14x18-inch pieces of quilt batting; 2¼ yards of 2-inch-wide crocheted lace; embroidery floss in pink, orange, brown, black, green, yellow, and gray; needle;
continued

1SQ.= 1/2 IN.

211

Continued from page 211
Fresh and Fanciful Trims

pillow stuffing; dressmaker's carbon.

Instructions: Stitch together one long edge of wallpaper fabric to floor fabric in a ¼-inch seam. Remaining design details are appliquéd or embroidered onto this background piece.

Enlarge pattern on page 211; transfer outlines of design (centered) to background fabric using dressmaker's carbon. Use outlines as placement guides for all design details.

Cut a 14x18-inch piece of muslin for backing. Sandwich 3 layers of batting between backing and top; baste layers together. Using 2 strands of white thread, quilt the floor; space rows and stitches ½ inch apart. Quilt wallpaper in vertical rows of stitches.

When cutting design details for appliqué, add ¼-inch seam allowances. Begin by appliquéing muslin wall moldings along the floor and ceiling.

For the fireplace, cut muslin ½ inch higher and 3 times longer than the fireplace. Tuck fabric as shown on the pattern, turn under raw edges, and appliqué in place. Cut out and appliqué mantel and moldings. Cut brick area from a print scrap; appliqué in place. Using cotton floss, embroider andirons (gray), log (brown), and flame (yellow).

For the clock, appliqué a brown print square in place; sew brown print moldings to top and bottom. Add a muslin square for the face; embroider details in brown and black thread. Appliqué a strip of fabric for the tabletop; embroider base in brown. Appliqué fabric rectangles for vases; add embroidered flowers and stems.

Appliqué sofa fabric in place, embroider wood edging and legs, and finish with a small pillow appliquéd to seat.

For picture, appliqué square fabric frame; top with muslin square and small flowers. Add embroidered stems and leaves. To make braided rug, appliqué ovals in contrasting prints atop one another. For hearth rug, appliqué print fabric; add muslin border.

For narrow print frame around scene, backstitch 1¼-inch-wide strips to top, bottom, and sides. Turn under raw edge ½ inch before stitching.

Cut 2½-inch-wide strips of muslin for top and bottom. Turn under one long edge ½ inch; backstitch to narrow frame. Add muslin strips to sides.

Baste crocheted lace to pillow front, ½ inch from edge. Cut muslin pillow backing to match front. With right sides together and lace tucked inside, stitch back to front, leaving an opening. Turn, stuff, and slip-stitch the opening.

Hardanger Embroidered Ornaments
page 205

Materials: 12x12 inches of #22 count Hardanger cloth (16 ornaments); sixteen 2½- or 3-inch wooden drapery rings; #5 and #8 white or ecru pearl cotton; tapestry needle; embroidery hoop; fabric glue; scissors; white double-fold bias tape; screw eyes; narrow white ribbon.

Instructions: Each pattern (below) represents one quadrant of a design. Repeat as necessary for a complete pattern.

Lightly pencil 3-inch squares on fabric; *don't* cut out squares. Starting in center of square, work satin stitches in #5 thread. Patterns are basic shapes; for variations use lacy filling stitches. Work satin stitches *before* cutting.

Mount fabric in hoop. For open areas, cut away threads bound on 2 sides by satin-stitched blocks (cut threads are missing in diagrams). Using #8 thread, weave over and under pairs of threads remaining in cut areas. Add

picots, festoons, and doves' eyes to centers as desired. (See the photograph for ideas.) Or leave squares uncut and fill them with eyelets.

Cut fabric into squares; glue to backs of rings. Trim excess. Cut bias tape in half lengthwise; glue tape over edge of fabric. Attach screw eye to ring; trim with a ribbon bow.

Fabric Bows
page 205

Materials: 1 yard of 44/45-inch-wide fabric (18 bows); fiberfill or potpourri; slender wire or narrow ribbon.

Instructions: Enlarge pattern (below); cut out pieces. Stitch bow front to back with right sides facing, leaving an opening. Turn, stuff lightly with fiberfill or potpourri; blindstitch.

Stitch tie front to back with right sides facing, leaving an opening. Turn right side out, blindstitch the opening. Fold center along pleat lines.

Wrap tie around center of bow and anchor in place with small stitches. Add ribbon or wire loop for hanging.

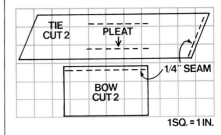

Tea-Party Pillow Dolls
page 205

Note: Finished size is approximately 11x18 inches.

Materials: (for 3 dolls) 1 yard of 45-inch-wide unbleached muslin; fabric scraps in assorted colors and prints; embroidery floss; embroidery needle; scraps of ribbon and lace edging; 1 yard of polyester quilt batting; polyester fiberfill; fabric glue; tracing paper; brown wrapping paper.

Instructions: Cut six 12x20-inch pieces of muslin for front and back doll pieces. Enlarge patterns on page 213 onto brown paper; these are master patterns. Trace them onto tissue paper; cut tissue apart, making patterns for appliqué pieces.

Cut shapes for appliqué from assorted fabric scraps (refer to photograph on page 205 for color and fabric suggestions). Do not add margins to appliqué pieces, except along edges of those pieces that overlap other pieces.

Glue appliqués in place on the doll fronts, using the master patterns as guides. (Be sure to keep dolls A, B, and C separate.) Machine zigzag around each appliqué and along dotted lines on patterns, using matching or contrasting thread. To prevent puckering, place paper beneath muslin while stitching. Add lace and ribbon trims.

Embroider facial features and other details as shown, using floss or a double strand of thread. Color cheeks with a crayon or colored pencils.

Repeat for doll backs.

Using a pencil, lightly draw a stitching line around each doll, starting about ¾ inch from the appliquéd skirts, to mark the edge of the pillow. (Make the front and back shapes the same for each individual doll.)

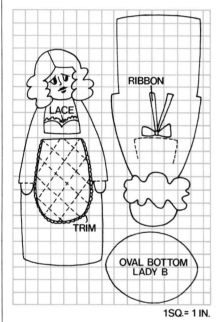

1SQ.= 1 IN.

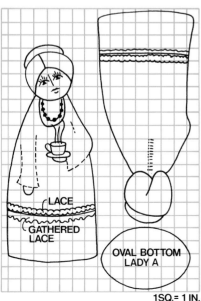

1SQ.= 1 IN.

Cut and pin a piece of quilt batting to each appliquéd panel; machine-stitch along penciled outlines to keep dolls from puckering when stuffed. Trim excess batting.

With right sides facing, match fronts and backs, and stitch them together along outlines, leaving bottoms open. Trim seams and clip curves.

Cut ovals from muslin, adding ¼-inch seam allowance to each piece. Pin to base of dolls and stitch, leaving an opening for turning. Turn, stuff, and slip-stitch openings closed.

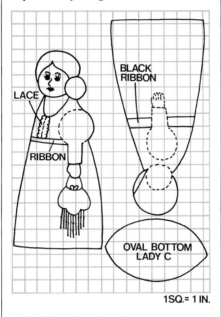

1SQ.= 1 IN.

Tea-Party Tea Cozy
page 205

Note: Finished size is approximately 9x11 inches.

Materials: Four 13-inch squares of muslin; two 13-inch squares of quilt batting; small scraps of fabric in assorted prints and colors; scraps of narrow laces, ribbons, and trims; 1 yard of ⅝-inch-wide lace for cozy edge; stick fabric glue; tissue paper; embroidery floss in black, pink, and colors to match fabrics; embroidery needle; dressmaker's carbon.

Instructions: Enlarge patterns (right) for tea cozy front and back. Using dressmaker's carbon, transfer outlines and facial details to 2 muslin squares (front and back); transfer *only* cozy outlines to remaining 2 squares (lining). *Do not cut out tea cozy shape.*

Using the pattern and the photograph on page 205 as guides, cut design shapes from assorted scraps. For the most attractive results, use diminutive prints in harmonizing colors. Do not add margins, *except* add ¼-inch margins to each piece that overlaps another

piece and to pieces that are next to outside edges.

Arrange and glue fabric pieces to front and back muslin pieces.

Machine satin-stitch over raw edges with matching or contrasting thread. To prevent puckering, place paper behind muslin before stitching. Satin-stitch sleeves and hair detail. Rather than machine stitching the cup and saucer, embroider around these shapes with stem stitch.

Embroider facial details with stem and satin stitches, using black and pink embroidery floss. Color cheeks with crayon or pencil.

Trim dresses. Add buttons and "necklace" of embroidered French knots or coral knots.

Cut quilt batting in shape of tea cozy. Place one piece behind the tea cozy front and one behind the back. Hand- or machine-quilt around the large shapes; quilt apron front along dotted lines shown on pattern.

Baste lace along outlines of tea cozy front. With right sides facing, sew front to lining along bottom outlines; repeat for back. Open up front/lining piece and back/lining piece, creating oval outlines. With right sides facing, stitch the 2 pieces together along the outlines, leaving the top of the lining open for turning. Trim excess fabric, turn, and blindstitch the lining closed. Push lining into tea cozy.

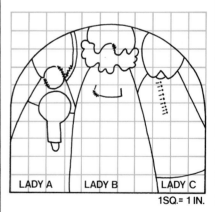

1SQ.= 1 IN.

1SQ.= 1 IN.

A Child's Fantasy Christmas

Treasures for Play and Pretend

Christmas is coming—and flights of fancy abound wherever there are children. Join in the imaginative spirit of Christmas by making your youngsters a soft fireplace, complete with stockings that button onto the mantel. Or "build" a charming Christmas house, with a miniature Santa and his bag full of toys. Directions begin on page 224.

Treasures for Play and Pretend

Cookie-loving crews can combine tastes and talents at Christmastime to come up with a whole troupe of munchable marionettes baked of sugar-cookie dough. Some cookies are destined for special gifts; others star in impromptu cookie capers, which the boys are rehearsing (below).

You and your children will have a ball dressing these puppets in bright, whimsical costumes made with tinted sugar icing (flavored if you wish). Accent their attire with red cinnamon candies, silver cake beads, chocolate sprinkles, or colored sugar crystals—whatever fancy dictates.

Start by mixing up a large batch of cookie dough (1). Place it in the freezer to set for an hour or so, until it is firm.

Next, sketch simple paper patterns for each puppet—one shape for the body and head, and separate shapes for arms and legs (2). Make some figures from the traditional cast of Christmas characters, or design your own shapes from color-book or comic-strip heroes.

Arrange paper patterns on ¼-inch slabs of dough; carefully cut out the dough pieces using a toothpick (3). Add small holes where arms and legs are joined to the body.

Bake and cool the cookies (4), then paint them using tinted icing (5). When icing shapes are completely dry, join the puppet pieces using twists of pipe cleaner held in place with gumdrops. Add colorful strings and crossed wooden slats and puppets are ready to wrap (6) or perform!

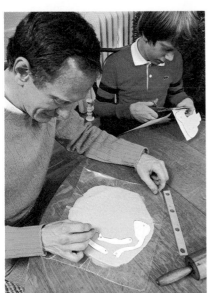

217

Treasures for Play and Pretend

In many homes, reading the story of the birth of Christ to the children in the family is a beloved part of the holiday ritual. This holiday season make the Christmas story come alive for your child with this very special marionette theater. You can craft the stage and scenery and an entire cast of easy-to-make-and-manipulate string puppets. Then let your young producer dramatize his own special version of the Christmas story.

The puppets are made from soft flannel, with felt features and yarn hair. Mary, the shepherd, and the angel (not shown) are 14 inches tall; the remaining figures measure 18 inches. Using a simple basic pattern, make clothing from fabric scraps and embellish the costumes with braids, ribbons, or other trims. Use soft terry cloth for the lamb, and felt and satin scraps for the camel.

When the puppets are completed, suspend them from control bars using nylon fishing line attached to the head, arms, and legs of each figure. Special cuphooks on a rod at the rear of the stage allow some characters to be on stage while the action in the story takes place elsewhere.

The theater for these delightful marionettes is four feet wide—large enough for a couple of youngsters to stage a production together. Build the stage from ½-inch plywood, and the stable and cradle from balsa or ¼-inch plywood. Make movable scenery from small pieces of wood painted with tempera paints, and finish the stage with front and rear curtains mounted on spring rods.

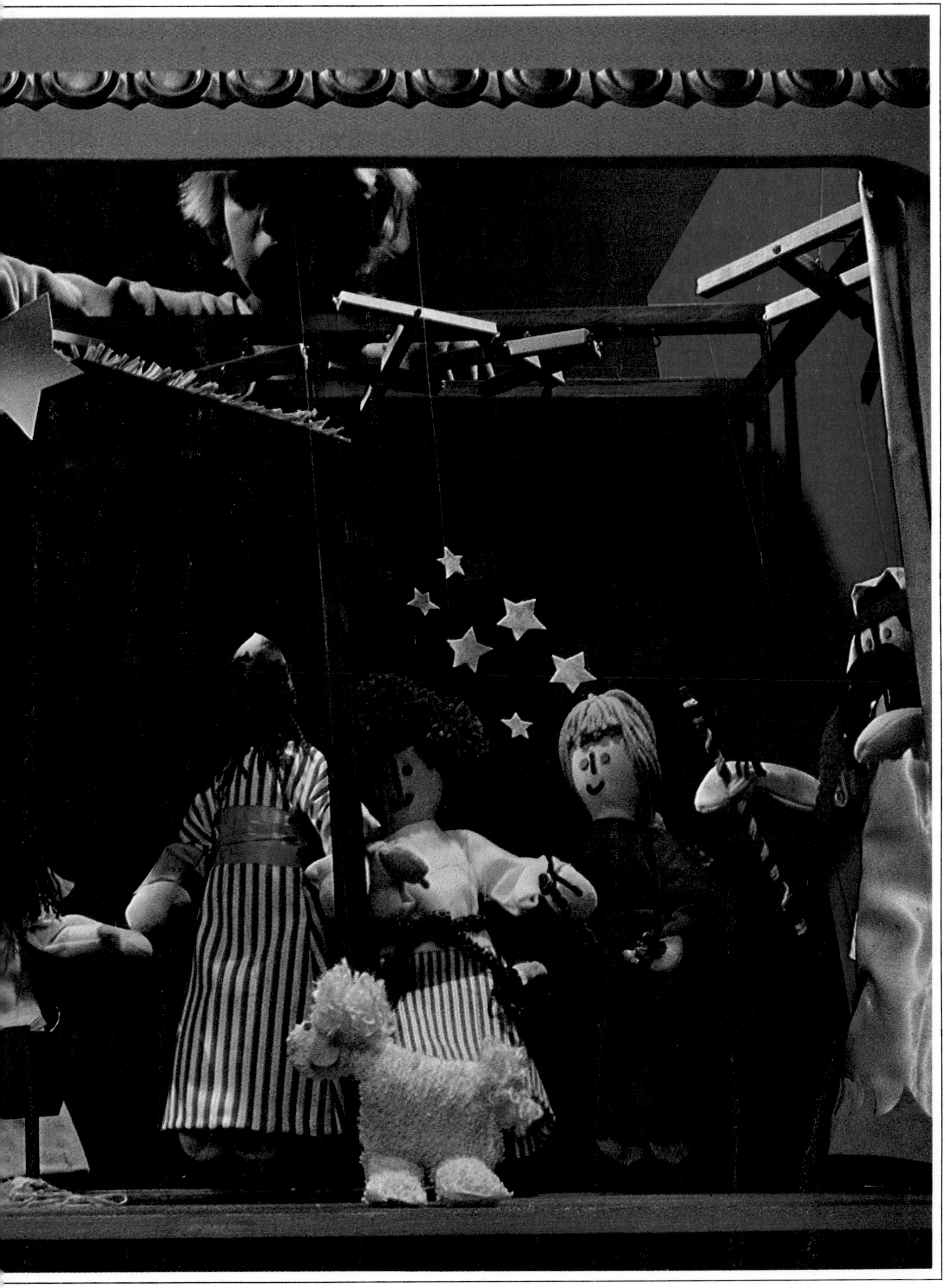

Treasures for Play and Pretend

Just looking at these whimsical Christmas angels will make you feel good all over! Their gingham and lace costumes, heart-stopping smiles, bright button eyes, and flower-bedecked halos are completely captivating—as any child will tell you in a minute.

Make them to hang above the mantel, to brighten a nursery wall, or simply to charm your own little cherubs this Christmas.

From the tips of their toes to the tops of their halos, these angels measure about 30 inches, a delightfully huggable armful for any youngster. If you are a collector of pretty laces and trims, or a saver of remnants from previous projects, you'll find these angels a snap to make.

The sweet little girl angel wears a demure, dotted Swiss apron; a lace-and-heart-trimmed dress; and lacy pantaloons. Dress the boy angel in a ruffled shirt, red velour pants and suspenders, and sporty red canvas baby shoes and infant's socks.

Make the heads, hands, and legs of muslin. Embroider broad grins on each of the faces and trim them with heart-shaped appliqués. Stitch gingham-covered buttons in place for eyes.

Sew the curly hair to the angels' heads with knitting yarn, using a loop stitch. Then tie pretty embroidered ribbon into bows for the girl's hair and a Christmasy bow tie for the boy.

Entwine silk roses, carnations, and other dainty artificial flowers and leaves around a wire frame to make the halos.

Treasures for Play and Pretend

When is a stocking not a stocking? When it's a shoe, of course, inhabited by a little old lady and her band of merry mischief makers! This lady and her six bright-eyed youngsters (below) live in an easy-to-make soft gingham shoe that's been spruced up with embroidered and appliquéd hearts and flowers to please any child who loves nursery rhymes.

This miniature home is only 14 inches high, but there's lots of room inside for toys and other Christmas-stocking stuffers.

If you have a car-crazy kid in your family, why not make him a Christmas "mountain" (opposite), complete with a snow-covered highway and tiny trees? The spiraling mountain road is a perfect place to display a fine collection of pint-sized cars and trucks at Christmastime.

This 30-inch table decoration is made with quilt batting wrapped around a plastic foam cone and trimmed with red felt. Use twisted lengths of green yarn for the guard railing.

Instructions for a Child's Fantasy Christmas: Treasures for Play and Pretend

The instructions below and on the following pages are for the decorations and gifts shown on pages 214–223. For directions for enlarging and transferring designs and patterns, see the glossary, pages 370–371.

Soft Fireplace
page 214

Note: Finished size is approximately 44x60 inches.

Materials: (all fabric measurements refer to 44/45-inch-wide cotton broadcloth) 2⅔ yards green, 1 yard brown, ⅞ yard black, ¾ yard light print, ½ yard red print, ⅓ yard gold, ¼ yard blue, ¼ yard red, ⅛ yard white, ⅛ yard khaki, ⅛ yard red polka dot; #5 DMC perle cotton in the following colors—white, gold, brown, blue, red, green, black, khaki; basting thread; three #003 (⅝ inch) buttons to cover for stockings; polyester fiberfill; pieces of 44x60-inch polyester quilt batting; brown wrapping paper; tissue paper; quilting hoop or frame; needles.

Instructions: The background for the quilt top is pieced by machine. All detail pieces are appliquéd during the quilting process.

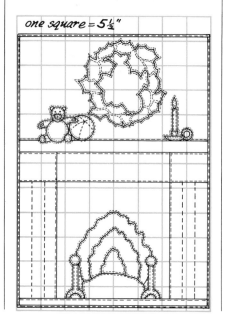

one square = 5½"

Enlarge pattern (below left) on brown paper. Lay tissue paper over brown paper pattern; trace around pattern pieces for holly leaves, candle, candle holder, candle flame, logs, bear, ball, andirons, 3-part fire flame, bear face, paws, and ears. Add ¼-inch seam allowances to all sides of these pieces.

Cut fabric as follows: Green—cut 2 pieces each 32x47 inches, 6 stocking pieces (use pattern on page 17), 18 holly leaves, and 1 candle; brown—cut 1 piece 7½x27 inches, 2 pieces 7½x10½ inches, 2 pieces 10½x26 inches, and 1 each of log and bear patterns; black—cut 1 piece 26x27 inches; light print, cut 1 piece 24¾x44 inches; red print, cut 1 large flame; gold—cut 1 candle holder, 2 andirons, and 1 medium flame; blue—cut 1 ball and 2 stocking pieces; red, cut 4 stocking pieces, 1 small fire flame, and 1 candle flame; white—cut 1 piece 3½x 44 inches; khaki—cut 1 piece 2¼x44 inches and bear face, paws, and ears; red polka dot—cut 12 circles for berries.

With right sides facing, stitch 2 green pieces together (½-inch seam) to form backing piece measuring 47x63 inches.

With right sides facing, stitch quilt top together in the following sequence (½-inch seams): Stitch 7½x27-inch-piece of brown to 27-inch side of black; press seam open. Then, stitch 7½x 10½-inch-piece of brown to 10½x26-inch-piece of brown; press seam open. Repeat with two like pieces. Then, stitch these pieces to opposite sides of first black and brown section. This completes basic fireplace. Add 2½x44-inch khaki strip for floor at bottom of fireplace.

Stitch 3½x44-inch white mantel to top of fireplace section, and stitch 24¾x44-inch light print wallpaper to mantel. Press all seams open.

Carefully turn under ¼-inch seam allowances on all detail pieces except stockings and holly berries. Pin and baste these detail pieces in position.

To assemble: Lay green backing wrong side up on a table and spread 2 layers of batting on top; spread fireplace top face up, centered atop batting and backing. Pin and baste through all 4 layers, taking long running stitches di-agonally from corner to corner and through horizontal and vertical centers. Mount on quilting hoop or frame.

Following quilting lines on pattern, quilt through all 4 layers using perle cotton to match each color of quilt top. Surface-stitch contrasting bear face, eyes, ball, and log details.

Remove quilt from frame and remove all basting stitches. Trim batting to match quilt top size, if necessary. Fold backing fabric to front, forming a half-inch seam binding on all sides of quilt. Pin and baste binding into position, making certain raw edges are concealed. Miter or butt corners; quilt through all layers with perle cotton.

● *Holly berries*

Baste along seam line of each berry circle using heavy thread. Pull up stitches slightly to form a pouf; stuff lightly with fiberfill. Pull gathers together more tightly; stuff pouf until firm and full. Tie off ends of gathering thread. Stitch berries to holly leaves.

● *Stockings*

You'll need 3 stockings: 1 green with red lining, 1 red with green lining, and 1 green with blue lining. To make green stocking with red lining, place 2 green stocking pieces with right sides together and stitch (½-inch seams) down back side, across foot, and up front, leaving top free. Turn.

Embroider "MAMA" at top of red lining using satin stitches and perle cotton. (Be sure to embroider in an upside-down fashion as this red cuff will be turned to outside of stocking when finished. Embroider "PAPA" and "BABY" on other stockings.) Stitch 2 red stockings together; do not turn.

Cut 2 layers of quilt batting from stocking pattern on page 17 (omit seam allowances). Slip the red stocking (lining) inside the green one, sandwiching a layer of batting between stocking and lining. Align tops of stocking. Turn raw edges of both stockings toward each other to inside; slip-stitch opening closed. Turn cuff down about 3 inches. Make a small hanging loop from perle cotton; attach to upper cuff corner.

Cover 3 buttons with white fabric and tack them to center and sides of mantel. Hang stockings from buttons.

Christmas House
page 215

Materials: ½ yard yellow fabric; ⅔ yard white piqué; scraps of calico, sheer, and green fabrics; 1½ yards white medium rickrack; ¼ yard red baby rickrack; quilt batting; ⅔ yard interfacing; 8x12x12-inch cardboard box; 18-inch cardboard circle; white, green, and black embroidery floss; ¼ yard red cotton; scrap of pink cotton; ½ yard synthetic fur trim; 1¼-inch plastic foam ball; black and green felt; ½ yard of ¼-inch-wide black ribbon; ½ yard of ¼-inch-wide red ribbon; white pompon; scraps of 1-inch plastic foam; white yarn.

Instructions: Enlarge patterns (right and on page 226). Make patterns for shutters, windows, and bushes. Cut house from cardboard box; tape sides so they're secure. Cut cardboard to size for roof. Tape.

Adding ½-inch seam allowance, cut house of yellow fabric, interfacing, and batting. Baste together, with batting in middle. Cut windows from sheer fabric; sew them to the house with a running stitch and black floss. Divide them into fourths for panes.

Cut curtains from calico; sew ⅛-inch hem in top and bottom. Slit the center, and hem both sides of the opening. Gather curtains so they fit windows. Tie back sides with yarn. Sew to windows.

Cut each green shutter double, adding ⅛-inch seam allowance. With right sides together, sew 3 sides. Turn, press, and fold raw edges inside. Sew to windows, covering side edges of curtains, using a short running stitch.

Cut dormers, door, and cornices from piqué, adding ⅛-inch seam allowance. Cut door and cornices double. Sew door to facing; turn and press. Stitch cornices to facings along curves; turn and press. Sew dormer (raw edges turned under), door, and cornices to house using running stitches. Use black floss on door and dormers, and white floss on cornices, as shown.

Cut bushes from green calico, adding seam allowances. Turn under raw edges and sew to house, stuffing lightly.

Baste side seams of house and fit fabric over box. Make adjustments for snug fit, remove from box, and stitch. Sew rickrack along corners. Again slip house over box and glue raw edges to top and bottom of box, using pins to hold them in place until the glue dries.

Cut a 20-inch circle of piqué and 18-inch circles of batting and interfacing. Baste long stitches around edge
continued

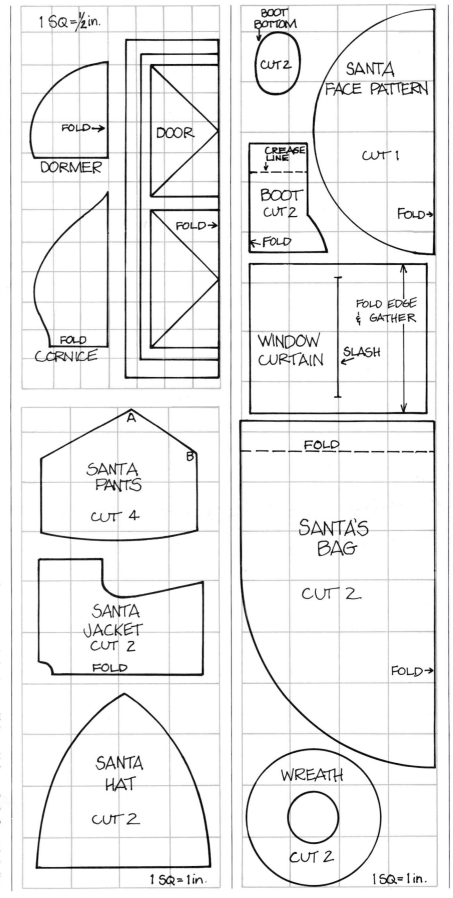

225

Continued from page 225
Play and Pretend

of piqué. Tack the 3 layers together using white French knots. Stretch the fabric over the cardboard circle, pulling up the gathers in the piqué for a snug fit. Tape raw edges. Glue calico circle to bottom of base.

Slip-stitch house firmly to base.

Stitch together wreath pieces on inner and outer edges; trim outer edge using pinking shears. Glue rickrack to front; add bow; sew wreath to door.

For Santa, cut out red Santa suit, adding ⅛-inch seam allowance. Sew hat together. Sew pants, first stitching along A–B on pattern, then sewing inseams and sides. Cut center front of jacket; sew front to back at shoulders.

Cut fur in half lengthwise. Bind raw edges of jacket sleeves with fur. Sew sides of jacket; bind front and lower edges. Bind lower edge of hat with fur.

Cut face from pink fabric. Lightly pad foam ball with batting and wrap face fabric over it, securing with a twist of wire at the neck. Make hands by covering small pieces of batting with pink fabric. Tie tightly with a short length of embroidery floss.

Tack hands into sleeves, then tack jacket to head and sew up jacket front. Stuff jacket lightly.

Cut black felt boots. Whipstitch boot fronts to crease line; add bottoms. Stuff lightly. Fold down tops; tack pant legs into boots. Stuff pants lightly.

Slip jacket over pants and stitch the two firmly together.

For beard, wrap yarn around a 2x3-inch piece of paper. Machine-sew ¾ inch from long edge; tear away paper. Fold short loops over longer ones and tack beard to head with ends in center back. Pull hat over head and tack. Add tiny pompon to top of hat.

Make black French-knot eyes on Santa's face. Gather ½-inch circle of red cotton into a ball for nose. Tack in place. Tie black ribbon around waist for belt. Tack or snap Santa to round base.

Cut out Santa's bag, sew sides, and make casing for ribbon. Plump with stuffing. Tack or snap to base.

For packages, cut plastic foam into tiny "boxes," wrap with fabric, and tie with ribbon. Tack or snap to roof and base. Make doll head of fabric wrapped around stuffing. Add a dress accented with lace.

Cookie Puppets
pages 216–217

Materials: For cookie dough—6 cups flour, 1 cup butter *or* margarine, 2 cups brown sugar, 2 eggs, 1 cup milk, 1 tsp. vanilla, 1 tsp. salt, 1 tsp. baking soda, 1 tsp. baking powder; for frosting—1 lb. confectioners' sugar, 3 egg whites, ⅛ tsp. cream of tartar; food coloring in red, yellow, orange, blue, green, and purple; small gumdrops; pipe cleaners; six 8-inch sticks; colored string for hanging; white glue; waxed paper; paintbrushes.

Instructions: To make cookie dough, cream butter; add sugar. Beat till fluffy. Add vanilla and eggs; mix. Stir in milk. Sift together flour, salt, baking soda, and baking powder. Mix till thoroughly blended. Cover and freeze for at least 30 minutes.

Keep dough refrigerated, taking out 1 cup of dough at a time for each puppet. (Cold dough is more manageable.)

Place chilled dough between 2 sheets of waxed paper. Roll dough to ¼-inch thickness.

Design your own cookie puppet patterns on tracing paper. Basic puppets consist of head and body (5 inches long by 2½ inches wide), 2 arms (3½ inches long), and 2 legs (4 inches long). Draw patterns onto flattened dough with a toothpick. Make holes where indicated on drawing. Remove excess dough.

Bake on foil-lined cookie sheet in a 400-degree oven for 10 minutes or until light brown. Let cool before removing.

Mix all icing ingredients till smooth. Divide icing into 7 small bowls. Add food coloring to all but one bowl. As you "paint" the cookies, keep the icings covered. For puppet details, use toothpicks and sturdy brushes.

To connect puppet sections, cut four 3-inch lengths of pipe cleaners. Form a small loop in one end of the cleaner; bend it back toward the cleaner at a 90-degree angle. Thread the pipe cleaners through the parts to be connected from the cookie backs. Place a gumdrop over the blunt end of the pipe cleaner to hold it in place.

To string puppets, place cookies on flat surface with puppet arms and legs hanging downward. Using square knots, tie strings to ends of puppet limbs and to hole in head. Cut strings so each extends 12 inches above the puppet head. For extra strength, place a dab of white glue on top of the knot.

Drill 1 hole ½ inch from the end of each stick and another hole in the middle of each stick. Cross the sticks. Bring puppet head string through the center stick holes and tie to upper stick, using a square knot. Bring arm strings up through the ends of 1 stick, leg strings to the other. Secure in place with square knots; add white glue to knots. Allow to dry.

1 SQ = 1½ in.

ROOF

FOLD

HOUSE

Marionette Nativity
page 218

Materials: 2½ yards soft flannel; yarn; felt and fabric scraps; 17 feet of ⅝-inch-diameter dowel; self-hardening clay; screw eyes; fiberfill; ¾x6x48 inches pine lumber (control bars, stage and stable supports); 4x7 feet of ½-inch plywood (stage); 1x2 feet of ¼-inch plywood or balsa (stable and crib); nylon fishing line; nails; wood glue; cup hooks; two 47-inch spring curtain rods.

Instructions: To make puppets, enlarge patterns (right); cut 6 large puppets and 3 small ones from flannel. For small puppet, cut eight 2¼-inch lengths of ⅝-inch dowel; for large puppet, cut eight 3-inch lengths.

Sew around body front and back, right sides together, leaving 2 inches open at top. Turn; stuff hands with fiberfill. Topstitch on dotted line at wrists. Insert dowel in lower arm and topstitch along line. Insert dowel above elbow and stitch. Insert dowel in lower legs; topstitch at knees. Insert dowels in upper legs; stitch.

Stuff body and head firmly. Close head by hand. Make hair using yarn and referring to photograph for design ideas. Cut facial features from scraps of felt and glue into place; or embroider features using floss.

Make feet from clay in proportion to body and insert screw eye firmly into top back of foot. Bake or let air dry. Paint feet a dark color and cover the soles with felt. Sew screw eye by hand onto the bottom of the leg.

● *Clothing and trim*

Using basic pattern, stitch clothes to fit puppets. Add fabric, braid, and other trims to clothing, referring to photograph for ideas. Tack clothes to puppets at neck and wrists.

Cut wings from light cardboard and cover with shiny fabric or paper. Sew to back of angel body.

● *Lamb*

Following pattern, cut 2 lamb body pieces and four 2x3-inch legs from terry cloth or white fur fabric. Fold leg pieces in half lengthwise; stitch along bottom and side. Turn; stuff almost to top.

Place legs into base of lamb body. Stitch body closed, leaving an opening. Turn right side out. Stuff and close.

Decorate lamb with wool yarn atop head and tail. Add felt ears and eyes.

● *Camel*

Cut camel parts from wool or satin and assemble the same as lamb. Topstitch at knees and add small clay feet. Attach cotton or satin bundles using hand stitching and cord.

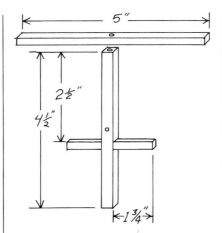

● *Puppet control bar*

Following diagram cut parts from ¾x¾-inch wood. Screw long bars together as shown. The bars should move freely.

Glue on short bars. Attach screw eyes to ends of long and short crossbars, and at center point between short crossbars. Place cup hook on top opposite from screw eye.

To string puppets, cut five 20-inch lengths of transparent fishing line. Sew line to wrists, knees, and top of head. Tie head string to screw eye in middle of short crosspiece. Tie hand strings to ends of small crosspiece and leg strings to ends of long crosspiece. Cut off excess.

● *Stage*

Cut stage parts from ½-inch plywood, following diagrams. Glue and nail front over sides and base.

On front piece inside stage, nail and glue on ¾x¾x47-inch supports (cut from pine board) where shown.

Cut two ¾x¾x16-inch bars, and nail and glue in place.

Cut one ¾x¾x46½-inch rod. Screw angle irons ¾ inch from each end. Screw on cup hooks 5 inches apart to hold puppets.

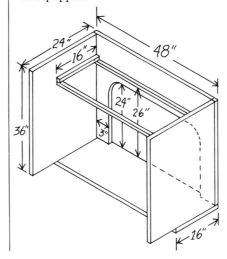

● *Curtains and background*

Mount spring-type curtain rods inside front and back of stage. Sew curtains to fit; attach fringe to front curtain.

Cut dome-shaped hills from ¼-inch plywood to fit in stage. Nail 1x2-inch boards between hills so they stand. Paint green; decorate with flowers.

From plywood or balsa, cut star to fit on manger. Paint star white and rays gold. Trim with gold cord if desired.

continued

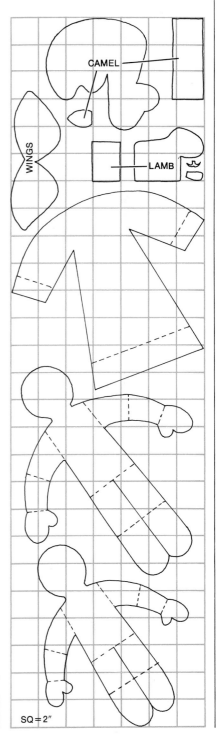

CAMEL

WINGS

LAMB

SQ = 2"

Continued from page 227
Play and Pretend

● *Crib*

Cut pieces from ¼-inch plywood or balsa. Make sides 2½ inches wide at the bottom, 4¼ inches wide at the top, and 2 inches tall. Cut end pieces to fit between sides. Cut a 2½x2½-inch bottom and glue all parts together. Glue short legs to bottom.

● *Stable*

Follow diagram (below), cutting parts from ¼-inch plywood or balsa. Use ¾x¾-inch wood for posts. Glue and nail parts together.

When stage and stable are assembled, sand all edges smooth (or apply veneer tape to plywood edges). Then stain the pieces or paint them in the colors of your choice. Varnish if desired.

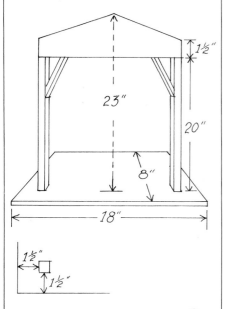

Gingham and Lace Angels
page 220

Materials: *For each angel*—¼ yard unbleached muslin; ⅜ yard eyelet or lace; ⅜ yard white cotton; ½ yard 3-inch-wide lace trim; two ⅝-inch button forms; scrap of green gingham; brown 4-ply knitting worsted; fiberfill; green floral wire; artificial flowers and leaves; red embroidery thread; 2 small heart appliqués; yarn needle; monofilament fishing line.

For girl angel: 1 yard red and white gingham; ¼ yard white dotted swiss; 1½ yards of 1¼-inch-wide lace; 1 yard of 2½-inch-wide gathered lace; 1½ yards of 1¼-inch-wide beader eyelet; 2 yards red ribbon; ½ yard white ribbon; 1½ yards green ribbon for beader eyelet; 1½ yards of 1½-inch-wide lace; 1 yard of 1¼-inch-wide green gingham

ribbon; ½ yard heart and leaves appliqué trim.

For boy angel: ¼ yard red and white gingham; ¼ yard red cotton terry velour; 1 yard of 1¼-inch-wide beader eyelet; 1½ yards red ribbon; 1 yard green ribbon for beader eyelet; ½ yard of 1¼-inch-wide green gingham ribbon; three ⅝-inch brass buttons; two 1¼-inch brass buttons; size 1 red baby shoes; infant's red stretch socks.

General Instructions: Enlarge the pattern, and cut the head, arms, and legs of muslin; the wing of eyelet; and wing lining of white cotton. Cut remaining pieces as noted in the specific instructions that follow. Add ¼-inch seam allowance to all pieces.

Embroider the mouth on the head front. Cover buttons with green gingham; sew to the face. Tack heart appliqués at ends of the mouth. Sew head front to back, right sides together, leaving a small opening. Turn, stuff, and whipstitch the opening closed.

Using a double strand of knitting worsted and the loop stitch, make hair as shown on front of head. Cover top half of the head back. Set aside.

Pin and stitch lace trim to the arm, referring to the photograph for placement. Pin sleeve to the arm, wrong sides facing. Stitch the center of the sleeve, dividing arms. Stitch sides of the sleeve to the arm. Stuff arms.

Pin wing to wing lining. Add beader eyelet. Complete wing and rest of body as noted in specific instructions.

Hand-stitch head to the body, as shown in the photograph. Add bows and shoes as noted below.

Bend floral wire into an arc and twine it with artificial flowers and leaves for a halo. Using yarn, attach ends firmly to the back of the head at the position shown. Make more hair loops, if needed, to hide the ends of the halo.

Hang angels with fishing line.

● *Girl Angel*

Cut body back, dress, and sleeve from red gingham. Cut apron from dotted swiss.

Assemble head, sleeves, and wing, according to the general instructions. Baste gathered lace trim to top and end of wing. (It will be sewn into the wing seam later.) Run ribbon through beader eyelet and tack eyelet in place.

Stitch legs to dress. Pin and stitch lace, beader eyelet, and appliqués on skirt and legs. Stitch center of legs.

Refer to the photograph on page 221 as you sew, if necessary.

Sew lace around 3 sides of the apron and down the apron front. Gather the apron top to fit the side of the dress where arms will be attached (about 7

inches). Place the right sides of the arm and dress together and pin at the ends. Slip the apron top between the arm and the dress; pin. Baste and stitch the 3 layers together.

Pin the lower edge of the wing to the upper dress, right sides together; stitch, completing the front of the angel.

Pin and stitch front and back of angel together (right sides facing), leaving an opening between wing base and dress bottom. Clip curves and corners. Turn; stuff. Whipstitch opening closed. Topstitch seam between wing and dress. Sew head to body. Add bows on head, arms, dress, and pantaloons.

● *Boy Angel*

Cut shirt front, back, and sleeve of red gingham; feet of muslin; pants of red velour.

Make head and sleeve, following the general instructions. After sewing eyelet to the wing, weave red ribbon through it; tack in place. Stitch wing front to

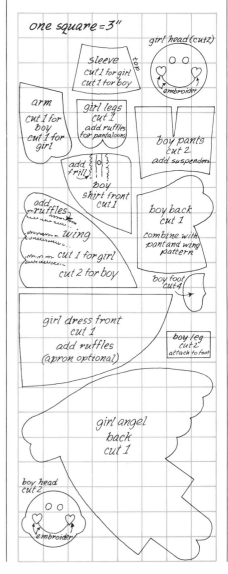

back and back lining, with the right sides of eyelet wings together. Leave the bottom of the wing open. Turn and stuff. Machine-stitch bottom edge closed. *Do not* turn seam allowance to the inside. It will be sewn into the body during final assembly. Set wing aside.

Pin and stitch beader eyelet and lace to shirt front. Weave ribbon through eyelet; tack in place. Sew small brass buttons in place.

Sew shirt front to pants front, right sides together. For suspenders, fold a narrow piece of red velour in half lengthwise, right sides together. Stitch the long seam; then stitch ends into a "V." Turn, press, and pin to shirt front. Tack ends to pants with brass buttons. Pin top of suspenders to top of shirt.

Pin and stitch right sides of arm and shirt front together.

With right sides together, stitch 2 pieces for one foot around bottom curves. Repeat for second foot.

Fold legs in half, right sides together; stitch. Sew legs to feet, matching leg seam with back of foot seam. (The new seam between the foot and leg makes the ankle.) Turn; stuff the foot only. Sew the front of the legs to the center of the front pant leg bottoms.

Stitch shirt back to pants back, right sides together.

Sew stuffed wing to right side of body front. With right sides together and wing tucked inside, sew body back to front. Stitch around outside edges, leaving an opening along the lower pants side and at the leg back. Stuff, and whipstitch the openings closed.

Sew the head to the body according to general instructions. Tack bow tie and bows to the arms and wing. Add shoes and socks.

Old-Lady-in-the-Shoe Stocking
page 222

Materials: ½ yard green and white gingham; ⅓ yard red and white polka-dotted fabric; ⅛ yard green and white polka-dotted fabric; ⅛ yard small brown print; pieces of felt in assorted colors; quilt batting; black, red, pink, yellow, brown, and green #5 pearl cotton; 2 yards ¼-inch-wide red grosgrain ribbon; scraps of eyelet lace; fusible webbing; white glue.

Instructions: Enlarge the patterns (right) and lightly trace the stocking, tongue, and design details onto the gingham. Include the ⅝-inch seam allowance when tracing the patterns.

Embroider stems and leaves in green and flowers in red, pink, and yellow using simple stitches such as stem and chain stitches and French knots.

Cut 4 pairs of shutters from the green and white polka dot, and 4 windowsills and a doorway from the brown print. Iron them to the stocking using fusible webbing. Embroider a black line across the top of each window. Cut and glue 8 red felt hearts to the shutters.

Cut the children's heads, hands, and clothes from felt, and embroider black French knots for eyes. Then embroider black, brown, and blond hair. (You may find it easier to embroider the features before you cut out the felt pieces.) Braid six 6-inch pieces of pearl cotton and tack them to one of the girls' heads. Glue felt pieces to windows.

Cut a cat from brown felt; embroider brown eyes and whiskers. Glue cat inside doorway. With red thread, buttonhole-stitch eyelets.

Transfer roof and roof designs onto polka-dotted material. Embroider roof tiles and chimney in black. Cut a gingham dormer and a brown print dormer roof. Fuse in place.

Cut the old woman's head, hands, and dress from felt, and embroider black French knots for eyes. Tack 2 rows of narrow lace to the head and 1 row to the dress for a cap, collar, and cuffs. Glue pieces inside window.

Cut 4 red and white polka-dotted roofs (including embroidered one) and 2 roofs from batting. Cut 4 gingham shoes (including embroidered one) and 2 shoes from batting. Cut 2 tongues of gingham and 1 of batting.

Pin the front of the shoe to the lining and the batting, layering the pieces in the following order: front of shoe, right side up; lining, right side down; and quilt batting. Sew the pieces together in a ⅝-inch seam, leaving a 2-inch opening for turning. Layer and sew all the pieces this way; then turn, and slip-stitch the openings.

Blindstitch the front and back of the shoe to the tongue, keeping the tongue's straight (back) edge even with the top of the shoe. Blindstitch the front of the roof to the front of the shoe, across the top. Repeat the same procedure with the back.

Thread a needle with red ribbon and lace the front of the shoe by moving the ribbon in and out of each eyelet. Attach a hanger to the top.

Christmas "Mountain"
page 223

Materials: ⅓ yard 72-inch-wide red felt; 24 small trees; 1 skein green yarn; 5 yards polyester fiberfill; 30-inch-high foam cone; wire stems.

Instructions: Start at top of cone twist 1½ yards fiberfill over cone. On first 2 rows use 2 thicknesses—on third row, 3 thicknesses; fourth row, 4 thicknesses. Push V-shaped pieces of wire into cone to hold batting.

Cut felt into 4-inch-wide strips. Roll felt to cover batting, then attach to cone with wire stems. Braid lengths of yarn down spiral to simulate railing.

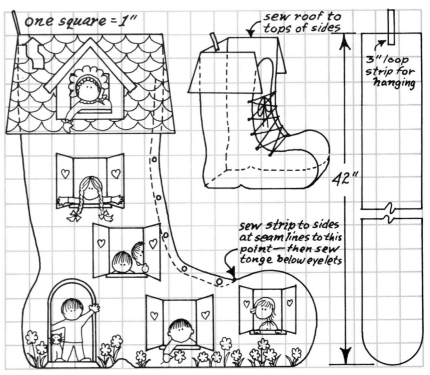

A Child's Fantasy Christmas

Stockings

In most homes with children, Christmas begins very early in the morning on December 25th. Scarcely have Santa's tracks been covered before youngsters, previously restrained by weeks of good behavior, are dashing out of bed ready to claim their just rewards. Chances are the kids make a beeline straight for their Christmas stockings, bulging with treasures and treats from the toys spilling over the top to the plump, juicy orange in the toe.

Children are so fond of stockings that in many families Christmas isn't complete without them. Large or small, plain or fancy, old or new, they are an essential part of the Christmas celebration.

Making stockings can be just as much fun as exploring their contents on Christmas morning. The ribbon stockings shown here, for example, are so simple to make that the kids easily can help put them together. The other stockings shown in this section also are guaranteed child-pleasers.

Directions for the projects begin on page 236.

Stockings

If your children are eager to make their own Christmas stockings, give them a handful of ribbons or fabric strips and set them to weaving new fronts for their old stockings. All you'll have to do is help the kids fuse the ribbons in place and add the cuffs.

Knitted stockings (opposite) require a little more effort on your part. These stockings are stitched in graduated sizes, just like "real" knitted socks.

To transform threadbare stockings from Christmases past into crisp and colorful "new" ones, start with four to six pretty patterned ribbons (½ to 1½ inches wide) for each stocking. Or use fabric that's been cut into strips with pinking shears. You'll also need some fusible webbing, cable cord, and scraps of velveteen or corduroy for the cuffs.

Cut a piece of fusible webbing the same size as the front of the stocking and pin it to a piece of cardboard. Arrange four to six patterns of ribbon or fabric diagonally across the webbing and pin the ends in place. Then weave a top layer of ribbons in and out of the first layer on the opposite diagonal, so the edges of the ribbons meet at right angles.

Trim the ends of all the ribbons about ¼ inch beyond the webbing, and stitch around the edge to hold the ribbons in place.

Cover the cable cord with fabric or ribbon and tack it around the stockings with both raw edges toward the front of the stocking. Cut a rectangle of cuff fabric about 3 inches wide and long enough to go around the top of the stocking. Seam the short ends together and baste the cording to the upper and lower edges as shown in the photograph.

Assemble the stockings by laying webbing and ribbons atop the stocking with the webbing in the middle. Pin the new front in place to hold it while you turn under the raw edges ¼ inch. Then iron the ribbons, fusing them to the front of the stocking. Hand-tack the folded edges of the ribbons to the covered cording, and stitch the cuff in place along the top.

The angel-trimmed stocking (below left) is the perfect cache for

232

an infant's first Christmas treasures. On the right is an easy-to-stitch plaid design for an older brother or sister; Mom and Dad rate snowflakes and a Christmas tree design.

Directions for the stockings begin here and are continued on page 236. To make all four socks, use Columbia Minerva's "Great Ideas" 100-percent Acrilan acrylic yarn. You'll need two skeins of white and avocado, and three skeins of red.

Use needles in the following sizes: 1 set (4 double pointed) size 9 for Dad's sock (Christmas Tree); 1 set (4 double pointed) size 6 for Mom's sock (Snowflakes); 1 pair size 2 for Baby's sock; 1 pair size 6 for plaid sock.

For Dad's stocking the gauge is 9 stitches = 2 inches. Starting at top edge with Red, cast on 44 sts. Divide sts evenly among 3 needles

(15–15–14). Being careful not to twist sts, join and k 12 rnds. Break off Red, join White; k 2 rnds. Break off White, join Avocado; k 1 rnd. Break off Avocado, join White; k 2 rnds. Break off White, join Red; k 2 rnds. Break off Red, join White; k 2 rnds. Break off White, join Avocado; k 1 rnd. Break off Avocado, join White; k 17 rnds.

Repeat same strip sequence as above, starting with 1 rnd Avocado, 2 rnds White, 2 rnds Red, 2 rnds White, 1 rnd Avocado, 2 rnds White.

Break off White, join Red. Divide sts for heel as follows: With 4th needle, k 11 sts from 1st needle, slip 11 sts from 3rd needle onto other end of 4th needle. There are 22 sts on heel (4th) needle. Rem 22 sts are for instep. Divide instep sts on 2 needles. Turn. Purl across heel sts only.

Continue working heel sts with Red in St st (k 1 row, p 1 row) for 14 rows; end with p row. Turn.

To turn heel: Row 1—k 13, k 2 tog, k 1. Turn. *Row 2:* Sl 1, p 5, p 2 tog, p 1. Turn. *Row 3:* Sl 1, k 6, k 2 tog, k 1. Turn. *Row 4:* Sl 1, p 7, p 2 tog, p 1. Turn. *Row 5:* Sl 1, k 8, k 2 tog, k 1. Turn. Continue same way; work one more st bet dec on every row until 14 sts remain, ending with p row. K across. This is heel needle (1st needle).

Instep for Dad's stocking: With heel needle (1st needle) pick up and k 11 sts along side edge of heel; with free needle (2nd needle) k across sts on two instep needles; with 3rd needle, pick up and k 11 sts along other side edge of heel. With same needle (3rd needle) k first 7 sts from heel needle. There are 18 sts on first and third needles; 22 sts on second one.

233

Stockings

Good things—including stockings—come in all sizes at Christmastime. The elegant black velveteen shorties (opposite) are only 14 inches tall, and the king-size stocking (below) is large enough for the whole family. Tuck tiny, whimsical dolls representing your own family inside.

Make the black velveteen stockings using the basic pattern on page 17. Line them with swishy taffeta or shiny printed satin and trim with crocheted lace, ribbons, or gold braid.

Hearts and flowers bedeck the appliquéd felt stocking. Pockets sewn inside hold the dolls.

Instructions for a Child's Fantasy Christmas: Stockings

Instructions on these pages are for the stockings shown on pages 230–235. For directions for enlarging and transferring designs, see pages 370–371.

Knitted Stockings
page 233

A list of materials for all the stockings is on page 233. Also, directions for the Dad's stocking begin on page 233 and are continued here. For knitting abbreviations, **see** page 371.

To shape instep: Rnd 1—K to within last 3 sts on 1st needle, k 2 tog, k 1; k across sts on 2nd needle; on 3rd needle k 1, sl 1, k 1. psso, k to end of needle. *Rnd 2:* K around. Repeat last 2 rnds alternately until there are 11 sts on 1st and 3rd needles. Sts on 2nd needle remain the same. Now k around all 44 sts until length from center back of heel measures 9 inches.

To shape toe: Rnd 1—K to last 3 sts on 1st needle. K 2 tog, k 1; on 2nd needle, k 1, sl 1, k 1, psso, k to last 3 sts on same needle, k 2 tog, k 1; on 3rd needle, k 1, sl 1, k 1, psso, k to end of needle—4 dec made.

Rnd 2: K around. Repeat last 2 rnds alternately 6 more times—16 sts remain. Leaving a 12-inch length of yarn, break off. Thread darning needle with this end; draw through rem sts. Pull tightly tog; fasten securely. Steam sock lightly through damp cloth.

Finishing: Roll top of sock down; tack to right side so rolled edge forms border with ribbed sts (wrong side) showing. Using Avocado, crochet a 5-inch chain, leaving about 4 inches of yarn at each end of ch. Attach ch to rolled edge, forming loop for hanging. Using 4-inch ends, tie bow.

● *Mother's sock (snowflakes)*

Gauge: 4 sts = 1 inch.

Starting at top edge with White, cast on 44 sts. Divide sts evenly among 3 needles (15, 15, 14). Be careful not to twist sts. Join.

K 18 rnds. Break off White, attach Red, k 9 rnds. Break off Red, attach Avocado, k 8 rnds. Break off Avocado, attach Red, k 9 rnds. Break off Red, attach White, k 6 rnds.

Divide sts for heel: With 4th needle, k 11 sts from first needle, sl 11 sts from 3rd needle onto other end of 4th needle. There are 22 sts on heel (4th) needle. Rem 22 sts are for instep. Divide instep sts on two needles. Turn. P across heel sts only. Continue working heel sts with White in St st (k 1 row, p 1 row) for 14 rows, ending with p row. Turn.

To turn heel—Row 1: K 13, k 2 tog, k 1. Turn. *Row 2:* Sl 1, p 5, p 2 tog, p 1. Turn. *Row 3:* Sl 1, k 6, k 2 tog, k 1. Turn. *Row 4:* Sl 1, p 7, p 2 tog, p 1. Turn. *Row 5:* Sl 1, k 8, k 2 tog, k 1. Turn. Continue in this manner, working one more st bet dec on every row until 14 sts rem, ending with a p row.

Instep: With heel needle (1st needle), pick up and k 11 sts along side edge of heel; with free needle (second needle), k across sts on 2 instep needles; with third needle, pick up and k 11 sts along other side-edge of heel. With same needle (3rd) k first 7 sts from heel needle. There are 18 sts on the first and third needles and 22 sts on the second needle.

To shape instep—Rnd 1: K to within last 3 sts on first needle, k 2 tog, k 1; k across sts on second needle. On third needle, k 1, sl 1, k 1, psso, k to end of needle. *Rnd 2:* K around. Repeat last 2 rnds alternately until there are 14 sts on first and third needles; sts on second needle rem the same. Break off White. Join Red. Continue dec as on rnds 1 and 2 until there are 11 sts on needles one and three. Now work around all 44 sts until there are 8 rnds of Red. Break off Red. Join Avocado. K 8 rnds Avocado. Break off Avocado. Join Red. K 8 rnds Red. Break off Red. Join White. K 6 rnds White. Start toe shaping.

To shape toe—Rnd 1: K to last 3 sts on first needle, k 2 tog, k 1; on second needle. K 1, sl 1, k 1, psso, k to last 3 sts on same needle, k 2 tog, k 1; on third needle, k 1, sl 1, k 1, psso, k to end of needle—4 dec made. *Rnd 2:* K around. Repeat last 2 rnds alternately 6 more times—16 sts remain. Leaving a 12-inch length of yarn, break off. Thread a darning needle with this end; draw through rem sts. Pull tightly tog; fasten securely. Steam press lightly.

Finishing: Roll top of sock down; tack to right side so that rolled edge forms border with ribbed sts (wrong side) showing. Using White yarn, sew cross-stitches scattered across both Red stripes at top of sock. With Red yarn, crochet a 5-inch ch leaving about 4 inches of yarn at each end. Attach ch to rolled edge, forming a loop for hanger. Tie bow with 4-inch ends.

● *Plaid sock*

Gauge: 4 sts = 1 inch. Starting at top with Avocado yarn and No. 6 needles, cast on 36 sts. Work in St st (k 1 row, p 1 row) for 8 rows.

*Drop Avocado, attach White, k 1 row White. Drop White, attach Red, p 1 row, k 1 row. Drop Red, pick up White, p 1 row. Break off White. (When cutting yarn to join new color, leave 8 inches for weaving.) Join Avocado, work 6 rows *. Repeat * to * 2 more times.

Drop Avocado, attach White, k 1 row. Drop White, join Red, p 1 row, k 1 row. Drop Red, join White, p 1 row. Drop White, join Avocado, k 1 row, p 1 row.

Next Row: Sl 10 sts at each end of needle to separate holders or threads, then work across center 16 sts for instep 3 inches; break off yarn. On right side of work k across 10 sts from first holder, pick up 11 sts along side of instep piece, work across center 16 sts of instep, pick up 11 sts along other side of piece, then work across 10 sts on 2nd holder. K across sts in St st 5 rows.

Dec row: K 1, k 2 tog, k 16, sl 1, k 1, psso, k 14, k 2 tog, k 16 to within 3 sts of end of row, sl 1, k 1, psso, k 1. Rep dec row *every* other row three times, having 2 sts less bet center dec each time. Work 2 rows more. Bind off.

To weave plaid stripes: Thread darning needle with 24-inch length of Red. Working loosely, starting ½ inch below top of sock, bring needle up in 2nd st from vertical side of sock. Weave needle over and under (vertically) in threads of rows to point where heel sts are separated from instep sts, always staying in 2nd vertical st. *Sk 4 vertical rows; rep running st in 5th vertical row with Red, in 6th vertical row with White, in 7th vertical row with Red*. Skip 4 vertical rows; finish with Red, running st in next to end vertical row. Weave all loose ends into wrong side of sock. Sew back and sole seams. Weave White running st along back seam.

Finishing: Same as Dad's sock, using Red for loop and bow.

● Baby's sock (angel)

Gauge: 9 sts = 2 inches. Starting at top with Red and No. 2 needles, cast on 38 sts. Work in St st (k 1 row, p 1 row) for 12 rows. Drop Red, join Avocado, k 1 row, p 1 row. Drop Avocado, pick up Red, k 1 row, p 1 row. Break off Red, join White; work 16 rows. Break off White, join Red, k 1 row, p 1 row. Drop Red, join Avocado, k 1 row, p 1 row. Break off Avocado, pick up Red, k 1 row, p 1 row.

Next row: Sl 13 sts at each end of needle to separate holders or threads, then work across center 12 sts for instep 2½ inches; break off yarn. On right side of work, k across 13 sts of first holder, pick up 14 sts along side of instep piece, work across center 12 sts of instep, pick up 14 sts along other side; work across 13 sts on 2nd holder. K across all sts in St st for 7 rows.

Dec Row: K 1, k 2 tog, k across to center 12 sts, sl 1, k 1, psso, k 8, k 2 tog, k to within 3 sts of end of row, sl 1, k 1, psso, k1. Repeat dec row every other row 3 times having 2 sts less bet center dec each time. Work 2 rows more. Bind off. Sew back and sole seams.

Finishing: Same as Dad's sock. Using Avocado yarn, embroider angel on wide White stripe. See diagram.

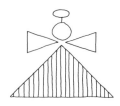

Black Velvet Stockings
page 234

Materials (for each stocking): ⅓ yard black velveteen; ⅓ yard taffeta or satin lining fabric; assorted lace edgings, ribbons, and braids in lengths from 18 to 36 inches.

Instructions: Enlarge the basic stocking pattern on page 17, but alter it so it is only 14 inches high from the toe to the top. Add ½-inch seam allowances to the pattern and cut a front and back from velveteen and from taffeta or satin lining fabric.

Hand- or machine-stitch a variety of trims to front of velveteen stocking, referring to color photograph for design suggestions. Floral motifs also may be cut out of lace yardage and appliquéd in a band to stocking. Baste lace trim along top seam line to make a lacy ruffle or edging along top of finished stocking.

To assemble the stocking, stitch stocking front to back, leaving top open. Clip curves, trim seams, turn, and press lightly. Stitch lining front to back, leaving top open. Insert lining in stocking, turn under top seam allowances, and slip-stitch lining to stocking. For hanging, add a ribbon or velveteen loop to the back corner of the stocking.

Family Stocking and Dolls
page 235

Materials: ½ yard each of pink and red felt; ¼ yard orange felt; scraps of yellow felt; red, yellow, and orange yarn; 30 inches red bias tape; round elastic. *For dolls:* natural or white knit fabric scraps, stuffing, fabric scraps (clothes); embroidery floss; yarn (hair).

Instructions: Enlarge pattern (below); cut 2 pink stockings (outside) and 2 red stockings (lining). Cut 2 orange and pink cuffs. Cut 2 red pockets.

Sew bias tape to top edge of inner pockets; thread with elastic. Stitch one pocket to each side of red lining socks, matching dots.

Carefully cut out hearts, circles, heel, and toe on one pink sock (front). Pin this pink piece to one red lining, matching edges. Embroider red lines beneath rows of motifs, using running stitches across each line twice; always stitch through both layers of felt.

Using red yarn, stitch around heel and toe. Using yellow, stitch around circles and orange toe and heel. Using orange, stitch around hearts.

For each heart, cut 1 pink and 1 yellow pattern. Place yellow heart atop pink one; pin to red in center of cutout. Using yellow thread, whipstitch through all layers around yellow heart. Whipstitch yellow leaf shapes to stocking.

Cut out orange and yellow petals and flower centers. Whipstitch orange flower shapes to stocking; add yellow petals and centers. Note that bottom circle has no yellow petals.

Pin stocking pieces together with red liners in center and pink stockings on outside. Stitch all layers together with red yarn.

Stitch side seams of cuffs to each other, turn and press seams open. Put orange cuff over pink cuff matching side seams, scallops, and edges. Embroider around scallops with red.

Cut 2 strips red felt 1½x6 inches. Fold in half lengthwise, stitch with ¼-inch seam, turn, and press. Fold strips into loops and tack to inside top back of stocking at sides.

Slip orange side of cuff inside sock with right side toward lining. Pin edges, matching side seams of cuff to lining and with loop ends between cuff and lining. Stitch orange cuff edge to sock. Turn cuff straight up; whip pink edge to outer sock front and back.

To make dolls, enlarge pattern and cut front and back for each doll from knit scraps. Stitch pieces together using ¼-inch seams; leave an opening in head. Turn; stuff arms and legs. Stitch joints at shoulders and hips. Stuff torso and head, turn in seam allowance at top of head, and sew opening closed.

Embroider eyes and mouth using floss; make hair with different colors of yarn (perhaps to match hair color of members of your family). Sew dresses, shirts, and pants for dolls from assorted fabric scraps. Tuck dolls into pockets of completed stocking.

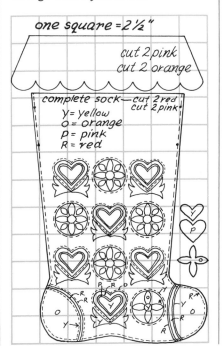

one square = 2½"
cut 2 pink
cut 2 orange
complete sock—cut 2 red
cut 2 pink
Y = yellow
O = orange
P = pink
R = red

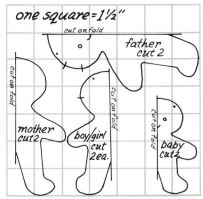

one square = 1½"
cut on fold
father cut 2
cut on fold
cut on fold
cut on fold
mother cut 2
boy/girl cut 2 ea.
baby cut 2

A Child's Fantasy Christmas

Heritage Gifts

Gifting children with toys is one of the special pleasures of Christmas. And among the most popular presents are old-fashioned playthings that have been treasured by generations of youngsters. All of the very special gift ideas in this section have such a heritage. All are toys that echo the style of another era, bringing to mind warm memories—for parents and grandparents —and bestirring the imaginations of children.

When you make any of these designs— investing the care, skill, and materials each requires—you will capture their timeless charm. And because these toys and gifts have been made to last, your children can enjoy them now, then pass them on to their own children in years to come.

What youngster, for example, wouldn't love homesteading with this pint-sized Early American furniture and these adorable parlor dolls? The dry sink, hutch, cradle, and settle are all made from pine. Fabric scraps no bigger than postage stamps are used for the tiny patchwork quilt and sewing remnants for the dolls. Directions for all the projects begin on page 246.

Heritage Gifts

Wooden playthings may not be the fanciest ones that your child owns, but they're apt to be among the best loved. Sturdy and tough to withstand lots of active play, wooden toys are subtly colored and wonderfully textured to stir the imaginations of children and to nourish an appreciation of natural things.

If you give your youngster one of these projects made from a fine furniture wood such as mahogany, maple, or birch, you'll enjoy making it as much as your child will love using it.

A child's first independent excursion is likely to be astride a gentle steed in the nursery. To make those first rides truly memorable, build your youngster or grandchild a rocking horse like this one (below), smooth of form and fleet of line.

The horse measures $12 \times 28 \times 48$ inches and is built of ¾-inch mahogany. When construction is complete, rub on a rich, warm stain, and seal the wood with varnish. Buff the final coat using steel wool to put a sleek, mellow finish on your thoroughbred.

The building blocks (above, left) have an interesting bonus: They're also a puzzle. To store the blocks neatly, a youngster must complete the puzzle, carefully fitting each piece into its appointed place.

The blocks are cut from a fir 2×4; the tray is ¾-inch pine; dowels are 1×3 inches. The blocks may be left unfinished or given a protective coating of satin varnish.

Watch a youngster at play, and you'll see that much of the time he's hard at work. To encourage that natural industriousness, build him a sturdy, child-size wheelbarrow so he can move mountains of sand or haul big loads with ease.

This 12×17×34-inch wheelbarrow is made from 1-inch pine. It's been stained and varnished, but it could easily be painted and decorated with whimsical motifs.

Many an infant has rocked safe and securely in a bonneted cradle like this one (left). The design for this adaptation, made of ¾-inch maple, goes back to 1800—and possibly beyond. The cradle has a 16×32-inch base; the bonnet is 28 inches high. Finish this project with a 3-inch-thick foam mattress covered in your favorite fabric.

If your youngsters have outgrown the cradle, consider crafting an heirloom for their dolls.

241

ᴴHeritage Gifts

Dolls have long been a cherished symbol of childhood. They not only serve as casual playthings but also frequently become intimate confidantes with whom children love to share their most-secret thoughts and fantasies.

Handcrafted dolls are special gifts. Like real people, such dolls are unique—each has a person-ality all its own depending on who makes it and the materials and techniques of construction.

No child could resist one of these rag dolls (below) or old-fashioned wax dolls (opposite), particularly if the doll you make is dressed to resemble an imaginary friend or made from remnants of your child's own clothing.

Rarely will you meet old-fashioned rag dolls with as much chic as this pair of dainty and demure young ladies (below). Dressed to the nines in outfits that include fancy aprons, slips, and pantaloons, these prim ladies can provide hours of fascinating company for a youngster.

The dolls' faces and hands are embroidered in cotton floss. On the muslin body of each doll your youngster will find a special surprise—an embroidered heart (which you can embellish as much or as little as your own heart desires).

Trim the costumes with bits of old lace, pretty buttons, or even a tiny corsage of silk flowers.

Wax dolls have been popular for centuries and much admired for their extraordinary beauty. Any one of these (below) would be welcomed by a young collector. The mama doll stands about 25 inches tall. Hansel and Gretel and the schoolgirl doll are each approximately 16 inches tall.

The waxed heads of these charming dolls are all made in the same way using 3-inch plastic foam balls covered with papier mâché. The facial features are modeled and sculpted in the papier mâché using your fingers or small modeling tools.

When the papier mâché is dry, gently sand the faces until they are smooth. Then stroke on flesh-colored paint and bright eyes, mouths, and cheeks. The mama doll's complexion should be delicate, but the children can have ruddier faces. Dip each head into melted beeswax two or three times to coat the papier mâché. As the wax coatings build up on the heads, the colors on the faces will mellow and take on the soft amber hue traditionally associated with wax dolls.

If this is your first experience making wax dolls, you may wish to practice dipping fruit into wax before you dip the heads. Once you've mastered the technique of coating the fruit in one smooth motion, you'll be able to coat the painted heads with ease.

The dolls' bodies are made of muslin and can be stuffed with fine sawdust or polyester fiberfill. Use the same pattern for the bodies of each of the children. All you need to vary on these dolls is the clothing and the hairstyles.

Make the hair for each doll of soft mohair yarn. Stitch it to a wig base first, styling as you go; then glue it to the heads.

When you make the costumes, bring all your creative needlework skills into play. Embellish Hansel's and Gretel's clothing with peasant-style embroidery, outfit the schoolgirl in an old-time middy blouse, and dress the mama doll in dainty lace threaded with narrow satin ribbon.

"Roughing it" is a favorite pastime of youngsters interested in the pioneers and fascinated by tales of the hunters, trappers, and traders who explored the American frontier. If your child listens spellbound to the adventures of Daniel Boone and other early settlers, he or she will whoop with delight upon discovering this miniature cabin under your tree. Its rustic design and the homey furnishings inside are straight from the wilderness.

Like real frontier houses of yesteryear, this cozy one-room cabin is built of logs around a stone fireplace and chimney. It has a loft for storage, a bearskin rug to warm the floor, and old-fashioned, hand-hewn wooden furniture. The cabin measures 24 inches long, 16 inches wide, and 16½ inches high.

Build the cabin from the ground up using plywood aged with antiquing stain for the floor and ⅝-inch dowels for the logs. Craft the fireplace and chimney by painting "stones" onto a wooden base, using modeling clay to make the stones three-dimensional. After the clay is dry, age the stones with antiquing stain.

Once you've completed basic construction of the cabin, finish the roof using cardboard shingles. Use odd bits of balsa, plywood, Popsicle sticks, and dowels to craft the miniature furniture, and fake fur to make the rug.

Instructions for a Child's Fantasy Christmas: Heritage Gifts

The instructions below and on the following pages are for the toys and gifts shown on pages 238–245. For directions for enlarging and transferring designs, see the glossary, pages 370–371.

Doll Furniture
pages 238–239

Note: Finished sizes are as follows: settle—16×17×6 inches; hutch—24×12×6 inches; cradle—9½×8×12 inches; dry sink—12½×18×7 inches.

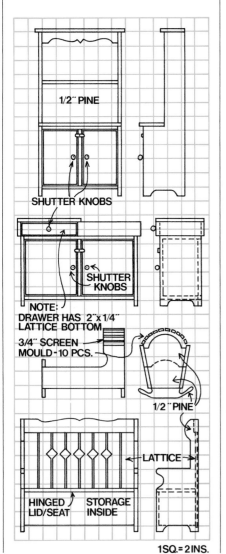

1/2" PINE

SHUTTER KNOBS

SHUTTER KNOBS

NOTE: DRAWER HAS 2"x1/4" LATTICE BOTTOM

3/4" SCREEN MOULD-10 PCS.

1/2" PINE

LATTICE

HINGED LID/SEAT

STORAGE INSIDE

1SQ.= 2INS.

Materials: ½-inch C-select pine; 2-inch-wide lattice (settle and dry sink); ¾-inch-wide screen molding (cradle); 5 shutter knobs; jigsaw; nails; glue; sandpaper; stain; varnish.

General instructions: Enlarge diagrams (left). Cut out pieces; assemble using butt joints, nails, and glue.

After assembling, sand edges to give pieces a soft, aged look and make them safe for children's play. Countersink nails; fill holes. Stain; varnish.

● *Settle*

Assemble from pine *except* cut back from strips of lattice. Make V cuts in lattice as shown; assemble with cutouts in diamond pattern. Back is dadoed into bench top and sides.

After assembling back and sides, attach front of seat and bottom. Seat is 6 inches above the floor and is mounted with pivoting nail hinges to make a lid for the storage box inside.

● *Hutch*

Assemble entirely using ½-inch pine, adding a 2½-inch-deep shelf to the top as shown. Mount doors on pivoting nail hinges and attach a small wood dog between doors to keep them closed. For handles, use shutter knobs.

● *Cradle*

Assemble from pine except for top, which is cut from ¾-inch screen molding. Cut rockers from a separate piece, with grain running horizontally, to prevent breaking.

● *Dry sink*

Assemble from pine except for bottom of drawer, which is made of lattice. Build 2-door chest first; mount tray-and-drawer piece on top. Mount doors on pivoting nail hinges; add a wood dog between them to hold doors closed. Add shutter knobs to doors and drawer for handles.

Parlor Dolls
pages 238–239

Materials for each head: 5-inch-egg-shaped plastic foam head; other foam scraps; brown grocery bag; wallpaper paste; glue; lightweight cardboard; acrylic paints; air-drying clay or papier mâché powder to form nose;

water-base varnish, 6 yards jute or yarn; ¼×12-inch dowel for each head; miscellaneous items (wig and jewelry).

Instructions: Carve thumb-size hole in narrow end of egg slightly behind point for chin, using scissors' points or kitchen knife. Model nose of plastic foam scraps, air-drying clay, or papier-mâché powder. Attach with straight pins. Cut ears about 1 inch long from cardboard; insert into place.

Soak 3×5-inch pieces of grocery bag in warm water. Meanwhile, mix small amount of wallpaper paste with ⅛ quantity of white glue. Remove paper from water, crumple; return to water. Rub paste mixture into hole of egg. Wring out paper; tear into small pieces; dip in paste mixture. Cover entire head with paper pieces, overlapping ¼ inch. Smooth edges with fingers.

Cover dowel using paper; dry and insert into neck. Stand dowel in weighted tumbler. When dowel is dry, sand rough spots. Repeat twice more.

Coat with water-base varnish to seal; sand lightly before applying base coat of white water-base enamel. Paint head flesh color; rub red into cheeks for a rosy blush. Paint eyes and brows with brush or markers.

Hair for doll with purple blouse: Cut 6 yards jute into 9-inch lengths. Set 1 piece aside; stitch other fiber on wig base strip (*see sketch, below*).

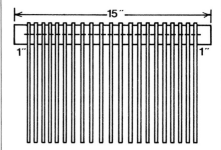

15"

1"   1"

Trim the base strip ¼ inch on each side. Bead glue along the stitching (hair side up); set aside for a few minutes. When glue is tacky, pin center of wig to head, hair side down, with long ends hanging over center of forehead.

Continue around head, at hairline, behind ears, to nape of neck, overlapping ends slightly. Allow hair to dry completely before removing pins. Smooth hair using wide-tooth comb; comb hair back into a loose ponytail. Wind ponytail into a circle, gluing and wrapping as you go. Glue this topknot to back of head, above nape of neck.

Braided hairstyle: Cut 6 yards fiber into 36-inch lengths. Make 1 braid of 3 lengths; make 2 smaller braids of remaining 3 lengths that you divide in two. Apply glue to back of large braid; when tacky, press center of braid to center of forehead; pin into place. Continue around hairline, behind ears, to nape of neck. Turn braids upward along back center part, continue to top of head, then follow around, filling in previous oval to end of braid on both sides. Wind the braids around the doll's head, pinning and gluing as you go. Let glue dry before removing pins.

Jewelry: Pierce earlobes using large needle. Cut ¼ inch off regular ear wires; rebend to hook. Hang small bead on wire, insert in ear, and close.

Earring studs: Make indentation in earlobe using sharp object. Drop in spot of glue; apply small rhinestone.

Materials for each body: ¼ yard unbleached muslin; ⅛ yard of striped cotton for stocking legs; small bag polyester fiberfill; acrylic paint—both flesh and red; 2 chenille stems.

Instructions: Cut arms and neck from muslin. Stitch, clip, turn. Stuff arms to elbow, insert chenille with half on either side of elbow. Stitch across elbow so arm seam runs through middle of flattened area. Stuff upper arm firmly to 1 inch from top. Stitch stocking legs to torso at thigh, right sides together. Stuff legs firmly and torso lightly.

Stitch arms into shoulders, leaving opening at neck. Insert glue-coated neck into head; dry. Insert dowel; stuff neck leaving rod in center. Work dowel into torso. Dowel rod should come to ¼ inch of torso bottom. Cut to length. Pin neck inside shoulders, add more stuffing, if needed; stitch. Paint arms from elbow to fingertip in flesh tone. Rub a little red into backs of hands for blush; paint neck, matching head.

Materials for wardrobe: ⅜ yard blouse fabric; ⅛ yard for ruffled apron; ¼ yard for plain apron; ⅜ yard each for skirt and petticoat; 1 yard lace for petticoat; ¼ yard lace for handkerchief; ¼ yard of ¼-inch-wide elastic; 1 kid glove from thrift shop for shoes; small beads for necklace; 3 blouse buttons.

Instructions: *For doll with braided hair:* Cut skirt (10¼×36 inches), petticoat (10½×33 inches), apron sash (2×30 inches), bow tie (3×25 inches), apron ruffle (1½×32 inches), and tied cuffs (2¾×4 inches). Cut blouse, apron, and handkerchief from pattern. Stitch ¼-inch hem on skirt. Sew the lace trimming onto the petticoat.

Run gathering thread along top of skirt, petticoat, and apron. Gather petticoat and skirt to 12 inches. Anchor elastic, then stretch and sew.

Stitch right sides together at ends. Press under ¼ inch around pocket; stitch to apron. Gather ruffle to fit edge of apron (first turn up ¼-inch hem; press and stitch). Stitch apron to ruffle.

Stitch sash to apron, right sides facing, matching center fronts. With right sides facing, stitch sash; leave piece already sewn to apron free. Turn sash through free piece; press. Turn under raw edge of waistband front; sew.

Insert hankie into pocket. Sew blouse. Gather wrists 1 inch above edge of fabric; put blouse on doll. Pull gathers tight, knot firmly; trim ends. Sew, clip, turn, and press cuffs. Wrap cuff around wrist; tuck in raw edges, stitch closed. Add buttons.

Tuck in raw edges around neck. Overlap blouse front; fold under one edge, tack at neck. Sew buttons to front, tacking blouse closed. Sew neck bow tie, leaving an opening; turn. Tie bow around neck. Put skirt on doll, then petticoat.

For doll with purple blouse: Follow directions for above doll for making skirt, petticoat, and basic blouse. When attaching bow tie, simply loop it 4 times, tacking instead of tying a bow. Cuffs are wrapped around wrist, then knotted instead of buttoned. Make apron from a scrap of print (¼-inch hem). Press, stitch, and gather to 5 inches. Attach waistband as for doll above.

Shoes: Using an old kid glove, cut 2 of larger fingertips off at 2¼ inches; slit down front 1½ inches. From the glove cut 4 strips ⅛ to ¼ inch wide and as long as you can cut them. Stuff tip of shoe with cotton. Put shoe on foot, tacking corners at top of slit. Tack long strips at back of slit. Tack long strips at back of ankle. Bring strips forward; lace up leg. Tack to leg at bow.

Postage Stamp Quilt
page 239

Materials: Fabric scraps in assorted colors and prints; complementary fabric for backing; quilt batting.

Instructions: Make 10-inch-square miniquilt by cutting and joining 1-inch fabric squares. Use ¼-inch seams.

Quilt shown has a red center block surrounded by a 5-inch square of blocks in assorted prints. Prints are bordered by green, pink, red, purple, blue, and black squares.

Stitch blocks into diagonal rows. Sew rows together. Trim outer edges so they are straight. Cut backing fabric to size. Assemble layers into quilt.

Wooden Rocking Horse
page 240

Materials: Two ¾×15-inch (O.D.) pieces of black pipe; four ¼×3-inch carriage bolts; glue; sandpaper; finishing nails; stain; varnish; clear mahogany or other wood such as oak, maple, walnut, birch, or cherry in the sizes listed on page 248. If 2-inch wood is unavailable, use 2 pieces of ¾-inch wood glued together.

continued

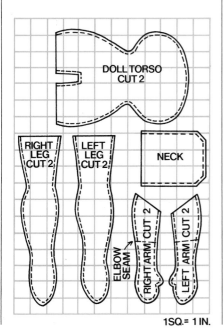

DOLL TORSO
CUT 2

RIGHT LEG CUT 2   LEFT LEG CUT 2   NECK

ELBOW SEAM   RIGHT ARM CUT 2   LEFT ARM CUT 2

1 SQ.= 1 IN.

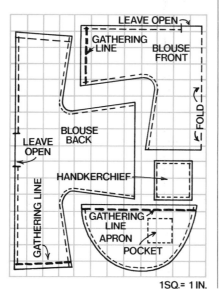

LEAVE OPEN

GATHERING LINE   BLOUSE FRONT

FOLD

LEAVE OPEN   BLOUSE BACK

HANDKERCHIEF

GATHERING LINE

GATHERING LINE   APRON   POCKET

1 SQ.= 1 IN.

Continued from page 247
Heritage Gifts

Instructions: Enlarge the patterns (below and opposite) onto brown paper. Using carbon paper and a pencil, trace patterns onto wood. (If you are using ¾-inch lumber, glue pieces together before transferring patterns to wood.)

Cut out all pieces (except base platform and base ends) using a band saw or fine-toothed sabre saw. Cut out base platform and ends using a table saw.

Nail and glue the platform base to the base ends. Sand rockers until all sides are smooth and free of blemishes. Nail and glue rockers to base.

Referring to diagrams for correct placement, drill ¾-inch holes in platform base; install ¾-inch pipe. Drill

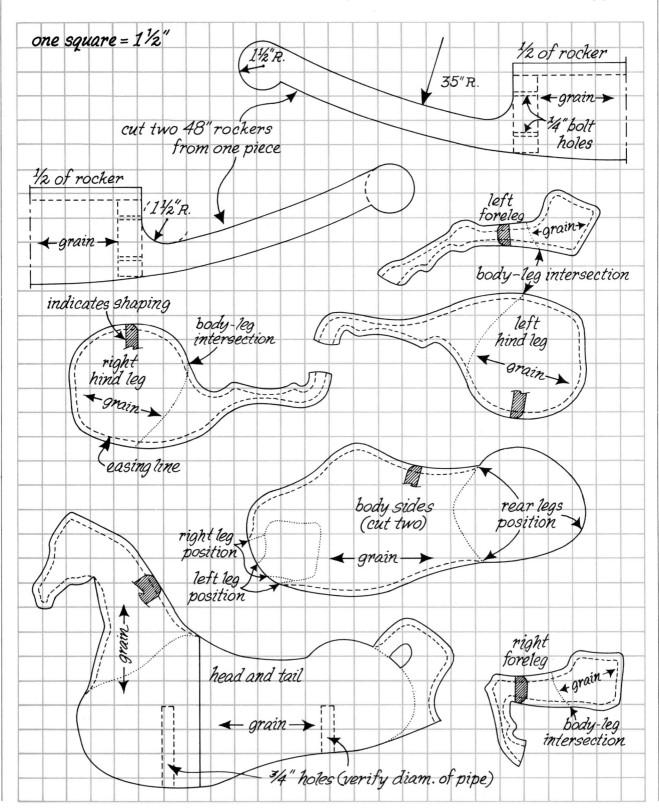

one square = 1½"

1½" R.

35" R.

cut two 48" rockers from one piece

½ of rocker

←grain→

¼" bolt holes

½ of rocker

←grain→

'1½" R.

left foreleg

←grain→

body-leg intersection

indicates shaping

body-leg intersection

right hind leg

←grain→

left hind leg

grain→

easing line

body sides (cut two)

rear legs position

right leg position

left leg position

←grain→

grain→

head and tail

right foreleg

←grain→

body-leg intersection

←grain→

¾" holes (verify diam. of pipe)

¼-inch holes through base ends and pipe. Install carriage bolts.

Drill ¾-inch holes in the chest and tail as shown on the diagram.

Sand all horse parts to exact size; ease edges of parts with a 1-inch-diameter shaper bit for a router, or use a fine-toothed wood rasp and sandpaper. Pattern of each part shows where easing starts and stops.

Assemble horse parts with glue and finishing nails; clamp sections firmly together until glue dries. Mount horse on ¾-inch pipes; tighten carriage bolts.

Sand the horse with fine sandpaper; apply wood filler if necessary. Stain wood if desired; apply sealer. Apply several coats of varnish, sanding between coats. When varnish is *thoroughly* dry, buff with steel wool.

continued

Materials:
Lumber in the following amounts and sizes:
2 pieces 1×8×48" for rockers; 1 piece 2×6×24" for base ends; 1 piece 1×12×14" for base platform; 1 piece 2×10×16" for tail section; 1 piece 2×12×18" for head; 1 piece 1×10×26" for hind legs; 1 piece 1×8×11" for right foreleg; 1 piece 1×6×15" for left foreleg; and 1 piece 1×10×44" for 2 body sides.

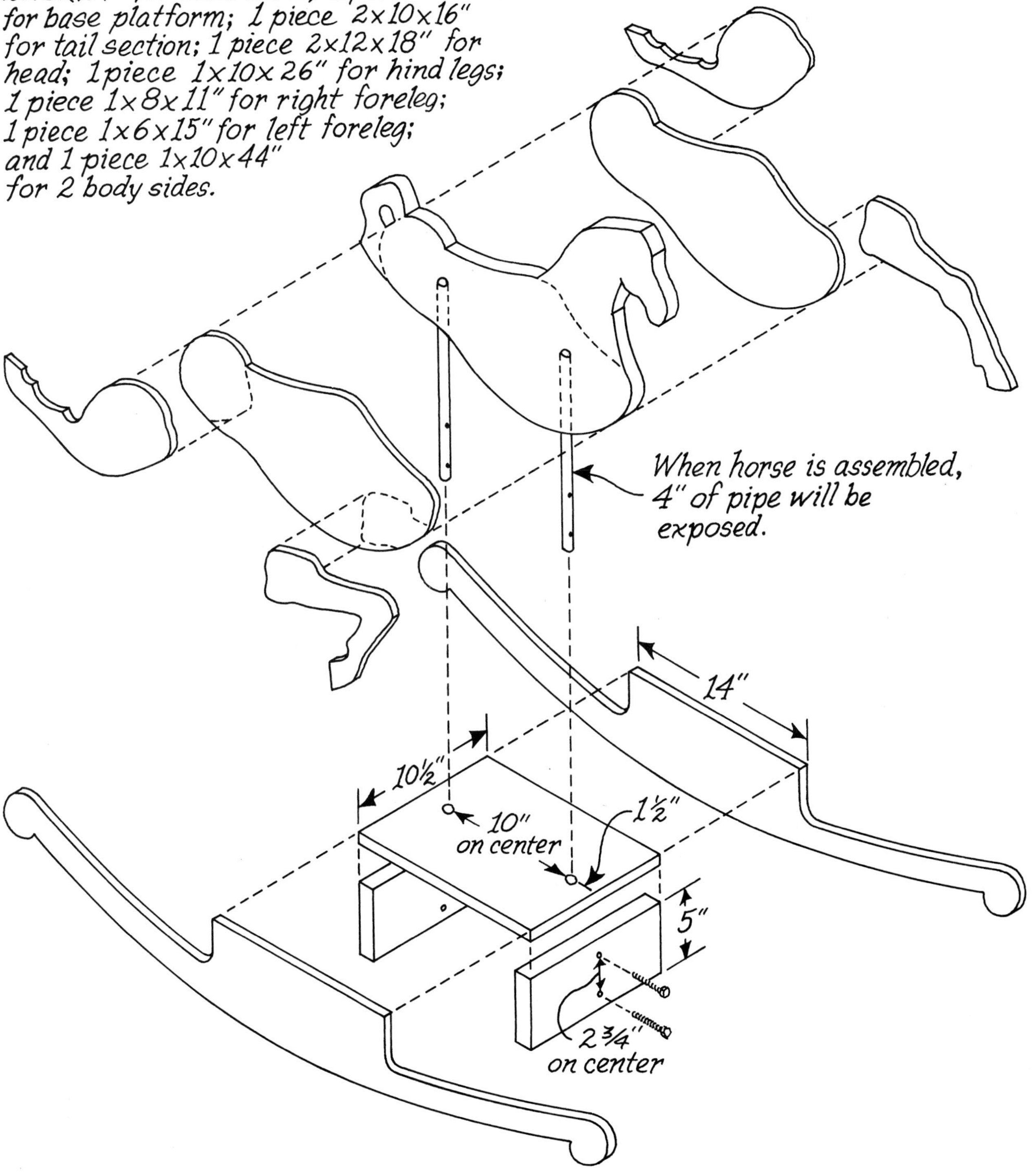

When horse is assembled, 4" of pipe will be exposed.

14"

10½"

10"
on center

1½"

5"

2¾"
on center

Continued from page 249
Heritage Gifts

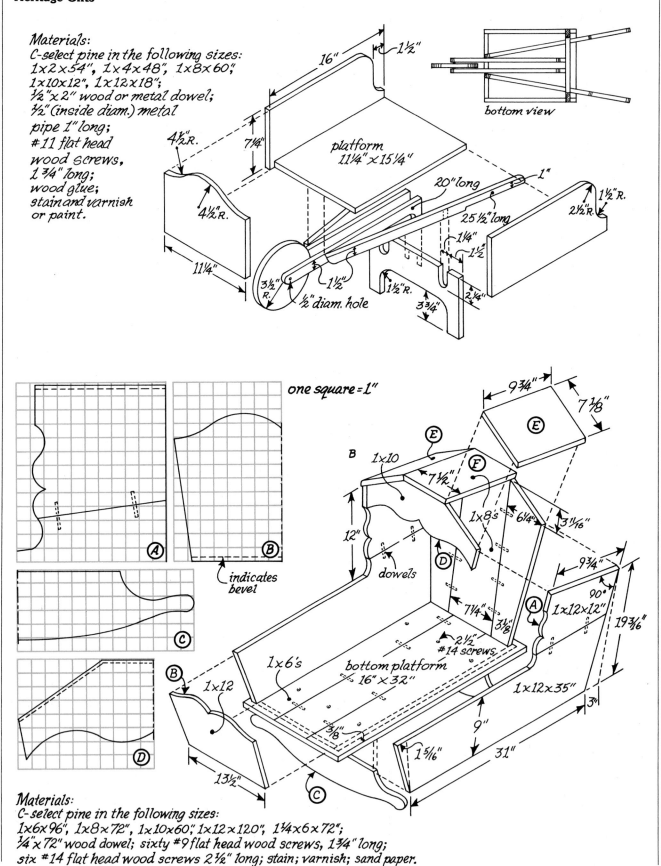

Materials:
C-select pine in the following sizes:
1x2x54", 1x4x48", 1x8x60",
1x10x12", 1x12x18";
½"x2" wood or metal dowel;
½" (inside diam.) metal
pipe 1" long;
#11 flat head
wood screws,
1 ¾" long;
wood glue;
stain and varnish
or paint.

16"
1½"
platform
11¼" x 15¼"
7¼"
4½"R.
4½"R.
11¼"
20" long
1"
25½" long
1½" R.
2½"R.
1¼"
1½"
3½" R.
1½"
½" diam. hole
1½"R.
3¾"
2¼"

bottom view

one square = 1"

9¾"
7⅛"
E
E
B
1x10
F
7½"R.
1x8's
6¼"
3 ¹¹⁄₁₆"
12"
D
9¾"
dowels
90°
1x12x12"
19³⁄₁₆"
A
7¼"
3⅛"
2½
#14 screws
1x6's
bottom platform
16" x 32"
1x12x35"
3"
B
1x12
9"
3⁄8"
1 ⁵⁄₁₆"
31"
13½"
C

A

B
indicates
bevel

C

D

Materials:
C-select pine in the following sizes:
1x6x96", 1x8x72", 1x10x60," 1x12x120", 1¼x6x72";
¼"x72" wood dowel; sixty #9 flat head wood screws, 1¾" long;
six #14 flat head wood screws 2½" long; stain; varnish; sand paper.

Wheelbarrow
page 241

Instructions: (See diagram opposite for materials.) All connections should be flat head set flush, and glued into place. Follow diagram (opposite) for cutting pieces. Assemble front and side panels to screw and glue to platform. Place upside down and assemble remaining pieces as shown.

Before placing wheel between wheel supports, insert the 1-inch long metal pipe through the hole in the wheel. This serves as bearing and spacer. There should be a ⅛-inch space on each side of wheel. Place ½-inch-diameter dowel through one wheel support, then the wheel, then the other wheel support. Connect this dowel from the underside to both wheel supports using small screws.

Sand lightly all edges and entire wheelbarrow to receive finish. Stain and varnish, or paint and decorate.

Blocks
page 241

Materials: 2×4×33 inches fir; 1×2-inch pine for tray sides; 1-inch pine shelving for tray bottom; three 1×3-inch dowels; sandpaper.

Instructions: Cut eleven 3×3-inch fir blocks according to pattern (below). Drill holes to accommodate dowels.

Cut bottom of tray; piece should measure about 9×12 inches, or slightly larger than assembled blocks. Cut sides of tray; attach to bottom with glue and finishing nails; countersink nails, fill holes. Varnish if desired.

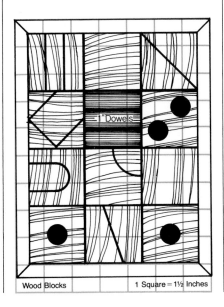

Wood Blocks   1 Square = 1½ Inches

Wooden Cradle
page 241

Instructions: (See diagram for materials.) Transfer diagram (opposite) onto brown paper, making full-size pattern. Cut each piece, checking against other pieces for fit.

Portions of cradle are too large to cut from a single piece of lumber. If using stock lumber, join pieces using dowels, edge gluing, and clamping. When edge gluing boards, reverse the heart grain of boards to increase their strength. Insert ¼×2-inch dowels into 1-inch deep holes drilled into edges to be glued together. Glue; clamp until dry.

When cutting the 2 side panels (A), edge glue two 1×12s that are long enough (about 48 inches) to cut both side panels (A) from. Before gluing, note position of dowels in order to have them placed properly in the finished piece. Be sure bevels on both side panels are on opposite sides.

The hood sides (E) also are cut opposite to each other. Note the "top front" on the cut piece for assembly. Round the lower edge of the hood sides (E) to a ¾-inch radius.

Rockers (C) are cut from 1¼-inch stock. *Do not use wood any thinner than this* because rocking is controlled by narrow part of this piece.

Refer to diagram for assembly. All joints are butt type and glued and screwed. Use #9 screws everywhere, except on rockers (C) use #14. Countersink screw heads; make plugs (from wood dowels) to glue over screw heads.

Position side panels (A), head panel, and foot panel (B) together, then glue and screw. Place on bottom platform; drill holes (³⁄₁₆-inch) around perimeter as marked, angling into side and end panels. Predrill holes (¼-inch diameter) in bottom platform for rockers (C) to be attached later.

Glue and screw hood front (D) into place, then assemble hood sides (E) and top (F). Glue and screw.

The rockers (C) are attached last. Use predrilled holes in bottom platform. Glue and screw. To finish cradle, sand thoroughly, seal, and varnish.

Rag Dolls
page 242

Materials: 1 yard muslin; 2 skeins rya yarn; blue, brown, red, and black embroidery floss; ⅔ yard print fabric; ⅓ yard coordinated fabric; fabric, lace, and ribbon scraps; 8 small buttons; fiberfill; ¼-inch elastic.

Instructions: Enlarge pattern (pieces include ⅜-inch seam allowance). Cut doll front and back from muslin.

Take a small tuck along dotted line on neck on both front and back pieces, stitching from seam allowance to seam allowance but not to cut edge. Tucks keep head from wrinkling when stuffed.

Embroider facial features, using 3 strands of floss. Use satin stitches for mouth; outline stitch other features. Embroider the heart.

With right sides facing, pin and stitch body pieces together, leaving lower end of body open. Clip seams, turn, and stuff. Head and neck must be stuffed firmly, or head will not stay upright.

Cut 4 legs from muslin and 4 shoes of black or brown fabric. Join leg parts to shoe parts. With right sides together, sew the 2 completed leg pieces together. Clip seams, turn, and stuff until seams are smooth. Add shoe buttons.

Pin tops of stuffed legs so seams meet and toes point forward. Sew legs into base of body, closing bottom seam of body at same time.

Cut out 4 arm pieces. Stitch 2 pieces together, leaving shoulder end open. Clip seams, turn, and press. Put a tiny amount of stuffing into end of doll's hand; embroider fingers over stuffing. Stuff remainder of arm; slip-stitch.

continued

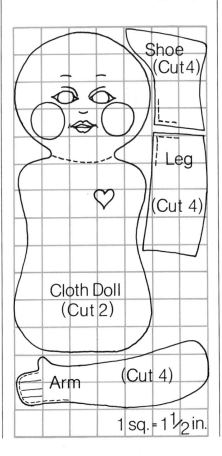

Shoe (Cut 4)

Leg (Cut 4)

Cloth Doll (Cut 2)

Arm (Cut 4)

1 sq. = 1½ in.

Continued from page 251
Heritage Gifts

Slip-stitch arms to body at shoulder; sew firmly with double thread at top edge only, so arms swing free.

To make clothing: Cut bodice front and back pieces from print fabric. Join at shoulders only. Add decorative lace trim, ribbon, and buttons to bodice front. For collar, cut fabric 2×10½ inches; sew one edge to neckline. Clip seam, fold collar over, press, and slip-stitch raw edge to seam.

For sleeves, cut 2 pieces 9×10¼ inches (longer edges are shoulder and wrist seams). Turn under wristband; add decorative trim to edge. Add lace or trim at other points along sleeve, if desired. Cut 5 inches of elastic; stitch to wrong side of sleeve about 3½ inches above wrist. Mask stitches on right side of fabric using additional lace or trim.

Gather top of sleeve; set into bodice, distributing gathers evenly. Stitch sleeves to bodice; stitch side seams of bodice and sleeves.

Cut out 8½×44-inch skirt. Sew a ½-inch hem along one edge of skirt; add decorative trim. Gather top edge; stitch to bodice, leaving back of dress open from top to bottom. Turn under back edges of dress ¼ inch; stitch.

Slip dress on doll. Because sizes will vary slightly according to the amount of stuffing and width of seams, overlap back edges of dress to determine the exact amount you'll need to turn the edges under (about ½ inch). Pin and slip-stitch this facing down, turning collar as well. Add snaps, or tiny hooks and eyes, at collar and waist, and wherever necessary in between.

Add ribbon at waistline, and lace or trim at neck.

For slip, cut fabric 10×36 inches. Turn one long edge under 1 inch to make casing for elastic. Sew lace and trimmings on slip (which will peek out beneath dress); stitch side seam, leaving casing open. Insert an 11-inch piece of elastic, stitch ends together, and slip-stitch casing closed, covering elastic.

Cut pantaloons from print fabric. Add wide lace trim and ribbons to bottom of each piece, as shown on pattern. Join front and back seams; turn under top edge for elastic. Insert an 11-inch piece of elastic, stitch ends, and slip-stitch casing closed. Sew legs.

For apron, cut fabric 8½×36 inches. Add pocket made from 4-inch square of fabric trimmed with lace or ribbon. Hem lower edge and sides of apron.

Cut fabric 3×38 inches for waistband and ties. Gather top of apron to 10 inches; center on band. Fold band in

half over gathers, turn under raw edges; slip-stitch together on 3 sides.

When doll is clothed, it is easier to determine the kind of hair style you'll want to add. Hair styles of dolls shown require 2 skeins of yarn each.

For curly hair (doll at left in photo): Cut a length of yarn about 8 yards long. Double it back and forth into a 3-foot-long piece, 8 strands thick. Lay one end of this skein on doll's forehead; tack into place. Make a loop and stitch again; pull stitches tight. Make loops small and close for short, tight curls. Continue until top of head and sides are covered (making new skeins as necessary). Use second full skein on back of head. Open skein to make large loop. Lay it across back of doll's head; back-stitch or catch-stitch to hold yarn. Tie pigtails; trim yarn.

To duplicate hair style of doll on right: Place a full skein of yarn over forehead. Sew in a line to suggest a center part. Tack at side. Double back remaining yarn at back of head; stitch into place. Use second skein on back of head. Line up the part with front part; stitch and tack into place. Tie remaining yarn into a ponytail; trim the ends so they are even.

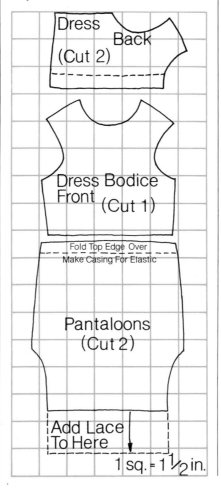

Wax dolls
page 243

Materials for each head: 3-inch plastic foam ball; lightweight cardboard; papier-mâché mix (1 pound makes 4 heads); 1×6 inches grosgrain ribbon; white glue; black, blue, brown, red, white, crimson, yellow acrylic paints; tape; 1 pound beeswax and 1 pound hard candle wax; candy thermometer; sandpaper; apples (to practice dipping into wax).

Instructions for heads: Cut cardboard rectangle 2½×5 inches for mother—2×5 inches for children. Roll into cylinder for neck. Tape edges; glue. Cut shoulder piece from cardboard; cut slashes in shoulder piece, overlapping ¼ inch to slope; glue and tape. (See sketch.) Pull shoulder piece over cylinder so bottom edge meets bottom edge of cylinder. Glue and tape shoulder piece to cylinder.

Cut ½-inch-deep hole in bottom of foam ball, large enough to fit over neck (cardboard cylinder). Glue neck cylinder in hole; let dry. Child's neck measures ½ inch from foam ball to neck piece; mother's measures 1 inch.

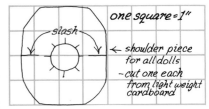

When covering head with papier-mâché mix, shoulders tend to collapse. Stuff crumpled paper towels under shoulder piece to retain shape. Mix mâché as directed on package. Keep mixture just wet enough to be pliable. (Have a bowl of water handy to rinse hands while working.) Working with small amount, cover surface of head, neck, and shoulders evenly with a layer ¼ inch thick. Build up cheeks, nose, and shoulder piece. Eye area should be slightly concave. Build mother's breast-piece to form bosom. Dry head in 250-degree oven for 2 to 4 hours.

Sand head to remove rough edges. Cut away cardboard cylinder under shoulder piece to leave opening for setting the head on to the body.

To paint head, use either a premixed flesh color or mix a little crimson and yellow into white. Flesh tone should be bright and a little on the pink side. When head is dipped in wax, colors will soften and have an amber hue. Spread base coat on evenly. To blend red or pink into cheeks, thin out color; then apply gently with a dry, soft brush. Mother's features should be delicate. Children's coloring should be ruddier. Paint features clearly, but not overly detailed. Use warm colors for painting eyes on all of the dolls.

When paint dries, cut two 3-inch pieces of ribbon; glue one edge of ribbon to bottom of shoulder piece in front and back, leaving other edge free for attaching to body.

Combine 1 pound hard wax with 1 pound beeswax, and heat in a coffee can or other container deep and wide enough to accommodate head. Put container in pot of water; heat slowly over burner. Or, place wax container into foil-lined electric frypan; turn dial to 300°. Heat wax to 190°. Before dipping heads into wax, experiment with an apple (or other fruit) on a stick. Remove wax from burner. Immerse object completely into wax; remove in one continuous movement. Tilt apple; let drips run to back. When you've mastered getting an even coat, you're ready to begin dipping head.

Reheat wax to 190°; remove from burner. Hold doll's head firmly by ribbon from upside-down position; dip head into wax up to where ribbon begins; remove in one continuous movement. Tilt head, features upward, so excessive wax will drip to back.

Hold head up until drips harden. Wax will cloud over but clears when cool. Heads require 2 coats of wax. If on first dipping, drips appear on face, carefully scrape them off with a paring knife before second dipping.

For second dipping, reheat wax to 190°. Second dipping must be smooth. Coat head a third time if desired, but wax coats cannot be removed.

● "Mother" doll

Materials: ⅓ yard muslin for body; fine sawdust or fiberfill; 2 ounces carded wool or mohair yarn for hair; ½ yard rose velveteen for skirt; ¼ yard printed fabric for blouse; ¼ yard velvet ribbon for belt; 1¾ yards casing lace and ribbon for blouse; 8×12-inch felt piece for boots; hooks, eyes, snap fastener, embroidery floss for lacing belt; 12 tiny pearl beads for boots.

Instructions: Make head according to basic head instructions. Head should measure 5½ inches to base of neck.

Overlap darts of cap that you cut from muslin; glue darts in place. Spread layer of glue around edge of cap to avoid fraying. Set cap on doll's head where hair will go. Trace outline of cap on head. With sharp knife, gently scrape off wax within outline, since wig must be glued onto mâché (glue will not adhere to wax).

Pull wool or yarn into 8-inch sections and lay them on cap in circle around edge of cap, with half hanging over edge of cap. Hand-sew wool around very edge of cap; gather inside fringe of wool together at top of head. Stitch wool to cap in circle.

At this point, glue wig to head, covering bald spot with glue. Set wig on head; smooth cap to fit. Wipe off any

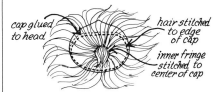

glue drips. When glue dries, smooth outside fringe of hair to crown of head. Gather hair loosely in bun at crown of head. Tack into place. Braid a lock of yarn to coil around bun, if desired.

For body: Enlarge patterns (below) and trace on brown wrapping paper. Cut out pieces from muslin fabric. Stitch

the center front and back seams and the darts in the torso. Sew side seams, leaving an opening along upper sides where indicated on pattern for attaching arms later. Stitch seam across upper edge of torso. Clip curves; turn right side out.

Sew arms, leaving open at shoulders for stuffing. Clip curves; turn. Stuff firmly. Overcast outside of arm seam with heavy thread. Stitch fingers in hands. Place arms in slits on side of body. Hand-sew the arms to the body. Thumbs should face up as shown.

Stuff torso firmly. Leave bottom open for legs; overcast center and side seams. Stitch front and back leg seams. Hand-sew sole to bottom of foot. Clip curves; turn. Stuff legs firmly; baste closed at upper edge. Hand-sew legs to lower edge of torso.

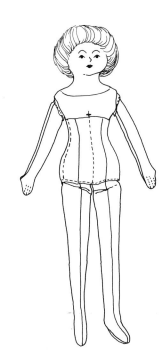

Set head on body. Pin so that it is very taut; firmly tack bottom of ribbon to body. Completed doll body should look like sketch (above).

Skirt: Cut skirt from rose velveteen fabric, using pattern (below). Be sure the nap of the fabric runs the same way on all 4 pieces. Sew 4 panels together at sides, leaving one side open at top; this will be center back. Ease top edge of panels, pulling most of fullness toward back. Sew on waistband; secure with snap fastener.

Blouse: Cut blouse from pattern (below). Thread ribbon through lace. Sew lace around bottom yoke edge

continued

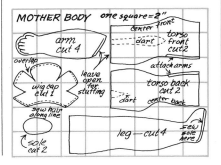

Continued from page 253
Heritage Gifts

only. Sew facing to yoke. Turn right side out; tack center back together at bottom. Sew shoulder seams.

Gather front and back at upper edge, as indicated on pattern. Right sides together, sew yoke to blouse piece.

Sew darts in sleeves. Sew lace around mid-sleeve and edge of sleeve. Gather upper edge; with right sides together, sew sleeve on bodice. Sew side and sleeve in continuous seam, matching lace.

Thread ribbon through collar lace. Hand-sew collar lace on outside to neck edge, forming stand-up collar.

Hem bottom edge and sleeves. Sew hooks and eyes along back opening.

Cinch belt: Cut from green fabric. Face with blouse fabric; sew right sides together. Turn; finish by hand. Lace back with embroidery floss.

Boots: Cut boots from felt. Sew 2 outside pieces together as indicated. Sew 2 halves down center front and back. Hand-stitch sole to boot. Clip corners; turn boot right side out. Sew pearl beads into place, simulating buttons. Put boot on foot; tack closed.

● *"Hansel" doll*

Materials: ¼ yard muslin for body; fine sawdust or fiberfill; two ½-inch buttons; 1 ounce carrot-colored mohair yarn; 12×15-inches muslin for shirt; ½ yard orange satin ribbon for tie; baby socks; two 9×12-inch dark green felt squares for shorts; 9×12-inch brown felt for boots; 4 buttons for suspenders and boots; embroidery thread.

Instructions: Make head according to basic instructions. Features should be rounded and complexion ruddy.

Cut cap from white muslin as for mother to go on top of head for gluing yarn to. Glue darts; spread thin layer of glue around edge of cap to avoid fraying. Cut cardboard rectangle from pattern (right, above). Wrap yarn around this piece, then machine-stitch a seam down center. Cut yarn along upper and lower edges of cardboard. Boy's hair will take about 20 inches of fringe. Hand-sew yarn to cap in circles,

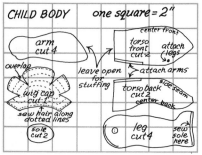

following guidelines on sketch (below). Glue wig to head, as for mother. Trim and shape hair—shorter on sides and back, longer on top.

Note: Children's bodies use same patterns. Stitch center front and back seam. Sew torso sides together; leave open at upper edge and at upper sides for stuffing and attaching arms. Turn.

Sew arms; leave open at top for stuffing. After stuffing, pin arms to sides where indicated, with thumbs facing up. Hand-sew opening at top closed.

Sew leg front and back seams. Hand-sew sole to bottom of foot. Clip curves; turn. Stuff legs firmly; turn under raw edges on opening; slip-stitch.

Pin legs to lower edge of body where indicated. With long upholstery needle, sew straight through from hip to hip, putting button on outside of each leg where attached. Sew back and forth 3 times. Legs should fit snugly against body. Attach head to body. Child's body looks like sketch (below).

Shorts: Cut from green felt; embroider. Use satin stitches for flower, chain stitches on stems, buttonhole stitches around edges. Sew center front and back. Sew leg seam.

Cut 2 sets of suspenders; put both together, topstitch along edge. Cut 2 suspender fronts; embroider. Top-stitch along outer edge. Cut slits for buttonholes. Tack suspenders to back of shorts. Buttonhole-stitch along waistline. Attach front piece to suspenders as marked on one side (other side is tacked on after shorts are placed on body). Sew buttons to front of shorts.

Shirt: Gather sleeve on lower edges. Set on cuff. Take a tuck at back of shirt where indicated. Turn under; stitch front edge. Set on collar. Sew side and

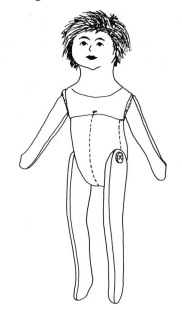

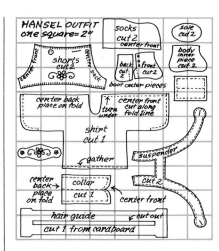

sleeve in one continuous seam. Hem bottom of shirt and cuff.

Cut socks from a pair of baby socks. Sew back seam; fold down top edge.

Cut out boots; with right sides together, sew pieces of outside piece where indicated. Put both halves of boot together; sew down center front and back. Hand-stitch sole to bottom; clip and turn. Tack boot closed on foot. Attach button at top.

● *"Gretel" doll*

Materials: ¼ yard white fabric for body; fine sawdust or fiberfill; 2 buttons for fasteners; mohair yarn; ½ yard white cotton for shift; 9×20 inches red felt for skirt; 9×12 inches black felt for vest and shoes; 13 inches white lace for trim on panties; ¼×12 inches white velvet ribbon for apron tie; shoe buttons or beads; embroidery floss.

Instructions: Make head, using basic head instructions. For hair, cut yarn into 20-inch sections. Backstitch center part. Stitch semicircle around part, beginning and ending where hair falls at chin of doll; see sketch.

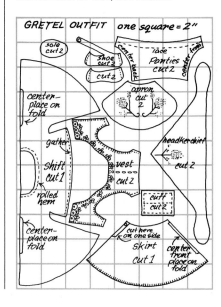

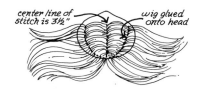

center line of stitch is 3½" — *wig glued onto head*

Set hair on doll's head; trace semicircle into wax. Using sharp knife, scrape away wax within semicircle. Glue wig onto bald spot, making sure none seeps through. Let dry. Braid in 2 braids. Secure braids with ribbon or embroidery thread.

Cut out and assemble body as for "Hansel" doll, using same pattern.

Dress: Cut out all pieces. Gather bottom of sleeve edge. Set on cuff; sew side and sleeve in one seam. Hem skirt; finish off cuff. Turn under neck edge. Beginning and ending at center front, sew a running stitch at neckline edge using 3 strands embroidery floss. Pull for drawstring. Leave 4-inch thread on each end for tying bow.

Head scarf: Transfer embroidery design, shown in sketch, to white fabric. (Or purchase one of the new iron-on embroideries that require no sewing.) Draw shape of scarf along cutting lines on pattern; do not cut top piece until needlework is completed. Work design in cross-stitches. Cut and stitch edges, as indicated. Turn right side out. Overcast edges with pale pink embroidery thread.

Skirt: Sew back seam to where indicated on sketch. Buttonhole-stitch in dark blue around lower edge of skirt. Attach at top with button.

Vest: Cut from black felt. Embroider as indicated, using 4 strands embroidery floss. Stitch side seams; turn. Braid 8 inches of 6-strand embroidery floss; lace up front. Tie in bow at top.

Apron: Draw cutting line on white fabric. Transfer embroidery pattern; cross-stitch as in diagram. Cut 2 apron pieces, right sides together. Sew edges, leaving top open; turn under raw edges at top, then overcast. Overlap ribbon on top edge of apron; hand-sew into place for apron strings.

Shoes: Stitch front and back seams. Hand-sew sole to bottom of shoe. Turn; sew buttons to straps; tack shoes closed.

Panties: Sew front and back seam. Turn under raw edges on legs; trim with lace. Sew inseam. Turn under raw edge at top, starting and ending at center front. Sew a running stitch along top edge, using 6 strands embroidery floss. Pull for drawstring; tie in bow.

● *Schoolgirl doll*

Materials: ¼ yard white fabric for body; fine sawdust or fiberfill; carrot color mohair yarn for hair; ¼ yard navy fabric for skirt; ⅓ yard white fabric for blouse; pair baby socks or 5×10-inch piece small-stripe cotton to make your own socks; 13 inches of ½-inch white lace for panties; package of navy middy braid; ½ yard satin ribbon for tie at neck; 2 pieces 9×12-inch navy felt for hat; 1½ yards ½-inch-wide navy or red grosgrain trim for hat; red buttonhole twist for top-stitching; 6 shoe buttons; skirt closure.

Instructions: Make head according to basic head instructions. For hair, cut yarn into 16-inch lengths. Hand-stitch a part down the center.

Stitch semicircle around center part, beginning where hair meets chin and ending semicircle in same spot on other side. Set wig on head; trace semicircle in wax. Using sharp knife, scrape away wax inside semicircle. Glue wig onto bald spot. Gather front section to back of head. Tie with pieces of ribbon or yarn. See sketch (above left).

For body, follow instructions given for "Hansel" doll.

Blouse: Gather bottom of sleeves along lines; attach cuff. Gather top edge of blouse back. Sew front of blouse to dot. Sew middy braid along guidelines on collar. Turn under front edges. Set collar on blouse, easing at back to fit. Pin one side of blouse; sew side and sleeve (1 seam). Ease lower edge along guidelines. Cut 9½ inches of braid; sew along guideline. Sew other side seam; hem. Finish cuff.

Skirt: Sew box pleats to lower arrows. Cut pleat; open seam, iron flat. Using red thread, topstitch arrow on pleat. Sew side seams, leaving open to dot. Set on waistband. Attach with snap at top. Hem skirt.

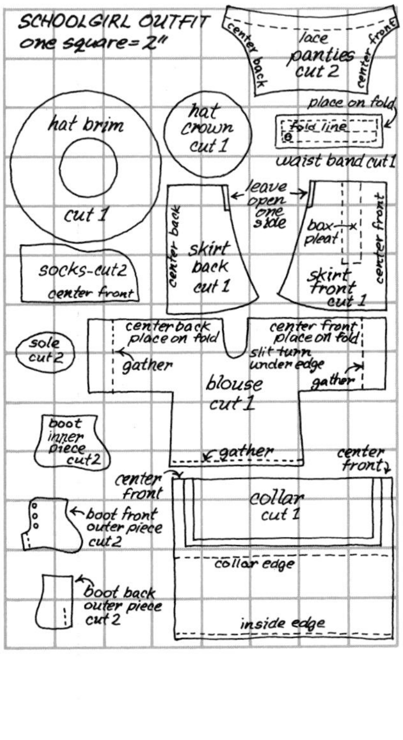

Boots: Sew 3 tiny buttons on outside of each boot.

Panties: Follow instructions for Gretel.

Hat: Cut crown and brim from navy felt (see sketch). Shape hat by dipping pieces into mixture of 1 part white glue to 2 parts water. Press out excess water. Smooth brim into bottom of lightly oiled glass mixing bowl; smooth out wrinkles but do not stretch. Using a lightly oiled inverted glass or jar, stretch crown on hat over jar bottom. Pull and stretch taut. Set in warm place to dry.

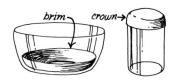

brim — *crown→*

Before pieces are entirely dry, lift off bowl and jar; let pieces finish drying by resting lightly on jar or bowl. When dry, brush inside of crown with more glue mixture to strengthen. Let dry again.

With the brim cupped upward, push the crown through from underneath. Stitch the brim to the crown.

Sew flat braid around the brim, binding the edge of the felt. Tack a piece of braid around crown. Fold another piece of braid (11 inches long) in half. Tack to ribbon around crown. Tack hat to head through hair.

Log Cabin
pages 246–247

Materials: (for log cabin and furnishings) ¼ sheet ¼-inch plywood; ¼ sheet ⅜-inch plywood; ¼ sheet ½-inch plywood; ½×⅜×48 inches pine or fir; 7 feet ½×½-inch pine or fir; 9 feet 1×1-inch pine or fir; 8 feet ⅜×1½-inch pine or fir; 6 feet ¼×⅝-inch pine, balsa, or basswood; seventeen ⅝×36-inch dowels; 4 feet ¼×¼-inch quarter-round molding; 1 foot ⅛-inch dowel; 3 feet ¼-inch dowel; ⅛×3×18 inches bass or balsa wood; two ¼×3×18-inch pieces bass or balsa wood; 2 feet ¾-inch half round; 2 feet ¼×¾-inch pine or fir; 1 foot ¼×¼-inch balsa or basswood; 4 feet ¼×¹⁄₁₆-inch balsa or basswood (optional); 20 frozen pop sticks; glue; twine; fur cloth; fabric scraps; fiberfill; medium-weight wire; aluminum foil; masking tape; stain; cardboard; brads; water-base putty (or papier-mâché); antiquing kit; white and black paint; varnish.

continued

SCHOOLGIRL OUTFIT
one square = 2"

hat brim
cut 1

hat crown
cut 1

lace panties
cut 2

place on fold

fold line

waist band cut 1

socks–cut 2
center front

skirt back
cut 1

leave open one side

box pleat

skirt front
cut 1

sole
cut 2

center back
place on fold

gather

center front
place on fold

under edge

gather

blouse
cut 1

boot inner piece
cut 2

gather

center front

collar
cut 1

center front

boot front outer piece
cut 2

collar edge

boot back outer piece
cut 2

inside edge

Continued from page 255
Heritage Gifts

Log cabin assembly (drawing below):
¼-inch plywood, cut as follows:
  A one piece 7½×15¾ inches
  B one piece 6×16 inches
  C two pieces 5½×7 inches
  D one piece 3¼×6½ inches
  E one piece 5×16 inches
  F one piece 4⅜×5 inches
  G one piece 4×11⅝ inches
  H two pieces 1½×4⅜ inches
  I two pieces 1×7¾ inches
  J two pieces 1×⅞ inch
  K one piece 1⅝×5½ inches
  L one piece 2¾×5 inches
  M two pieces 1×3⅞ inches
½-inch plywood, cut as follows:
  N one piece 16×24 inches
⅜-inch plywood, cut as follows:
  O two pieces 11×25 inches
Pine or fir, cut as follows:
  P one piece ½×⅜×7½ inches
  Q one piece ½×⅜×16 inches
  R one piece ½×⅜×24 inches, and
two pieces ½×⅜×16 inches
  S four pieces ½×½×11 inches
  T two pieces 1×1×22 inches
  U two pieces 1×1×16 inches
  V one piece 1×1×24 inches
  W two pieces ⅜×1½×24¾ inches
  X two pieces ⅜×1½×16 inches
  Y seven pieces ¼×⅝×4 inches
  Z six pieces ¼×⅝×4½ inches
  AA two pieces ¼×⅝×6⅝ inches
  BB see instructions for dimensions
Quarter-round screen molding:
  CC one piece 16 inches
  DD two pieces 7 inches

General construction: Exploded drawing shows overall construction of this 3-sided log cabin. First build the floor. Then assemble loft and fireplace. Build sidewalls of cabin using dowel "logs," notched to fit at corners. Add loft and assemble roof; shingles go on last.

To ensure a perfect match of pieces, measure each piece accurately; use assembly list only as a general guide.

Build base: Assemble the 1×1-inch underfloor braces with butt joints. Glue and nail plywood floor to braces.

To build loft: Assemble loft braces under loft floor at front and inside edges, notching ends as shown. Braces extend ¼ inch beyond loft floor at back and sidewalls.

Sand, fill front edges of loft; prime both loft and cabin floor. When they are dry, apply base coat of antiquing kit, using directions in package. When base coat is dry, measure and mark ½-inch floor boards at random lengths. Press hard enough with pencil to make dents in wood. Mark nail holes at ends of "boards" with tiny dents. Wipe with antiquing glaze; allow to dry.

Nail floor fascia boards into place; stain fascias and outer edges of loft.

Fireplace: Assemble fireplace parts using glue and nails. Cut sidepieces as needed to fit. Carefully stain mantel. Paint fireplace interior. Sketch rocks on all other portions of fireplace to within ⅝ inch of both back sides and to within ⅞ inch at top back sides against roof ends. Thin modeling paste slightly with water; paint on rocks (¹⁄₁₆ inch thick).

Paint white. When paint is dry, apply antiquing glaze; rub it off "rocks."

Sidewalls: Stain dowels and trim pieces before cutting. Cut trim pieces for door and window frames as indicated in assembly list. Cut dowels (notching as shown) as follows: For front wall, cut 6 at 10 inches, with 1 end notched; 16 at 3½ inches with 1 end notched; 16 at 2½ inches without notches; and 2 at 24 inches with both ends notched. For fireplace wall, cut 14 at 5½ inches, with 1 end notched; 2 at 6 inches with both ends notched; 5 at 6 inches with 1 end notched; and 5 at 6 inches without notches. For end wall, cut 5 at 16 inches with 1 end notched; 8 at 6 inches without notches; and 8 at 6 inches with 1 end notched. For loft post, cut 1 about 8½ inches, without notches.

Assemble door, door frames, and window frames. Detail door planks as you did floor planks. Cut a 3½-inch spacer from scrap material for door. Glue finished fireplace and door frame with spacer into position on their respective sides. Glue first row of logs to floor with notched edges together and plain ends glued to fireplace and door frame. Allow glue holding a group of logs in place to dry thoroughly before adding next row throughout construction. Glue second and third courses of logs into place. Be certain that walls are vertical; check after adding each row.

Next, glue window frames into place. Add logs, a course at a time, up to top of door frame. At this point, remove spacer; fit door to frame. Drill hole in floor and through top of door frame for "pin" hinges. Tap brads into holes. Cut head off bottom brad; remove upper brad. Fit door into frame, dropping upper pin hinge through door frame into door. Sand door to fit.

Add remaining logs until 13 courses are in place. Notch trim pieces for top row as shown (½-inch face is up). Notch back wall for front inner-loft support. Glue trim into place. This top trim supports roof ends and loft. Dry.

Roof: Cut triangular roof ends as follows: piece B is a triangle with a 16-inch base, 6-inch altitude; piece C (cut two) is a right triangle with a 7-inch base and 5½-inch altitude.

Cut roof end beams. Miter ends to match roof-peak angle. Glue and nail braces on outer edge of larger triangle. Glue and nail quarter-round top to bottom inside edges of chimney-side roof ends, mitering at back corner. Position and nail; then glue roof end beams, leaving room between triangles for chimney. Use opposite roof end for placement pattern. Glue and nail roof ends, chimney, and top of wall.

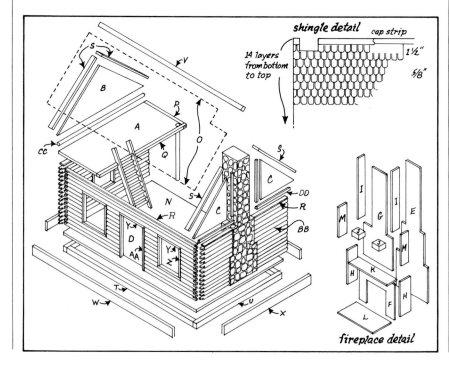

shingle detail

cap strip

14 layers
from bottom
to top

1½"

⅝"

fireplace detail

On loft side, mark center line along top of side and back. Spread glue on inner side of line and on notched ends of loft braces. Glue loft into place; glue and nail loft post into place.

Glue and toenail roof end to top of wall. Place quarter round along loft side; mark sides of roof end on quarter round and cut off ends. Glue and nail to loft and roof end.

Glue and nail back roof to roof ends and braces, lining up roof edges to edges of end-roof beams. Check measurement for center roof beam; cut to correct length. Glue to inner roof edge; glue and nail ends of roof end and toenail to chimney end. Glue and nail front roof into position.

Measure and mark at ¾-inch intervals both sides of roof for shingles from lower-eave edge to ridge. Each side will have 14 rows of shingles.

Cut cardboard shingles from pattern given. (If you wish, you may use wood shingles. Apply them in the same manner.) Glue shingles into place starting at lower eave and ending at ridge. Glue and nail cap strips into position.

Prime-coat cardboard shingles, then paint with base color and antique in the same way as you did floor. Touch up stain on logs; trim as needed. Cover completed cabin with 2 coats of low-sheen polyurethane finish.

● *Furnishings:* All furniture is made from balsa or basswood, pine, dowels, and fabric scraps. Cut balsa or basswood with a craft knife or jigsaw.

Cut all pieces as indicated on drawings (right). Assemble pieces, using butt joints, with glue and brads, if necessary. Sand rough edges smooth. Stain or paint as desired, using photographs on page 244 as a guide.

Trunk: Use 16 frozen pop sticks for top and borders. Use ⅛-inch material for other pieces. Cut rounded ends of top; cut sticks to length and glue to ends. Sand down inner edges after glue has dried. Assemble bottom of trunk, cut trim and set aside.

Purchase hinge or cut ½-inch strip of fabric to fit length of trunk. Glue back of trunk top and bottom before adding trim strips. Drill holes for twine handles; thread knotted twine through holes. Line trunk interior with fabric scraps if desired.

Bed: Drill holes for rope strings before assembling bed; glue bed pieces together. Cut a 50-inch-piece of twine. Tie knot in one end; weave twine back and forth the length of the bed. Pull taut; knot end. Cut second piece of twine 55 inches long. Tie knot in one end; weave back and forth going over and under lengthwise ropes. Knot end.

Secure knotted ends with glue. Cut mattress and pillow from fabric scraps, stitch 3 sides; turn and stuff. Slip-stitch opening closed.

Table: Stain pieces, then assemble.

Ladder: Cut ten 2-inch half-round ladder rungs. Assemble as shown.

Sampler: Assemble frame. Paint design on heavy card; glue to frame back.

Hat rack: Stain frozen pop sticks. Mark dowel placement. Make holes at center of dowel marks using a brad. Push brads through holes from back, joining all pieces. Start holes in ends of dowels using an awl. Put glue on ends of dowels; force dowels down on brads to form hanging pegs.

Moose head: Form wire into antlers. Squeeze foil around wire at center and bring ends to front. Add more foil, modeling head and neck. Wrap horns using masking tape. Stain back mounting piece. Pound nail through center of mounting so it will go into center of moose's neck. Force head on nail. Remove head; spread glue on back of neck. Attach head to mounting piece.

Mix small amount of putty or papier-mâché; apply to head and neck. Use modeling tool, spatula, and orangewood stick for modeling details. When head and neck are dry, paint.

Gingerbread men on tree: Cut four 1×6-inch strips of brown paper. Laminate pieces together with glue. Cover top piece using glue; allow to dry. Draw gingerbread figure on back of strip; cut out. Apply glue on uncoated side, allow to dry. Add features.

Bearskin rug: Cut from fur fabric.

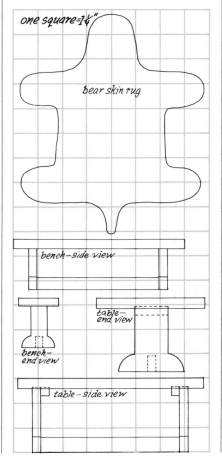

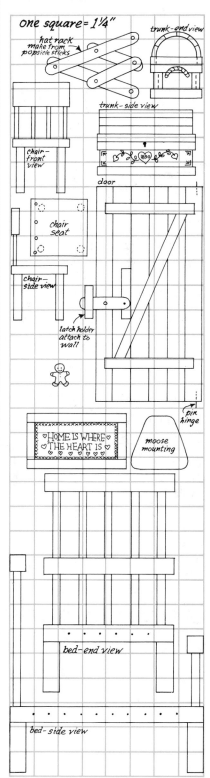

257

A Child's Fantasy Christmas

Gifts for Imaginative Play

Fanciful animals, lovable dolls, and sturdy wooden toys are the kinds of gifts kids love to get. So, if you want to guarantee smiles of satisfaction on Christmas morning, create fantastical presents for the children on your list. You'll find lots of great ideas here.

A nature-loving child (or two if they're small) will tumble happily into this sleeping bag adorned with all his favorite friends from the zoo. (Who could resist talking to these delightful animals?) Each of these whimsical creatures is machine-appliquéd to the top of this cozy 50×68-inch bag. Four layers of quilt batting inside (two on top and two on the bottom) make it warm enough for even the coolest of Christmas nights. To make your child's overnight excursions complete, stitch one design onto a pajama tote and another into a fat, jolly pillow.

Directions for all the projects shown in this section begin on page 268.

Gifts for Imaginative Play

High on the most-wanted list of many youngsters at Christmastime are lovable animals in all shapes and sizes. Make your child's wish come true by creating one of these easy-to-make gifts.

Mama duck and her three ducklings are only eight and six inches tall. Stitch and stuff them using gingham checks in different sizes.

The stick reindeer is a whimsical substitute for a hobbyhorse. Use a wooden drawer pull, painted shiny red, for his nose, and bright fabric for his soft antlers. Or gift your animal-loving child with his own moose head; it's a perfect scarf, mitten, and cap catcher. Tiny tots will love these soft muslin bunnies and bears. They're only six, nine, and 12 inches tall.

Gifts for Imaginative Play

What child can resist a fat and sassy goose with such an incredible gift of gab that she's always chock-full of secrets to share with young admirers? This glib goose (opposite) even sports a cleverly hidden horn to "honk" when she wants to corner the kiddies' conversation.

The soft and huggable bunnies (right) have floppy ears, powder puff tails, and a handful of velvety carrots to amuse your bunny-loving child. Make the goose or the mama bunny and her baby as puppets (they make great pajama bags, too), or stitch and stuff them into toys.

The gabby goose and the mama rabbit are large puppets—your child's arm will be hidden when inserted into the goose's neck or the base of the rabbit to make the animal chatter and move. When completed, the goose is about 35 inches tall, the mama rabbit about 25 inches tall, and the baby bunny about 11 inches high. Make all three from plush fake fur, using the simple patterns on pages 271 and 273.

To make the goose, stitch up the body, sewing by hand if the fabric is too bulky to stitch by machine. Then stuff the body at least three-quarters full of plastic pellets or fiberfill.

After assembling the neck and head, make the beak by stitching canvas triangles together. Insert cardboard liners to make the beak stiff, then paint the canvas bright orange and black using acrylic paints. To make the eyes sparkle, coat black buttons with clear nail polish before sewing them to the head.

Make the goose's legs and feet from orange rubber gloves. Cut "toes" from the fingers and thigh and calf pieces from the palms and backs of the gloves. Gather and glue the pieces together, and stitch them to the body. Then anchor a tricycle horn into the body of the goose to give her a voice all her own. Once the horn is in place, your youngster will be able to squeeze the bulb with his free hand.

Make fluffy wings by cutting individual fake fur "feathers" and sewing them in layers onto the goose's wings. To complement her flighty appearance, finish her up

with three festive collars gathered about her neck in a ruff.

For the bunnies use short-pile fur—white for the mama and beige for the baby. Line the ears with shiny pink satin or soft velveteen. Then, to make the ears perky, support them with pipe cleaners twisted together and tacked into the seam, out of sight. Your child will be able to cock the ears of his new toy however he pleases.

The legs on the bunnies are separate pieces, stitched and stuffed, and then sewn to the body through a button on the inside. That way the legs move freely when your child wiggles his hand inside the body.

Each of these puppets is easily sewn into a toy, such as the baby bunny (left), simply by closing the seam that's left open to make it a puppet.

Gifts for Imaginative Play

Soft and cuddly, just right for hugging and squeezing and rocking to sleep—chances are that's your youngster's idea of a doll. And these brother and sister dolls (opposite) and the little miss perched on her very own bed (below) are exactly that—lovable, huggable friends.

This pair of old-fashioned dolls (opposite), made of muslin, has high-button shoes, yarn hair, and sweet embroidered faces. The little girl is dressed in lacy pantaloons, a polka-dotted shift, and rickrack-trimmed pinafore. Her brother wears corduroy pants (held up by ribbon suspenders) and a gingham shirt topped off with a casual polka-dotted tie.

The perky doll (below) wears a nightie and robe to match her cushy upholstered bed. Construct the bed from stock lumber, pad it with quilt batting, and cover it with a pretty print. Then your tiny tot will have a comfortable spot to sit and chat with her new friend, as well as a special place for her doll to sleep.

Make the doll of soft brushed flannel, using the pattern on page 105. For her hair, use black yarn—or yarn in a color that matches your child's hair.

Gifts for Imaginative Play

Your junior train engineer, car enthusiast, or airplane pilot will be off on a fantastic imaginary adventure when he opens a package with one of these toys on Christmas morning. This old-time steam engine (opposite) can be built in just an evening or two in your workshop—as can the horseless carriage (right) or the biplane (below). And the kids will delight in hearing stories of early flights, and about the golden spike joining the East and West coasts by rail.

Because these toys are made of sturdy pine, they'll last until your child outgrows them. Use stock lumber and dowels for the basic construction and build them using the diagrams on pages 276 and 277. To safeguard tiny tots, assemble the parts with nontoxic glue. Then sand off all the rough edges.

Seal the finished toy using two coats of satin varnish, sanding well between coats. When the varnish is thoroughly dry, buff with steel wool until your child's new toy is smooth as glass.

Pine is an excellent wood for Christmas toys, but you also may wish to work with one of the fine furniture woods such as gum, poplar, willow, or basswood. All are slightly harder than pine, but they're every bit as easy to work with. In addition, they have fine, even grains and are generally knot free; so the clear finish you put on the toys looks especially attractive.

Instructions for a Child's Fantasy Christmas: Gifts for Imaginative Play

The instructions below and on the following pages are for the gifts and toys shown on pages 258–267. For directions for enlarging and transferring designs, see pages 370–371.

Zoo Sleeping Bag
pages 258–259

Materials: 3½ yards of bright blue fabric; 2½ yards of orange fabric; 2½ yards of yellow fabric; 3 yards of green fabric; scraps of white and red fabric; 6 yards of 36-inch-wide fabric for lining; 4 yards non-woven interfacing; 2 king-size quilt batts; 108-inch zipper (or Velcro); ½ pound polyester fiberfill; thread to match fabrics; blue quilting thread; brown wrapping paper.

Instructions: Cut fabric as follows: 2 pieces blue, 38½×56 inches; 4 pieces yellow, 2½×50 inches; 4 pieces yellow, 2½×68 inches; 4 pieces orange, 3×50 inches; 4 pieces orange, 3×68 inches; 4 pieces green, 3½×50 inches; 4 pieces green, 3½×68 inches.

Enlarge designs (opposite) on brown paper; this will be your master pattern. Trace designs on tissue paper; cut apart. Cut appliqués from remnants, using photograph on page 259 as a guide. Cut basic shape from one color, then cut detail pieces to appliqué. (For example, cut tiger from orange, then cut stripes from blue.)

Pin detail pieces to animal shapes; then pin animals to interfacing. Lightly mark non-appliquéd detail lines with pencil. (Each animal is stitched and padded before it is applied to bag.)

Set machine on medium-width zigzag and medium-length stitch. Stitch around all details, leaving a small opening for stuffing. Next, stuff details lightly and baste openings closed. Set machine on satin stitch (widest zigzag, closest stitch) and stitch over all basting lines to close openings.

Zigzag-baste along detail lines and again around outside edges of animal shapes, leaving an opening. Stuff lightly; baste opening closed. Then satin-stitch along all detail lines. Trim excess interfacing from edges of animals. Baste animals in position onto pieces of blue

fabric; machine-zigzag into place, then satin-stitch outside edges.

Cut out "My Zoo" and pin or glue into place. Satin-stitch.

Next, stitch yellow, orange, and green strips together, using ½-inch seams, to make bands for front and back of bag. Make four 50-inch strips and four 68-inch strips. Press seams.

With right sides together, pin strips to outer edges of blue center sections. Stitch, starting ½ inch from each corner. Next, miter all corners; stitch. Trim excess fabric from mitered seams.

With right sides of front and back together, stitch one long side.

Cut lining fabric into 3 pieces, each measuring 34×68 inches. Stitch all 3 pieces together, making 1 piece that is 68×100 inches. Press seams open.

With right sides facing, pin lining and sleeping bag cover together along the top and sides. Stitch across top and down 10 inches from top on both sides. Turn to right side; press.

To pad bag: Slip 2 layers of batting into bag; pin to wrong side of lining. Trim batting ¾ inch narrower than lining. Baste batting to lining. Pin bag cover to lining and batting.

Press outer seam allowances on cover and lining to inside. Open zipper; place bottom of zipper at bottom of bag's center seam. Pin zipper between lining and cover; baste and stitch zipper into place, catching cover and lining with a row of stitching. Or, substitute nylon fastening tape for zipper.

To quilt: Using quilting thread and medium-length straight stitches, quilt around all animals and bands. Start quilting in center of bag; work toward outside edges. When quilting is finished, remove all basting.

Hippo Pillow
page 259

Materials: 1 yard of yellow fabric; 1¾ yards of non-woven interfacing or 1 yard of lining fabric; scraps of green and red fabric; orange thread; 2 pounds polyester fiberfill.

Instructions: On brown wrapping paper, enlarge hippo pattern (opposite)

following this scale for the pillow: 1 square equals 3¼ inches. Add ½-inch seam allowances. Pin pattern on double thickness of yellow fabric; cut it out. Repeat for interfacing or lining.

Transfer all markings to one yellow hippo piece. Cut out appliqués. Pin them onto hippo front which has been backed with interfacing or lining.

Set sewing machine on medium-width zigzag and medium-length stitch; baste appliqués into place. Also baste along detail lines. Set machine on satin stitch; stitch over basting.

Pin hippo front and back together, right sides facing. (Interfacing or lining should be on outside top and bottom.) Stitch around outside edges, leaving an opening.

Trim seams, clip curves, and turn. Stuff with polyester fiberfill. Slip-stitch the opening closed.

Gingham Ducks
page 260

Materials: ¼ yard each of gingham checks in 3 different sizes; fiberfill.

Instructions: Using 8½×11 inches paper for large duck and 6½×8½ inches paper for small duck, draw duck shape (body, head, beak). Mark separation line of beak from head. Cut pattern apart, add ¼-inch seam allowance, and cut body and head, beak, and eye from different-size checks. Stitch eye and beak to head. Sew body back to front, leaving an opening. Turn, stuff, and slip-stitch.

Make wings and feet from circles. For large duck, cut three 4½-inch circles and two 7-inch circles. For small duck, cut three 3½-inch circles and two 4½-inch circles. Cut all circles in half.

To make wings, appliqué small half-circle to large half-circle, turning under raw edges ⅛ inch. Sew plain half-circle to appliquéd half-circle along curved edge in ¼-inch seam. Turn, stuff; slip-stitch opening and tack to body. For feet, sew 2 halves of small circles together on curved edge. Turn, stuff lightly, slip-stitch. Fold stuffed wedge in half (into quarter circle); tack to body.

continued

MY ZOO

1 Square = 2¾ Inches

Continued from page 269
Gifts for Imaginative Play

Stick Reindeer
page 261

Materials: 2×8×12-inch pine board; 6- and 36-inch long ⅝-inch dowels; 3-inch drawer pull (nose); ⅛×2-inch dowel; 10×24 inches quilted fabric (antlers); 3×5-inch strip matching antler fabric; 18 inches bias tape; fiberfill; rivet; red and white acrylic paint; beige and white felt; plastic eye pupils; black chenille bump for eyebrows; ribbon; jingle bells.

Instructions: *Head*—Cut head from 2×8×12-inch board. Drill hole for crossbar (A). Drill hole for 36-inch stick (B). Sand top and edge of head. Place small dowel in hole (A). Drive nail through head and crossbar to secure.

Glue long dowel in head (B). Stain head, crossbar, and stick. Varnish when dry. Drive rivet into nose (C).

Paint drawer-pull nose red; give second coat, if necessary. Dip end of small dowel in white paint; touch red nose at random, let dry. Spray with sealer. Place small amount of glue in hole of "nose"; force end into rivet.

Antlers—Cut 2 sets of antlers from 10×24-inch quilted fabric (back and front) with pinking shears. With wrong sides together, stitch, using ¼-inch seam. (Let seam on outside show.) Leave a 2-inch opening at bottom (center), then stuff firmly with fiberfill. (Do not stuff firmly in center of antlers.) Stitch opening closed. Gather center together by hand; tie with double length of string. (See diagram, below.)

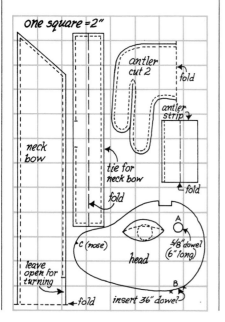

one square = 2"

antler cut 2 · fold · antler strip · fold · neck bow · tie for neck bow · fold · fold · leave open for turning · fold · insert 36" dowel · c (nose) · head · ⅝" dowel (6" long) · A · B

To hold antlers in place, fold and stitch a 3×5-inch fabric strip with a ¼-inch seam. Finished size is 5×1¼ inches. Turn and press. Using staple gun, attach 1 inch of strip into groove at top of head. Place tied antlers into groove; pull strip tightly over antlers, folding edge under. Staple.

Tie an 18-inch polka-dotted ribbon bow at neck, then glue on white felt eyes, beige felt eyebrows, plastic pupils, and chenille bump eyelid. Attach jingle bells to the ends of the ribbon, if desired.

Moose Cap Rack
page 261

Materials: ¾-inch plywood in following sizes—28×9½ inches, 12½×11 inches, four 4×6-inch pieces; scraps of ¼-inch dowel totaling 20 inches; primer; paint; 2 screw eyes.

Instructions: Cut pattern pieces; sand, and fill where necessary. Apply primer coat. Drill dowel holes for face and hooks. Dowel and glue parts, face, and hooks to horns.

Paint finish coat on assembled parts and on features. When paint dries, glue eyes and nostrils to face. Add screw eyes on back for hanging. (See pattern, below.)

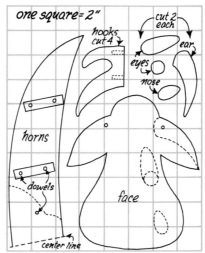

one square = 2"

hooks cut 4 · cut 2 each · ear · eyes · nose · horns · dowels · face · center line

Bunnies and Bears
page 261

Note: One yard of 45-inch-wide fabric will yield fronts and backs for the following: 4 large rabbits; 8 small rabbits; 3 large bears; or 5 small bears. Purchase fabric accordingly.

Materials: 45-inch-wide broadcloth; #5 pearl cotton embroidery thread; fiberfill for stuffing; embroidery needle;

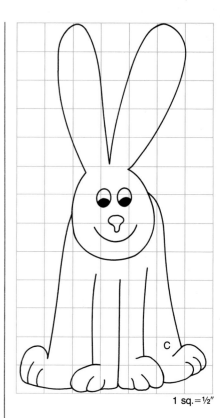

1 sq. = ½"

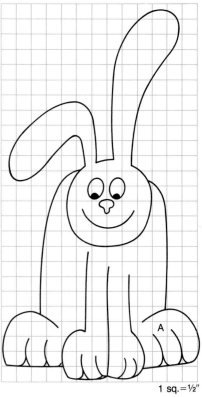

1 sq. = ½"

embroidery hoop, dark-colored waterproof marker; tissue paper.

Instructions: Enlarge patterns (above and opposite); transfer to tissue paper. Go over outlines with marker to darken them. For small bear, reduce pattern so height equals 9 inches.

1 sq. = ½"

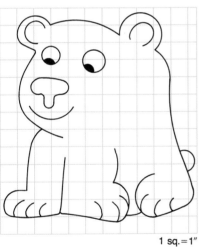

1 sq. = 1"

Place pattern under fabric; *lightly* trace pattern's outline (embroidery lines) onto fabric with a pencil.

Using a hoop, embroider design lines using outline or stem stitches. Clip knot "tails" close to fabric, so ends won't show from right side of fabric.

Cut 2 inches around embroidered outline through both fabric layers for animal's front and back.

With right sides together, stitch animal front to back ½ inch away from embroidered lines. Leave small opening along bottom edge of animal for turning. Trim seams, clip curves. Turn; stuff with fiberfill. Slip-stitch opening.

Goose Puppet
page 262

Note: Finished size is 35 inches.

Materials: 1 yard (60-inch-wide) white fake fur; 1 yard unbleached muslin; ¼ yard heavyweight cotton canvas or duck; 1 pair orange rubber gloves; 1 bag plastic pellets *or* polyester fiberfill for stuffing; 1 small plastic tricycle horn with rubber bulb; 2 black buttons; cotton balls; 5×9 inches of medium-weight cardboard (¹⁄₁₆-inch-thick); four 18×36-inch pieces of lightweight cardboard; 1½×3 inches of soft foam; acrylic paints in white, black, and orange; paintbrush; yellow felt-tipped marker; heavy-duty white thread for machine stitching; white button or carpet thread for hand stitching; white glue; masking tape; contact cement.

For 3 collars: Two 4½×39-inch fabric strips; two 4×33-inch fabric strips; two 3½×31-inch fabric strips; pins; three 10-inch pieces of ¼-inch elastic.

Instructions: Enlarge patterns (below); transfer them onto lightweight cardboard. Place patterns on *wrong* side of fabric; trace around patterns using yellow marker. This line is your stitching line. When cutting out the patterns, leave an extra ½ inch *beyond* the yellow line for the cutting line.

Stitch seams twice for extra strength. If goose becomes too bulky to machine stitch, finish by hand. Trim seams to ¼ inch unless otherwise indicated.

Cut pattern pieces A, B, C, D, E, F, and G from fur. Cut 2 of G and 1 of H from muslin. Pin and stitch pieces A and B (top and bottom of body), right sides together, matching pattern dots. Make a 4½-inch slit (as marked on pattern) in *only one* of piece A. Turn body right side out through slit. (Slit is line without arrows on the pattern.)

Pour plastic pellets through slit into goose, or stuff with fiberfill, until body is three-quarters full.

Pin H (neck tunnel) along slit edges, right sides together; stitch the shorter sides of H together to form circular piece. Rip open 4½ inches of the seam directly in front of the slit, which begins where the body seams meet (see pattern piece). Push H through the slit and then through the 4½-inch opening in the seam. (See pattern for line marked with arrows.) Pin H to edges of opened seam; stitch into place.

Right sides together, stitch neck seam on piece C between dots. Pin head piece D into neck—right sides together—matching dots; stitch into place. Pin neck C to H, tucking under raw fur edges. (*Note:* Neck is sewn to the opening you made in the seam—not in the slit.) Head triangle must be at top of head with neck's seam running down neck.

Trace I onto foam. Clip this piece into a ½-ball shape. Insert ½ foam ball into neck, matching ball center to the point of the triangle D. Pin foam into place; sew into place.

To form the beak, cut beak pieces J, K, L, and M from heavy cotton fabric. With right sides together, ease and pin outer top beak J to inner top beak L; ease and pin outer bottom beak K to inner bottom beak M. Baste into place. Stitch with small stitches, trim seams to ⅛ inch, and turn. For beak liners, cut one piece L and one piece M from ¹⁄₁₆-inch cardboard. Coat both sides of each with white glue; insert into stitched beak. Push liners to beak tips; dry. Hand-sew the 2 beak halves together at the seam line; trim to ⅛ inch. Paint

continued

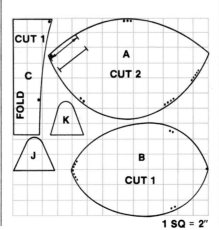

1 SQ = 2"

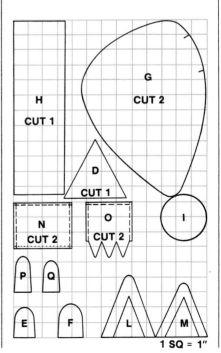

1 SQ = 1"

Continued from page 271
Gifts for Imaginative Play

beak with orange acrylic; dry. When orange paint is dry, paint black acrylic triangles on insides of beak (see pattern). Prop beak open until paint dries.

Insert beak into head and pin along seam line, tucking under raw fabric edges. Stitch into place.

Pin button eyes to head above the beak. Trim fur around eyes for better visibility. A coat of clear nail polish adds sparkle to the eyes. Let nail polish dry thoroughly before sewing eyes to head.

Cut thigh piece (N) and calf piece (O) from rubber gloves (note ⅛-inch seam allowance). Run gathering thread along upper thigh piece. (Stitch rubber by hand if machine bogs down as you work.) Stitch right sides of O together; turn right side out. Stitch sides of N, right sides together. Slip unturned thigh (N) over calf piece (O). Pull gathering thread to fit closely to calf; knot the thread. Pin, then stitch into place. Flip thigh piece *up* to form finished leg.

To form the toes, cut fingertips from rubber gloves to the length shown on patterns P and Q. Insert half of a cotton ball into the tip of each toe. Pinch the open toe end slightly to form a pleat; pin and stitch pleat. Place one short toe on either side of one long toe to form each foot. Pin together; stitch into place.

Apply contact cement to the upper portion of the toes. Insert the feet into the calves. Apply cement under each of the 3 calf flaps and gently press down onto the toes. Carefully remove the toes from the calf, setting them aside for 10 minutes to get tacky. Reinsert toes into calf, press cemented parts firmly together to bond. To attach feet and legs to goose, place goose upside down on your lap. Pin thighs to center goose bottom (B), tucking under the raw rubber edges. Hand-stitch each of thighs into place.

Attach tricycle horn to the goose body as you would stitch buttons onto clothes. To form "buttonholes," heat an ice pick and pierce 3 pairs of holes in the flared plastic part of the horn. Apply masking tape to the area where the bulb meets the horn to keep the bulb on the horn.

Place goose upside down. Find the spot where the body seams meet. Rip open a hole in this seam that's large enough to insert the horn. Push horn into the body until the horn's flared end rests against the outer fur fabric. Hand-stitch horn to the body as you would 3 buttons (through the melted holes). To ensure that horn is completely en-closed, take small gathering stitches around horn and pull tightly. Knot thread; trim excess.

Pick up the goose by the exposed horn and shake to distribute pellets or fiberfill so you can feel the bulb inside goose. With your fingers find the area where the horn is taped. Attach this area to goose body using needle and thread. To camouflage exposed horn, coat with white acrylic paint.

Place each of muslin piece G (wing) and fur piece G right sides together. Stitch together, leaving a small opening. Turn; slip-stitch opening.

To form fluffy feathers, make a small pleat in straight end of each feather piece (E and F). Secure pleat using 1 or 2 stitches before arranging on wing. Stitch feathers to each wing, beginning with F pieces at broad end of wing and working toward wing tip with E pieces. (Four large stitches across top of each feather and 2 or 3 small stitches to bind off are enough to attach each feather securely.)

Position one wing on body's center front; pin and stitch into place. Place second wing on strip behind neck to hide your child's arm when it goes into neck. Pin and stitch.

Each of the 3 collars is reversible, and has a side with a solid color and another with a print. Fold each fabric strip in half lengthwise, right sides facing; stitch 3 sides; leave a 3-inch opening. Turn and press.

Run a line of stitching from lower end of one ½-inch opening to the other to form elastic casing. Safety-pin one end of 10-inch elastic piece next to one of the ½-inch openings. Put second safety pin in opposite elastic end. Using the pin as a needle, thread elastic through the casing. Remove pins; stitch elastic ends together. Tack collar ends together to hide elastic. Distribute gathers evenly along length of collar piece.

Large Bunny Puppet
page 263

Note: Finished size is 25 inches.

Materials: ½ yard (60 inches wide) white fake fur cloth; scraps of pink satin or velveteen for ear lining; scraps of black velveteen or felt for nose; two ½-inch black buttons for eyes; two ⅝-inch white buttons; polyester fiberfill for stuffing; one package 6-inch pipe cleaners; black and white sewing thread; large needle; masking tape; brown wrapping paper; waterproof yellow felt-tipped pen.

Instructions: Enlarge pattern pieces (opposite) onto wrapping paper; add ½-inch seam allowances to all pieces except F. Cut pieces A, B, C, D, and E from fur fabric after placing patterns on *wrong* side of fabric and outlining with the felt-tipped pen. Mark position of eyes, ears, tail, and hind legs on right side of fur (see black dots on pattern pieces). Cut bunny ear linings (E) from pink fabric; cut bunny nose and nose lining (F) from black fabric.

With right sides together, stitch the A pieces at the center back. Stitch back to front (B), right sides together. Trim seams to ¼ inch; turn.

With right sides facing, sew ear linings to ears; leave bottom edge open. Trim seams to ¼ inch; turn. Twist 4 pipe cleaners together to form a circle. Wrap joints with masking tape; bend circle into ear shape. Insert into ear. Tack pipe cleaners into place at the ear tip. Turn raw edges of ear base to the inside, covering the end of the pipe cleaner circle. Sew ear to body using carpet thread. Repeat for other ear.

Baste along seam allowance of tail (C) with carpet thread, leaving 1 inch of thread at ends. Pull thread to form a puff; leave an opening for stuffing. Stuff; gather threads tightly and knot. Stitch tail to bunny back.

With right sides together, stitch each leg, leaving bottom end open. Trim seams, turn. Stuff legs using fiberfill; slip-stitch openings closed. Attach legs by hand-stitching through to a button located on the body's *inside.*

Baste nose to nose lining. Turn slashed edges under; stitch nose to face. Sew button eyes into place.

Make a circle of double rows of pipe cleaners for rabbit bottom. Twist pairs of pipe cleaners together to make a circle that's 5 groups around. Wrap joints with tape. Place circle inside rabbit's lower edge along seam allowance. Pin seam allowance to inside; hem. Gently fluff any fur that's caught in the stitches. (*Note:* Large bunny also may be made into a stuffed toy by adding a bottom oval piece. See small bunny how-to opposite.)

● *Carrots*

Materials: (Makes 4 carrots of varying sizes.) Square of orange felt or velveteen; square of green felt; polyester fiberfill; orange and black sewing thread.

Instructions: Enlarge carrot and leaf patterns; transfer to brown paper. Trace carrot patterns onto orange fabric. Cut carrots out ½-inch *beyond* pencil lines.

With right sides together; stitch carrot front and back on penciled line; seam is ½ inch. Leave straight end open. Trim seams to ¼ inch; turn and stuff, leaving

½ inch at top empty. Baste along the top; leave 1 inch of thread at each end.

Cut out green leaves; do *not* add ½ inch to pattern Match leaf pairs together. Place matching leaves atop each other, then raise one leaf ¼ inch above the other so foliage is staggered. Pin leaf pairs into this position; stitch, using black thread, along leaf center. If desired, place a tiny bit of fiberfill between the leaf pieces then outline stitch in black.

Place finished leaf into open carrot end. Draw up basting threads; knot. Hand-stitch carrot and leaf together. Arrange carrots in a basket, or attach singly to bunny puppets.

Small Bunny Toy
page 263

Note: Finished size is 11 inches.

Materials: ¼ yard (60 inches wide) white fake fur; ¼ yard (60 inches wide) beige fake fur; scraps of pink satin or velveteen for ear lining; scraps of black velveteen or felt for nose; 2 black ⅜-inch buttons for eyes; 2 white ⅝-inch buttons; black and white thread; fiberfill for stuffing; white carpet thread; yellow felt-tipped pen.

Instructions: Enlarge patterns (below); add ½-inch seam allowances to *all* the pieces except pattern piece F.

Arrange the patterns on the wrong side of the fabric: cut pieces A, D, E, and H from beige fur; cut B, C, and G from white fur (see photograph). Trace pieces using yellow pen. Cut out pieces using sharp scissors and cutting only through backing fabric of fur.

On right side of fur, mark position of ears, eyes, tail, and legs (black dots on patterns).

Cut ear linings from pink satin or velveteen and nose and nose lining from black fabric. With right sides facing, sew ear linings to ears; leave bottom open. Trim seams to ¼ inch; turn right side out.

continued

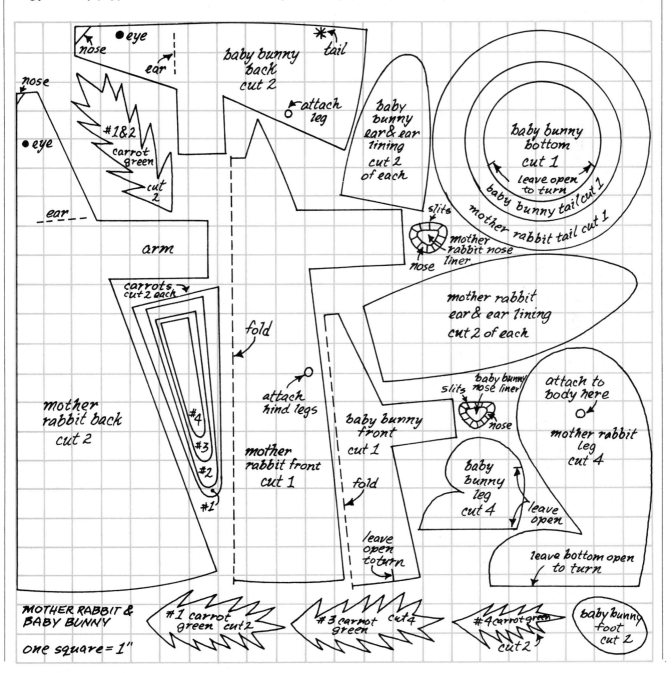

273

Continued from page 273
Gifts For Imaginative Play

With right sides together, stitch A pieces at the center back. Sew back to B, right sides together. Pin H to body bottom and stitch; leave an opening for turning. Trim seams to ¼ inch; turn to right side. Sew ears to body.

Baste along seam allowance of tail (C); leave an inch of thread at both ends. Pull basting to form a puff, leaving a small opening for stuffing. Stuff and gather tightly; knot thread. Stitch tail to back.

With right sides together, stitch legs (D), leaving bottom ends open. Position feet bottoms (G) into this opening, right sides facing; stitch. Turn to right side; stuff legs. Slip-stitch opening closed. Attach legs to body by stitching through to button on inside of body.

Baste nose to nose lining (F). Turn slashed edges under and stitch nose to bunny face. Sew button eyes into place using carpet thread.

Stuff body through bottom. Slip-stitch opening closed. Fluff any fur that caught while being stitched. (*Note:* Baby bunny also may be made into a puppet by omitting the bottom piece H. See large bunny how-to page 272.)

Brother and Sister Dolls
page 264

Note: Finished size is 26 inches.

Materials: (Enough for both dolls.) 1¼ yards of 45-inch-wide muslin; ½ yard each of green polka-dotted, green print, and brown corduroy fabrics; ½ yard each of green gingham, rust, and brown fabrics; thread to match; embroidery floss in blue, rust, coral, and pale yellow; four ⅜-inch gold buttons for boy's pants; one ½-inch green button for girl's pinafore; ten ⅜-inch black buttons for boy's boots and ten ⅜-inch pearl buttons for girl's boots.

Two yards of ivory rickrack; 1¼ yards of 1-inch-wide ivory eyelet; 1 yard of ½-inch braid for suspenders; 1 yard of ⅜-inch grosgrain ribbon for hair; 1½ yards of ¼-inch elastic; snaps; bias tape; 1 pound of polyester fiberfill for stuffing; 1 skein of #325 Rust and #320 Burnt Orange Aunt Lydia's Rug Yarn for the doll's hair.

Instructions: Enlarge doll patterns (right); use same body pattern for both dolls. Pattern pieces include ¼-inch seam allowances. Transfer patterns to paper or tissue, and cut doll bodies from muslin fabric.

Using blue floss for eyes, rust for eyebrows and eyelids, yellow for nose,

and coral for mouth, embroider doll faces using satin and outline stitches (refer to color photograph, page 264).

With right sides together, stitch front and back of each doll together (¼-inch seam allowances), leaving openings where the arms will go and also at the base of the body for stuffing. Turn bodies right side out; press. Stitch, turn, and press arms.

For boots, zigzag machine-stitch or hand-appliqué brown heel and toe designs onto rust boots following "foot" pattern. Sew boot top to appliquéd foot. Stitch boot to leg. With right sides facing, stitch around each leg-and-boot piece, leaving top open for stuffing. Turn, press, and stuff with fiberfill. Stitch buttons up outside of each boot (use pearl buttons for girl, black buttons for boy).

Stuff doll arms and stitch to body. Stuff head and body. Stitch legs to front of body, turn under back seam, and slip-stitch closed.

Hair for girl: Open a skein of rust rug yarn. Spread yarn on table and smooth out strands until they form a 7½-inch-wide strip. To form yarn wig, place a piece of tape down the center of yarn strands; stitch through both yarn and tape; repeat for extra strength. Remove tape; slip-stitch wig to doll's head. Arrange hair in ponytails; tie with ribbons. Trim yarn ends and tack hair to head with matching thread where necessary.

Hair for boy: Thread a single strand of burnt orange rug yarn double in a large tapestry needle. Beginning at base of hairline, stitch hair to back of boy doll's head by making 2-inch-long rya knots in evenly spaced rows every ½ inch up to top of head. On front of doll, stitch from "earline" around the front, following the seam line. Yarn hair should be trimmed to about 1½ inches long all around.

Clothing for girl: Cut bloomers from muslin, stitch seams, and add double

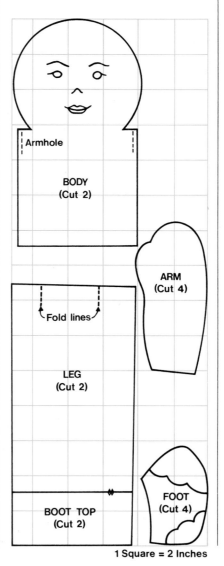

1 Square = 2 Inches

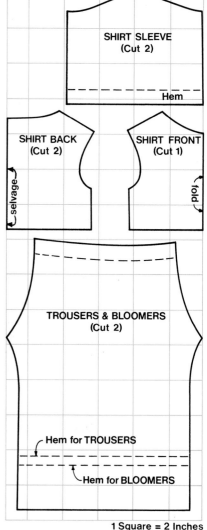

1 Square = 2 Inches

274

rows of eyelet trim. Turn under top edge to make casing for elastic waistband. Insert elastic and trim to fit; slip-stitch casing closed.

For green polka-dotted dress, stitch back seam up to opening along selvage line. Stitch front to back at shoulders. Gather sleeve top and stitch to dress. Turn under edges of sleeves and finish; stitch band of elastic ½ inch from

bottom of sleeve and fit to doll arm. Stitch side and sleeve seams; hem dress and finish neck edge using bias tape. Add snaps for back closing.

For green print pinafore, sew side and shoulder seams. Turn up hem. Finish bottom edge, back edges, neckline, and armholes using white rickrack. Place button and buttonhole at neck top in back. Appliqué pocket to front of pinafore; add a hanky cut from dress scrap with pinking shears.

Clothing for boy: Cut trousers from brown corduroy fabric; stitch same as for girl doll's bloomers, omitting eyelet. Turn up 3-inch hem, then turn back again to form cuffs. Cut 2 pieces of braid for suspenders. Cross suspenders in back; tack into place. Sew 2 yellow buttons below each point where suspender is tacked to front of trousers.

For boy doll's shirt, stitch shoulder seams, insert sleeves, then stitch side and sleeve seams. Turn under sleeve edge and stitch. Neck edge is finished with bias tape. With pinking shears, cut bow tie from fabric scrap.

Little Miss Doll
page 265

Materials: Two 1×6×12-inch pieces of lumber; two 1×6×16½-inch pieces of lumber; ⅜×12×18 inches plywood; ⅜×12×22 inches plywood; two 1-inch screws; 4 small, right angle braces; quilt batting; stapler; 12×22 inches cardboard; glue; 2 yards print fabric; 2 yards broadcloth or batiste in solid color to complement print; 1 yard gingham in color to complement print, or substitute 8⅓ yards 1½-inch gingham ribbon for ruffle on flounce and narrower ribbon for nightgown and hairbows; light pink flannel for doll's body; black felt for slippers; black yarn for hair; embroidery floss; small scraps of print fabric for neckbow, pocket and bias binding on robe; double fold bias tape.

Instructions: Construct base for bed using 1×6-inch lumber. Butt join sides to ends so bed frame measures 6×12×18 inches. Do not add top and headboard yet.

Cut quilt batting to fit around sides and one end of bed frame (about 6×48 inches). Staple batting to wood.

Next, cut a strip of print fabric 12×52 inches to fit around 2 sides and end. Staple one narrow end of the fabric strip to the unpadded end of the bed frame. Pull fabric tight around sides and end; staple other narrow end to unpadded section. Stretch fabric over edges of sides and end; staple to inside of frame.

Cut 2 or 3 layers of quilt batting to fit the top of the bed (12×18 inches); staple into place.

Cut print fabric for top of bed 16×22 inches. Stretch fabric tightly over padding; staple to back of top. To minimize wrinkling, begin stapling in center of each side and work toward corners. Staple corners last, folding fabric into neat, flat mitered corners (trim excess if necessary).

Pad headboard using quilt batting beginning 6 inches above bottom edge; staple batting into place. Cut print fabric 16×26 inches, stretch over padding and staple into place on back of headboard. Next, fit headboard to unpadded end of bed frame. Drill holes for screws; screw headboard to bed.

Cut print fabric 14×24 inches to cover cardboard. Center card on wrong side of fabric; stretch extra fabric over the edge, mitering the corners. Glue to cardboard. When glue is dry, glue covered cardboard to back of headboard, hiding the raw edges of the upholstery fabric.

Finally, join the top of the bed (mattress) to the sides with angle braces, using 2 on each side.

● Bedding

Cut fabric for bedding as follows: From print, cut one piece 13½×19 inches for spread top, two pieces 7×7 inches for pillow, one piece 6×36 inches for ruffle on pillow, and one piece 12×13½ inches for bolster. From solid-color fabric, cut one piece 26×28 inches for sheet, one piece 9×120 inches for flounce on bedspread (cut and piece fabric strips to necessary length), and two 4¼-inch circles for bolster. From gingham, cut and piece a 3×300-inch length for ruffle on flounce (or use ribbon).

To make the pillow, fold ruffle in half lengthwise; gather along raw edges. Fit ruffle to edge of pillow front; baste. Stitch pillow front to back, right sides together (with ruffle tucked between); seam allowance is ½ inch. Leave an opening for turning. Turn, press, stuff, and slip-stitch the opening.

To make bolster, fold fabric in half (to 6¾×12 inches); stitch along 12-inch edge, leaving ends open. Pin circles into ends, stitch, turn, stuff, and whipstitch opening closed.

To make the sheet, put sheet on bed (width is 26 inches). Pin sheet to fit at corners at foot of bed. Stitch, cut off excess fabric close to seam. Sew a 3-inch hem in top of the sheet. Turn up a narrow hem along sides and end. Or, if desired, add a row or two of decorative eyelet ruffling along top of sheet.

continued

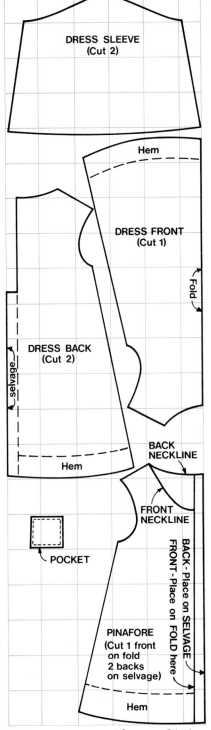

DRESS SLEEVE
(Cut 2)

Hem

DRESS FRONT
(Cut 1)

Fold

DRESS BACK
(Cut 2)

selvage

Hem

BACK
NECKLINE

FRONT
NECKLINE

POCKET

BACK - Place on SELVAGE
FRONT - Place on FOLD here

PINAFORE
(Cut 1 front
on fold
2 backs
on selvage)

Hem

1 Square = 2 Inches

Continued from page 275
Gifts For Imaginative Play

To make the bedspread, sew a 2½-inch hem in one edge of the flounce. Then sew a ½-inch hem on both sides of the ruffle (omit this step if you are using ribbon). Gather the ruffle ¾ inch from one edge. Pull up the ruffle to fit the flounce; stitch into place. Gather flounce to fit sides and one end of spread top. Stitch flounce to spread. (If desired, stitch lining piece to underside of spread top.) Bind top edge of spread using bias tape.

● *Doll*

Using pattern on page 105 for small doll, stitch and stuff doll. Embroider facial features and make hair from yarn according to directions on page 106. Make nightgown and robe from remaining bed fabrics, referring to photograph on page 265 for design ideas.

Steam Engine
page 266

Note: Size is 9¾×6×2⅜ inches.

Materials: ¾×2⅜×20 inches C-select pine; ⅜×3½×26 inches C-select pine; ¼×9-inch dowel; ⅝×3-inch dowel; 1 inch of 1¼-inch-diameter dowel; 1¾×1⅝×4 inches of handrail stock; one 1½-inch flat head wood screw; white wood glue; sandpaper; varnish; 0000 steel wool; carbon paper.

Instructions: Enlarge pattern (right); transfer to wood using a soft pencil and carbon paper. Cut pieces.

Assemble train engine by following the exploded isometric drawing shown at right. Predrill wheel carriage, then screw and glue it to the base. Assemble remainder of the train engine with nontoxic glue.

Sand all the edges smooth. Finish with 2 coats of clear varnish. After the varnish is completely dry, buff with steel wool for extra smoothness.

Horseless Carriage
page 267

Note: Finished size is 10×7×5 inches.

Materials: ⅜×4×42 inches C-select pine; ¾×4×16 inches pine; ¼×12-inch dowel; ¾×1½-inch dowel; ⁵⁄₁₆×3-inch dowel; wire brads; coat hanger; nontoxic white wood glue; sandpaper; varnish; 0000 steel wool.

Instructions: Enlarge pattern pieces (opposite); transfer to wood. Cut out the wood pieces.

Glue and nail the seat to the body parts, and the seat support to the

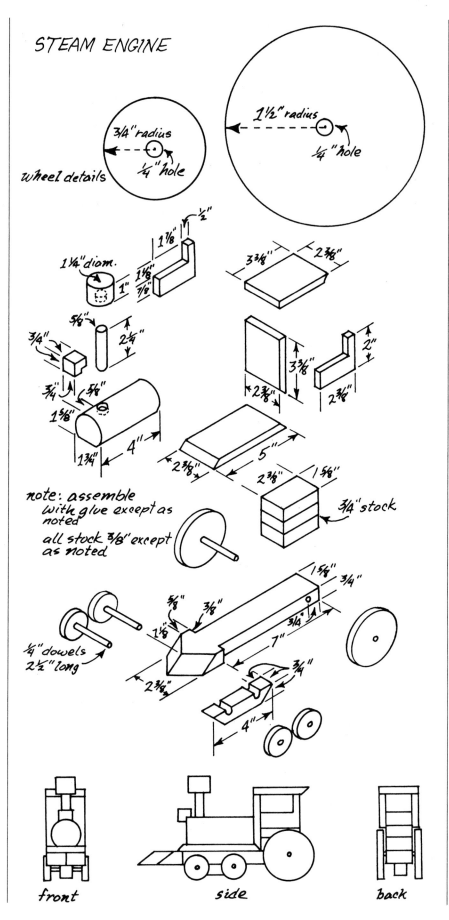

STEAM ENGINE

chassis. Glue these 2 assemblies together, as shown in the drawing (below, right). Next, glue dashboard to chassis.

Make tiller of 5/16-inch dowel and 2 inches of coat hanger wire. Glue and nail wheel carriage to chassis. Glue wheels to axles as shown. Glue headlights to the chassis.

Sand edges smooth; finish with 2 coats of varnish. Buff with steel wool when varnish is completely dry.

Biplane

page 267

Materials: 36 inches of 2⅜×⅜-inch pine; 10 inches of 1½×¾-inch pine; 2 inches of 2¼×¾-inch pine; 16 inches of 5/16-inch-diameter dowel; 4 inches of ¾×⅛-inch pine; ⅛×¾-inch roundhead screw with washer; one 1½-inch flathead wood screw; nontoxic white wood glue; sandpaper; varnish; 0000 steel wool.

Instructions: Enalrge pattern (below); transfer to wood; cut pieces.

Assemble the 2 wings with 5/16-inch dowel struts, as shown in drawing. Glue wings to fuselage; assemble all other parts as shown using white glue.

Sand edges smooth. Finish with clear varnish. After varnish is completely dry, buff with steel wool.

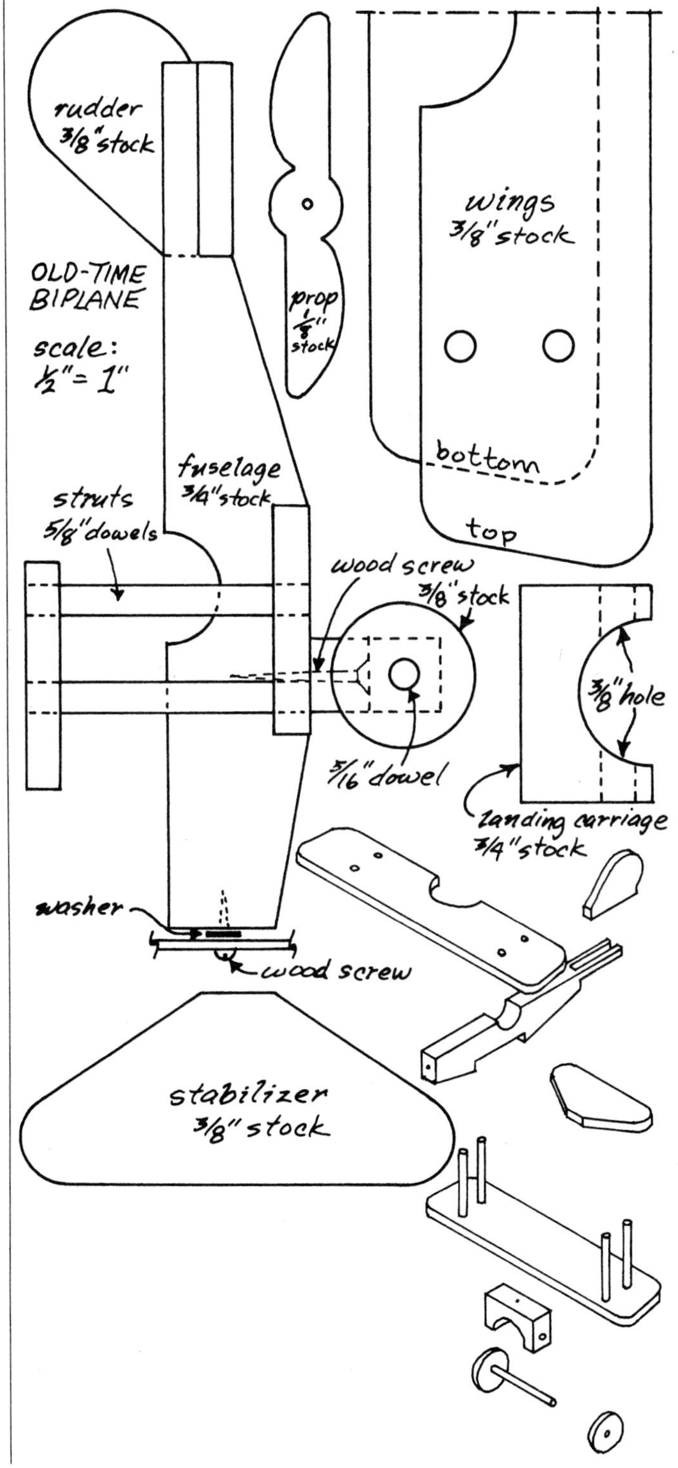

rudder 3/8" stock
OLD-TIME BIPLANE
scale: 1/2" = 1"
prop 1/8" stock
wings 3/8" stock
bottom
top
fuselage 3/4" stock
struts 5/8" dowels
wood screw
3/8" stock
3/8" hole
5/16" dowel
landing carriage 3/4" stock
washer
wood screw
stabilizer 3/8" stock

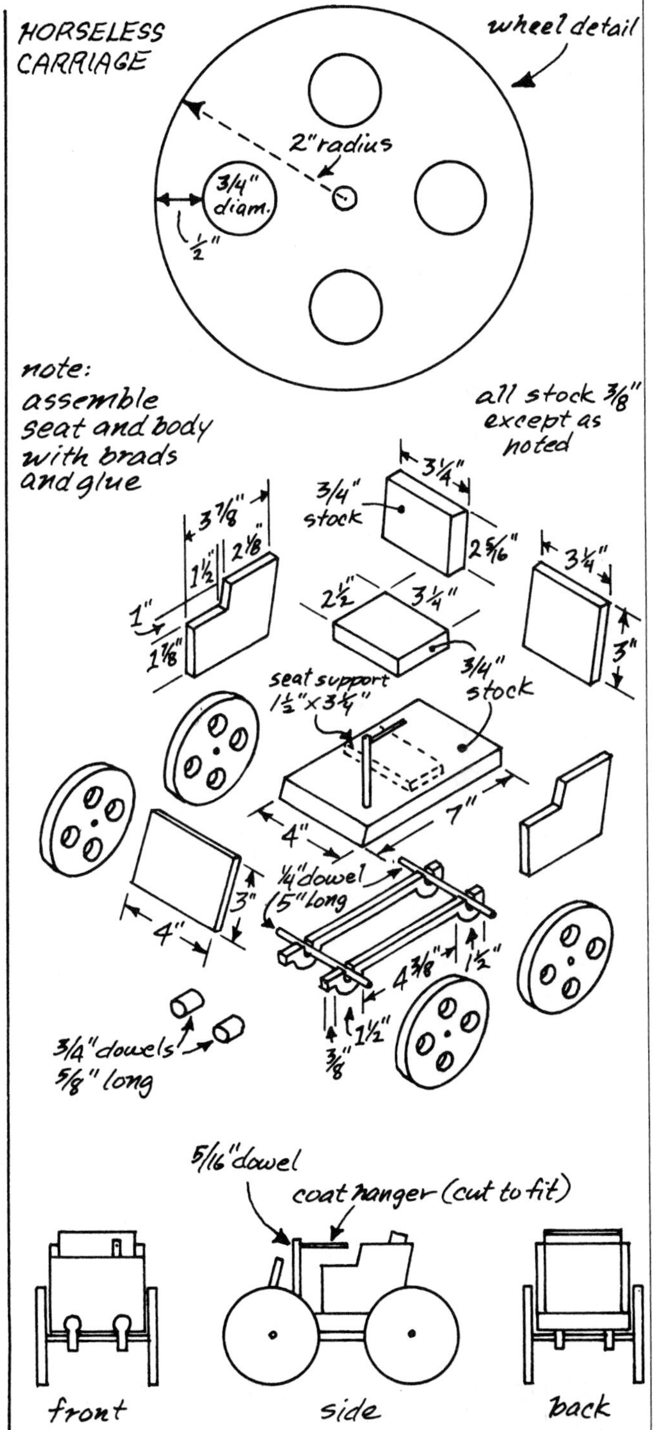

HORSELESS CARRIAGE
wheel detail
2" radius
3/4" diam.
1/2"
note: assemble seat and body with brads and glue
all stock 3/8" except as noted
3/4" stock
3 1/4"
3 7/8"
2 1/8"
1 1/2"
1"
1 1/8"
2 5/16"
3 1/4"
2 1/2"
3 1/4"
3"
seat support 1 1/2" x 3 1/4"
3/4" stock
4"
7"
1/4" dowel 5" long
3"
4"
4 3/8"
1 1/2"
1 1/2"
3/8
3/4" dowels 5/8" long
5/16" dowel
coat hanger (cut to fit)
front
side
back

The Christmas Story

Beautiful Crèche Figures

Nativity scenes have been popular Christmas symbols since 1224, when St. Francis of Assisi erected a manger and played out the first Christmas with a cast of characters that included live animals and real people. The crèches shown in this section are today's versions, and include a grotto scene (below), crafted to display ceramic figures, and an elegant but easy-to-make triptych (opposite).

Directions for all the projects begin on page 288.

Beautiful Crèche Figures

Crèche, the French word for cradle, has come to mean a nativity scene depicting the infant Jesus in a lowly manger, surrounded by Mary, Joseph, the animals, and adoring shepherds and magi—just as in this charming scene (below).

Simple materials and a little time are all you need to create these crèche figures. The figures have bottle foundations and foam-ball heads and hands. They are imaginatively draped with prestarched fabric that is available by the

yard in craft stores. Shape snippets of fake fur into hair and beards, and swirl acrylic modeling paste into curly lamb's wool.

Embellish the kings' costumes with bits of braid, plastic or glass jewels, and other trims.

Use fabric to craft a graceful turban and paper to shape a crown. Tiny "gifts" are small pieces of foam covered with fabric and trimmed with braid.

When costuming is completed, the figures are elegantly painted with artist's acrylics and then wiped with antiquing stain. Fine features go on with an artist's brush or felt-tip pen.

Heights of the figures vary from 7 inches for the lambs to 18 inches for Joseph.

Beautiful Crèche Figures

Generation after generation of people have created nativity scenes to symbolize the beauty of the birth of Christ. This present-day interpretation wins the prize for its stunning simplicity, gemlike brilliance, and striking contemporary look.

All of the figures and the triptych and star in the background are made with a framework of lead came wrapped around pieces of richly colored stained glass and "jewels." To cut the glass, use an inexpensive cutter found in hardware or craft stores.

Figures range in height from 2 to 8 inches. The mirrored triptych, hinged together with solder, stands 9½ inches high. When assembled, the three sections measure about 20 inches across.

Small braces at the base of the figures allow them to stand easily.

Beautiful Crèche Figures

If you're an avid needlepointer, you won't want to bypass this stately crèche. Each of the eight figures is a soft-sculpture work of art. Together they make an heirloom collection your family will treasure now and for many Christmases to come.

Although this stunning crèche features a rainbow of beautiful colors and elegantly stylized designs, the figures are worked only in continental stitches. Even a novice can make them easily. Use Persian yarn and interlock canvas, which retains its shape well and won't ravel when the pieces are cut out and stitched together.

To assemble a completed figure, apply a line of white glue ⅛ inch from the edge of the needlepoint around all sides. After the glue is thoroughly dry, trim around the figure with small, sharp scissors. Cut Vs at the top as shown on the patterns and stitch the darts to give the heads their rounded shape. Stitch the back seam, stuff lightly with fiberfill, and whipstitch the base in place.

285

Beautiful Crèche Figures

Many early crèches were made from papier-mâché or plaster. Today a crèche can be made of almost any material. Scraps of inch-thick white pine were used for these figures. The natural beauty of the wood was enhanced with transparent stain in rich, subdued colors.

The figures in this nativity scene range in height from 6⅝ inches for Joseph to 4 inches for the kneeling shepherd. Use a jigsaw or coping saw to cut out each figure, then sand and round off all edges of the figure sections. When finished sanding, stain the figures with wood stains or acrylic paints in a variety of mellow shades. Some parts of each figure can be left natural.

If you use acrylics as wood stain, thin them with water and test them on a scrap of wood to be sure color is transparent.

Reassemble and glue together the figure sections using any white household glue that dries clear. If desired, apply a finish coat of satin varnish or clear acrylic. Then sand smooth when dry.

Instructions for the Christmas Story: Beautiful Crèche Figures

The instructions below and on the following pages are for the nativity scenes and crèche figures shown on pages 278-287. For directions for enlarging and transferring designs, see the glossary, pages 370-371.

Grotto for Crèche Figures
page 278

Materials: Purchased crèche figures; 1- and 2-inch-thick plastic foam sheets; white glue; plywood or hardboard large enough to accommodate crèche figures; scraps of chicken wire; colored stones; tree bark; pieces of wood; moss; sand.

Instructions: For the grotto assemblage, find natural materials such as stones, wood, and bark in parks, woods, and fields.

To make the grotto, cut the white foam sheets into pieces large enough to accommodate groups of the figures. Glue the foam sheets to a piece of hardboard or plywood, building up a variety of levels for the figures to rest on, as shown in the photograph.

Form a mountain and a cave opening using chicken wire; cover wire with 1½×3-inch strips of papier-mâché made from paper towels or newspapers that have been dipped into white glue or modeling paste. Let dry. Mold 3 layers of paper strips over the "mountain," hiding the chicken wire.

Conceal the edges of the foam sheets using rocks or wood chips; use papier-mâché to keep them in place. For greenery dampen moss so ferns will stand. Allow the moss to dry, then glue into an upright position.

Paint uncovered areas of the board using white glue; sprinkle with sand. Large rocks or pieces of bark placed behind the scene create depth.

Triptych
page 279

Materials: Religious print designed to be cut apart for a triptych (available in craft or art supply stores); purchased triptych frame (in 3 parts) to fit print, or sufficient wood to build your own frame; wood carving tools (optional); gesso; sandpaper; red acrylic paint; gold leaf; gold leaf adhesive; soft bristle brush or scraps of velvet; clear, spray sealer; decoupage glue; brayer; varnish; antiquing materials; 4 sets of hinges.

Instructions: If you are constructing your own frame, cut wood pieces large enough to accommodate sections of print plus 3 or 4 inches above print for a carved motif (see photograph, page 279).

Using small chisels and other wood carving tools, carve a design at the top of the 3-piece screen.

Prepare the frame before mounting the prints. First, sand wood until it is smooth. Apply 2 coats of gesso, sanding each coat smooth after it dries. Next apply 2 or 3 coats of red acrylic paint, sanding lightly between each coat.

When red paint is dry, brush on gold-leaf adhesive. Let it dry to the tacky stage, 20 to 30 minutes. Then, gently place gold leaf on the adhesive surface, one sheet at a time. Cut gold leaf into small pieces to fit corners and angles. Using a dry, clean, soft bristle brush or a small piece of velvet, gently dab gold leaf onto adhesive. Let a bit of red paint show through, if desired. Do not use gold leaf on areas where print will go.

After 24 hours, brush off loose pieces of gold leaf. Softly burnish the gold using velvet or a soft cloth.

To prepare prints: Cut print into 3 pieces to fit triptych. (The print was designed to be used this way, so you won't lose any of the picture.) Seal both sides of each part of the print using 2 coats of spray sealer.

Glue prints in place, using either decoupage glue or spray adhesive. Then roll surface of print using a brayer, working from center to outer edges, to remove any air bubbles.

Allow glue to dry. Then apply 2 or 3 coats of varnish over gold leaf and prints. Let dry between coats. Antique the triptych if desired.

When antiquing dries, join panels together with small hinges at top and bottom, as shown in the photograph.

Fabric-Draped Crèche
pages 280-281

Materials: Quart-size soda pop bottles for all figures except Mary and camel; gallon bleach bottle (Mary); 1½ gallon bleach bottle (camel); 5-inch-diameter plastic foam balls (heads for wise men, shepherd, Mary, Joseph); prestarched fabric, ready to dip into water (available at craft supply stores); sequin pins; scraps of fake fur; glue; gesso; 2-inch-diameter foam balls (hands for figures); 18-gauge florist's wire; slender dowel; acrylic paints; scraps of braid and other trims for costumes; 2½-inch foam ball (infant's head); 1½-inch foam ball (Mary's hands); 3-inch oval foam egg (shepherd's feet); three 5-inch oval foam eggs (lamb, camel); 4-inch foam ball (lamb); acrylic modeling paste; 3-inch foam ball (camel); 2-inch foam ball (camel).

Instructions: *To make heads* for wise men, Joseph, and shepherd, roll a 5-inch white foam ball along the edge of a table. *Press hard,* making an indentation that extends halfway around the ball (figure A, opposite). Roll again, this time pressing one side of the indentation flat for the forehead (B). Make nose from part of a tiny foam ball; fold and roll foam to about ½-inch diameter. Position nose in space created by cheeks; pin in place.

Cut a piece of prestarched fabric large enough to cover half the ball; dip it into cold water, then remove—*do not soak or wring it.* Let starch in fabric soften for about 45 seconds, then lay fabric over face. Using 8 to 10 short sequin pins, attach wet fabric to ball around nose. Push pins into foam until there are no bumps as these pins will not be removed. Smooth fabric over facial curves, and secure the outside edges with pins.

Cut hair from fake fur with pile about 2 to 3 inches long. If adding a turban, hat, or scarf, do not cover entire head with hair; attach only enough to show beneath head covering. Glue and pin hair in place. Make beards and mustaches from long-pile fabric.

Paint hair and face using gesso. (For ease while painting, push a dowel into bottom of head and stand dowel up in a bottle.) While fake fur mustaches and beards are wet with gesso, clip and trim them; shape attractively. Let heads dry for several hours or overnight.

To make hands, cut a 2-inch foam ball in half; notch one side of each half, being sure to cut a right and left hand (C). Wrap each hand with a 3½-inch circle of wet fabric. Cut off any excess. While fabric is still wet, score hand using scissors' blade to make "fingers"; lines slant *toward* index finger (D).

To make bodies, bend an 18-inch length of 18-gauge flower wire around neck of bottle; twist tightly on back side of figure (E). Bend wire on each side at halfway point (elbows). Wrap each arm using 1 facial tissue; secure with ¼-inch strip of wet fabric. Leave 1 inch uncovered at bottom end of each wire; insert wire into hands later.

Wet a piece of fabric 18 inches long and 1 inch taller than bottle. Fold under an inch "hem"; gather top together and drape around bottle. No glue is needed. Wet an 8-inch square for each sleeve. Turn under an inch "hem" at top and bottom; join sides to make a tube. Slip over arm; pinch together at top. Arrange arm and sleeve to fold gracefully. Let dry several hours.

To attach head to body, remove dowel from head, then hold head over body. Tilt at various angles until it looks natural. Press down hard; bottle will leave mark on foam. Cut hole in head, spread thick glue over top of bottle; press head down onto bottle. Let dry.

To finish costumes, refer to color photograph and see instructions that follow. Make side panels of wet fabric, turning edges under to resemble coats when painted. To vary heights of figures and make turbans look high and full, pad top of head with facial tissues before draping it with fabric. Add texture to coats and turbans with braids.

For "gifts," cover small foam pieces with wet fabric, then trim with braids.

To add hands, try various angles first as with heads. Punch holes in hands with scissors' point; put glue on wire, then insert wire into hand.

For Mary and Infant, use a 5-inch foam ball for Mary's head and 2½-inch size for Babe. Follow directions for wise men. Child has only a tiny "button" for nose. Mary has more hair than wise men; it is parted in center. Use 1½-inch foam ball, cut in half, for Mary's hands.

For body, cut handle off a gallon bleach bottle. Do not add wire arms. Wet a 30×14-inch piece of fabric; fold up "hem," gather top, then drape around bottle. Let dry several hours. Glue head to body (see wise men instructions above). Bend head down and tip slightly to one side (F). Let dry.

Make a crinkled paper-towel "body" for infant; wrap head and body in a 12-inch square of wet fabric. Make sleeves for Mary as for wise men but without wire. Pad slightly with facial tissue, then pinch together at top and glue to body. Lay child in lap, fold arms around him; glue hands in place.

For shepherd, follow directions for wise men, except that robe is shorter and feet are exposed. Make feet from 3-

inch foam egg, cut in half lengthwise. Break small end off each half egg; glue to front of figure. Cover feet and lower bottle using wet fabric. Add robe.

For the lamb, cut ⅓ off side of a 5-inch-long foam egg, then cut 1 inch off tip (G). Pin tip to a 4-inch foam ball; cover with a 5-inch square of wet fabric, stretched taut. Pin around edge of fabric. Fasten ball onto small end of egg with glue; wire and cover head and body, except face, with acrylic modeling paste (much like icing a cake). When head and body are covered, swirl stick through modeling paste to create woolly look (H). Let dry. Ears are double thickness of fabric, glued together but not wet. Poke hole in side of head; insert ear.

For the camel's body, use a 1½-gallon bleach bottle. (If bottle has a hump in neck, trim to have a smooth curve.) Cover holes with wet fabric (I).

Cut the bottom end of the handle from the bottle. Lay bottle on side with neck down on table. Bend handle back until line of neck is formed for head (J). Slip a heavy wire into handle to hold the neck in this position.

Glue the following to bottle: Cut a 3-inch foam ball in half for humps. Cut a 5-inch foam egg in fourths lengthwise; use 2 pieces for hind legs. Pad back with 4 or 5 crinkled paper towels (K).

For the camel's head, whittle a 5-inch foam egg until the face below the eyes is thinner than the egg, and the top of the face is flat. Glue half of 2-inch foam ball to bottom tip of egg (L). Make hole in bottom of head; glue onto end of handle. Wrap with paper towels until neck measures about 2 inches in diameter. Wrap the head and neck smoothly with wet strips of fabric.

Wet a 24-inch square of fabric; drape over body. Smooth down over humps; pull it down around base of neck; tuck closely around bottom of figure. Trim off any excess. Let dry.

Eyes can be purchased in craft shops or make your own from fabric-covered foam balls. Ears are double thicknesses of fabric, not wet, but glued together. Braid indicates harness and trappings.

Painting instructions: When figures are completely dry, coat with gesso. (Hair has already been coated with gesso, but faces need 2 coats.) Let dry.

Paint all figures with acrylic paints. If tube acrylics are used, thin with a small amount of water. For good flesh tones, mix white with a tiny bit of light red. Let dry overnight.

To antique: Spray a small area using gold leaf antiquing glaze. Wipe top surfaces clean, leaving glaze in corners.

continued

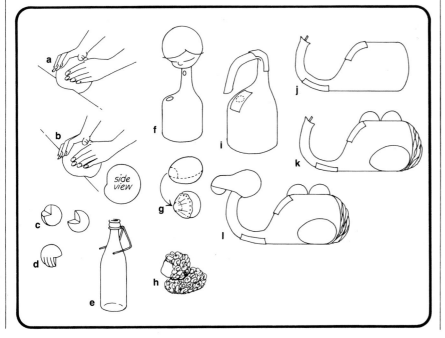

side view

Stained-Glass Tips

Stained glass is staging a comeback! If you're ready to try your hand at this beautiful craft, you'll find some valuable tips here to help make the crèche on pages 282-283—or the other stained-glass projects in this book.

Kinds of Stained Glass

Several types of glass are widely used by home glass crafters. Select the glass that best suits your project, your skills, and your budget.

Antique glass is handmade today in much the same way as in ancient times. Richly colored and containing bubbles, streaks, and other fanciful irregularities of color, texture, and thickness, the spectacular beauty of antique glass attracts many seekers.

Cathedral glass is machine made, so the color, texture, and thickness of individual sheets are uniform. Easier to cut and less expensive than antique glass, it is available in a wide variety of colors and textures.

Opalescent glass is milky and marbelized with streaks of colors. It often is used for hanging lamps and accents in panels and small projects.

Novelty pieces, such as faceted glass jewels, rondels (flat round discs), and glass beads, can be incorporated for interesting effects.

Tools and Equipment

In addition to glass, you'll need heavy paper for patterns and an art knife or single edge razor blade for cutting templates. Use steel glass cutters (from the hardware store) for scoring glass, and kerosene or household oil to lubricate the wheel and preserve the edge of the glass cutter.

Remove sharp edges that remain after breaking glass using grozing, needle nose, or regular pliers.

For wrapping glass, use adhesive-backed copper foil tape or lead came. You'll need H-shaped (double channel) lead came for inside edges and U-shaped (single channel) lead came for the outside edges of your design, unless directions specify otherwise.

For soldering pieces together, use a medium-weight soldering iron, flux, and 60/40 (tin/lead) solid-core wire solder. Do not use resin or acid core solder for stained-glass work.

A Few Words About Safety

Many of the tools and supplies used in glass crafting can be dangerous. To reduce the likelihood of accidents, select a work area that is not in a high traffic area of your home. Also, store glass, flux, solder, and other potentially harmful materials well out of children's reach. Work in good light and be sure work area is well ventilated.

Work on a table that is sturdy, level, and close to an electrical outlet (for the soldering iron). Nail a strip of lath along one edge of the table to keep glass from slipping off and to give you a firm edge to push against when you're fitting glass pieces together before soldering.

Wear heavy gloves to protect your hands while moving glass or cleaning up, and safety glasses to protect eyes.

Cutting the Pieces

When enlarging the design for your project, be sure outlines between shapes are $1/16$ inch wide to allow for lead came. But for copper foil, mark outlines with a regular (narrow) pen or pencil. Make a master pattern and templates for all glass pieces.

Before cutting a piece of glass, first clean it with detergent. Then lay the template on the glass at least an inch from the edge; hold it firmly in place. Dip the cutter in kerosene or household oil; blot on paper.

Hold the glass cutter between your forefinger and middle finger, with your thumb pressing the cutter from behind. Hold the cutter handle perpendicular to the glass, and begin and end the score slightly in (about $1/8$ inch) from the edge of the glass.

Draw the cutter toward or away from you, whichever enables you to see the line you're scoring on the glass. Score in a continuous motion, using constant pressure throughout. Score the hardest cuts first—usually inside curves. Use a metal ruler for straight lines. Do not re-score a cut; doing so will result in ragged break and damaged cutter.

Break the glass immediately after scoring, so the separation is crisp and clean. Using breaking pliers on small pieces and just your hands on large pieces, sharply snap the glass in two. Use a continuous motion, and break glass away from your face while rolling your wrists outward. Along straight edges, position glass so the score falls along a table edge; pull glass down sharply to break it.

Edges on cut pieces must be clean for the lead or foil to fit correctly. Use grozing pliers, needle nose pliers, or sandpaper to remove any fragments of glass that did not separate cleanly from the piece you're cutting.

Check each newly cut piece against the master pattern and make any necessary corrections in the shape. When all pieces have been cut to size, you're ready to assemble the project.

Leading

If you're using lead came, first stretch rolled came by stepping on one end and pulling the other end up over your head. Open the channel by running the end of an orange stick or other small, blunt tool along it.

If possible, assemble your project over the master pattern so you can judge how well the pieces are fitting together as you work. Begin leading in a corner of the design or, if there are no corners, begin with an outside shape. Slide outer edge of glass into a U-came. Use H-came to bind inner edges. Using a lead knife to cut the came, miter or butt join corners where cames meet.

As each came is fitted to glass, apply gentle but firm pressure on the came and the glass so pieces fit together snugly.

Foiling

Wipe glass with detergent, then cut lengths of adhesive-backed foil tape to wrap around each piece. Center the strip along the edge of the glass; press down all around, overlapping slightly at the ends. Since foil is wider than glass is thick, crimp excess over sides of glass. Use an orange stick or other tool to smooth foil to glass. Wrap one piece at a time, and replace it on the master pattern.

Soldering

Paint soldering flux generously over edges of came or foil to make them receptive to solder.

Using solid-core wire solder, and following the soldering iron manufacturer's directions, tack pieces together. If you're using lead came, solder all joints so they're smooth and well sealed. For foil, flow solder over all exposed copper to fill gaps and hold pieces securely together. As you are soldering over copper, let solder build up to form a smoothly rounded seam. Repeat on the reverse side.

Stained-Glass Nativity
pages 282-283

Materials: Red, orange, orange opaque, rust, brown, gold, lavender, purple, purple opaque, light blue, medium blue, gray-blue, turquoise, milky white, clear, flesh, pale yellow, and green opaque stained glass; 4 glass "jewels"; three 8⅞×5⅛-inch mirrors (for arches); 2mm lead H-came; 50/50 (lead/tin) solder; 50- to 80-watt soldering iron with steel or copper tip; flux; copper wire; graph paper; tape; glass cutter; hammer; 1¼-inch horseshoe nails; flux or paste brush; wooden work board; nibbling pliers and glass pliers.

Instructions: Enlarge and trace patterns (right) onto graph paper with felt-tip pen. Work one figure at a time. Lay glass on pattern, smooth side up. Score glass with glass cutter along edge of pattern moving cutter toward you. Extend cut from one edge of glass to another or from score to score. Avoid sharp angles and curves; apply constant, even pressure. Never recut same score line. Hold glass on each side of score; break by pushing down.

If glass is opaque, tape cutout pattern to glass; score around outline. Make another set of patterns for taping to work board for leading step.

Cut pieces for one opaque figure; check size and fit against pattern. Smooth edges using nibbling pliers; then rub edges using scrap glass.

Unroll H-came; stretch to eliminate slack and to straighten curves. Step on end or secure it in vise; pull other end with pliers. Stretch taut, then reroll.

Tape pattern to board; lay glass pieces on it. Start leading on large piece with many outside edges (few pieces joined to it). Wrap lead strip around glass; cut strip and fit to glass over pattern. Hold lead in place with nails around edges. Outline adjoining glass using lead in same way, except don't line side that abuts first piece. Hold glass and lead in place with nails at edges. Outline all pieces using lead; nail snugly in position. Use lead knife to firm pieces into position. Brush flux on joints where lead meets lead. Solder joints.

Color key for glass:

GB	Gray-blue	O	Orange
T	Turquoise	F	Flesh
LB	Light Blue	BR	Brown
OO	Orange Opaque	R	Rust
MW	Milk White	G	Gold
MB	Medium Blue	RD	Red
GO	Green Opaque	Y	Yellow
PO	Purple Opaque	P	Purple
L	Lavender	CL	Clear

Remove nails; turn piece over. Solder joints on back side. Solder a U-shaped brace to back so pieces stand. Wash completed pieces using soap and warm water. Dry all pieces carefully with a lint-free cloth.

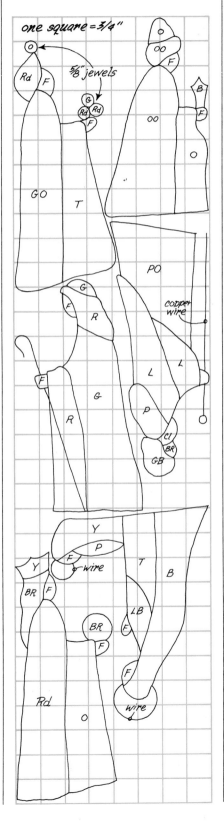

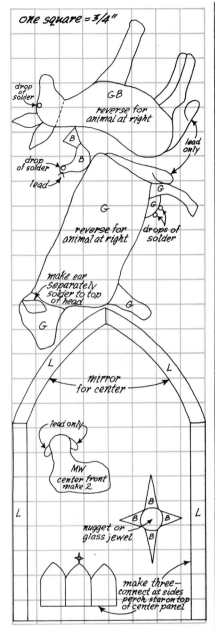

Needlepoint Crèche
pages 284-285

Materials: 3-ply Persian wool in the colors and amounts listed on the chart on page 293; 1⅔ yards 36-inch-wide canvas (12 or 14 meshes per inch); #17 tapestry needle; 9×12-inch felt pieces in the following amounts and colors—1 orange, 1 yellow, 1 turquoise, and 2 navy blue; 8½-inch piece of 1/16-inch-diameter brass wire for staff; 24-inch piece of 1/32-inch-diameter aluminum wire for angel wings; lightweight cardboard; white glue; cotton batting; waterproof pen; masking tape; needlepoint frame (optional).

continued

Continued from page 291
Beautiful Crèche Figures

Instructions: Enlarge patterns on the following pages. Cut canvas pieces 2 inches larger on all sides than patterns; bind raw edges using masking tape. Position canvas over enlarged patterns, leaving 2 inches of canvas all around. Make sure horizontal and vertical threads run square to facial detail.

Trace outlines of patterns and design details using *waterproof* pen. As an alternative, do not cut canvas pieces apart; transfer up to 4 patterns to 1 large piece of canvas. Mount in frame; stitch all figures at once.

Using 2 strands of 3-ply wool, work figures in continental stitches.

To assemble, carefully apply a thin line of glue ⅛ inch from edge of completed needlepoint around all sides; let dry. This glue prevents raveling (if you are using interlock canvas, eliminate this gluing step). Trim around needlepoint ¼ inch from all outside edges, being careful not to cut into glue or stitches. To give the head its rounded shape, make a ⅜-inch-deep cut into each V at top of figure. Fold Vs inward (making a dart); stitch together with 1 strand of yarn to match adjoining needlepoint. Close back seam similarly.

Turn figure upside down and stuff. For bottom, trace and cut cardboard oval to fit; cut felt oval also, adding ¼-inch margin to cardboard pattern. Glue cardboard, centered, to felt oval. Allow to dry. Position felt bottom on inverted figure (with cardboard to the inside), and tuck the extra felt inside. Using 1 strand of yarn, sew felt bottom to edge of figure, keeping raw edges of felt and canvas inside.

For halos, glue and trim around edges of needlepoint halos as for the figures. Fold under raw edges and glue. Cut matching halo from felt; glue lightly to back of needlepoint halos. If desired, place a stack of books or other heavy objects on halo to keep it flat until glue dries. Stitch together edges of felt and needlepoint. Using 1 strand of matching yarn, attach halo to head.

Glue and trim angel wings as for halos. Fold under raw edges of canvas. Before gluing them down, cut aluminum wire to fit around outer edges of wings for stiffening. Bend wire to match outline of wings. Position shaped wire inside folded canvas edges; glue edges down. Cut felt to fit wings. Sew felt to needlepoint; attach wings to angel.

For shepherd's staff, cut an 8½-inch piece of brass wire; bend into shape as shown on pattern. Attach to hand section of shepherd with matching yarn.

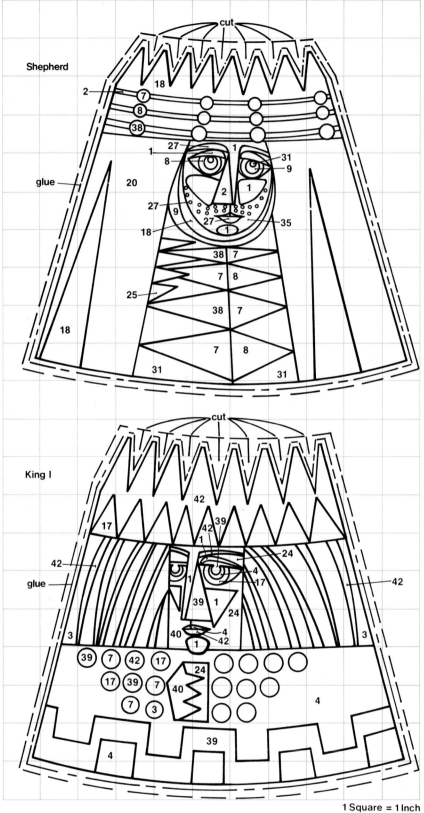

1 Square = 1 Inch

292

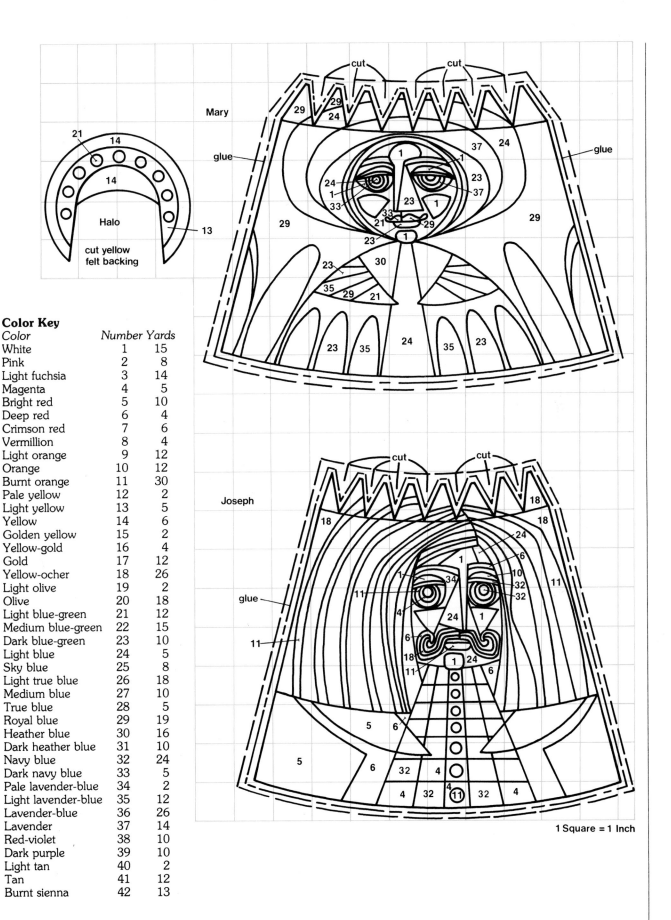

Mary

Joseph

Halo

cut yellow
felt backing

Color Key

Color	Number	Yards
White	1	15
Pink	2	8
Light fuchsia	3	14
Magenta	4	5
Bright red	5	10
Deep red	6	4
Crimson red	7	6
Vermillion	8	4
Light orange	9	12
Orange	10	12
Burnt orange	11	30
Pale yellow	12	2
Light yellow	13	5
Yellow	14	6
Golden yellow	15	2
Yellow-gold	16	4
Gold	17	12
Yellow-ocher	18	26
Light olive	19	2
Olive	20	18
Light blue-green	21	12
Medium blue-green	22	15
Dark blue-green	23	10
Light blue	24	5
Sky blue	25	8
Light true blue	26	18
Medium blue	27	10
True blue	28	5
Royal blue	29	19
Heather blue	30	16
Dark heather blue	31	10
Navy blue	32	24
Dark navy blue	33	5
Pale lavender-blue	34	2
Light lavender-blue	35	12
Lavender-blue	36	26
Lavender	37	14
Red-violet	38	10
Dark purple	39	10
Light tan	40	2
Tan	41	12
Burnt sienna	42	13

1 Square = 1 Inch

continued

Continued from page 293
Beautiful Crèche Figures

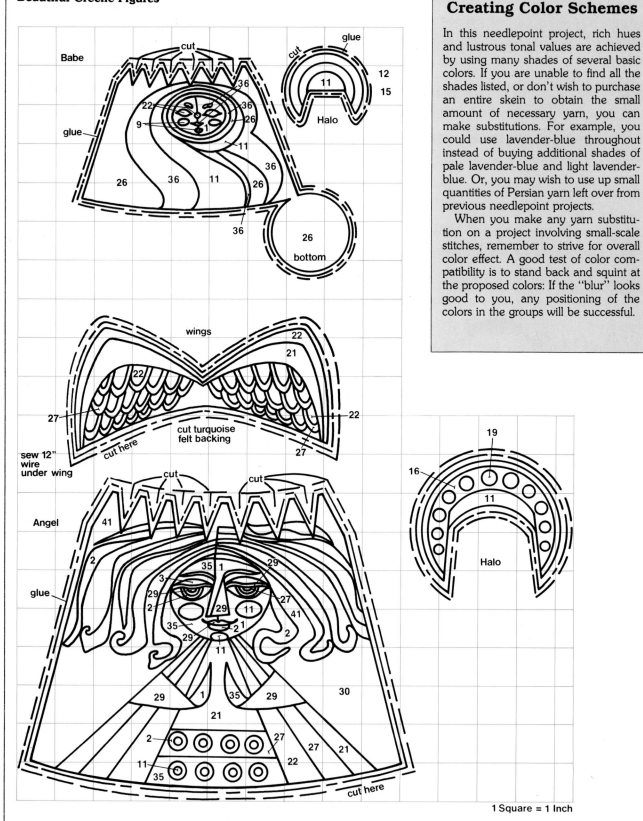

Babe

cut

glue

cut

glue

36
22
36
9
36
26
11
36
26
36
11
36
26
26
36
26
bottom

11
Halo
12
15

wings
22
21
22
27
22
27
cut turquoise
felt backing
cut here
cut here

sew 12"
wire
under wing

Angel
41
2
cut
cut
35
1
29
3
29
27
2
29
11
41
35
2
29
2
1
11
29
1
35
29
30
21
2
27
11
27
21
35
22

19
16
11
Halo

1 Square = 1 Inch

Creating Color Schemes

In this needlepoint project, rich hues and lustrous tonal values are achieved by using many shades of several basic colors. If you are unable to find all the shades listed, or don't wish to purchase an entire skein to obtain the small amount of necessary yarn, you can make substitutions. For example, you could use lavender-blue throughout instead of buying additional shades of pale lavender-blue and light lavender-blue. Or, you may wish to use up small quantities of Persian yarn left over from previous needlepoint projects.

When you make any yarn substitution on a project involving small-scale stitches, remember to strive for overall color effect. A good test of color compatibility is to stand back and squint at the proposed colors: If the "blur" looks good to you, any positioning of the colors in the groups will be successful.

King II

32

22

36

34

26

1

24

26

24

22

36

26

glue

32

38

28

9

36

32

28

32

28

32

34

28

24

11

26   32

36   22

32

38   9

11

36

cut

Materials: Scraps of 1-inch pine, or alternative woods suggested on **page 18**; wood stains or acrylic paints in a variety of colors and shades; white glue; sandpaper; jigsaw or coping saw.

Using the patterns (below), cut out and assemble the crèche figures. Directions are on page 287.

one square = ¾"

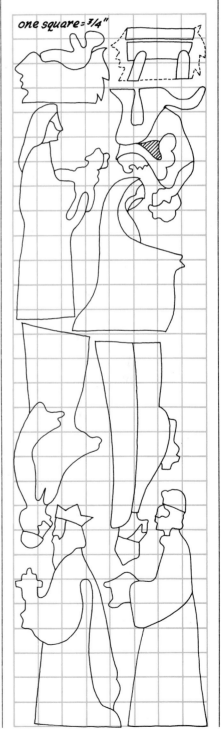

King III

cut

11

38

32

9

11

1

25

36

10   9

9

38

36

1

25   37

10

35

25

1

10

38

11

37

32

37

25

35

38

36

36

36

32

36

1 Square = 1 Inch

The Christmas Story

Simple Manger Scenes

Many families follow a tradition of making small manger scenes to display in their homes during the Christmas season. Youngsters especially love to create tiny crèche figures, which need not be complicated or time-consuming to be beautiful. Simple craft techniques and down-to-earth materials, such as bread dough, wood, straw, or fabric, can be used to create lovely and charming nativity scenes that the whole family will enjoy.

In miniature, here is a crèche that is as simple and beautiful as the Christmas story itself. Though bread-dough tree ornaments have been popular for years, these diminutive figures look unique and are every bit as exquisite as more elaborate crèches.

These nativity pieces range in height from 1 inch for the sheep in the foreground to 3 inches for the figure of Joseph. Small but beautiful is this most-enchanting Christmas craft.

The other manger scenes in this section are equally as appealing and simple to make as the crèche shown here. Directions for all the projects begin on page 304.

Simple Manger Scenes

Simple materials provide the ideal means of recapturing the primitive scene of Christ's birth in the manger. Coarse burlap is used for the figures at left, and the nativity below is crafted of soft balsa wood and trimmed with brown markers to resemble woodburning. The golden sheen of straw and balsa wood against a flat black background enhances the primitive effect of the straw marquetry scene (opposite).

Classic simplicity is the hallmark of the burlap crèche. Make the frames for the figures using coat-hanger wire, then wrap the bodies in fabric draped in graceful folds. Mary measures about 8 inches tall and Joseph is about 10 inches tall.

The wooden nativity (opposite) looks as if a master craftsman had created it. Actually it was made from a few sheets of balsa. When completed, the figures were surrounded with pine cones and votive lights for a seasonal arrangement to go on the table or mantel. Instructions for making this crèche follow.

To make the freestanding crèche, you'll need a brown, waterproof marking pen, some contact cement, sandpaper, scissors, a knife, matte-finish acrylic spray, and balsa wood in the following sizes: two pieces $\frac{1}{8} \times 4 \times 36$ inches, one piece $\frac{1}{8} \times 3 \times 36$ inches, two pieces $1 \times 1 \times 36$ inches, three pieces $\frac{1}{4} \times 1 \times 36$ inches, and one piece $\frac{1}{8} \times 1 \times 36$ inches.

Begin by enlarging the patterns on page 305. Then, using scissors, cut out the figures. For the three arches and the angel, crib, sheep, and cow use $\frac{1}{8} \times 4 \times 36$-inch pieces of balsa. For Mary, Joseph, and the lamb use the $\frac{1}{8} \times 3 \times 36$-inch piece of balsa.

Lightly sand each piece and decorate it, using a brown marking pen and referring to the photograph for ideas.

To assemble the crèche, cut three 15-inch strips from a piece of balsa $1 \times 1 \times 36$ inches and five 15-inch strips from a piece $\frac{1}{4} \times 1 \times 36$ inches. Build the base to hold the figures from the back to the front, sandwiching the figures between strips of balsa.

To begin, glue the largest arch to the center front of a $1 \times 1 \times 15$-inch strip. Fill each side of the arch with a $\frac{1}{8} \times 1$-inch strip glued to the front of the first base piece. Use scrap pieces to fill in any gaps in the base.

Glue the remaining arches to this narrow strip. Fill any gaps. Then glue a $\frac{1}{4} \times 1 \times 15$-inch strip in front of the arches. Glue the angel and Joseph to the front of the strip, and fill any gaps.

Glue two $\frac{1}{4} \times 1 \times 15$-inch strips in front of the angel and Joseph. On the last layer, glue Mary, the sheep, and the cow into place. Fill any gaps, add two $\frac{1}{4} \times 1 \times 15$-inch strips, and glue the crib and lamb into place. Fill any gaps.

Before gluing the last $1 \times 1 \times 15$-inch piece of balsa onto the front, draw a border design on one side. Then glue it into place and sand the edges of the base. To finish, coat the entire crèche with acrylic.

The manger scene below is worked on a 12×24-inch plywood background. Mary is $9\frac{1}{4}$ inches tall and Joseph $9\frac{3}{4}$ inches. Cut the pieces for the Holy Family, angels, and shed from balsa or cardboard. Paint all pieces black, leaving faces and hands natural. Before assembling, work straw marquetry by cutting straw into geometric shapes with a craft knife and gluing to figure parts. Finish with a coat of plastic sealer.

Simple Manger Scenes

For an unusual and imaginative way to celebrate the nativity this year, make these soft, subtly elegant figures and suspend them from a graceful pine bough or a beautiful piece of weathered wood in front of a window or above the mantel.

If you have a family of young artists skilled in the use of paints, pens, or a needle, you'll probably find them eager to help. The figures are simple and easy to make using muslin, pillow stuffing, fabric paints or pens, and a little embroidery thread.

The figures, ranging in height from 5 to 12 inches, are first outlined on muslin with a black pen and then colored with acrylic paints. All eight pieces are stitched and stuffed separately, so they can be grouped in any arrangement that pleases you.

An important thing to remember when working with fabric paints and marking pens is to make sure your art supplies are waterproof. Acrylics are waterproof once they are dry. To test your pen, mark on scraps of muslin and dampen the ink with water. If the ink does not bleed, the pen is safe to use.

Also, when choosing a pen for this project, select one with a very fine tip. Apply pressure lightly for a crisp, clear outline.

Mix paints to get a variety of different shades, then apply just a light wash of color to the fabric using smooth, even strokes. To set colors, press with a warm iron.

Simple Manger Scenes

This cheerful manger scene is made of the small-scale prints that are most often used in quilts and other patchwork designs. Unlike most nativities, this one can be mounted on a wall or above a mantel. The stable is approximately 20 inches wide and 13 inches high. Figures are a child-pleasing 4 inches tall.

Patterns for this quilter's crèche and a list of the materials you'll need to make it are on page 307. Directions, however, are given here, so you can refer to the photograph as you work.

To make the manger scene, first enlarge the patterns on page 307. Add ¼-inch seam allowances to all pieces except those to be cut from the felt.

Using a variety of calico fabrics, cut two body pieces (triangle A) for Mary, Joseph, the shepherd, wise men, and angel. Cut two body pieces (triangle B) for the sheep, manger, and cow. Cut one side of the sheep from fake fur and the other from black felt.

With right sides facing, sew corresponding body pieces together. Leave 2 inches open along the bottom of each triangle. Turn, press, and stuff lightly.

Cut pieces for seven pairs of feet from felt; insert one piece into the bottom of each triangle. Slip-stitch openings closed.

Cut two sleeves for each figure, and sew a ¼-inch hem in each. With right sides together, fold the sleeve in half and sew ¼-inch

side seam. Turn sleeves right side out and glue a felt hand onto the front of each one.

Cut nine round faces, one sheep face, and one cow face from felt. Make French-knot eyes; cut mouths and cheeks from felt. Glue the features into place.

Cut three circles (B) from felt

302

and glue them to the backs of Mary's head, the infant's, and the angel's. Arrange ½-inch pieces of yarn (hair) around the faces; stitch. Cut ½-inch pieces of yarn for each beard; stitch pieces around the faces.

Cut and glue the crowns and head pieces into place. Then glue the heads onto the bodies. Tack wings to the back of the angel.

Braid nine 4-inch pieces of yarn for the cow's tail. Cut and glue four felt legs to the sheep. Attach a twig to the shepherd for a staff. Then sew a piece of eyelet to the back of the infant's head and Mary's. Trim the bodies using small pieces of lace and rickrack as shown in the photograph.

For the stable, cut three roof pieces: one of monk's cloth, one of blue calico, and one of batting. Sew trim to the face of the monk's cloth; this will be the front.

Layer the pieces in this order: monk's cloth, face up; calico, face down; and batting. Stitch the edges, leaving 6 inches open. Turn, slip-stitch the opening, and quilt, as shown on the pattern.

Cut three star pieces, sew them atop one another, and stitch the radiating lines as shown in the photograph. Hand-stitch them to the center of the roof. Cut two walls from monk's cloth and one from batting. Cut four windows of blue calico; machine-sew them to the front wall. Stitch radiating lines as shown. Then pin the walls, right sides together, and lay batting atop them. Sew the top and sides; turn. Hand-sew the roof to the walls, folding in the two sides, as shown in the photograph.

Cut two small holes in the upper back of the wall, close to the seam between the roof and the wall. Then cut away the bottom wire of a coat hanger. Insert the top of the hanger through the holes so the hook is centered behind the star. Tack the hanger into place behind the star so it is hidden from view.

Insert a piece of florist's wire through the front of the roof between the two quilting lines.

Place the bottom of the coat hanger along the bottom of the wall, between the layers of monk's cloth. Turn under each layer ¼ inch toward the inside and machine-stitch them together.

Tack the figures to the front of the stable wall, as shown.

Instructions for the Christmas Story: Simple Manger Scenes

The instructions below and on the following pages are for the manger scenes and nativity figures shown on pages 296-303. For directions for enlarging and transferring designs, see the glossary, pages 370-371.

Bread-Dough Crèche
pages 296-297

Materials: Salt; flour; aluminum foil; white bread; white glue; salad oil; tempera paints, or suitable substitute, in a variety of colors; spray lacquer.

Instructions: Two kinds of dough are needed for the crèche figures. Make basic shapes from baker's clay (salt dough), then add clothing and hair made of breadcrumb dough.

To prepare baker's clay for basic shapes, mix ½ cup of salt with ¾ cup boiling water. Stir occasionally until the mixture cools; salt will not dissolve completely. Add 2 cups flour all at once. Mix using a spoon, then shape dough into a ball using your hands. Turn dough out on a bread board and knead for 6 to 8 minutes until the dough reaches a smooth consistency.

Pinch off a small piece of dough and place it in a clean cup. Mix hot water into this dough until it is the consistency of whipped cream, similar to the slip (liquid clay) used in ceramics. This slip will be used later to patch any cracks that might develop in the figures during the baking process.

Cover the remaining dough with an inverted clean bowl to prevent dough from drying out.

To make the figures, cut a number of 4-inch squares of aluminum foil; shape a figure of baker's clay on each foil piece. Make the head by pinching off a small amount of dough; roll dough between the palms of your hands, forming a ball. If there are any cracks, roll until they disappear.

Make the body by shaping a fat, sausage-shaped piece of dough. Lay the dough on your work surface and flatten it slightly with your fingers; transfer dough to a square of foil.

Using a single-edge razor blade, cut away one end of the sausage to form a flat base (see diagram). Then cut slashes in sides to form arms, spreading them away from the body. To vary the position of the arms (see color photograph), prop them on "pillows" made by rolling strips of foil around a pencil. Cut a vertical slash in the base to form legs. Trim sides of figure if necessary.

Join the head to the body using a

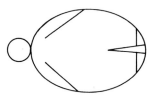

round toothpick to push the two pieces of dough together.

Place the figures, still on foil, on a cookie sheet and bake in a 325-degree oven for 20 minutes. Remove from the oven and check for cracks on the back of the pieces. If necessary, repair cracks with slip (liquid dough) mixed earlier. Then return figures to the oven for an additional 20 minutes.

Figures should bake (and dry) rather than cook. If you find the figures are baking too fast and turning brown, bake them at a lower temperature for a longer time. When figures are done, remove them from the oven and let them cool. Spray with lacquer.

Press small bits of breadcrumb dough (instructions below) against the bottom of each foot, using a dot of glue, if necessary, to make the dough stick. Stand the figures carefully on a small piece of foil to dry overnight.

While figures are baking in the oven, prepare breadcrumb dough for garments and hair. Remove crusts from 4 slices of white bread; tear bread into bits in a mixing bowl. Add 4 tablespoons white glue, and mix using a spoon until dough forms a ball. Put the dough into a plastic bag and place it in the refrigerator until ready to use.

After figures have dried overnight, color the breadcrumb dough and add decorative details to each figure.

To add color: Remove dough from refrigerator. Rub a little salad oil into your hands; knead tempera paints in a variety of colors into small portions of dough. Store dough of different colors in separate plastic sandwich bags. (You'll note the dough looks white before any color is added, but as it dries, it becomes beige in color. Use white tempera in the dough you wish to look white, as in the sheep.)

Clothing: Roll colored dough flat between two pieces of smooth foil. Small pieces of flattened dough can then be pressed against figure, or wrapped around it, leaving lower edge loose for shawls or skirts. Paper rectangles can be "tried on" the figures to determine size of dough piece needed.

Stripes: Press thin "snakes" of dough in contrasting colors against flattened piece. Do this before piece is put on figure, or after figure has been dressed and dried completely.

Assembly-line dressing: Do basic garments on all figures first, let dry somewhat, then add hair. Next, add shawls, robes, or mantles. Paint colored dough with more glue diluted with a few drops of water per tablespoon of glue. Avoid getting glue on baker's clay hands, faces, or feet. When figures are dry, spray with lacquer.

● *Sheep*

Roll thin legs of black dough and small bits of black dough for nose and ears. When dry enough to be firm, press legs into a ball of white dough to form sheep's body. Press nose and ears into a smaller ball of white dough for head. Let dry partially; glue head to body. Allow to dry thoroughly, then spray with lacquer.

Burlap Crèche
page 298

Materials: 1 yard of good-quality natural-colored burlap; polyester fiberfill; 2 metal coat hangers; small box; packing excelsior; masking tape; white glue; pliers; small wire cutters.

Instructions: For Mary and Joseph, cut armature pieces from hangers—one 10-inch piece (arms), one 9-inch piece (body), and two 6-inch pieces (leg supports). Round sharp ends with a metal file, and wrap with tape to contour hands and feet.

Cut four 1-inch-wide bias burlap strips to wrap the wires, making them ½ inch longer than wires. Fold raw edges inward; stitch the burlap strip tightly around wires with heavy thread.

Sew two 6-inch burlap-covered wires to body wire; keep ends flush at bottom. Separate wires into tripod so figures are stable. Bend Joseph's feet ½ inch from wire ends. For Mary, bend leg wires 2 inches above end. Bend front wire so figure is kneeling.

Enlarge the pattern (below); cut head pieces. (Use 1-inch seam allowances. After stitching, trim to ¼ inch.) Double-stitch head pieces together from A to B. Trim seams; apply glue to cut edge to prevent raveling. Turn inside out (tweezers are helpful); stuff tightly. Place heads on body wires. Joseph is 10 inches tall, Mary 8 inches tall. Fold under raw edges of head; sew seam. Stitch to body.

Center arm piece on body; stitch tightly ½ inch below head. Sew long seams on sleeves; hem. Place sleeves on arms; stitch to neck, chest, and back.

For Joseph's tunic, cut a 9×13-inch rectangle on the bias; seam short sides, stitching twice. Fold under top edge ¼ inch; gather tightly and tack to waist. Hem tunic. Repeat for Mary's skirt, using an 8×11-inch rectangle.

For Joseph's hair, glue strands of burlap across head from front to back; trim evenly. Repeat for Mary's hair; stitch along center part.

For Joseph's beard fold 4-inch burlap threads in half; drape over burlap bearer cord. Glue one side of beard and let dry. Apply glue to face and position beard on glue; let dry. Trim.

For Joseph's coat, cut a 6×20-inch bias rectangle. Glue edges to prevent fraying. Drape coat over head and shoulders, making tucks in back to form hood. Tack to head and shoulders.

For Mary's veil, cut a half circle 19 inches across. Turn under raw edges and glue. Place on head and secure.

For infant, cut a 3-inch circle from burlap. Run a row of gathering stitches around the edge, stuff firmly, and pull gathers tightly, keeping folds to the back. This will be the head.

Sew side seams of body piece, stuff firmly, and gather the neck edge. Sew the head to the body. Pull individual threads from a scrap of burlap; sew burlap thread loops to head for hair.

To make the swaddling clothes, cut a 7-inch burlap square and tack it in place around the infant.

For manger, cover the box with burlap; fill with excelsior.

When figures are complete, bend arms into position using pliers. Bend neck wire forward. Stitch a small twig to Joseph's hand.

Balsa Crèche
page 298

To make the balsa wood nativity scene use these patterns (below center and below). Materials and instructions for cutting out and assembling the pieces are on page 299.

continued

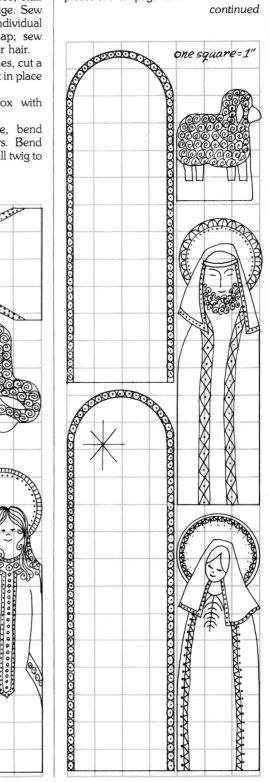

one square=1"

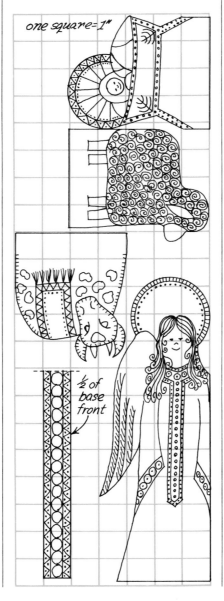

one square=1"

½ of base front

SLEEVE CUT 2 ON BIAS

NECK

BODY FOR INFANT

PLACE ON FOLD

HEM

SEAM

HEAD CUT 2 ON BIAS

B   A

1 SQ.= 1/2 IN.

Continued from page 305
Simple Manger Scenes

Straw Nativity
page 299

Materials: ¼×12×24-inch plywood sheet; ¼×3×36-inch balsa (pattern pieces); two ½×½×36-inch pieces pine or balsa (frame); ¼×¼×36-inch piece of balsa (shed); ¼-inch graph paper; medium weight cardboard; sandpaper; glue; black, water-base paint and primer; clear plastic coating; scissors; single-edge razor; straw.

Instructions: Enlarge the patterns (left). Paint plywood, frame, and shed pieces. Cut #1 pieces from cardboard; cut the remaining parts from balsa.

Fit sections together; sand edges. Shape hands, carving palms on angel's hands for horns and cutting hands of Madonna so right hand will fit over left hand (remove top half of left hand and lower half of right hand).

Paint all parts black except leave hands and faces natural.

Work straw marquetry details before assembling the scene. Dampen straw; slit one side with a razor blade. Press straws flat with a moderately hot iron. Glue straws side by side to graph paper, graph side down. Then cover straw-coated paper with waxed paper; weight with books until the glue is dry.

Most patterns on figures are geometric and based on ¼-inch and ½-inch squares (whole or cut into triangles). Cut straw for figures, angels, and floor base along ¼-inch and ½-inch squares, according to the grid on the paper. Cut long strips for other pieces.

Glue straw to wood pieces; remove excess glue with damp tissue paper. Then mark position of figures, angels, and shed on backdrop; glue shed in place, then add figures.

Make twenty-two 1-inch diameter, 8-pointed stars using 2 straw Xs glued together. Cut points as shown in the diagram (left). Glue stars around shed.

For large star, glue 4-inch straw over shed. Complete star with three 3-inch straws, eight 1½-inch straws, and 16 straw pieces cut on diagonal to fit between each arm of star.

Glue and nail frame to backdrop; miter or butt corners. Touch up black paint if necessary; glue straw strips to frame. Finish with plastic coating.

Painted Fabric Crèche
pages 300-301

Materials: 1½ yards 36-inch-wide unbleached muslin; polyester fiberfill;

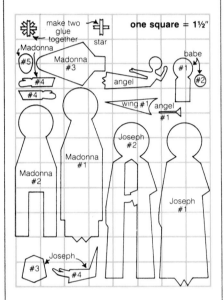

1 Square = 1 Inch

seam line

black waterproof pen; acrylic paints or waterproof marking pens in assorted colors; paintbrushes; embroidery floss; ¼-inch wide beige grosgrain ribbon; 20-inch-long wooden dowel.

Instructions: Enlarge patterns (below) onto tracing paper and transfer to muslin. Go over all outlines using a black waterproof pen. (To test pen, mark on scraps of muslin and dampen the ink using a few drops of water. If ink does not bleed, pen is safe to use.)

Color each figure as desired using acrylic paints or permanent felt-tipped pens. (Refer to photograph on pages 300-301 for colors.) If you use acrylics, thin them first to the consistency of light cream. Paint a section at a time using black outlines as a guide.

Let each section dry before painting adjoining ones. Embroider details as shown on patterns using simple stitches (see page 374 for stitch ideas).

Cut out each piece, leaving ½-inch seam allowance. For backings, cut matching pieces of muslin for each figure. With right sides facing, sew front and back pieces together, leaving small openings for turning. Turn right side out, stuff, and slip-stitch openings.

To hang, stitch ribbon loop to top of each figure so figure hangs at desired length. Insert wooden dowel or pine branch through ribbon loops.

Patchwork Crèche
pages 302-303

Materials: Scraps of small print fabrics; black, white, pink and gold felt; lace, rickrack, and other trims; scraps of pillow stuffing; scrap of gray synthetic fur; black embroidery floss; black, gold, and purple yarn; white glue; ⅓ yard blue calico; ⅔ yard quilt batting; 1⅓ yards unbleached monk's cloth or similar fabric; coat hanger; florist's wire; 1 yard ribbon or trim.

Instructions: Enlarge pattern (below) and use directions on pages 302-303 to assemble crèche.

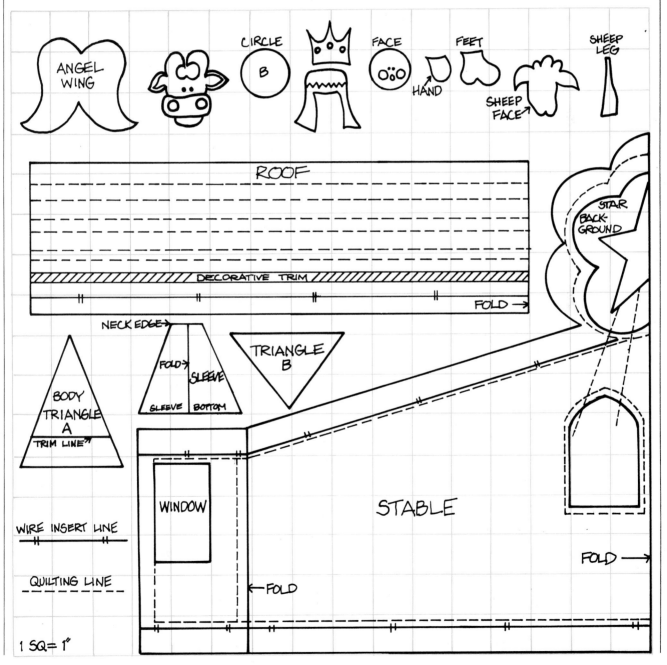

The Christmas Story

Symbols of Peace and Goodwill

Whether you live in the snowiest mountain region of Montana or along a sunny Florida shore, one of the nicest ways to herald Christmas and to share the joys and hopes of the holidays with family, friends, and neighbors is with beautiful banners and other decorations inspired by the Christmas story. Angels, wise men, and madonnas are traditional symbols of the season. Just as popular are Christmas messages of peace, joy, and brotherhood.

Show off your holiday spirit this year with bright Christmas banners like these. Crafted of rainbow-hued felt and yarn, each measures a stunning 3 by 6 feet. But despite their great size they are easy to make. Glue felt appliqués to a background fabric, then trim the borders and some of the motifs using rows of plump craft yarn glued into place.

For additional banners, angels, and other trims that celebrate the Christmas story, please turn to page 310. Directions for all the projects shown in this section begin on page 319.

Symbols of Peace and Goodwill

When you think banners, think big! Banners should be enjoyed from a distance, so make the designs bold, colorful, and dramatic. And use them as people have for years: to commemorate special events, carry important messages, or inspire all who see them.

Banners are easy to make if you stick to simple designs and materials (such as felt) that do not require time-consuming and complicated sewing or other finishing. And if you can enlist the aid of family or club members, portioning out parts of the project to each of your helpers, you'll find you can create even the largest of Christmas banners in very short order indeed.

These 35×60-inch hangings would make a wonderful display in your home, church, or club during the holidays. They celebrate the story of Bethlehem and the hopes of people everywhere during the Christmas season for peace on earth, goodwill toward men.

Each of these banners is made from felt, scraps of printed cotton, silver rickrack and other trims, and bits of mylar—a metallic, mirror-like material sold in art or craft supply stores. You'll find the banners easy to make if you construct parts of each section separately and then stitch completed sections together.

Because the banners are large, it is easier to work from a master pattern. Enlarge the diagrams on pages 320–321 and trace sections of this master pattern onto tissue paper. Cut the tissue apart into patterns for the individual motifs.

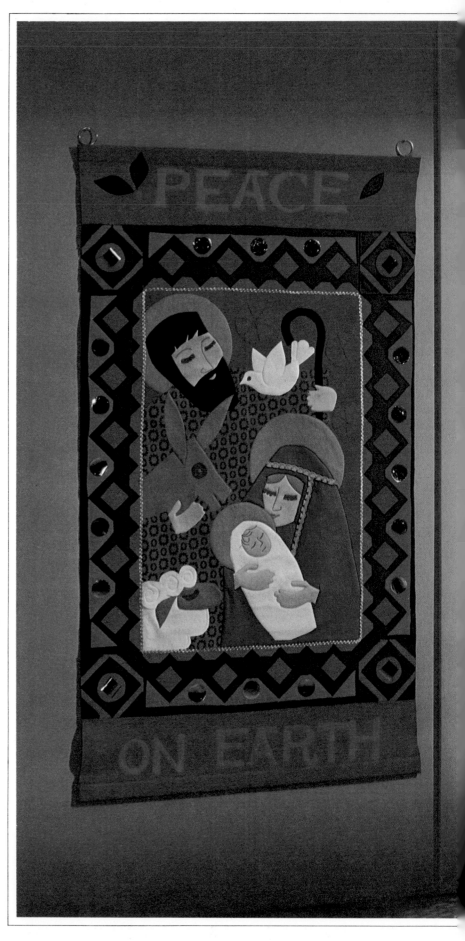

First construct the scene on each banner. Cut out and assemble each figure by appliquéing smaller shapes onto larger ones. Use transparent thread or brown thread for appliquéing pieces into place. Machine satin-stitch facial features using brown thread.

For example, on the banner depicting the holy family, construct the infant first, then Mary. Appliqué the infant into position, adding Mary's hands last. Cut out and assemble the sheep, dove, and Joseph separately. Then pin all the figures onto the magenta background and stitch them into place. Finally, turn the panel over and carefully trim away the excess magenta fabric from beneath the appliquéd figures to eliminate unnecessary bulk. Trim the background fabric so the edges are perfectly straight and the corners are square.

Center the completed scene on the background fabric used for the border and satin-stitch into place. Then lay this large piece on a table or the floor, and arrange all the border shapes in position. (If you're unable to find mylar, you can substitute silver fabric or even aluminum foil kitchen pans.) Glue the border motifs to the felt using white glue. Then glue silver rickrack around the edge of the center scene as shown in the photograph.

To make the panels with the lettering, stitch letters onto the background strips, using the master pattern to position them correctly. There will be a margin of ½ inch along the long edge that will be sewn to the geometric border and a margin of 2 inches for the casing on the other long edge. Turn under the 2-inch underlap for the casing, and stitch 1¾ inches from the fold.

To assemble the banner, stitch lettered panels to the top and bottom of the border panel, placing the border panel on top. Trim ½ to ¾ inch from the sides of the completed banner so the edges are straight. Insert pieces of lath (cut to size) into the casings at the top and bottom of the banner, and sew brass rings to the upper corners of the banner for hanging.

Symbols of Peace and Goodwill

Felt is a wonderful fabric to use for banners because it's available in such a wide variety of colors and doesn't ravel. These quick-and-easy hangings can be created just days before your holiday decorating begins.

The stylized angel (below) measures 29½ × 33 inches. To make it, cut out and position the felt appliqués on the purple background. Then glue or stitch the pieces onto the fabric.

The panels of the three wise men (opposite) are designed to simulate stained-glass windows. Like leading on real stained glass, the black background is visible around the felt pieces in the design. Each panel measures 14 × 36 inches.

When colored appliqués are in place, reinforce the panels at the top with a piece of cardboard cut into a curve. Attach the cardboard to the back of each panel, and add drapery weights in the lower corners so panels hang well.

Symbols of Peace and Goodwill

Straw, one of the most workable and popular design materials available, is widely used in Europe and Latin America for Christmas decorations. Beautifully and intricately woven angels, kings, and madonnas are available in import and basketry shops.

If you like the natural effect of straw trims, but find Christmas crafting time scarce, then begin with purchased straw figures. You can turn a single straw ornament, such as the one shown here, into a dramatic decoration for the holiday season or year-round.

Accent the central figure with small stars. You'll find them easy to make using straw that's been peeled and dampened with water.

Show off an elegant straw figure by surrounding it with greenery and a ring of bright stars. Begin with a straw tray or shallow basket large enough to accommodate the figure, some real or artificial greenery, floral stem wire, and purchased straw stars or enough straw to make your own stars.

Using floral stem wire, anchor the figure to the center of the tray or basket. Add a wire loop on the back of the container at the center top for hanging.

Next, wire bits of greenery around the rim of the tray or basket. Then, if you're using purchased stars, wire these around the figure as well, snuggling them into the greenery as shown.

Making your own straw stars is fun and not at all difficult. Use the straw of wheat, rye, barley, or oats. If you live in or near the country, you may be able to find grain in empty fields in your area. If so, when the grain is almost dry,

cut it as close to the ground as possible using a hedge trimmer or a pair of kitchen shears for cutting. Tie the straw in bundles and hang it in a dry place for about ten days. Also, you can purchase straw at a florist supply store or feed store where straw is sold for bedding. It can be stored for several months in a dry place.

When you're ready to begin making stars, cut off the heads of the grain (the top, feathery part) using a razor blade or art knife. Peel down the outer coating of straw to the shiny inner stalk.

Soak the straw in water 20 minutes or overnight, until the straw bends without splitting or breaking. Also soak the tying string or yarn that you plan to use to hold the straws in place when the star is assembled. Drain the stalks and wrap them in a wet towel for two to three hours before you make the stars.

Flatten the straws using the back of a spoon, then cut into 3-inch pieces. Each star requires six 3-inch pieces of straw.

Stack three straws atop one another in a star shape by threading a straight pin through the centers and pivoting the straws on the pin to make a six-pointed star. Then use just a drop of any white household glue to glue the straws together in the center (remove the pin). Arrange and glue a second set of three stars. Position this second set atop the first set so the star points radiate evenly in a circle.

Using damp yarn or string, weave around the points of the star. Weave under the lower straw, then over the upper straw all the way around. Pull the weaving thread tight (but the star should remain flat) and tie the ends into a knot. As the damp thread dries, it tightens around the straws, holding them firmly in place.

Finally, using a razor blade or sharp craft knife, trim the ends of the star points so they are all about the same length.

Make 20 to 30 stars, depending on the size of the ring of greenery around your straw figure.

Symbols of Peace and Goodwill

In stories, paintings, and pious chants, angels have been the bearers of momentous tidings; so it's not surprising that for generations they've also been a symbol of Christmas. Angels make an especially pleasing holiday decoration when they are crafted in stained glass, the traditional material used in church windows.

This stained-glass angel (opposite and right) is crafted in two shades of green glass and stands just a bit taller than 10 inches.

Cut the body and wings of the angel from sheet glass and wrap the pieces with lead came. Solder the body pieces together at an angle so the angel will stand easily on a table.

Use an amber glass jewel for the head, rose-colored tri-beads for the flowers, and slender wire for the halo and the streamers beneath the bouquet.

The candle sculpture, reminiscent of masses of blazing candles seen in churches during the holidays, is worked in amber with a ring of holly leaves and bright red berries around the base. A votive candle set in the center makes the glass sparkle and shine.

To make the angel or the candle arrangement, use either antique glass, which is hand blown, or cathedral glass, which is machine made. Both are available in a variety of rich colors and interesting textures.

Because antique glass is handmade, it has beautiful irregularities in it. But it is harder for a beginning glass crafter to work with than cathedral glass because it is not always uniformly thick. If this is your first venture in stained glass, you may wish to use machine-made glass, which is available in ¼-inch-thick sheets with a textured side and a smooth side. It can be easily scored and cut on the smooth side.

After cutting all the pieces for your project, wrap each one in ³/₁₆-inch U-channel lead came, snugging the lead close to the edge of the glass for a tight fit.

Then carefully solder all of the joints together.

Clean your completed project using a mild window cleaner or a mixture of vinegar and water.

Glass and the tools and supplies you'll need for cutting and wrapping the pieces and assembling the angel and candle sculpture are available from stained-glass suppliers or hobby shops.

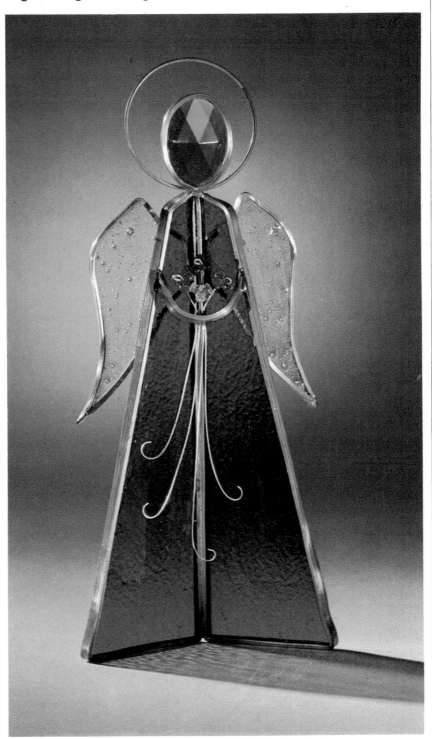

Symbols of Peace and Goodwill

These flighty angels hovering in the window (below) are delightful spin-offs of the American patchwork quilt. If this is the year you plan to enjoy a down-home, country-style Christmas, use the gingham and calico fabrics beloved of quilt makers to create these sophisticated soft-sculpture angels for your home.

Each angel measures approximately 38 inches from wing tip to hem. Hands and faces are muslin, costumes, halos, and hairdos (there are two to choose from) are of printed and colored fabrics.

To make the angels, start with a selection of small-scale posy prints, ginghams, and natural muslin. Then piece and appliqué the angels together, sandwiching quilt batting between the layers of fabric to quilt as you go. You may stitch the body and wing sections by hand or machine, but you'll want to work the angels' expressive eyes by hand, using cotton embroidery floss.

When the angels are finished, mount each on sturdy matt board and suspend them using loops of ribbon or nylon thread.

Instructions for the Christmas Story: Symbols of Peace and Goodwill

The instructions below and on the following pages are for the projects shown on pages 308–318. For directions for enlarging and transferring designs, see the glossary, pages 370–371.

Madonna and Child Banner
page 308

Materials: Felt in the following amounts and colors—1¾ yards purple (P on pattern), 2 yards red (R), two 9×12-inch squares white (W), ⅔ yard royal blue (B), 12×18 inches light blue (LB), ½ yard yellow gold (G); 36-inch dowel; white glue or thread to match fabrics; 7 yards each red and purple craft yarn; 15 yards blue craft yarn.

Instructions: Enlarge the pattern (below) and cut pieces to size. Use 2 yards of red felt for background.

Glue or stitch figure onto red background. Cut letters from bright gold; glue or stitch in place. Glue blue yarn around outlines of central figures; trim edges of banner using purple, blue, and red yarn. Make blue tassel.

Cut 3×9-inch hanging tabs, trim one end as shown, and stitch to top. Insert dowel through tabs.

Peace Banner
page 309

Materials: Felt in the following amounts and colors—⅝ yard yellow (Y), 2 yards spring green (G), 24×24 inches white (W), 2 yards peacock blue (B); 5 yards peacock blue craft yarn; 8 yards yellow yarn; white glue or thread to match fabrics; 36-inch dowel.

Instructions: Enlarge the pattern (below). Using blue felt as background, glue bird, leaves, tree, and blossoms in place. Note that tree limbs extend beyond the top of the banner. Extend cutting lines on green felt 4 inches at the top. Fold extra fabric to the back; stitch into loops to hold the dowel.

Cut letters out of a solid piece of yellow felt as for reverse appliqué. Glue yellow felt to blue background so letters show as blue.

Trim edges with yellow and blue yarns. Make yellow tassels if desired.
continued

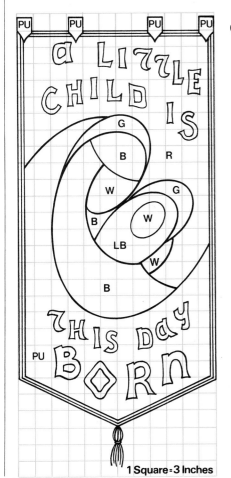

1 Square = 3 Inches

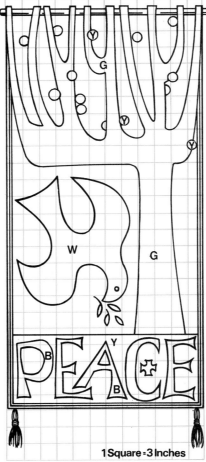

1 Square = 3 Inches

1 Square = 3 Inches

Continued from page 319
Symbols of Peace and Goodwill

Rejoice Banner
page 309

Materials: Felt in the following amounts and colors—2 yards yellow gold (G), 1¼ yards blue (B), 1 yard orange (O), two 12×18-inch pieces magenta (M); craft yarn in the following amounts and colors—20 yards yellow gold, 16 yards each orange and magenta, 2 yards blue; white glue or thread; 2 brass bells; 36-inch dowel.

Instructions: Enlarge pattern (page 319); cut out letters and abstract shape. Using yellow-gold felt for background, glue or stitch felt pieces into place.

Cut background to match pattern. Outline letters and trim edges of banner with yarn. Fill center of abstract shape with rows of yarn. Tack bells to lower corners; stitch tabs to top as shown.

Peace on Earth and Goodwill to Men Banners
pages 310–311

Materials: 72-inch-wide felt in the following colors and amounts—1 yard each green and turquoise; ⅝ yard each magenta and violet; ⅜ yard each ocher, white, red, and black; ¼ yard each hot pink, orange, tan, sienna, and pink (or use small squares); brown thread; nylon thread; mylar or silver fabric; 3¼ yards silver rickrack (each banner); ½ yard ocher edging (Mary's robe); white glue; ⅜×1½×72 inches wood lath (each banner); brass rings; ⅝ yard print fabric (Joseph's coat); ½ yard print fabric (right king's robe).

Instructions: Enlarge the patterns (right and opposite) to make master patterns. Transfer shapes to tissue paper; cut tissue apart to make patterns for individual pieces. Assemble using directions on pages 310–311.

● *Peace on Earth Banner*

Cut fabric as follows: *Green:* 36 × 46-inch background for border; 3 leaves. *Turquoise:* Mary's robe. *Magenta:* 22½×34-inch background for center scene; two 10×36-inch strips for top and bottom. *Ocher:* 3 halos. *White:* Sheep; dove; infant's wrap. *Red:* 3 circle shapes (cut into sixths) for center scene; 4 circles and 20 squares for border.

Black: Joseph's beard and crook. *Hot pink:* Upper lettering; 16 outer shapes and 8 triangles for border. *Orange:* Lower lettering; 16 corner strips and 40 inner shapes for border, 2 dots.

Tan: Donkey; sheep's face and ear. *Sienna:* Eyelashes; animals' and dove's eyes. *Pink:* Joseph's and Mary's faces and hands; infant's face.

Mylar: 16 circles and 4 squares. *Printed fabric:* Joseph's robe.

● *Goodwill to Men Banner*

Cut fabric as follows: *Green:* Right king's crown; lower king's gift. *Turquoise:* 36×46-inch background for border; right king's gift trim; left king's crown jewels and gift; lower king's

1 Square = 4 Inches

crown jewel; shepherd's hat. *Magenta:* Lower king's crown; 2 circle shapes (cut into sixths) for center.

Violet: 22½×34-inch background for center scene; two 10×36-inch strips for top and bottom. *Ocher:* Left and lower

kings' faces and hands; right king's crown and lips; lower king's earring. *White:* Eyes; right king's collar.

Red: Lower king's robe; 4 circles and 24 small squares for border. *Black:* Right king's hair; lower king's beard;

shepherd's beard; 4 eye pupils. *Hot pink:* Lower lettering; lower king's gift trim (4 circles) and crown trim (12 semicircles); 24 triangles and 9 small triangles for border.

Orange: Upper lettering; right king's crown jewels (4 dots), gift; left and lower king's gift trim (5 triangles); 28 squares for border. *Tan:* Right king's face, hand; shepherd's rough coat. *Sienna:* Upper king's hair; 2 eye pupils.

Pink: Shepherd's faces. *Printed fabric:* Right king's robe. *Mylar:* 28 squares and 4 circles for border.

1 Square = 4 Inches

Stylized Angel
page 312

Materials: Felt in following colors and amounts—⅓ yard 36-inch wide pink, ⅙ yard yellow, 4×36-inch piece orange, 1 yard reddish purple, ⅓ yard white, scraps of black and flesh tones; ½×34½-inch dowel; 2 wooden beads.

Instructions: Cut 2 inches off reddish-purple fabric for tabs. Cut 7 tabs 2×5 inches. Fold ½ inch on both sides; glue so tab is 1×5 inches.

Use remaining reddish-purple fabric for background. Hem top and sides using 1½-inch hem—bottom, 3 inches. Stitch side and top hems. Fold tabs in half. Stitch as shown on pattern, ½ inch down on back of top edge.

Enlarge pattern of angel (page 322); trace onto background. Cut dress pieces from pink. Cut out orange pieces; glue. Glue dress pieces in place.

Cut a 6-inch circle from yellow felt. Cut pattern from circle, retaining triangular pieces from outer edges. Glue the halo to the background fabric.

Cut an outline of face and hands from flesh-colored felt. Cut and glue features and hair on face. Position face; glue into place. Set hands aside. Cut and glue wings and border from white. Cut and glue horn and stars from yellow. Glue hands into place.

Glue wooden beads on dowel (the overall length measures 34½ inches).

Wise Men Hangings
page 313

Materials: Felt scraps or 9×12-inch squares in following colors—hot pink, red, aqua, green, purple, yellow, white, 3 shades of flesh tones; 1 yard 72-inch black felt for background; 3 pieces heavy cardboard that measure 8×14 inches cut in curved shape; fabric glue; 42-inch drapery weights (optional); fishline or carpet thread.

continued

Continued from page 321
Symbols of Peace and Goodwill

Instructions: Enlarge patterns of wise men (below). Cut backgrounds for the panels from black felt measuring 14×36 inches; curve tops.

From white paper, cut 1½-inch border to fit around background.

Trace pattern pieces for each color on tracing paper. Mark each piece using color as indicated in color key (below).

Cut shapes from colored felt using tracing paper patterns. Begin gluing at outer edges of background; spread glue over back of each piece. Continue gluing remaining pieces. Weight felt with books if necessary to keep pieces from curling.

Cut 2 pieces 1½ inches wide from black felt for side borders, noting dotted lines on patterns; cut curved border for top edge and one border for bottom. Use paper borders for patterns. Glue felt borders in place.

Using background pattern, cut curved top piece from cardboard. Mark line at center of cardboard. Make 2 holes on center line 1 and 2 inches down from top edge. Cover one side of cardboard using felt or paint black. Cut about 6 inches of carpet thread or fishline. Fold in half; tie overhand knot about 1 inch below loop. Thread ends through holes on finished side; knot ends together on back, forming loop.

Glue wrong side of top of felt panel to wrong side of cardboard. Tack optional drapery weights to back. Panels can be folded and stored in a small space. Also, if you wish, use ⅓ yard more black felt. Cut outline of wise men; glue figure pieces to outline; glue completed outline to background.

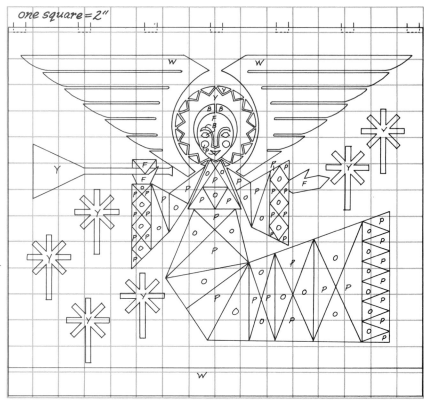

one square = 2"

color key: P-pink Y-yellow O-orange F-flesh W-white B-black

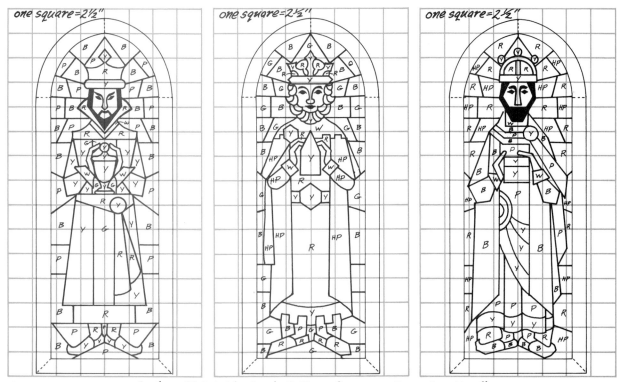

one square = 2½"

color key: HP-hot pink R-red B-blue G-green P-purple Y-yellow

Stained-Glass Angel
page 316

Materials: 2 shades of green glass 7×9 inches for body, 6×5 inches for wings; six 6-foot strips U-channel lead came; 5 feet solder, 20-gauge wire for flowers, 16-gauge wire for halo, 1 jewel 1¾ inches in diameter for head, tribeads for flowers.

Instructions: Cut each glass piece as in pattern. Wrap and solder each one. Cut and shape hands from lead. Make flowers; solder into bouquet.

Put angel body together at 45-degree angle; solder down center back. Attach hands, head, and halos with solder; solder wings onto center back. Solder bouquet, made from tri-beads, to angel's hands.

Stained-Glass Candle Sculpture
page 316

Materials: 3 shades of amber glass 6×10 inches for candles; 7×7-inch amber glass for circle base; 3×11-inch red or variegated glass for flames; 6×9-inch green for holly leaves; twenty-seven ⅜-inch red nuggets for berries; 55 feet of 3/16-inch U-channel lead came; 2 feet ¼-inch U-channel came; 5 feet 60/40 solder, silicone glue.

Instructions: Using patterns (below), cut glass—3 of each candle, 18 flames, 36 leaves, one 6-inch circle for base. Wrap candles and flames using 3/16-inch came. Glue lead to sides of glass. Solder joints closed. Wrap circle base with ¼-inch came; solder at joint.

Arrange 9 candles in assorted sizes and colors spaced evenly around base. Solder candles to base at inside edge of ¼-inch channel. Tilt candles outward.

Solder the remaining 9 candles behind the first ones, alternating sizes and colors. Stand candles upright. Wrap holly berries; solder closed. Arrange 9 sets of 3 berries each. Solder together into clusters. Wrap and solder leaves. Solder berry clusters and leaves to base and occasionally to candles.

Patchwork Angels
page 318

Materials: White, green, blue, black, and red embroidery floss; ¼ yard pink fabric (face and arms); eight to ten ½-yard pieces of gingham and calico prints; quilt batting; craft glue; poster board or medium-weight cardboard.

Instructions: Enlarge patterns and cut all the pieces from fabric except head. (There are 2 hair patterns.) Refer to the photograph for color suggestions. Cut bodice, halo, wings, sleeves, 2 skirt pieces, and 2 hand-and-arm pieces from quilt batting.

Pin each skirt batting to the wrong side of 1 skirt piece. Pin together the 2 skirt-and-batting pieces, right sides facing, and sew in a ⅝-inch seam, leaving the waist open. Trim seams, clip curves, turn, and press lightly.

Pin skirt overlays into position; sew using machine zigzag or by hand.

Pin batting to wrong side of bodice front. Stitch together bodice front and back, right sides facing. Leave waist open. Trim seams, turn, and press.

Pin bodice over skirt top. Wrap waistband over raw edges of bodice and skirt, folding ends to back of angel. Zigzag- or hand-stitch around edges.

Pin and sew the sleeves and batting together, leaving 1 inch open for arms. Clip, trim, and turn.

Assemble hand (and arm) with a layer of padding between pieces. Leave open at top of arm. Turn; top-stitch hand to make fingers. Pin arms into sleeve openings; whipstitch. Pin sleeves to bodice; zigzag- or hand-stitch.

Transfer head pattern to double fabric, but don't cut out. Using 3 strands of floss and satin stitch, embroider eyes. Cut out cheeks and red felt mouth; sew into place. Cut out head; pin to halo.

Pin hair to halo; zigzag-stitch around edges. Sew neck to bodice.

Assemble wings with padding between them, leaving 2 inches open at the bottom. Turn and press. Pin and sew feathers into place, using the photograph as a guide. Pin and sew wings behind sleeves and head, and zigzag- or hand-sew overlapping edges together.

To make the backing, trace around the angel on poster board. Cut backing shape ½ inch inside the traced line. Glue backing to back of angel; attach loops to wings for hanging.

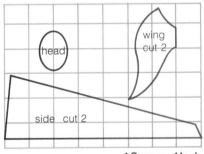

1 Square = 1 Inch

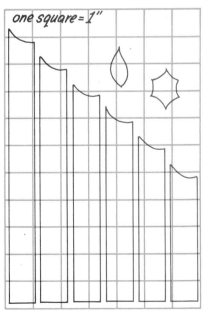

one square = 1"

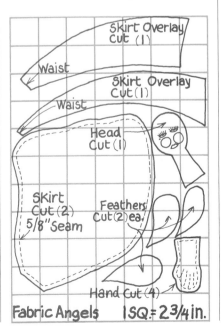

Fabric Angels   1 SQ.= 2¾ in.

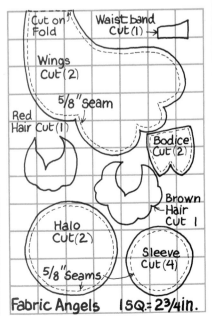

Fabric Angels   1 SQ.= 2¾ in.

Decorations to Delight Your Guests

All Around the House

It doesn't take much—just the right touch—to spruce up your home for the holidays. So, deck your halls with one of the merry Christmas trims in this section! Included are table toppers, tiny trees, and pretty wreaths to pleasure your family and friends, starting with an enchanting, potpourri-covered deer (below) in a thicket of green succulents, ribbons, and candles, and a whimsical teddy bear (opposite) made of pine cone petals glued to a papier-mâché base and adorned with a red velvet bow.

Directions for the projects begin on page 332.

All Around the House

Bamboo, wood, greens, and flowers are part of nature's finery all year round—and especially festive at Christmas. Gather an assortment of these down-to-earth materials to craft the merry decorations shown here.

The geometric trims (right) look like the handiwork of a master craftsman, but they're easy to make using lath, balsa, wood blocks, or strips of bamboo.

Or, circle an 18-inch green wreath (right, below) with a frame designed from thirty-two ½-inch balsa slats. Make eight squares; glue corners, clamping with clothespins until dry. Next, glue two of the squares together to form an octagon. Glue additional squares on top, placing corners between points of the octagon. Attach the frame to an evergreen wreath and add a decorative straw or bamboo figure.

The shapely tree (opposite) perched atop a drum (you can use any suitable base) is a feast for the eyes and delightfully scented with cinnamon sticks. To make one like it, begin by securing a 3-foot cone to the base. Arrange strings of lights in place and spiral a garland of greens around the cone. Cluster long sticks of cinnamon (from a spice company or florist) at the base, then hang small birds, berries, children's blocks, wrapped candies, or other ornaments on the tree.

To carry out the natural theme, create a decoration by tying together a stack of foot-high straw-flowers. Fan out stems of flowers, then insert a 3-inch clay pot beneath the stems to give the arrangement stability. Trim with twigs, ribbon, and birds atop an artificial nest.

All Around the House

Kitchens and dining rooms are pretty important places during the holidays because a lot of Christmastime fun is tied in with cooking and eating. When arranging goodies for your guests to enjoy, leave room on the counter, sideboard, or table for an eye-catching Christmas trim to set the mood for your festivities.

Do your guests migrate to the kitchen during a party? Then trim a tiny tree with spices and herbs for a potpourri of fragrance on your kitchen counter. Purchase a table-size tree from your florist or nursery and bedeck it with clusters of spices. Tie them to the tree using thread or fine wire.

On this small tree (right) are anise, nutmeg, stick cinnamon, blade mace, cardamom, coriander, gingerroot, allspice, juniper berries, cloves, fennel and caraway seeds, and vanilla and coffee beans. The spicy scent will last long after the holidays are over.

Team the spices with a variety of sweet treats—sugar cubes, gumdrops, popcorn, assorted soft candies, walnuts, and peanuts. You can snip these off the tree when guests drop in.

To add spots of color on the tree, arrange large ribbon bows at strategic spots on the branches. Tie some bows that you cut from lengths of plaid ribbon and other bows in a variety of sizes from solid-colored ribbon.

If you use a real tree be sure to water it regularly to keep it sprightly looking all through the season.

The corn husk Christmas tree (opposite) serves as the focal point for a bountiful buffet table. It's made by attaching rows of bleached corn husk loops to a plastic foam cone that stands about 24 inches high. For a base, use a miniature bushel basket.

Corn husk loops are easy to make. Just soften dried husks (available in grocery and craft stores) in boiling water, then wrap them in a towel to keep them damp while you work.

Tear the husks into 1½-inch-wide strips 6 to 8 inches long. Fold the strips in half over a piece of cardboard (so the loops will all be the same size), then pin the puffs to the foam cone using hair-pins or floral stems. (Arrange the loops in bands, as shown opposite, to leave room for the berries.) Trim the top of the tree with a foam ball wrapped in husks.

Add color to the tree by stringing rows of cranberries or wooden beads between the corn husk loops.

To complete your buffet centerpiece, wrap small gift boxes in brown paper. Trim the "packages" using velvet or paper ribbons, and arrange them around the tree's base.

All Around the House

Wreaths are traditional at Christmas, but they needn't be made of traditional green boughs. Stitch one of these stunning designs using beautiful old silk ties or needlepoint canvas and yarn, and you'll have an elegant and unusual wreath to enjoy for many Christmases to come.

The crazy quilt wreath (opposite) is a collage of old silks adorned with feather stitching and a lavish bow. The Della Robbia design (below) was inspired by the traditional wreaths of colonial Williamsburg. It has a beautiful array of fruits and greenery for you to needlepoint.

Instructions for Decorations to Delight Your Guests: All Around the House

The instructions below and on the following pages are for the table decorations, small trees, and wreaths shown on pages 324–331.

Potpourri-Covered Deer
page 324

Materials: Chicken wire and papier mâché mix (or substitute purchased deer figure about 16 inches high); gesso, potpourri mixture; 24-inch plastic foam ring; wire picks or medium-gauge wire cut into 5-inch lengths and bent into hairpin shapes; sphagnum moss; succulent plants such as hens and chicks; terra-cotta saucer; ribbon; 4 candle holders; candles; pine cones.

Instructions: Using chicken wire, construct a deer about 16 inches high; cover with papier mâché. When mâché dries, coat with gesso. Or, use a purchased figure; paint with gesso. While gesso is wet, pour potpourri mixture over the deer, covering it completely.

Wire sphagnum moss onto the plastic foam ring. Attach succulents with wire picks, covering the entire wreath. Set wreath into an inverted terra-cotta saucer. Insert candle holders into ring as shown in the photograph; add candles. Trim the deer and green ring using bows and pine cones.

Pine Cone Teddy Bear
page 325

Materials: Chicken wire and papier mâché (or substitute a purchased teddy bear figure about 14 inches high); glue; pine cones; ribbon.

Instructions: Using chicken wire, shape a teddy bear figure that measures about 14 inches high and rests in a sitting position, as shown in the photograph. Cover the chicken wire form with papier mâché until it is smooth.

When the papier mâché is completely dry, glue individual pine cone petals in place, following the shape of the bear (a glue you heat works best). Overlap petals a bit for a layered effect. Allow glue to dry overnight; tie a ribbon bow around the bear's neck.

Wood Trims
page 326

Note: Directions are given for projects, left to right in photograph.

Materials: Discarded bamboo blind or strips of ½-inch balsa; dowels for tree trunks; wood blocks for bases.

● *Star with curved rays*

Cut 5 equal pieces 10 to 12 inches long from ½-inch-wide bamboo slats, avoiding joints. Heat center of each piece (using hot water, steam, gas, or electric burner) till pliable. Cross ends at an angle; clamp till set.

Split each end in thirds; interweave these ends. Touch with glue; clamp till dry. Arrange the pieces in a star-shape, with bent middles at center and interwoven ends outermost. Cut 5 more equal pieces 10 to 12 inches long; soften centers with heat. Bend these pieces and place one around each ray. Glue and clamp at contact points.

Glue a single bamboo "trunk" between the 2 bottom rays. Reinforce it with another slat that you glue on each side. Glue into a wooden base.

● *Four-sided tree*

Draw a triangle with 10-inch base and 24-inch sides. Cover with ½-inch bamboo slats; set edge to edge starting at base. Hold temporarily with masking tape; mark triangle, then cut slats. Repeat to make second set.

Nail a 4-inch wooden base to "trunk" that is ⅝x⅝x22 inches. Starting 3½ inches up from base, glue longest slats of each set to opposite sides of trunk, the next 2 longest slats above and touching first slats at right angles. (See photograph.) Continue with other ascending sizes.

Near the top, split off increasing slivers of bamboo, gradually decreasing width as pieces get shorter. Discard shortest pieces; top tree with a wooden button mold and wooden bead.

● *Twelve-ray star* (24 inches high)

Cut 12 pieces 7 inches long from ½-inch bamboo slats; avoid joints. Arrange 3 pieces in a triangle (disregard projecting corners); glue, clamp till dry. Cut off projecting corners to leave a true triangle. Make 4 such triangles.

Draw a circle 7½ inches in diameter; divide into 12 equal sections (use protractor or compass). Set triangle to touch 3 radii on circle; set another triangle to touch the 3 adjacent radii; glue where triangles overlap. Continue with third and fourth triangles, etc. Glue each to the triangle under it. Glue to dowel set in a block.

● *Sixteen-ray star* (18 inches high)

Cut eight 10-inch pieces from ½-inch bamboo slats, avoiding joints. Make 4 crosses, gluing at center. Glue pairs of crosses together to make 8-ray stars; glue together for 16-ray star.

Split a slat to ³⁄₁₆-inch wide; make small 8-ray star for center. Glue to a ¼-inch dowel set in a wooden base.

● *Triangle tree* (22 inches high)

Cut 3 identical pieces from ½-inch bamboo slats. Arrange corner to corner in a triangle (disregard projecting corners). Glue, then clamp in place until dry. Cut off projecting corners.

Glue similar triangles ranging from 4 to 7 inches on a side at overlaps. Form stars from short pieces of wood strips about ³⁄₁₆ inch wide. Glue tree trunk to a short dowel set in a wood base.

Corn-Husk Tree
page 329

Materials: 24-inch plastic foam cone; 16-oz. metal can; masking tape; corn husks; cardboard; spool wire; about 450 red, wooden ⅜-inch beads; plastic foam ball; 8-inch piece of ¼-inch dowel; glue; U-shaped floral pins; container for tree; rubber bands; knife and scissors for cutting husks.

Instructions: Set foam cone on metal can. Press down, marking outline of can on cone. Cut an indentation 1 inch deep; cover can with masking tape. Fit can into indentation.

Soak husks in boiling water until pliable. Drain, wrap in a towel. Glue husks to can, overlap and pin to hold.

To cover ball for top of tree, insert dowel 3 inches into ball. Tear softened husks into 1-inch strips; glue to ball, starting and ending at dowel. Next, wire ends of husks to dowel. Set ball and dowel aside to dry.

Mark cone from bottom to top into alternating 2¾- and 1½-inch bands.

For corn-husk puffs, tear off outer edges of softened husks. Tear husks into 1½-inch-wide strips. Cut cardboard guide 2¾x2 inches. Fold a husk strip over the 2-inch side of guide. Pinch ends of husks together at edge of cardboard; wire together. Trim corn husk close to wire. Remove guide. Put thumbs inside husk at fold; pull husk.

Pin puffs along wider bands of cone, beginning at bottom. To add ball, cover top 2 inches of dowel with husks. Insert remainder of dowel into cone. Hold rows of beads or cranberries into position using hairpins or floral stems.

Insert trunk end of tree into a basket or other container.

Crazy Quilt Wreath
page 330

Note: Finished wreath measures approximately 23 inches in diameter.

Materials: Approximately 24 ties (garage sales, thrift shops, and the Salvation Army are good sources for old ties; scraps of any other light to medium-weight fabrics may be substituted for ties). One yard acetate tie silk (for bow); ⅔ yard lining fabric; 24-inch square of cardboard; 2 spools of #5 pearl cotton (gold); quilt batting; ¾ yard muslin; stapler.

Instructions: Ties should be free of spots and stains. Cut off 6 inches from both ends of each tie; remove backing and lining fabrics. Iron tie ends flat, leaving edges turned under at points and along sides of each tie piece.

Cut a circle of muslin 25 inches in diameter. From center, clip out a 9-inch circle. Beginning at top of wreath and working counterclockwise, lay tie points out on muslin pattern, alternating colors and patterns, and alternating wide and narrow points. Points should all face in same direction and completely cover muslin base. You will need 4 or 5 pieces across width of wreath; points should overlap 2 to 3 inches at base.

When you complete a round, tuck raw edges of last row of ties under points of first row at top. Pin and baste all pieces in place, clipping away excess where ties overlap. Leave about 1 inch unstitched at center of wreath, to allow for give when wreath is stretched on cardboard frame.

Cut a cardboard circle 22 inches in diameter, and cut out a circle with a 10-inch diameter from center. Cut 3 layers of batting slightly larger than cardboard frame. Stretch batting over frame and staple raw edges around on

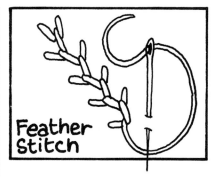

back of frame. Lay pieced tie wreath over padded frame; clip inside edges to ease, and make sure edges on pieced wreath will stretch comfortably to back of frame. Adjust where necessary.

Remove tie wreath and machine- or hand-tack ties down. Remove basting. Using #5 pearl cotton, work a row of featherstitching along all seams.

Gently iron patched wreath from back. Stretch over frame and staple raw edges of fabric to back of cardboard. Cut a piece of lining fabric to fit and slip-stitch to back of wreath.

To make the bow, cut a piece of tie silk 14 inches wide and 1½ yards long (piece at center, if necessary). With right sides together, fold in half lengthwise, and seam (½ inch). Turn right side out, press, and tie into bow. Adjust streamers to appropriate length, clip ends on the diagonal, turn raw edges in and slip-stitch closed. Hand-tack bow to wreath, slightly off center.

Needlepoint Wreath
page 331

Materials: 24x24-inch piece of #14 needlepoint canvas; waterproof marking pen; 24x24-inch piece of ⅜-inch plywood; quilt batting; 20x20-inch green felt; 4-inch-wide red velvet ribbon; staple gun; masking tape; #14 needles.

Also, 3-ply Persian wool in colors and amounts below. (Color code is for Paternayan yarn; any suitable substitute may be used. One strand of yarn is 32 inches long.)

Color code	Color	Amount
G74	Pale green	11 strands
G64	Light green	20 strands
R70	Light holly	9 strands
R10	Dark holly	9 strands
G54	Medium green	19 strands
504	Dark green	35 strands
865	Light golden red	6 strands
855	Light red	8 strands
845	Medium red	20 strands
810	Dark red	24 strands
590	Light olive green	11 strands
553	Medium olive	8 strands
540	Dark olive	9 strands
975	Pale orange	5 strands
965	Light orange	10 strands
960	Medium orange	7 strands
958	Dark orange	7 strands
528	Dark blue green	6 strands
532	Medium blue green	6 strands
535	Light blue green	4 strands
113	Dark brown	24 strands
405	Medium brown	12 strands
420	Light brown	10 strands
430	Pale brown	12 strands
433	Dark yellow (gold)	12 strands
427	Medium yellow	13 strands
441	Light lemon yellow	17 strands
437	Pale lemon yellow	17 strands
010	White	45 strands

Instructions: Tape edges of canvas using masking tape. Draw an 18-inch circle in center of canvas using a compass and a waterproof pen. Divide the circle into fourths. Draw a 7-inch circle in the center of the 18-inch circle. This will be the center of the wreath and is not filled in.

Count squares from the inside edge to the outside of the wreath to make sure they equal the number on the graph (pages 334–335). Make adjustments in size of circle on the canvas so it corresponds to size of graph.

Add an extra 7 spaces to the inner and outer edges of the graph and the circle on the canvas. Fill these spaces with additional white yarn so that when the wreath is cut and turned, none of the design will be lost from view.

Using 2 strands of yarn, begin the design in 1 quadrant of the wreath, following pattern for colors.

After finishing the first quadrant, label one end of the pattern A and the other B. To begin the second quadrant, move wreath clockwise and match end B of the first quadrant to end A of the second. Continue around the wreath until all 4 sections are complete. Be sure to work the white background an extra 7 spaces beyond inner and outer edges marked on the graph.

Block the wreath, if necessary. Cut the wreath, leaving a 2-inch border of unworked canvas around both inside and outside edges.

Cut a 17¼-inch diameter circle from the plywood. Cut a 6½-inch diameter hole in the center. Sand edges.

Pad the plywood with 3 layers of quilt batting. Lay the wreath over the padding and staple it to the back of the wood. Clip the center curve wherever necessary. Then cut a piece of felt to fit the back; glue it in place, covering the raw edges of the canvas.

Tie a bow with the ribbon and tack to the bottom of the wreath.

continued

Color	Symbol		Color	Symbol
Light holly	L		Medium green	+
Dark holly	/		Dark green	◢
White	□		Light golden red	—
Pale green	○		Light red	·
Light green	M		Medium red	▲
			Dark red	✕

This pattern is for 1 quadrant (1 quarter) of the wreath design. To complete the quadrant, fit together the 2 halves of the pattern along the notched edge down the center of each page.

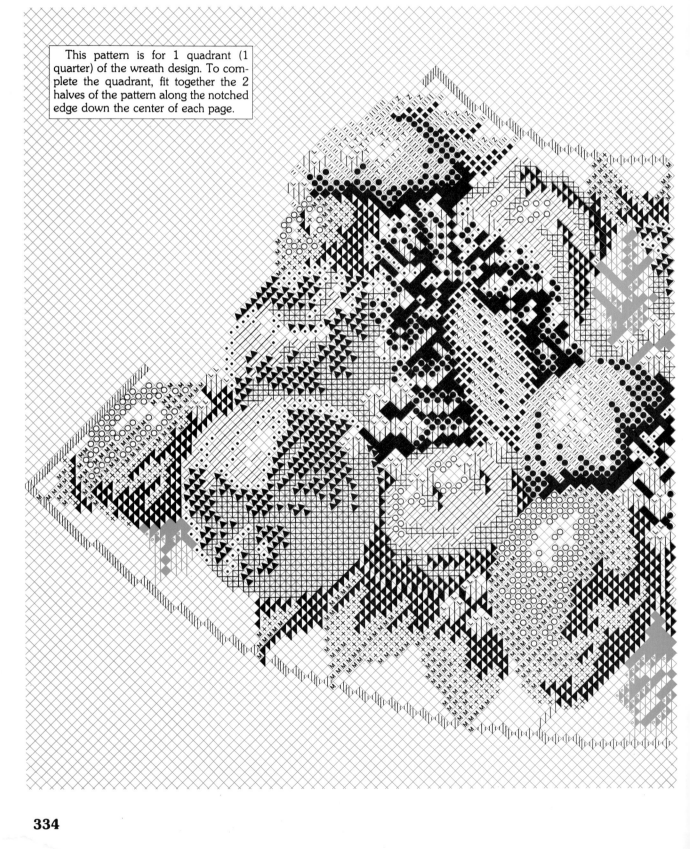

Pale orange	T	Light blue green	z	Medium yellow	✕
Light orange	=	Dark brown	■	Light lemon yellow	—
Medium orange	●	Medium brown	●	Pale lemon yellow	○
Dark orange	■	Light brown	/	Light olive green	⁄
Dark blue green	▪	Pale brown	·	Medium olive	◢
Medium blue green	‖	Dark yellow (gold)	◢	Dark olive	▨

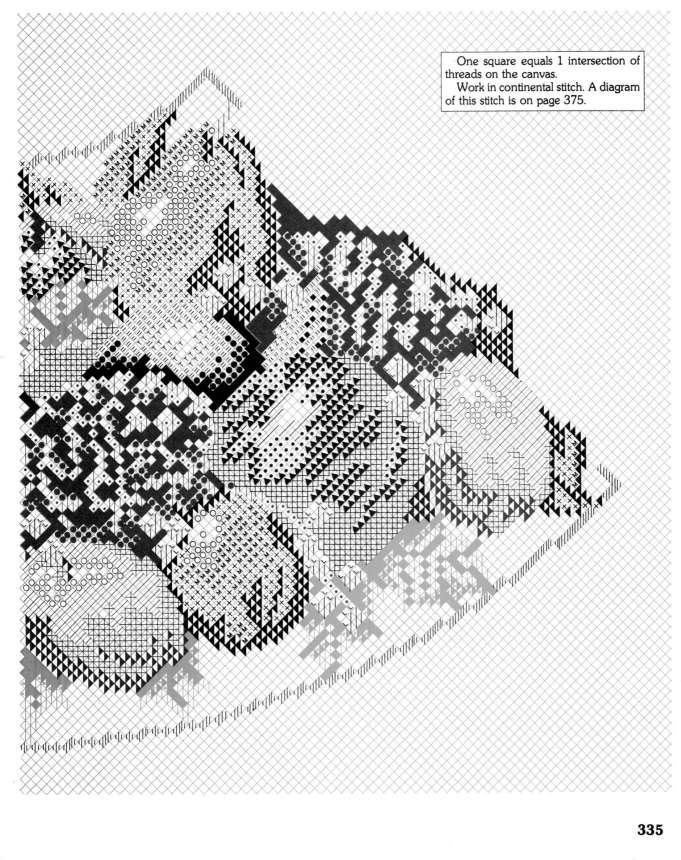

One square equals 1 intersection of threads on the canvas.
Work in continental stitch. A diagram of this stitch is on page 375.

Decorations to Delight Your Guests

Festive Table Settings

Get your Christmas parties off to a flying start with festive table decorations! Holiday table trims can be fun—even fabulous—and still be rather quick or easy to put together. You'll find lots of ideas for sensational tables in this section, and they'll take far less than a month of Sundays to complete.

This wreath, for example, is so simple to make you'll want to feature it at special-occasion parties all through the holidays. Combine fresh greens with whirligig candies to encircle a footed punch bowl. Tuck in a small pair of scissors adorned with a velvet bow so guests can help themselves to a sweet treat.

To make the basic green wreath, use a plastic foam ring (the one shown is 18 inches in diameter), heavy florist wire cut into 5-inch lengths and bent into hairpin shapes, and fresh or artificial evergreen sprigs. Anchor the greens to the foam using wire pins. For the candy wreath, tie wrapped sweets to a wire ring. Then snug the two wreaths together and set the punch bowl inside.

Directions for the other projects in this section begin on page 344.

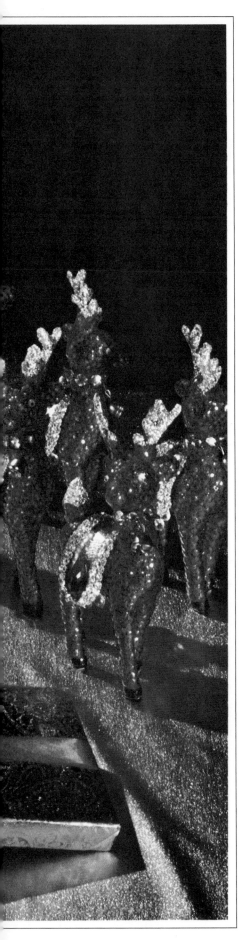

Festive Table Settings

Here comes Santa Claus—dashing across your Christmas table with all his reindeer—decked out in sequins, fur, and silver braid. This whimsical centerpiece takes a little time to make, but it's so easy even your youngsters can join in the fun.

If time is in short supply, see the suggestions (below, right) for quick-to-fix decorations for your table or buffet.

A ready-made sleigh, reindeer, and Santa figure form the base for this table decoration (left). In addition, you'll need red, black and silver cupped sequins; scraps of silver Mylar, leather, or vinyl; plastic jewels and beads; silver braid or ribbon; white fur; white glue; toothpicks; and tweezers.

Assemble all the materials and pour sequins into a shallow tray so they're easy to pick up one at a time. Also, pour a small amount of white glue into a jar cap or other shallow container.

Apply sequins to each of the purchased figures by dipping the end of a toothpick into the glue (picking up only a tiny amount) and dotting glue onto the figure (rather than the sequin). Then pick up a sequin (using tweezers) and attach it to the figure.

Cover each figure completely except for the eyes on the reindeer and the facial features on Santa. Avoid overlapping the sequins unless it's necessary to cover the figures.

For the reindeer, begin by covering the hooves using black sequins. Then cover the legs, body, and head using red sequins, except use silver on the tips of the tails and the antlers. Cut an oval

of silver Mylar, leather, or vinyl for a coat for each reindeer. Glue or hand-stitch a row of silver braid (or use silver sequins) around the edge of each coat.

Glue each coat onto the body of the reindeer, and decorate the coat using teardrop-shaped "jewels," beads, or additional braid.

Finish by sewing a collar of silver sequins for each reindeer. Add a tiny bell to the neckpiece and glue the collar into place.

Cover the sleigh using red sequins; add tiny red beads if desired. If the runners of your purchased sleigh are narrow and difficult to cover, you may wish to coat the entire sleigh using red paint before adding the sequins.

Cover Santa's suit, hat, and mittens using red sequins. Trim his suit and cap using narrow strips of fake fur glued into place.

Arrange Santa in his sleigh and tuck in a tiny lap robe made from a scrap of red velvet fabric.

Even when last minute company's coming you still can set a beautiful table in short order. Here are some ideas:

Fill an oversize brandy snifter, soup tureen, or clear glass dish with miniature packages. Wrap empty match boxes, spice boxes, and other tiny containers in pretty dollhouse wallpapers, diminutive calico prints, or elegant gift wrap papers. Trim these pretend presents with tiny bows tied in narrow ribbon or gold or silver cord.

Fill a beautiful dish with an arrangement of fresh Christmas greens. Tuck them into a block of florist's foam to hold them in place, and include candles, small glass or satin tree ornaments, or miniature birds if desired.

Show off a collection of small treasures—miniature dolls, paperweights, or vases just large enough for single blossoms, for example—by grouping it in the middle of your table. Or, skip a "centerpiece" altogether and opt for small arrangements in front of each place setting. However you decide to display your collection, you'll have a table decoration that is personal and unique.

Festive Table Settings

Get set for oohs and ahs of admiration when you put this bouquet of soft flowers on your Christmas table. Use yarn roses, daisies, and pompons with tiny lights and satin ornaments for this sweet, romantic centerpiece.

Craft these lovely roses in a variety of pink and red knitting yarns. Coil a strand of yarn into a flat circle using masking tape to hold the yarn in place while you work. Anchor the strands together with sewing thread, then stitch the newly formed petal to a knotted-yarn flower center. Shape 10 petals into a graceful flower, and anchor with a wire stem.

Pompons are easy to make by wrapping yarn around and around cardboard disks with holes in the center. For daisies, use floral looms from craft or hobby shops.

When all the flowers are finished, arrange them in a block of foam tucked into a small basket.

Festive Table Settings

One time during the holidays why not pull out all the stops and throw a party that will be the talk of the town? All you need to succeed without trying too hard is a little razzle-dazzle and your own enjoyable friends.

Set your table with splendiferous accessories like those shown here, and you have the beginnings of a dinner party to remember. The mirrored place mats are such a good idea you'll want to use them for special-occasion dining all year long. They're made of one-inch-square mirror tiles glued to felt backing fabric—as are the quickie napkin rings.

Use similar mirror tiles for the glamorous city-scape screen on the buffet. The screen is a project you can complete by the holidays but it's not so Christmasy that you can't use it in May as well as December.

To make the screen, glue blue and silver mirror tiles onto four 10x24-inch plywood panels using the pattern on page 345 as a guide. Then join the panels with silver piano hinges and arrange them on your buffet to reflect the candlelight and add sparkle to your dining room.

Those classy candle holders can be yours in an instant. All they require are some store-bought silver Christmas tree balls and a clever presto-chango trick: Remove the ornaments' hanging wires. Then glue a silver-colored washer or craft ring to the base of each ornament. (Be sure each Christmas ball sits upright.) Half-fill the ornaments with sand so they're stable, and add an assortment of white tapered candles.

To create a super snazzy centerpiece that's easy and inexpensive, cover a plastic tray, small paper box, and slender cardboard tube with silver adhesive-backed paper and arrange them as shown in the photograph. Tuck a few sprigs of holly into the box and a gorgeous red rose into the "vase." Then pile the tray high with lots and lots of small silver and blue packages.

Here's a heaven-sent idea for trimming those "presents"—paste store-bought paper stars on blue or white wrappings for custom gift wraps with class.

While you're doing up packages, also gift wrap your door in smashing silver and blue. Door-width paper like this can be purchased in gift wrap stores. For a door-size bow, select super-wide ribbon—either fabric or paper—and tie it on with panache.

Since you're jazzing up your dining room for Christmas entertaining, why not dress up the rest of the house too? Make your tree a star attraction, for example, by trimming it with a twinkling galaxy of shimmery stars.

If you can cut and paste or stitch and stuff, you're qualified to be a star-maker. To make cardboard glitter stars, cut out star shapes in a variety of sizes. (You can use the pattern on page 16 as a guide.) Paint both sides of the cardboard stars with white glue, and then simply sprinkle them with dime-store glitter.

You can fashion chic fabric stars from a variety of shiny materials such as silver lamé, readily available in fabric shops during the holidays or at costume-making establishments throughout the year.

Make star patterns in small, medium, and large sizes and cut fronts and backs from fabric. (Be sure to add at least ¼ inch around the outside of your pattern for the seam allowance.) Then stitch the stars together, leaving an opening for turning. Clip the corners, trim the seams, turn, and press. Stuff the stars with polyester fiberfill and hang them on the tree (and in the windows, too) using metallic silver cord, braid, or ribbon, or invisible nylon thread.

Instructions for Decorations to Delight Your Guests: Festive Table Settings

The instructions below are for the table decorations shown on pages 336–343. For directions for enlarging and transferring designs, see the glossary, pages 370–371.

Yarn Flowers
page 340

General instructions: (You will need 10 petals for each rose.) Assemble petals around a center that is constructed on a wire stem so roses may be placed in a basket or vase arrangement.

Petals: Cut a 2x3-inch piece of masking tape to hold yarn in place as you wind petal. Place one end of yarn on center of gummed side of masking tape. Holding tape in your left hand, keep end of tape in position with your left thumb (A). Take yarn in your right hand; carefully wind it in a circle around end that you place on tape (B). As you wind, keep yarn just touching adjacent turn; apply light pressure with your left thumb to hold it in place on the tape. Do not wind too tightly or petal will distort when you remove it from the tape. Wind in this manner until the diameter of the petal is the width of tape. Cut yarn (C).

Next, stitch yarn together so the petal will hold its shape when removed from

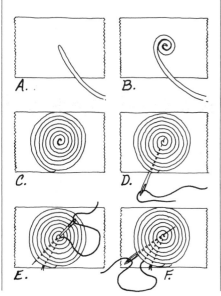

A. .

B.

C.

D.

E.

F.

tape. Starting at outside end of yarn on tape, pass needle through strands of yarn parallel to tape, bringing it out at center of petal. Pull thread through until knot is against end of yarn (D). Next, pass needle from center of petal to outer edge, bringing it out ¼ inch from where first stitch entered (E). Run next stitch from outer edge to center, ¼ inch from where other exited (F). Continue this stitch pattern all the way around petal; tie off thread, cutting it off close to petal. Carefully remove petal from the piece of tape.

Flower centers: To make center for a rose, cut a length of yarn that measures 48 inches long. Fold piece of yarn in half, then in half again. (You now have 4 strands of yarn 12 inches long.)

Tie 4 overhand knots in the center of this piece of yarn. Leave the ends free (G). Cut a piece of wire about 14 inches long. Slip one end of the wire through the center of the bottom knot, until it protrudes about 1½ inches. Bend the end of the wire down; twist it around the longer piece (H).

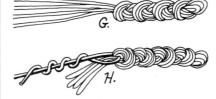

G.

H.

Cut off the ends of the yarn about 1 inch below the bottom knot. Position 4 knots straight up above the wire with the ends of the yarn down along wire. To form stem, cover base of bottom knot with floral tape; tape yarn for entire length of wire.

For centers of flowers to be used on plastic foam, use a 4½-inch piece of wire and make in same manner.

To assemble rose: Position the center of the rose in the middle of a petal with edge of petal slightly below bottom knot (I). Wrap the petal around the center; stitch around the center with matching thread (J). Next, start at side opposite from where first petal was started. Wrap the second petal around the center, overlapping the first; stitch into place (K). This completes first row of petals.

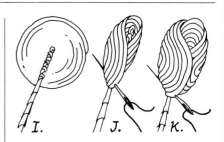

I.

J.

K.

For second row use 3 petals. Start anywhere; position first petal; stitch into place. Position second petal to overlap first by half; stitch. Place third petal to overlap both first and second equally; stitch into place.

Use 5 petals for third row. Position and attach same as for second row.

After third row is in place, hold petals close together; stitch around third row about ¾ inch above bottom of petals. This holds petals together so completed flower can be shaped.

To open and shape flower, start with third row. Roll petals back until open. Repeat with second and first rows.

● *Pompons*

Using a compass, draw two 2-inch circles on shirt cardboard; draw a ½-inch circle in the center of each (L).

Cut out two-inch circles. Next, cut a small circle from center of each disk. Cut a piece of yarn about 6 yards long. Thread 2 ends of yarn through the eye of a blunt tapestry needle. Position the 2 cardboard disks one atop the other.

To start the pompon, pass the needle through the center holes of the cardboard disks; draw yarn through hole. Pass needle through closed, looped end of yarn; draw snug around disks. Continue wrapping the yarn around disks and through the center hole until the disks are completely covered and the holes are almost full. Then cut the yarn between the disks along the outside edges (M).

Cut a piece of yarn about 12 inches long and fold in half. Separate the disks slightly; slide the 12-inch piece of yarn down between them as shown (opposite); wrap around yarn several times, then knot to secure. Leave ends free to use for attaching (N).

Mounting a pompon on a wire stem: Cut a piece of wire about 14 inches

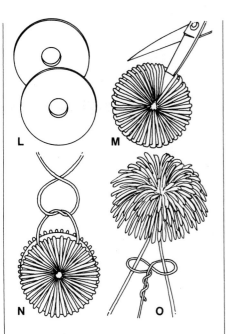

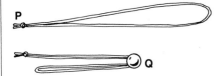

long. On one end of wire form 2 loops that are symmetrical around and perpendicular to wire. Position pompon where yarn tie comes off against loops on wire; knot around the center of loops (O). Cut yarn tie to about 3-inch length; wrap to stem with green floral tape, covering entire stem.

● *Twisted yarn cord*

Cut 7 yards of yarn; fold yarn in half, then tie 2 ends together (P). Fold doubled yarn in half; hook the center over a doorknob (Q).

Slip index and center fingers of your right hand through looped and knotted ends of yarn. With left hand, hold 4 strands loosely together about halfway between doorknob and fingers of your right hand. Draw back with right hand until yarn is taut; then with right hand twist yarn until it begins to kink.

With your right hand, keep yarn taut. Take hold of center of twisted yarn with your left hand; fold looped end up to doorknob. Slip loop off doorknob and onto fingers of right hand while still keeping the yarn taut.

Carefully and slowly let go of folded end held in your left hand. The 2 sides of the yarn will twist together.

● *Daisies*

Make yarn daisies of white and yellow yarn using daisy loom available in yarn or craft shops. Follow manufacturer's directions. Attach finished flowers to wire stems.

Mirror Tile Screen
page 342

Materials: Four 18x24-inch sheets of blue mirror tiles; four 18x24-inch sheets of silver mirror tiles; four 10x24-inch pieces of plywood (¾ inch thick); wood putty and sandpaper, or ¾-inch wood veneer; three 24-inch-long silver piano hinges; white glue; black paint.

Instructions: Using wood putty, seal edges of plywood pieces; after putty is dry, sand edges smooth. Or, cover edges with wood veneer. Then paint plywood pieces black on all sides.

Fasten the plywood pieces together using piano hinges to form a 40x24-inch screen. Alternate the direction of the hinges, with the 2 end hinges folding to the rear as shown in the photograph.

Using the pattern below as a guide, glue the mirror tiles onto the front of the screen with white glue.

Mirror Tile Place Mats
page 342

Materials: Four 18x24 inch sheets of silver mirror tiles (to make 4 place mats); two 18x24-inch sheets of blue mirror tiles; ½ yard felt fabric for backing; white glue.

Instructions: Using the pattern (above right) as a guide, arrange silver and blue mirror tiles. (Because the backs of the tiles must be coated with glue, work with the tiles upside down on your work surface.)

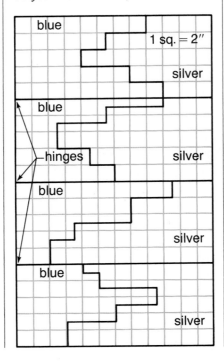

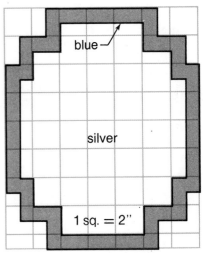

Cut a piece of felt that's ⅛ inch less than the dimensions of the place mat. Apply a coat of white glue to the back of the tiles. Cover back of tiles with felt backing. Allow glue to dry. If desired, glue on an additional backing of thin cork.

Mirror Tile Napkin Rings
page 342

Materials: Strip of 5 silver mirror tiles for each ring; felt fabric scraps; white glue.

Instructions: Cut felt ⅞x5½ inches; glue it to the back of a tile strip, leaving an extra ½ inch of felt at one end. Form a circle with the tile strip. Glue ½-inch felt "handle" to back of tile at opposite end. Allow glue to dry.

Glitter and Fabric Stars
page 342

Materials: 1 yard smooth silver metallic fabric; 1 yard fuzzy silver metallic fabric; white glue; cardboard; silver glitter; large needle; silver cording for hanging; fiberfill.

Instructions: Using star pattern on page 16 as a guide, cut out 4-, 6-, and 8-inch stars from fabrics and cardboard. (Note: For fabric stars, add ¼-inch seam allowance.)

● *Cardboard stars*

Cover both sides with a layer of glue; dip into silver glitter. Dry. Punch hole at one star point; make a silver loop from silver cord and hang.

● *Fabric stars*

With right sides together, sew fronts and backs of stars in a ¼-inch seam, leaving an opening for turning. Clip seams, turn, and stuff with fiberfill. Blindstitch opening. Attach silver cord and hang.

Foods for Holiday Entertaining

Open houses and cocktail parties at Christmas and New Year's are as much a part of the holidays as wrapping presents, trimming the tree, or making New Year's resolutions. In this section you'll find a mouth-watering collection of recipes that help you glide through your holiday parties without a hitch.

There are menus for festive buffets that range all the way from appetizer assortments to full dinners. Also, you'll find extra recipes for dips, party sandwiches, cheese balls or spreads, meatballs, and snack breads. You can choose from an array of both hot and cold punches. Combine some of these recipes with your own family favorites to create party menus your guests will long remember and rave about.

The foods pictured at right not only look spectacular, but also can be made ahead so you'll be relaxed and at ease when your guests arrive. Depending on the number of guests and the time of day, you may want to choose only some of these tempting snacks. Clockwise from back left are: Holiday Shrimp Rounds, Tamale Bites, Cranberry Banger Punch, Layered Cheese Dome, Cheese-Chili Cubes, Golden Cheese Wheel, and Spicy Apple Eggnog. See recipes, pages 348 and 349.

Holiday Party Menus

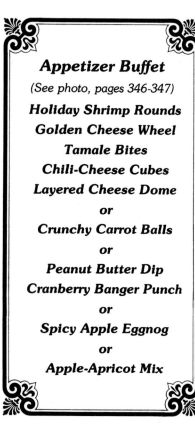

Appetizer Buffet

(See photo, pages 346-347)

Holiday Shrimp Rounds

Golden Cheese Wheel

Tamale Bites

Chili-Cheese Cubes

Layered Cheese Dome

or

Crunchy Carrot Balls

or

Peanut Butter Dip

Cranberry Banger Punch

or

Spicy Apple Eggnog

or

Apple-Apricot Mix

Spicy Apple Eggnog

2 **beaten eggs**
3 **cups milk**
2 **cups light cream**
⅓ **cup sugar**
½ **teaspoon ground cinnamon**
¾ **cup apple brandy**

Combine eggs, milk, cream, sugar, cinnamon, and dash *salt*. Cook and stir till slightly thickened; chill. To serve, stir in brandy. Top each serving with ground nutmeg, if desired. Serves 6.

Golden Cheese Wheel

1 **package active dry yeast**
⅔ **cup warm water (110° to 115°)**
2 **cups all-purpose flour**
2 **tablespoons cooking oil**
½ **teaspoon sugar**
½ **teaspoon salt**
1 **beaten egg**
3 **cups shredded muenster cheese (12 ounces)**
½ **cup snipped parsley**
½ **teaspoon garlic salt**
⅛ **teaspoon pepper**
• • •
1 **slightly beaten egg**
1 **tablespoon water**
1½ **teaspoons sesame seed**
1 **teaspoon sugar (optional)**

In a bowl soften yeast in the warm water. Beat in *1 cup* of the flour, the cooking oil, the ½ teaspoon sugar, and salt. Stir in as much of the remaining flour as you can mix in using a spoon. On lightly floured surface knead in remaining flour to make a moderately stiff dough. Continue kneading till dough is smooth and elastic (5 to 8 minutes). Place in a lightly greased bowl, turning once to grease surface. Cover; let rise in warm place till double (about 1 hour).

Punch dough down; divide into two portions. Cover and let rest 10 minutes. On a lightly floured surface, roll *one* portion to a 13-inch circle. Place circle on a greased 12-inch round baking pan. Combine 1 beaten egg, cheese, parsley, garlic salt, and pepper. Spread over dough.

Roll remaining half of dough to a 13-inch circle. Place atop filling. Trim and flute edges. Bake in a 400° oven 20 minutes. Remove from oven.

Brush top of wheel with a mixture of the remaining egg and the 1 tablespoon water. Sprinkle with sesame seed and sugar, if desired. Bake 12 to 15 minutes more. While wheel is still hot, cut it into narrow wedges. Serve at once. Makes 16 appetizer servings.

Tamale Bites

2 **cups crumbled corn bread**
1 **10-ounce can mild enchilada sauce**
½ **teaspoon salt**
1½ **pounds ground beef**
• • •
1 **8-ounce can tomato sauce**
½ **cup shredded monterey jack cheese (2 ounces)**

Combine corn bread crumbs, ½ *cup* of the enchilada sauce, and salt. Add ground beef; mix well. Shape into 1-inch balls. Place in shallow baking pan. Bake, uncovered, in 350° oven for 18 to 20 minutes or till done. Drain.

Meanwhile, in small saucepan heat together tomato sauce and remaining enchilada sauce. Place cooked meatballs in chafing dish; pour sauce over and top with cheese. Keep warm over low heat. Serve with wooden picks. Makes about 90 appetizers.

Cheese-Chili Cubes

8 **eggs**
½ **cup all-purpose flour**
1 **teaspoon baking powder**
¾ **teaspoon salt**
• • •
3 **cups shredded monterey jack cheese (12 ounces)**
1½ **cups cream-style cottage cheese (12 ounces)**
2 **4-ounce cans mild green chilies, seeded, rinsed, and chopped**

In large mixer bowl beat eggs using electric mixer 4 to 5 minutes, till light. Stir together flour, baking powder, and salt; add to eggs. Mix well. Fold in monterey jack cheese, cottage cheese, and chilies. Turn mixture into a greased 9×9×2-inch baking dish. Bake in 350° oven 40 minutes. Remove from oven; let stand 10 minutes. Cut in small squares; serve hot. Makes 3 to 4 dozen appetizers.

Layered Cheese Dome

2 8-ounce packages cream
   cheese, softened
2 teaspoons lemon juice
⅓ cup grated parmesan cheese
1 tablespoon chili sauce
½ cup cream-style cottage
   cheese, drained
⅛ teaspoon onion salt
⅛ teaspoon garlic powder
½ cup snipped parsley
   Assorted crackers

In small mixer bowl beat together cream cheese and lemon juice till fluffy. Divide into two portions. To one portion, stir in parmesan and chili sauce; turn into lightly oiled 2½- or 3-cup mold or bowl. To remaining cream cheese, add cottage cheese, onion salt, and garlic powder; beat till nearly smooth. Stir in parsley. Spoon atop first layer in mold. Cover and chill. To serve, unmold onto platter; serve with crackers. Makes 2½ cups.

Crunchy Carrot Balls

1 3-ounce package cream
   cheese, softened
½ cup shredded cheddar cheese
   (2 ounces)
1 teaspoon honey
1 cup finely shredded carrot
⅓ to ½ cup grape nuts cereal
2 tablespoons snipped parsley

In mixer bowl beat cream cheese, cheddar cheese, and honey together using electric mixer till blended. Stir in carrot. Cover; chill 30 minutes. Shape into 1-inch balls; cover and chill. Just before serving, roll balls in a mixture of cereal and parsley, pressing mixture into cheese to coat. Makes 14 balls.

Peanut Butter Dip

½ cup peanut butter
½ cup dairy sour cream or plain
   yogurt
¼ cup frozen orange juice
   concentrate, thawed
   Assorted fruit dippers

In mixer bowl beat peanut butter, sour cream or yogurt, and orange juice using electric mixer till fluffy. Cover; chill. Serve with fruit. Makes 1¼ cups.

Cranberry Banger Punch

1 12-ounce can frozen orange
   juice concentrate, thawed
2 juice cans water (3 cups)
½ cup orange liqueur
• • •
8 cups cranberry juice cocktail,
   chilled
1 fifth (750 ml) vodka
2 16-ounce bottles lemon-lime
   carbonated beverage,
   chilled (4 cups)

Combine orange juice concentrate, water, and orange liqueur. Pour into ice cube trays; freeze.

To serve, combine cranberry juice cocktail and vodka in large punch bowl. Slowly pour chilled lemon-lime beverage down side of bowl; stir. Float orange juice ice cubes atop punch. Makes 32 four-ounce servings.

Apple-Apricot Mix

½ cup water
⅓ cup sugar
12 inches stick cinnamon,
   broken
½ teaspoon whole cloves
3 cups apple juice, chilled
1 12-ounce can apricot nectar,
   chilled
¼ cup lemon juice
   Lemon slices
• • •
   Vodka, brandy, or rum
   Ice

In small saucepan combine water, sugar, cinnamon, and cloves; bring to boiling. Cover; reduce heat and simmer 10 minutes. Strain out spices; discard. Chill syrup. In glass pitcher combine apple juice, apricot nectar, lemon juice, and chilled syrup. Add lemon slices.

To serve, pour 1 jigger of your choice of vodka, brandy, or rum over ice in a glass. Add fruit mixture; stir. Makes about 4½ cups mix.

Holiday Shrimp Rounds

1 cup butter or margarine
1½ cups all-purpose flour
½ cup dairy sour cream
½ cup shredded sharp cheddar
   cheese (2 ounces)
• • •
   Milk
1 8-ounce package cream
   cheese, softened
¼ cup milk
1 teaspoon lemon juice
1 teaspoon worcestershire
   sauce
¼ teaspoon dried dillweed
   Dash garlic powder
1 4½-ounce can small shrimp,
   drained
   Dillweed (optional)

In mixing bowl cut butter into flour till mixture resembles small crumbs. Stir in sour cream and cheddar cheese. Divide mixture in half; wrap and chill 4 hours or overnight.

Working with half the chilled dough at a time, roll on floured surface with rolling pin to ¹⁄₁₆-inch thickness. With 2-inch floured biscuit cutter, cut half of the dough into 48 rounds. Using round hors d'oeuvre cutter, cut 1-inch circles out of centers of 32 dough rounds. Place remaining 16 rounds on ungreased baking sheet; brush with milk. Top each with two dough rounds with centers removed (making 3 layers in all), brushing with milk between layers. Repeat with remaining half of dough (and center cutouts). Bake in 350° oven for 22 to 25 minutes. Cool on wire rack.

Beat together cream cheese and the ¼ cup milk. Add lemon juice, worcestershire, ¼ teaspoon dillweed, and garlic powder. Stir in half of the shrimp; cover and chill.

Spoon shrimp mixture into pastry rounds. Garnish with remaining shrimp; sprinkle with additional dillweed, if desired. (Filled rounds may be stored up to 2 hours in refrigerator. Remove from refrigerator 10 minutes before serving.) Makes about 32.

Salmon Mousse

- 1 16-ounce can salmon
- 2 envelopes unflavored gelatin
- 2 cups mayonnaise *or* salad dressing
- ½ cup chili sauce
- 2 tablespoons lemon juice
- 1 tablespoon worcestershire sauce
- ½ teaspoon dried dillweed
- ¼ teaspoon pepper
- 1 6½- *or* 7-ounce can tuna, drained and finely flaked
- 4 hard-cooked eggs, finely chopped
- ½ cup pimiento-stuffed olives, finely chopped
- ¼ cup finely chopped onion
  Sliced pimiento-stuffed olives
  Pimiento strips
  Parsley
  Assorted crackers

Drain salmon, reserving liquid. Add water to reserved liquid to total ½ cup, if necessary. Bone and finely flake salmon; set aside.

In heatproof measuring cup combine gelatin and reserved salmon liquid. Place cup in a saucepan of hot water and stir to dissolve gelatin. Transfer dissolved gelatin to mixing bowl; gradually blend in mayonnaise or salad dressing. Stir in chili sauce, lemon juice, worcestershire sauce, dillweed, and pepper. Fold in flaked salmon, tuna, egg, chopped olives, and onion. Turn into a 6-cup mold. Chill till firm.

Unmold mousse onto platter. Garnish with additional sliced olives, pimiento strips, and parsley. Serve with crackers. Makes 6 cups spread.

For a light Christmas buffet serve this assortment of appetizers: Start with Ginger Dip *served with fresh fruit arranged on skewers (back left). Then add* Tiny Chicken Quiches *(front left), smoked oysters stuffed in cherry tomatoes (front center), and* Corn and Nut Crumbles *(front right). To quench your guests' thirst, end with* Christmas Sparkler *(back right).*

Tiny Chicken Quiches

- 2 sticks piecrust mix
- ½ of 4¾-ounce can (about ¼ cup) chicken spread
- 3 wedges gruyère cheese, shredded (3 ounces)
- 2 eggs
- ¼ cup light cream

Prepare piecrust sticks according to package directions. Roll dough thin. With 2½-inch round cutter, cut 24 circles. Fit one pastry round in each of twenty-four 1½-inch muffin cups. Add ½ teaspoon chicken spread and a small amount of shredded cheese to each.

Beat eggs; stir in cream and dash *pepper*. Fill each cup with about 1½ teaspoons of egg mixture. Bake in 400° oven 18 to 20 minutes. Cool 1 minute; remove from pans. Makes 2 dozen.

Ginger Dip

- ¾ cup dairy sour cream
- ½ cup mayonnaise
- ¼ cup shredded coconut, toasted
- 2 tablespoons finely chopped candied ginger
  Fresh fruits, cut into bite-size pieces

In a bowl combine sour cream, mayonnaise, coconut, and ginger. Cover and chill. Alternate fresh fruit pieces on skewers. Serve with chilled dip. Makes 1½ cups.

Corn and Nut Crumbles

- 1 8½-ounce package corn muffin mix
- 1 cup coarsely chopped salted peanuts
- ½ cup grated parmesan cheese
- 1 teaspoon garlic powder
- 3 tablespoons butter *or* margarine, melted

Prepare muffin mix according to package directions; spread batter evenly in well-greased 15×10×1-inch baking pan. Sprinkle with nuts, cheese, and garlic powder; drizzle butter over top. Bake in 375° oven for 20 to 25 minutes. Immediately cut into 48 pieces; cool slightly. Remove from pan. Makes 48.

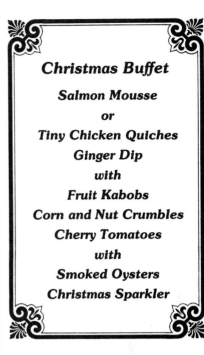

Christmas Buffet

Salmon Mousse

or

Tiny Chicken Quiches
Ginger Dip
with
Fruit Kabobs
Corn and Nut Crumbles
Cherry Tomatoes
with
Smoked Oysters
Christmas Sparkler

Christmas Sparkler

- 2 10-ounce packages frozen sliced strawberries, thawed
- 2 tablespoons lime juice *or* lemon juice

• • •

- 1 fifth (750 ml.) sparkling pink Catawba grape juice, chilled
- 1 28-ounce bottle lemon-lime carbonated beverage, chilled
  Lime *or* lemon slices, cut in half (optional)

In a bowl press strawberries through a sieve. Stir lime or lemon juice into pulp. Cover; chill.

Place strawberry pulp in a large punch bowl. Carefully pour grape juice and lemon-lime carbonated beverage into chilled pulp, stirring with an up and down motion. When serving punch, garnish each serving with a lime or lemon slice, if desired. Makes 18 four-ounce servings.

Blue Cheese Mold

1 envelope unflavored gelatin
¼ cup cold water
1¼ cups buttermilk
1 cup dairy sour cream
½ teaspoon garlic salt
¼ teaspoon onion salt
½ cup crumbled blue cheese
   (2 ounces)
Snipped parsley
Assorted crackers

In small saucepan combine gelatin and cold water. Add buttermilk. Stir over low heat till gelatin is dissolved. Remove from heat. Stir in sour cream, garlic salt, and onion salt. Fold in blue cheese. Pour into a 3-cup mold; chill till firm. Unmold onto plate. Garnish with snipped parsley. Serve with crackers. Makes about 3 cups spread.

Dipper's Delight

¾ cup all-purpose flour
1 tablespoon salt
1 tablespoon paprika
¼ teaspoon pepper
2 dozen chicken wings, tips
   removed and separated at
   joint
½ cup butter *or* margarine
1½ cups soft bread crumbs
   (about 3 slices)
½ cup milk
¼ cup finely chopped onion
2 eggs
1½ teaspoons salt
2 pounds ground beef
24 jumbo shrimp, cooked,
   shelled, and deveined
Barbecue Dip (see recipe,
   below)

For chicken wings, mix flour, the 1 tablespoon salt, paprika, and pepper in a plastic bag; add a few chicken pieces at a time. Shake to coat. Repeat with remaining chicken. Melt butter or margarine in a 15×10×1-inch pan. Place chicken pieces in pan; turn once to butter surface. Bake in 375° oven for 1 hour.

Meanwhile, to make meatballs combine bread crumbs, milk, onion, eggs, and the 1½ teaspoons salt. Add ground beef; mix lightly but thoroughly. Shape into 4 dozen small balls, about 1 inch in diameter. Place in 15×10×1-inch baking pan. Bake in 375° oven for 25 to 30 minutes.

On a large platter, arrange chicken wings, meatballs, and shrimp. Serve with Barbecue Dip. Makes 24 servings.

Barbecue Dip

2 cups catsup
1 8-ounce can (1 cup) whole
   cranberry sauce
⅓ cup lemon juice
2 tablespoons prepared
   horseradish
2 teaspoons worcestershire
   sauce

In saucepan combine catsup, cranberry sauce, lemon juice, horseradish, and worcestershire sauce. Bring to boiling. Serve warm. Makes 1½ cups sauce.

Potted Pepper Dip

4 large red *or* green peppers
2 tablespoons lemon juice
2 teaspoons olive *or* cooking
   oil
1 teaspoon sugar
1 teaspoon salt
½ teaspoon prepared
   horseradish
   Dash white pepper
1 small onion, cut up
1 8-ounce package cream
   cheese, softened
¼ cup mayonnaise
   Few dashes bottled hot
   pepper sauce
2 red *or* green peppers, tops
   removed and seeded
   Tortilla chips

Dip the first 4 peppers into boiling water a few seconds. Peel, seed, and cut up. In blender container or food processor, place lemon juice, olive oil, sugar, salt, horseradish, white pepper, and *one third* of the cut up peppers and onion. Cover; blend till smooth. Add another third of the peppers and onion to mixture. Cover; blend till smooth. Repeat with remaining third of peppers and onion.

Transfer mixture to mixing bowl. Let stand, covered, at room temperature for at least 2 hours. Place puréed vegetable mixture in a sieve, pressing gently to drain off liquid.

In mixing bowl combine cream cheese, mayonnaise, and hot pepper sauce. Stir in puréed vegetable mixture. Cover and chill.

Spoon cheese mixture into the two hollow pepper shells. Place peppers on serving platter. Surround with tortilla chips. Makes 2 cups.

Artichoke Spread

1 14-ounce can artichoke
   hearts (8½ ounces drained)
½ cup mayonnaise *or* salad
   dressing
¼ cup grated parmesan cheese
1 clove garlic, minced
   Assorted vegetable dippers

Drain artichokes thoroughly, pressing to remove excess liquid. In mixing bowl mash artichokes; stir in mayonnaise or salad dressing, parmesan, and garlic. Cover and chill several hours. Sprinkle with paprika, if desired. Serve with vegetables. Makes 1½ cups.

Caviar à la Crème

1 envelope unflavored gelatin
½ cup cold water
2½ cups cream-style cottage cheese
2 8-ounce packages cream cheese, softened
1 cup dairy sour cream
2 tablespoons sifted powdered sugar
1 teaspoon vanilla
1 2-ounce jar red caviar, chilled
Crackers *or* party bread

In heatproof measuring cup combine gelatin and water. Place cup in a saucepan of hot water; heat and stir till gelatin dissolves. Press cottage cheese through sieve.

In mixing bowl beat together sieved cottage cheese, cream cheese, and sour cream till smooth; beat in powdered sugar and vanilla. Gradually blend about *1 cup* of the cheese mixture into gelatin. Return to remaining cheese mixture. Stir till combined. Turn into a 5-cup mold. Chill till firm.

Unmold on platter; top with caviar. Serve with crackers or party bread. Makes 5 cups spread.

Hot Cranberry Wine Cup

4 cups cranberry juice cocktail
2 cups water
1 cup sugar
4 inches stick cinnamon, broken
12 whole cloves
Peel of ½ lemon, cut in strips
2 fifths (750 ml. each) dry red wine
¼ cup lemon juice

In saucepan combine cranberry juice cocktail, water, sugar, cinnamon, cloves, and lemon peel. Bring to boiling, stirring till sugar is dissolved. Reduce heat; simmer, uncovered, 15 minutes. Strain. Add wine and lemon juice; mix well. Heat through, but do not boil. Transfer to a heatproof pitcher. Makes 28 four-ounce servings.

Phony Bologna Pâté

1 pound unsliced bologna, cut up
½ small onion, cut up
½ cup creamy Italian salad dressing
1 teaspoon dry mustard
1 teaspoon prepared horseradish
½ teaspoon worcestershire sauce
⅛ teaspoon pepper
3 hard-cooked eggs
Assorted crackers

Grind bologna and onion through fine blade of food grinder or in food processor. In mixing bowl combine bologna-onion mixture, Italian dressing, mustard, horseradish, worcestershire sauce, and pepper. Turn *half* of the bologna mixture into the bottom of a well-oiled 7×3×2½-inch loaf pan. Place *2* of the eggs end-to-end lengthwise down the center of the pan. Top with remaining bologna mixture, spreading evenly. Cover; chill several hours or overnight.

Turn pâté out onto serving platter. Chop remaining egg, sprinkle over top. Garnish platter with parsley, if desired. Slice and serve with crackers. Makes about 3 cups.

Kir Spritzer

1 half-gallon dry white wine, chilled
1½ cups crème de cassis*
2 28-ounce bottles carbonated water, chilled
Ice

In large pitcher combine *4 cups* of the wine and ¾ *cup* of the crème de cassis. Gradually add *1 bottle* carbonated water, stirring gently to mix. Add ice. Serve over ice cubes. Mix remaining ingredients as needed. Makes 33 four-ounce servings.
Note: If you like, substitute blackberry brandy, sloe gin, cranberry liqueur, or raspberry liqueur for the crème de cassis.

Avocado Deviled Eggs

6 hard-cooked eggs, halved lengthwise
3 slices bacon, crisp-cooked, drained, and crumbled
3 tablespoons mayonnaise *or* salad dressing
1 tablespoon prepared mustard
¼ teaspoon paprika
⅛ teaspoon salt
Dash pepper
1 medium avocado, finely chopped
Paprika
Pimiento strips (optional)
Snipped parsley (optional)

Set aside hard-cooked egg whites. Sieve egg yolks. In a bowl combine sieved yolks with bacon, mayonnaise or salad dressing, mustard, the ¼ teaspoon paprika, salt, and pepper. Fold in avocado. Pile avocado mixture into egg whites. Sprinkle with additional paprika. If desired, top each with a pimiento strip and some snipped parsley. Arrange eggs on a platter; cover. Chill. Makes 12 halves.

Imitation Escargots

1 package refrigerated crescent rolls (8 rolls)
• • •
3 tablespoons anchovy paste
2 tablespoons butter *or* margarine, softened
Dash garlic powder

Unroll dough on lightly floured surface; pinch perforations together to form 4 rectangles. Blend together anchovy paste, butter or margarine, and garlic powder.

Spread ¼ of the mixture over each rectangle. Roll up, beginning at narrow end. Slice each roll into seven ½-inch thick pieces. Place, cut side down, on ungreased baking sheet.

Bake in 350° oven 11 to 12 minutes. (*Or* wrap rolls and refrigerate up to 48 hours. Then slice and bake for 12 to 14 minutes.) Serve hot. Makes 28.

Dinner Buffet

Scandinavian Salad
Swiss Chicken Cutlet
Broccoli
with
Deviled Cream Sauce
Brown Rice Pilaf
*Batter Rolls * Butter*
Pumpkin-Orange Cake
or
Dobos Torta
Spiced Wine Nectar
or
Mulled Beverage Mix

This no-bother buffet makes entertaining easy. The buffet features Swiss Chicken Cutlet *(bottom left),* Brown Rice Pilaf *(center left),* Scandinavian Salad *(top left),* Broccoli with Deviled Cream Sauce *(bottom right),* Pumpkin-Orange Cake *(center right), and* Spiced Wine Nectar *(top right). (See pages 356-357 for recipes.)*

Swiss Chicken Cutlet
see photograph, pages 354-355

5 chicken breasts, skinned,
   split, and boned
  Salt
2 beaten eggs
1 cup fine dry bread crumbs
¼ cup cooking oil
3 tablespoons butter *or*
   margarine
¼ cup all-purpose flour
½ teaspoon salt
⅛ teaspoon pepper
2½ cups milk
½ cup dry white wine
       • • •
1 cup shredded process Swiss
   cheese (4 ounces)
  Avocado slices
  Tomato wedges
  Parsley (optional)

Place each chicken breast half between two pieces of waxed paper. Pound out to about ¼-inch thickness using meat mallet. Sprinkle lightly with salt. Dip in beaten egg, then in bread crumbs.

In skillet heat *2 tablespoons* of the oil. Brown chicken cutlets, a few at a time, about 2 minutes on a side, adding remaining oil as needed. Set chicken aside.

In saucepan melt butter or margarine; blend in flour, the ½ teaspoon salt, and pepper. Add milk all at once; cook and stir till thickened and bubbly. Remove from heat; stir in wine. Pour about *half* of the sauce into bottom of 13×9×2-inch baking dish. Arrange chicken cutlets atop sauce. Top with remaining sauce.

Cover and chill several hours or overnight. Bake, covered, in 350° oven about 50 minutes till heated through. Sprinkle with cheese. Top with avocado and tomato. Return to oven for 2 minutes. Garnish with parsley, if desired. Makes 10 servings.

Scandinavian Salad
see photograph, pages 354-355

4 medium oranges
  Water
2 tablespoons sugar
2 tablespoons lemon juice
½ teaspoon aniseed, crushed
¼ teaspoon dry mustard
4 medium apples, cored and
   sliced
1 cup red grapes, halved and
   seeded
½ cup dried figs, sliced
  Bibb lettuce leaves

Section oranges over small bowl to catch juice. Measure juice. Add water to juice to total ½ cup liquid.

In small saucepan combine orange juice mixture, sugar, lemon juice, aniseed, and dry mustard. Bring to boiling. Remove from heat; cool.

Combine fruits; toss with syrup. Cover and chill. Spoon into lettuce-lined bowl. Makes 10 servings.

Broccoli with Deviled Cream Sauce
see photograph, pages 354-355

3 pounds fresh broccoli *or* 3
   10-ounce packages frozen
   broccoli spears
2 tablespoons butter *or*
   margarine
2 tablespoons all-purpose flour
1½ teaspoons dry mustard
1 teaspoon brown sugar
½ teaspoon worcestershire
   sauce
¼ teaspoon salt
1 cup milk
½ cup dairy sour cream

Wash fresh broccoli; trim and cut into spears. Cook in boiling, salted water, covered, about 15 minutes or till tender. (*Or* cook frozen broccoli spears according to package directions.) Drain. Arrange broccoli in a shallow serving dish; keep warm. In saucepan melt butter or margarine. Blend in flour, dry mustard, brown sugar, worcestershire sauce, salt, and dash *pepper*. Add milk all at once. Cook and stir till thickened and bubbly. Stir a small amount of hot mixture into sour cream. Return all to hot mixture in saucepan. Heat through but *do not boil*. Spoon sauce over broccoli in serving dish. Sprinkle with toasted slivered almonds, if desired. Makes 10 servings.

Brown Rice Pilaf
see photograph, pages 354-355

6 slices bacon
½ cup chopped onion
½ cup chopped celery
3 cups boiling water
1 tablespoon instant beef
   bouillon granules
1 cup brown rice
½ cup dry white wine
¼ cup toasted slivered almonds

Cook bacon till almost crisp; remove *two* of the slices. Drain on paper toweling. Arrange in curls; secure with wooden pick. Set aside for garnish. Cook remaining bacon till crisp; drain, reserving 2 tablespoons drippings. Crumble bacon; set aside. Cook onion and celery in reserved drippings till tender but not brown. Stir boiling water into bouillon granules. Add to vegetables in skillet along with uncooked rice, wine, almonds, crumbled bacon, and ½ teaspoon *salt*; heat to boiling. Turn into a 1½-quart casserole. Bake, uncovered, in 325° oven 1 hour. Garnish with bacon curls. Serves 8 to 10.

Batter Rolls

3¼ cups all-purpose flour
1 package active dry yeast
1¼ cups milk
½ cup shortening
¼ cup sugar
1 teaspoon salt
1 egg
  Milk
1 tablespoon poppy seed

In large mixer bowl combine *2 cups* of flour and the yeast. In a saucepan heat the 1¼ cups milk, the shortening, sugar, and salt just till warm (115° to 120°), stirring till shortening almost melts. Add to dry mixture in mixer bowl; add egg. Beat at low speed of electric mixer for ½ minute, scraping sides of bowl constantly. Beat 3 minutes at high speed. At low speed beat in remaining flour till smooth (2 minutes), pushing batter from beaters.

Cover; let rise till double (about 1 hour). Stir down batter; beat well. Let rest 5 minutes; drop batter into greased 2¾-inch muffin pans, filling half full. Cover; let rise till double (about 30 minutes). Brush tops with milk; sprinkle with poppy seed. Bake in a 400° oven 12 to 15 minutes or till done. Cool on wire rack. Makes 20.

Spiced Wine Nectar

see photograph, pages 354-355

 1 29-ounce jar spiced whole
       peaches
       Whole cloves
12 sticks cinnamon
 1 46-ounce can (5¾ cups) apple
       juice, chilled
 ½ gallon (8 cups) dry white
       wine, chilled
 2 12-ounce cans (3 cups)
       apricot nectar, chilled
 ¼ cup lemon juice

Drain peaches, reserving the syrup; chill syrup. Stud peaches with whole cloves; place peaches, cinnamon sticks, and additional cloves, in bottom of 5½-cup ring mold. Fill with about *3 cups* apple juice; freeze.

In punch bowl combine chilled peach syrup, the remaining apple juice, dry white wine, apricot nectar, and lemon juice. Unmold and float peach ring atop. Makes 28 four-ounce servings.

Mulled Beverage Mix

1½ cups water
 ¾ cup sugar
 6 inches stick cinnamon,
       broken
 6 whole cloves
       Peel of ¼ lemon, cut into
          thin strips
 ½ cup lemon juice
       Chilled *or* heated apple juice,
          cranberry juice cocktail,
          dry red wine, dry white
          wine, rosé, *or* sparkling
          pink catawba juice

In saucepan combine water, sugar, cinnamon, cloves, and lemon peel. Bring to boiling, stirring till sugar is dissolved. Reduce heat; cover and simmer 10 minutes. Strain through cheesecloth. Stir lemon juice into sugar-water mixture. Cover tightly. Refrigerate up to 6 weeks.

To serve, pour mix into glasses or mugs. Add desired beverage. Use 2 tablespoons mix to ¾ cup (6 ounces) beverage. (Serve chilled drink with ice, if desired.) Makes 1½ cups mix or enough for 12 servings.

Pumpkin-Orange Cake

see photograph, pages 354-355

1½ cups sugar
 ½ cup shortening
 2 eggs
          • • •
 1 cup canned pumpkin
 ½ of 6-ounce can (⅓ cup)
       orange juice concentrate,
       thawed
 ¼ cup milk
1⅔ cups all-purpose flour
 1 teaspoon baking powder
 1 teaspoon ground cinnamon
 ½ teaspoon baking soda
 ½ teaspoon ground allspice
 ½ teaspoon ground nutmeg
 ¼ teaspoon ground cloves
 ½ cup currants *or* raisins
          • • •
 1 cup milk
 3 tablespoons all-purpose flour
 1 teaspoon vanilla
 ¾ cup sugar
 ½ cup butter *or* margarine
 ½ cup pecan halves

In large mixer bowl beat together the 1½ cups sugar and the shortening till light and fluffy. Add eggs; beat well.

Add pumpkin, thawed orange juice concentrate, and the ¼ cup milk. Stir together the 1⅔ cups flour, the baking powder, cinnamon, baking soda, allspice, nutmeg, and cloves. Add to pumpkin mixture, beating till smooth. Fold in currants or raisins.

Spread batter into 2 greased and floured 8-inch round cake pans. Bake in a 350° oven for 30 to 35 minutes or till cakes test done with a wooden pick. Cool in pans for 10 minutes. Turn out of pans onto wire rack; cool.

Meanwhile, in a small saucepan blend the remaining milk into the remaining flour. Cook and stir till mixture is thickened and bubbly. Cool to room temperature (about 1 hour). Stir in vanilla. Beat together the remaining sugar and butter or margarine till light and fluffy. Gradually beat in the cooled milk mixture. Spread between cooled cake layers, and frost sides and top of cake. Garnish with pecan halves around edge.

Dobos Torta

 9 eggs
 ½ cup granulated sugar
 1 teaspoon finely shredded
       lemon peel
 ⅔ cup all-purpose flour
       Sifted powdered sugar
 1 cup butter *or* margarine,
       softened
 ½ cup granulated sugar
 2 eggs
 ⅓ cup unsweetened cocoa
       powder
 ¼ teaspoon instant coffee
       crystals
 ¼ cup granulated sugar

Bring eggs to room temperature. In large mixer bowl beat the 9 eggs till blended. Beating at medium speed of electric mixer, add the first ½ cup granulated sugar and the lemon peel. Beat at high speed, guiding mixture into beaters using rubber spatula, for 8 to 10 minutes or till thick and light yellow. Sprinkle flour over egg mixture; fold in. Divide batter among 3 greased and floured 9×1½-inch round cake pans. Bake in 350° oven 10 to 12 minutes. Loosen edges and turn out onto towel sprinkled with powdered sugar. Cool. Split each layer in half horizontally.

In small mixer bowl beat together butter and the second ½ cup sugar till fluffy. Add 2 eggs, one at a time, beating well after each. Beat in cocoa and coffee crystals; beat till smooth. To assemble cake, reserve one top cake layer. Spread one side of each of remaining 5 layers with about *3 tablespoons* of the mocha mixture, stacking one atop another. Frost sides with remaining mocha mixture. Decorate sides by drawing tines of fork through frosting; set aside.

Place remaining cake layer, cut side down, on plate. In heavy 1-quart saucepan heat and stir the remaining sugar over low heat till sugar melts and turns golden brown. Pour syrup over top of cake layer. Quickly spread to edges in one firm stroke. Cool till hardened. With hot knife, cut into 16 wedges. Arrange atop cake. Makes 16 servings.

Give a tree-trimming party and highlight the occasion with an Italian Buffet featuring Spaghetti Pie.

Insalata Verdi

- **4 cups torn fresh spinach**
- **4 cups torn iceberg lettuce**
- **1 15-ounce can garbanzo beans, drained**
- **1 cup sliced zucchini**
- **1 cup sliced fresh mushrooms**
- **½ cup cauliflowerets**
- **½ small red onion, sliced and separated into rings**
- **¼ cup sliced celery**
- **2 tablespoons snipped parsley**
- **3 hard-cooked eggs, quartered**

- **⅓ cup salad oil *or* olive oil**
- **½ cup red wine vinegar**
- **1 envelope Italian salad dressing mix**

In large salad bowl combine salad greens; arrange vegetables and eggs atop. In screw-top jar mix oil, vinegar, and dry salad dressing mix; shake well. Pour desired amount of dressing over salad and toss till greens are well coated. Season to taste with salt and pepper. Makes 6 to 8 servings.

Antipasto Tray

- **1 7-ounce can solid-pack tuna, drained**
- **¼ cup mayonnaise**
- **1 teaspoon lemon juice**
- **1 tablespoon capers, drained**
  Thinly sliced salami
  Thinly sliced boiled ham *or* prosciutto
- **1 2-ounce can rolled anchovies, drained**
  Mild pickled peppers
  Pimiento-stuffed olives
  Ripe olives

Place tuna in center of large serving tray. Stir together mayonnaise and lemon juice; dollop over tuna. Top with capers. In spoke-fashion around tuna, arrange salami, ham, anchovies, peppers, and olives. Makes 6 to 8 servings.

Cherry Savarin

2 cups all-purpose flour
1 package active dry yeast
¾ cup milk
¼ cup sugar
¼ cup butter or margarine
½ teaspoon salt
1 egg
½ cup dried currants or light raisins
½ cup chopped candied citron
½ cup water
¼ cup sugar
¼ cup kirsch, rum, or brandy
1 16-ounce can pitted dark sweet cherries
2 tablespoons sugar
2 tablespoons cornstarch

In small mixer bowl stir together *1½ cups* of the flour and the yeast. In a saucepan heat milk, the first ¼ cup sugar, butter or margarine, and salt just till warm (115° to 120°), stirring till butter almost melts. Add to dry mixture in mixer bowl; add egg. Beat at low speed of electric mixer for ½ minute, scraping sides of bowl constantly. Beat 3 minutes at high speed. By hand, stir in currants, citron, and the remaining flour. Cover and let rise in warm place till double (1 to 1¼ hours).

Stir down batter; spoon into a well-buttered 6½- or 7-cup fluted tube pan. Cover; let rise till almost double (30 to 45 minutes). Bake in 350° oven about 35 minutes or till golden brown. Cool in pan 5 minutes; then invert onto wire rack. Cool.

In saucepan combine water and the second ¼ cup sugar. Bring to boiling, stirring till sugar dissolves. Boil gently, uncovered, for 5 minutes. Remove from heat; cool slightly. Stir in kirsch. Prick cake with tines of long fork. Slowly spoon syrup over top and sides of cake, allowing syrup to soak in. Repeat till all syrup is used.

Drain cherries, reserving syrup. Halve cherries; set aside. Add enough water to reserved syrup to measure 1⅔ cups liquid. In small saucepan combine the 2 tablespoons sugar and the cornstarch; stir in reserved cherry liquid. Cook and stir till thickened and bubbly. Stir in cherries; cool slightly. Serve cherry sauce over savarin. Makes 12 servings.

Spaghetti Pie

6 ounces spaghetti
2 tablespoons butter or margarine
⅓ cup grated parmesan cheese
2 beaten eggs
1 pound ground beef or bulk Italian sausage
½ cup chopped onion
¼ cup chopped green pepper
1 8-ounce can (1 cup) tomatoes, cut up
1 6-ounce can tomato paste
1 teaspoon sugar
1 teaspoon dried oregano, crushed
¼ teaspoon salt
¼ teaspoon garlic salt
1 cup cottage cheese, drained
½ cup shredded mozzarella cheese (2 ounces)

Cook spaghetti according to package directions; drain (should yield 3¼ cups spaghetti). Stir butter into hot spaghetti. Stir in parmesan cheese and eggs. Form spaghetti mixture into a "crust" in a buttered 10-inch pie plate.

In skillet cook ground beef or sausage, onion, and green pepper till vegetables are tender and meat is browned. Drain off *excess* fat. Stir in *undrained* tomatoes, the tomato paste, sugar, oregano, salt, and garlic salt. Spread cottage cheese over bottom of spaghetti "crust." Fill "pie" with tomato mixture. Cover with foil and chill in refrigerator 2 to 24 hours. Bake, covered, in 350° oven for 60 minutes. Uncover; sprinkle with mozzarella cheese. Bake 5 minutes more. Serves 6.

Caramel Apple Fondue

⅓ cup evaporated milk
1 package creamy caramel frosting mix (for 2-layer cake)
2 tablespoons butter or margarine
3 large apples, cored and cut into chunks
¾ cup finely chopped pecans

In fondue pot gradually blend evaporated milk into frosting mix, stirring till smooth. Add butter or margarine. Heat and stir over low heat till butter is melted. Place over fondue burner. Spear apple with fondue fork. Dip in fondue, then nuts. Makes 6 servings.

Italian Buffet

Antipasto Tray
Insalata Verdi
Spaghetti Pie
Butter Logs
Caramel Apple Fondue
or
Cherry Savarin
*Coffee * Milk*

Butter Logs

2 cups all-purpose flour
3 tablespoons toasted sesame seed
1 tablespoon sugar
2½ teaspoons baking powder
½ teaspoon cream of tartar
½ teaspoon salt
¼ cup shortening
2 beaten eggs
½ cup milk
¼ cup butter or margarine, melted

In mixing bowl stir together the flour, sesame seed, sugar, baking powder, cream of tartar, and salt. Cut in shortening till mixture resembles coarse crumbs. Combine eggs and milk; add all at once to dry mixture. Stir just till dough clings together. Knead gently on lightly floured surface, 10 to 12 strokes.

Roll or pat dough to 10×6-inch rectangle. With floured knife, cut dough in half lengthwise. Then cut each half crosswise into eight 3×1¼-inch sticks. Place 1 tablespoon of the butter or margarine in 13×9×2-inch baking pan. Place sticks in pan; brush with remaining butter or margarine. Bake in 425° oven 18 to 20 minutes till light brown. Makes 16 butter logs.

Recipes To Round Out the Party

Harlequin Sandwiches

Tuna Filling (see recipe, right)
Deviled Ham Filling (see recipe, below)
Peanut Butter-Apple Filling (see recipe, right)
8 slices firm-textured white bread
8 slices firm-textured rye bread
1 4-ounce container whipped cream cheese
Green pepper strips
Snipped parsley
Sliced canned pimiento

Prepare one or more of the fillings. Using a cookie or biscuit cutter, cut bread slices into shapes.

Spread filling on white or rye bread shapes. Top with a matching shape of a contrasting color bread. Frost tops with cream cheese. Decorate tops with green pepper strips, snipped parsley, or pimiento slices.

Deviled Ham Filling

1 4½-ounce can deviled ham
¼ cup finely chopped celery
¼ cup finely chopped dill pickle
1 tablespoon mayonnaise or salad dressing

In a bowl combine deviled ham, celery, dill pickle, and mayonnaise or salad dressing. Cover and chill mixture. Makes 1 cup filling.

Tuna Filling

1 6½- or 7-ounce can tuna, drained and flaked
1 hard-cooked egg, chopped
¼ cup finely chopped cucumber
¼ cup finely chopped celery
2 tablespoons sweet pickle relish
¼ cup mayonnaise
1 teaspoon lemon juice

In a bowl combine tuna, hard-cooked egg, cucumber, celery, and pickle relish. Blend in mayonnaise and lemon juice. Cover and chill. Makes 2¼ cups filling.

Peanut Butter-Apple Filling

½ cup creamy peanut butter
2 tablespoons mayonnaise or salad dressing
2 teaspoons lemon juice
½ cup finely chopped peeled tart apple
4 slices bacon, crisp-cooked, drained, and crumbled

In a bowl blend together peanut butter, mayonnaise or salad dressing, and lemon juice. Stir in apple and crumbled bacon. Cover and refrigerate to store. To spread, remove from refrigerator and bring to room temperature. Makes 1¼ cups filling.

Crab Fondue

1 8-ounce package cream cheese
1 5-ounce jar American cheese spread
1 7½-ounce can crab, drained, flaked, and cartilage removed
2 tablespoons milk
2 tablespoons dry white wine
2 teaspoons worcestershire sauce
French bread, cut into bite-size pieces

In saucepan over low heat melt together cream cheese and American cheese spread, stirring constantly. Stir in crab, milk, wine, and worcestershire sauce. Heat through. Transfer to fondue pot or chafing dish; place over burner. Serve with bread pieces. Makes 2¼ cups.

Consommé and Cheese Pâté

1 teaspoon unflavored gelatin
¾ cup canned condensed beef consommé
1 4¾-ounce can liver spread
3 tablespoons mayonnaise
1 8-ounce package cream cheese, softened
3 tablespoons milk
1 tablespoon dry onion soup mix
Assorted crackers

In a heatproof 1-cup measure soften gelatin in 2 tablespoons *cold water*. Set measure in a pan of hot water; heat and stir till gelatin is dissolved. Stir in consommé. Chill till partially set (the consistency of unbeaten egg white).

Line an 8½×4½×2-inch loaf pan with waxed paper. Turn consommé mixture into pan; chill till almost set. Combine liver spread and mayonnaise; spread over consommé mixture. Mix cream cheese, milk, and dry onion soup mix. Spread over liver mixture. Cover; chill overnight.

Unmold pâté onto serving platter. Remove waxed paper. Serve with crackers. Makes 2 cups.

Beer-Sauced Links

2 pounds fully cooked Polish sausage or frankfurters, cut into ½-inch pieces
1 cup beer
¼ cup packed brown sugar
2 tablespoons cornstarch
¼ cup vinegar
¼ cup prepared mustard
1 tablespoon prepared horseradish

In skillet combine sausage and beer. Cover; simmer 10 minutes. Combine brown sugar and cornstarch. Stir in vinegar, mustard, and horseradish. Add to sausages; cook and stir till bubbly. Turn into fondue pot; place over fondue burner. Serve warm with wooden picks. Makes 36 pieces.

To make Harlequin Sandwiches, *cut bread into different shapes using cookie cutters, fill the sandwiches with* Deviled Ham Filling, Tuna Filling, *or* Peanut Butter-Apple Filling, *and decorate the tops with cream cheese and green pepper strips, snipped parsley, or pimiento slices.*

At your next holiday party, serve (pictured clockwise from bottom left) Appetizer Cheesecake, Chestnut Meatballs, Clam and Avocado Dip, Notches, Anchovy-Cheese Ball, *and* Shrimp-Cucumber Dip.

Notches

2 ounces cheddar cheese
24 taco-flavored tortilla chips
½ cup refried beans *or* canned bean dip
1 canned mild chili pepper, diced

Preheat broiler. Cut cheddar cheese into 24 pieces, each ¾×¾×⅛-inch. Arrange chips on baking sheets. Top each chip with 1 teaspoon beans, a piece of cheese, and a piece of chili pepper. Broil 4 inches from heat till cheese melts, 1 to 3 minutes. Serve hot. Makes 24 appetizers.

Clam and Avocado Dip

2 ripe avocados, seeded, peeled, and cut into pieces
1 7½-ounce can minced clams, drained
2 tablespoons mayonnaise *or* salad dressing
1 tablespoon chopped onion
1 tablespoon lemon juice
½ teaspoon salt
    Dash freshly ground pepper
    Dash garlic salt
    Corn chips *or* assorted crackers

In small mixer bowl or blender container combine all ingredients *except* chips. Beat with electric mixer or cover and blend till smooth. Pour into serving bowl. Cover; chill well. Serve with corn chips or crackers as dippers. Garnish with fresh onion rings, if desired. Makes 1½ cups dip.

Chestnut Meatballs

2 cups soft bread crumbs (2½ slices)
½ cup milk
1 tablespoon soy sauce
½ teaspoon garlic salt
¼ teaspoon onion powder
½ pound ground beef
½ pound bulk pork sausage
1 5-ounce can water chestnuts, drained and finely chopped

In a bowl combine crumbs, milk, soy, garlic salt, and onion powder. Add beef, sausage, and water chestnuts; mix well. Form into 1-inch balls. Bake on 15½×10½×1-inch baking pan in 350° oven for 18 to 20 minutes. Makes 60.

Appetizer Cheesecake

1 cup dairy sour cream
¼ cup finely chopped green
    pepper
¼ cup finely chopped celery
2 tablespoons finely chopped
    pimiento-stuffed olives
2 tablespoons finely chopped
    onion
1 teaspoon lemon juice
½ teaspoon worcestershire
    sauce
    Dash paprika
2 or 3 drops bottled hot pepper
    sauce
⅔ cup finely crushed rich round
    cheese crackers (about 16
    crackers)
    Assorted crackers or
    vegetables

In a bowl thoroughly combine sour cream, green pepper, celery, olives, onion, lemon juice, worcestershire sauce, paprika, and hot pepper sauce. Line a 2½-cup bowl with clear plastic wrap. Reserve some of the cheese crackers for garnish. Spread about ½ cup of sour cream mixture in bowl. Sprinkle with ¼ cup of cheese crackers. Repeat sour cream and cracker layers. Cover; chill overnight.

Unmold onto serving plate; remove wrap. Top with reserved crackers. Serve spread with crackers or vegetables. Makes about 2 cups.

Curried Appetizer Meatballs

½ cup crushed herb-seasoned
    stuffing mix
⅓ cup evaporated milk
1½ to 2 teaspoons curry powder
¼ teaspoon salt
1 pound ground beef

In a bowl thoroughly combine stuffing mix, evaporated milk, curry powder, and salt. Add ground beef; mix well. Shape meat mixture into 40 small balls. Place in a large shallow baking pan. Bake in 400° oven 15 minutes; drain. Keep warm in chafing dish. Makes 40.

Shrimp-Cucumber Dip

1 4½-ounce can shrimp
1 medium cucumber
1 cup cream-style cottage
    cheese
2 tablespoons finely chopped
    onion
2 teaspoons vinegar
½ teaspoon prepared
    horseradish
    Vegetable dippers

Drain shrimp; set aside 2 for garnish. Coarsely chop remaining shrimp; set aside. Cut unpeeled cucumber in half lengthwise; remove seeds and discard. Shred enough cucumber to make 1 cup; drain well.

In a small mixer bowl combine the shredded cucumber, cottage cheese, onion, vinegar, and horseradish. Beat till smooth using electric mixer. Stir in chopped shrimp. Spoon into serving bowl; garnish with reserved whole shrimp. Serve with vegetable dippers. Makes about 2 cups dip.

Anchovy-Cheese Ball

1 8-ounce package cream
    cheese, softened
½ cup butter or margarine,
    softened
1 tablespoon anchovy paste
1 teaspoon paprika
½ teaspoon caraway seed
½ teaspoon prepared mustard
    Parsley
    Sliced radishes
    Vegetable dippers

In mixer bowl beat cream cheese and butter or margarine with electric mixer. Beat in anchovy paste, paprika, caraway, and mustard; blend well. Line a small bowl with clear plastic wrap; turn mixture into bowl. Cover; chill several hours or overnight.

Unmold onto serving plate; remove wrap and smooth surface. Garnish with parsley and radish slices. Serve with vegetables. Makes 1½ cups.

Bridge Scramble

6 cups puffed oat cereal
3 cups pretzel sticks
3 cups mixed salted nuts
¼ cup butter or margarine,
    melted
¾ cup grated parmesan cheese
1 tablespoon Italian salad
    dressing mix

In 13×9×2-inch baking pan heat cereal in a 300° oven about 5 minutes till warm. Remove from oven. Stir in pretzel sticks and nuts. Pour the melted butter or margarine over cereal mixture. Sprinkle with parmesan cheese and dry salad dressing mix. Stir thoroughly. Return cereal mixture to oven and heat 15 to 20 minutes more. Makes about 12 cups.

Smoked Cheese and Wine Logs

2 8-ounce packages cream
    cheese, softened
2 cups shredded smoked
    cheddar cheese (8 ounces)
½ cup butter or margarine,
    softened
¼ cup dry red wine
1 tablespoon finely snipped
    chives
2 teaspoons prepared
    horseradish
1 cup finely chopped walnuts
    • • •
    Melba toast rounds

In mixer bowl combine cream cheese, cheddar cheese, butter or margarine, wine, chives, and horseradish. Beat using electric mixer till fluffy. Cover; chill slightly. On waxed paper shape mixture into 2 logs about 1½ inches in diameter. Roll logs in walnuts. Wrap in clear plastic wrap; chill well.

To serve, unwrap cheese logs. Serve as cheese spread with melba rounds. Or, slice using a wire cheese slicer or serrated knife into rounds. Place atop melba rounds. Broil 4 inches from heat 1½ minutes or till bubbly. Makes 2 logs.

Liederkranz Bread

¾ cup warm water (115° to
 120°)
1 13¾-ounce package hot roll
 mix
1 egg
 • • •
½ pound lean ground beef
1 tablespoon chili sauce
1 tablespoon prepared mustard
⅛ teaspoon pepper
4 hard-cooked eggs, chopped
2 4-ounce packages liederkranz
 cheese, diced
 • • •
1 slightly beaten egg

Place warm water in large bowl. Sprinkle yeast from hot roll mix over water. Stir till yeast is dissolved. Beat in the first egg. Blend in flour mixture from package. Cover; let rise in warm place till double (30 to 45 minutes).

Meanwhile, brown meat in skillet. Drain thoroughly. Stir in chili sauce, mustard, and pepper; mix well. Fold in hard-cooked eggs and cheese. Cool.

Divide risen dough in half. On lightly floured surface roll *half* of the dough to a 13-inch circle. Spread *half* of the meat mixture over *half* of the circle of dough, leaving ½ inch border around edges. Moisten edges of dough with water. Fold dough over filling to form a turnover; press edges together and seal using fingers or tines of fork. Repeat with remaining dough and filling. Place on an ungreased baking sheet. Brush tops with remaining beaten egg.

Bake in a 375° oven 20 to 25 minutes or till browned. Remove from baking sheet to cutting board. Garnish with fresh onion rings, if desired. To serve, slice into ½-inch portions. Makes 2 loaves.

If you enjoy cheese, try one of these hearty appetizers. Liederkranz Bread (top) features a ground beef and liederkranz filling. Chili-Cheese Spread (center left) is made with shredded sharp cheddar cheese. Blue Cheese Bites (center right) sports a blue cheese and butter topper. And Italian Gouda Spread (bottom) is made in a hollowed-out gouda cheese shell and served with fruit or crackers.

Chili-Cheese Spread

2 cups shredded sharp cheddar
 cheese (8 ounces)
¼ cup milk
2 tablespoons butter *or*
 margarine
1 clove garlic, minced
½ cup seeded, chopped, canned
 green chili peppers
 • • •
 Assorted crackers

Bring cheese to room temperature. In saucepan heat milk to boiling. Pour over shredded cheese in mixer bowl. Beat using electric mixer till nearly smooth. Add butter or margarine and garlic; beat well. Stir in chili peppers. Mixture will be thin. Cover and chill thoroughly. Serve as spread for crackers. Makes 1½ cups.

Blue Cheese Bites

1 8-ounce package refrigerated
 biscuits
¼ cup butter *or* margarine
3 tablespoons crumbled blue
 cheese

Cut each biscuit in quarters. Arrange in two 8-inch round baking dishes. Melt together butter and blue cheese. Pour over biscuit pieces, coating well. Bake in 400° oven for 12 to 15 minutes or till golden. Serve warm. Makes 40.

Italian Gouda Spread

1 8-ounce gouda cheese, at
 room temperature
½ cup dairy sour cream
1½ teaspoons Italian salad
 dressing mix
 Assorted crackers *or* apple
 wedges

Cut circle from top of gouda; reserve any cheese cut off. Hollow out bottom of cheese, leaving about ¼ inch cheese on all sides; set aside.

In small mixer bowl combine cheese from inside of shell and from top slice with sour cream and dry salad dressing mix. Beat using electric mixer till smooth. Spoon into cheese shell. Cover; chill. Serve with crackers or apple wedges. Makes about 1¼ cups.

Saucy Ham Nibbles

1 slightly beaten egg
¾ cup soft bread crumbs
 (1 slice bread)
1 teaspoon dry mustard
2 ¾-ounce cans chunked ham,
 drained and flaked
 • • •
2 tablespoons cooking oil
1 cup cranberry-orange relish
½ cup dry white wine
2 tablespoons dried parsley
 flakes
2 teaspoons worcestershire
 sauce

In a bowl combine egg, bread crumbs, and mustard. Add ham; mix well. Shape into 1-inch balls. In skillet quickly brown meatballs in hot cooking oil. Combine cranberry-orange relish, wine, parsley flakes, and worcestershire sauce. Pour over ham balls; cover. Simmer 10 minutes or till hot. Transfer to chafing dish; place over burners. Serve warm with wooden picks. Makes 3 dozen.

Curry-Cheese Slices

2 3-ounce packages cream
 cheese, softened
2 tablespoons milk
1 tablespoon dried parsley
 flakes
1 teaspoon curry powder
¼ cup chopped peanuts
 Party rye bread slices
 • • •
¼ cup water
1 tablespoon lemon juice
 Thinly sliced apple wedges

In a bowl combine cream cheese, milk, parsley flakes, and curry powder. Stir in peanuts. Spread on rye bread slices.

In a small bowl combine water and lemon juice. Dip apple wedges into lemon mixture. Place 1 wedge atop each sandwich. Makes 15.

Lemon-Maple Christmas Punch

4 cups lemon juice
3 cups maple-flavored syrup
4 cups whiskey
• • •
Ground nutmeg (optional)
Lemon slices (optional)

In large saucepan mix the lemon juice and maple-flavored syrup. Heat just to boiling. Stir in whiskey; heat through. *Do not boil.* Serve at once in small mugs. Sprinkle with ground nutmeg and garnish with lemon slices, if desired. Makes 20 four-ounce servings.

Brandy Milk Punch

2 cups milk
¾ cup brandy
¼ cup sifted powdered sugar
3 tablespoons anisette
1 egg white
½ teaspoon vanilla
¼ teaspoon ground nutmeg
4 ice cubes

In blender container combine milk, brandy, sugar, anisette, egg white, vanilla, nutmeg, and ice cubes. Cover; blend till frothy. Pour into tall glasses. Sprinkle with additional ground nutmeg, if desired. Makes 9 five-ounce servings.

Strawberry-Lemon Tea

2 10-ounce packages frozen sliced strawberries, thawed
4 cups pineapple-orange drink, chilled
4 cups strong black tea, chilled
¾ cup lemon juice
½ cup sugar
Ice cubes

Press thawed strawberries through a sieve. Mix with pineapple-orange drink, tea, lemon juice, and sugar. Serve over ice. Makes 21 four-ounce servings.

Christmas Cooler

1 3-ounce package lime-flavored gelatin
1 cup boiling water
1 6-ounce can frozen limeade concentrate
½ teaspoon almond extract
½ teaspoon vanilla
8 large ice cubes (2 cups)
2 7-ounce bottles ginger ale, chilled
2 cups cold water
Maraschino cherries with stems

In a bowl dissolve gelatin in boiling water; cool. In blender container combine gelatin mixture, frozen limeade concentrate, almond extract, and vanilla. Cover; blend at high speed, adding 1 ice cube at a time till smooth and frothy. Transfer to serving bowl. Gently stir in ginger ale and water. Garnish with cherries. Makes 16 four-ounce servings.

Spiked Grape Punch

5½ cups water
4 cups grape juice
1 cup sugar
1 6-ounce can frozen lemonade concentrate
1 6-ounce can frozen orange juice concentrate
4 inches stick cinnamon, broken
1½ cups vodka

In a saucepan combine water, grape juice, sugar, lemonade concentrate, and orange juice concentrate. Add cinnamon. Simmer, covered, 15 minutes. Remove cinnamon; stir in vodka. Makes 25 four-ounce servings.

Hot Buttered Lemonade

¾ cup sugar
1½ teaspoons finely shredded lemon peel
¾ cup lemon juice
2 tablespoons butter

In saucepan mix 4½ cups *water*, sugar, lemon peel, and lemon juice. Cook and stir till hot. Pour into mugs; top each serving with 1 teaspoon of the butter. Serve with stick cinnamon, if desired. Makes 12 four-ounce servings.

Champagne Party Punch

Fresh cranberries
Green grapes
Oranges, cut into wedges
• • •
2 fifths (750 ml each) sauterne, chilled
3 cups cognac, chilled
• • •
6 fifths (750 ml each) champagne, chilled
8 cups carbonated water, chilled

Place cranberries, green grapes, and orange wedges on a foil-lined baking sheet. Freeze fruit.

Before serving, combine sauterne and cognac in a punch bowl. Resting bottles on rim of bowl, carefully pour in champagne and carbonated water. Add frozen fruits, stirring gently to mix. Makes 60 five-ounce servings.

Festive Fruit Punch

4 cups unsweetened pineapple juice
1 cup orange juice
½ cup lemon juice
¾ cup sugar
• • •
1 ice ring
1 28-ounce bottle ginger ale, chilled

In a bowl combine pineapple juice, orange juice, and lemon juice. Stir in sugar till dissolved. Cover; chill.

To serve, place ice ring in a punch bowl. Pour juice mixture over ring. Slowly pour ginger ale down side of punch bowl. Stir gently to mix. Makes about 18 four-ounce servings.

Share the cheer of the season with all your guests by serving either of these punches. Champagne Party Punch (front) features a mixture of sauterne, cognac, and champagne garnished with frozen fruits. Festive Fruit Punch (back) is a blend of pineapple, orange, and lemon juices, mixed with ginger ale and served over an ice ring.

Pineapple Nog

2 quarts dairy *or* canned
   eggnog, chilled (8 cups)
1 cup orange liqueur
1 6-ounce can frozen pineapple
   juice concentrate, thawed
½ cup water
½ teaspoon ground allspice
   Frozen whipped topping,
   thawed
   Ground nutmeg

In bowl stir together eggnog, orange liqueur, pineapple juice concentrate, water, and allspice. Chill. At serving time, stir eggnog mixture and pour into punch bowl. Garnish with dollops of whipped topping; sprinkle with nutmeg. Makes 20 four-ounce servings.

Golden Wassail

8 inches stick cinnamon,
   broken
½ teaspoon whole cardamom,
   coarsely crushed
2 12-ounce cans apricot nectar
3 cups orange juice
1 24-ounce bottle white grape
   juice
¼ cup lemon juice
2 tablespoons brown sugar
   Lemon slices (optional)
   Stick cinnamon (optional)

Tie the 8 inches stick cinnamon and the cardamom in a cheesecloth bag. In a large saucepan combine apricot nectar, orange juice, grape juice, lemon juice, brown sugar, and spice bag. Bring to boiling. Reduce heat; cover and simmer 15 minutes. Remove spice bag. Transfer to punch bowl. If desired, float lemon slices with short pieces of cinnamon stick inserted in center. Makes 18 four-ounce servings.

You can serve anything from a cold eggnog to a hot wassail if you choose from these punches for your next holiday gathering. Pictured (from back to front) are: Pineapple Nog, Double Berry Punch, Golden Wassail, Apple Wine Brew, and Spiced Wassail.

Apple Wine Brew

6 inches stick cinnamon,
   broken
1 teaspoon whole allspice
1 orange, cut into wedges
16 whole cloves
6 cups apple cider
2 fifths (750 ml each)
   apple-flavored pop wine
   (6½ cups)

Tie the stick cinnamon and allspice in a cheesecloth bag. Stud orange wedges with cloves. In large saucepan combine spice bag, orange wedges, and cider. Bring to boiling. Cover and simmer 10 minutes. Stir in wine and heat through. Remove spice bag. Pour into a warm serving bowl. Makes 24 four-ounce servings.

Spiced Wassail

6 small baking apples
1 cup packed brown sugar
1 cup brandy

• • •

1 cup water
12 inches stick cinnamon,
   broken
1 teaspoon whole cloves
1 teaspoon whole allspice,
   crushed
2 fifths (750 ml each) dry red
   wine
1 fifth (750 ml) dry sherry

Core apples; peel a strip around the top of each. Place apples in a 10×6×2-inch baking dish. In saucepan combine brown sugar and brandy. Bring to boiling. Pour over apples. Cover with foil. Bake in 350° oven 35 to 40 minutes or till tender. Drain, reserving syrup.

In large saucepan or Dutch oven combine reserved syrup (about 1½ cups) and water. Tie spices in cheesecloth; add to saucepan. Bring to boiling. Cover and simmer 10 minutes. Stir in wine. Heat through. Remove spice bag. Pour into punch bowl. Float apples atop. Makes 24 four-ounce servings.

Double Berry Punch

8 cups cranberry juice cocktail,
   chilled
3 cups raspberry-flavored
   carbonated beverage,
   chilled
1 10-ounce package frozen
   raspberries, thawed
1 quart raspberry sherbet

Place chilled cranberry juice cocktail in a punch bowl. Slowly pour in carbonated beverage. Top with raspberries. Stir gently with an up-and-down motion to mix. Serve over scoops of sherbet. Makes 24 four-ounce servings.

Peach Spike

2 10-ounce packages frozen
   peach slices, partially
   thawed
2 6-ounce cans frozen
   lemonade concentrate,
   partially thawed
2 lemonade cans (1½ cups)
   vodka
24 ice cubes

In blender container combine 1 package of the peaches, 1 can lemonade concentrate, and half the vodka. Cover and blend till chopped. Add half the ice cubes, one at a time, blending at lowest speed till slushy. Pour into punch bowl. Repeat with remaining ingredients. Makes 16 four-ounce servings.

Bloody Mary Punch

2 12-ounce cans bloody mary
   cocktail mix, chilled
2 cups vodka, chilled
1 14-ounce can (1¼ cups) beef
   broth, strained and chilled
   Bottled hot pepper sauce
   Ice cubes
   Lime slices, celery sticks, *or*
   green onions (optional)

In a punch bowl combine cocktail mix, vodka, and beef broth. Add hot pepper sauce to taste. Serve over ice cubes. Garnish with lime slices or vegetable stirrers, if desired. Makes 14 four-ounce servings.

Glossary

Enlarging, Reducing, and Transferring Designs

Here and on the following pages is a glossary of basic information to help you complete the projects in this book. Contained are: instructions for enlarging the scaled-down patterns in the book and transferring the designs to fabric; knitting and crochet abbreviations; and stitch diagrams for knitting, crochet, embroidery, and needlepoint.

Successful completion of a craft project often begins with accurately enlarging (or reducing) a pattern. Changing the size of a needlework pattern is easy when you use a grid. And once you've mastered the grid technique, the design possibilities are endless. Besides enlarging scaled-down designs from craft books and magazines, you can transfer designs from postcards, art books, or posters and scale them up or down by using a grid. Here are tips for enlarging, reducing, and transferring designs with or without a grid.

Enlarging or Reducing Designs

● *Patterns with grids*

Most of the patterns in this book appear on grids—small squares laid over the design. Enlarge the patterns by drawing a grid of your own on tissue or brown paper, using the scale indicated on the pattern. For example, if the scale is "one square equals 1 inch," draw a series of 1-inch squares on your pattern paper to enlarge the drawing to the recommended size.

When enlarging, be sure to choose paper that can accommodate all of your finished pattern. Or, tape sufficient small pieces of paper together to get a piece large enough for the full-size pattern. You also can use preprinted graph paper for the pattern. If you do, mark the paper off in squares that correspond to the scale called for in the original design.

To avoid drawing a grid line by line, buy sheets of graph paper at an office supply, art store, or fabric or needlework shop. It is available in many sizes, ranging from 1 square to 14 squares per inch. Graph paper that has heavy line divisions every 5 or 10 squares makes transferring easier. If the paper has no divisions, mark off every fifth line with a ruler. Be sure the paper is as large as your finished pattern.

Large graph paper is sold by the yard at many art stores and engineering supply companies. Also, some fabric shops carry pattern-enlarging tissue with small dots at 1-inch intervals.

To form a working grid, first count the number of horizontal and vertical rows of squares on the original pattern. With a ruler, mark the exact same number of horizontal and vertical rows of larger squares on the pattern paper.

Number horizontal and vertical rows of squares in the margin of the original pattern. Then transfer these numbers to corresponding rows that appear on your pattern.

Begin by finding a square on your grid that corresponds with a square on the original. Mark your grid with a dot wherever a design line intersects a line on the original. (Visually divide every line into fourths to gauge whether the design line cuts the grid line halfway or somewhere in between.)

Working one square at a time, mark each grid line where it is intersected by the design. After marking several squares, connect the dots, following the contours of the original, as shown in the diagrams below. Work in pencil so you can erase any errors.

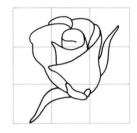

The original design

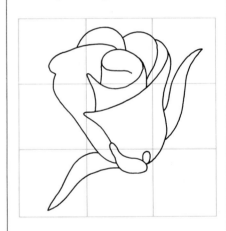

The enlarged design

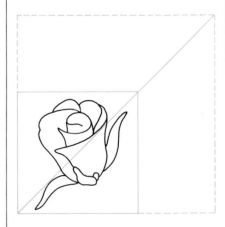

Enlarging without a grid.

● *Patterns without grids*

Even if the pattern for your craft project has no grid, it can be enlarged if you know any one of the dimensions of the final pattern. Draw a box around the design. Then draw a diagonal line between two of the corners on the grid.

On pattern paper, draw a right angle; extend bottom line to length of new pattern. Lay the original in the corner; using a ruler, extend the diagonal. Then draw a perpendicular line between the diagonal and the end of the bottom line (see below, left).

Divide the original and the new pattern into quarters and draw a second diagonal between corners. Number the sections, and transfer the design as explained above (see diagrams, right).

Another method for adapting a design without a grid is to sketch over the original on tracing paper and then pencil in a border. Mark off the bordered area in a series of 1- or 2-inch squares on a sheet of paper that's the same dimension as your finished design (the size you want it to be when it's enlarged). Try to keep the design simple and uncluttered. Intricate detailing and subtle shading are often difficult to translate into a piece of needlework.

Designs also may be enlarged by photostating. Take your pattern to a blueprint company and have it enlarged to the size you need for your project.

Transferring Designs

● *Dressmaker's carbon paper*

Use dressmaker's carbon (not typists' carbon paper) as close as possible to the color of the fabric you intend to mark (yet still visible). Place it face down between fabric and pattern.

Trace design lines using a tracing wheel or pencil and just enough pressure to transfer design lines to the fabric.

● *Hot transfer pencil*

Keep the transfer pencil sharp so design lines do not blur. Lightly trace outlines of the design onto back of pattern. Then iron the transfer in place, being careful not to scorch the fabric.

It's a good idea to test your transfer pencil on scrap fabric before you begin

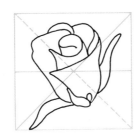

The original design

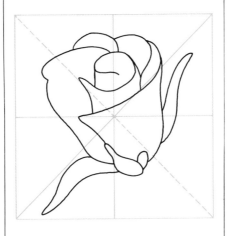

The design enlarged

because the color deposited on the fabric does not always fade when the article is washed or dry-cleaned. Practice drawing on paper, varying the pressure on the pencil and the sharpness of its point. Also practice ironing the transfer onto your fabric until you have marked a design line that is dark enough to see while you work the project but faint enough not to show when the project is completed.

● *Blue lead pencil*

A colored pencil is effective on light-colored, lightweight fabrics. Tape the pattern to a window; then tape the fabric over it (centering the design beneath the fabric). Trace the pattern using the pencil, making dotted lines instead of solid ones.

● *"Disappearing" pen*

This is a somewhat new product available for transferring designs. It is a blue felt tip marker especially designed for needlework and craft projects. Draw or trace directly onto light-colored fabric (use a light touch), work your design, and when you are finished simply dampen the fabric and the blue lines disappear. Look for this pen in needlework, fabric, and quilt shops.

● *Basting*

This is an efficient way to transfer design lines to dark, soft, highly textured, stretchy, or sheer fabrics. Use this method whenever other methods suggested above will not work.

Draw the pattern on tissue paper and pin it to fabric. Hand- or machine-baste around design lines. Tear away the tissue paper and proceed with the project. Remove basting stitches when you've finished working.

Knitting and Crocheting Abbreviations

Abbreviations given here are for the knitted and crocheted Christmas decorations and gifts shown in this book. For stitch diagrams, please turn the page.

Knitting Abbreviations

beg . . . begin(ning)
dec . . . decrease
dp . . . double pointed
inc. . . . increase
k . . . . . knit
MC . . . main color
p . . . . . purl
pat . . . pattern
psso. . . . pass slip st over
rem . . . remaining
rep . . . repeat
rnd . . . round
sk . . . . skip
sl st . . . slip stitch
sp . . . . space
st(s) . . . stitch(es)
st st . . . stockinette stitch
tog . . . together
yo . . . . yarn over
* . . . . . repeat from * as indicated

Crocheting Abbreviations

beg . . . begin(ning)
ch . . . . chain
dc . . . . double crochet
dec . . . decrease
dtr . . . . double treble
hdc . . . half double crochet
inc. . . . increase
lp(s). . . loop(s)
pat . . . pattern
rnd . . . round
sc . . . . single crochet
sl st . . . slip stitch
sp . . . . space
st(s) . . . stitch(es)
tog . . . together
yo . . . . yarn over

Glossary

Basic Knitting Stitches

Casting on

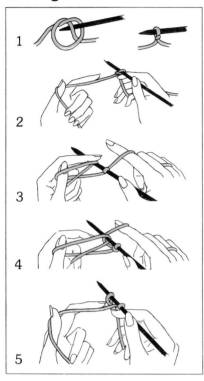

Make a slipknot around the needle at a distance from the yarn end that equals 1 inch for each stitch to be cast on (1). Hold the needle with the slipknot in your right hand; make a loop of the short length of yarn around your left thumb (2). Insert the point of the needle in your right hand under the loop on your left thumb (3). Loop yarn from the ball over the fingers of your right hand (4). Wind yarn from the ball under and over the needle and draw it through the loop, leaving the stitch on the needle (5). Tighten the stitches on the needle and bring the yarn end around your thumb. Repeat steps (2) through (5) for the desired number of stitches. Switch hands, so stitches are on your left.

Knitting

Knitting (continued)

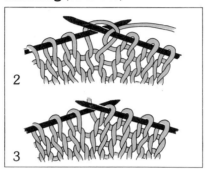

Hold the needle with the stitches on it in your left hand and the other needle in your right hand. Insert the right needle through the stitch on the left needle from the front to the back. Pass the yarn around the point of the right needle to form a loop (1, below left).

Pull this loop through the center of the stitch on the left needle and draw the loop onto the right needle (2, above). Now, slip the stitch completely off the left needle (3). Repeat until you have transferred all the stitches from the left needle to the right needle. This completes one row. When working the next row, move the needle holding the stitches to the left hand, and the other needle to the right hand.

Purling

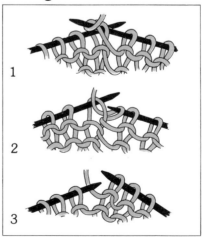

Hold the needle with the stitches in your left hand and the other needle in your right hand. Insert the right needle through the stitch on the left needle from the back to the front. Wind the yarn around the point of the right needle to form a loop (1, below center). Draw a loop through the stitch on the needle in your left hand and transfer it to the needle in your right hand (2). Slip the stitch completely off the left needle (3). Repeat these steps until all the loops are transferred to the right needle.

Increasing & decreasing

In order to increase a stitch, knit or purl as usual, but do not slip the stitch off the left needle. Instead, insert the right needle into the back of the stitch and knit or purl into the stitch again as shown. Slip both onto the right needle, making 2 stitches.

To decrease, knit or purl 2 stitches together at the same time.

To slip a stitch, insert the right needle into the stitch on the left needle from the back, as if to purl (unless directions say as if to knit). Then slip the stitch onto the right needle without working or twisting it.

Binding off

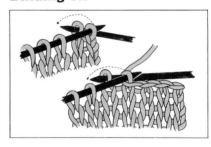

Work 2 stitches in pattern loosely. With the left needle, lift the first stitch over the second stitch and off the right needle. This binds off one stitch. Repeat this procedure for the required number of stitches.

To bind off a row, continue until 1 stitch remains; break the yarn and draw the end through the last stitch.

Basic Crochet Stitches

Chain stitch

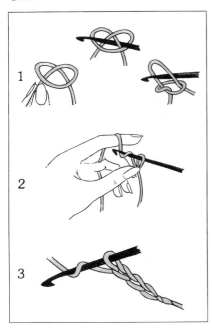

Make a slipknot on the crochet hook about 6 inches from end of yarn (1). Pull one end of yarn to tighten knot. Hold hook between right index finger and thumb, as you would a pencil. Wrap yarn over ring finger, under middle finger, and over index finger, holding short end between thumb and index finger. For more tension, wrap yarn around little finger. Insert hook under and over strand of yarn (2).

Make the foundation chain by catching the strand of yarn with the hook and drawing it through the loop (3). Make chain as long as pattern calls for.

Single crochet

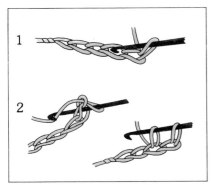

Single crochet (continued)

Insert hook into second chain from hook, under 2 upper strands of yarn (1, below left). Draw up a loop (2). Draw yarn over hook (3, above). Pull yarn through 2 loops, completing the single crochet stitch (4). Insert hook into next stitch and repeat the last four steps.

Half-double crochet

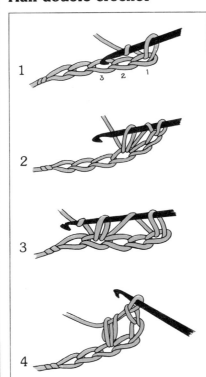

With yarn over hook, insert hook into third chain, under 2 upper strands of yarn (1). Draw up a loop (2). Draw yarn over hook (3). Pull through 3 loops, completing half-double crochet (4).

Double Crochet

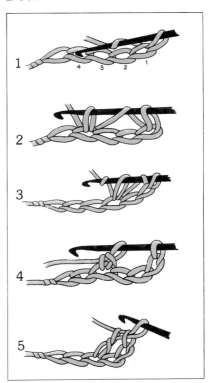

Holding yarn over hook, insert hook into fourth chain, under 2 upper strands of yarn (1, above). Draw up a loop (2). Wrap yarn over hook (3). Draw yarn through 2 loops as shown (4). Yarn over again; draw through the last 2 loops on hook (5) to complete.

Slip stitch

After you've made the foundation chain, insert the crochet hook under the top strand of the second chain from the hook and yarn over. With a single motion, pull the yarn through the stitch and the loop on the hook. Insert the hook under the top strand of the next chain, then yarn over and draw the yarn through the stitch and loop on the hook. Repeat this procedure to end of chain. Use this stitch for decreasing.

373

Glossary

Basic Embroidery Stitches

Backstitch

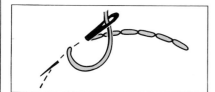

Buttonhole Stitch

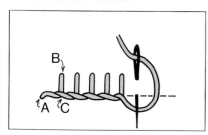

Chain Stitch

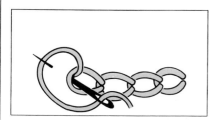

Couching Stitch

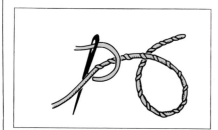

Laid Work

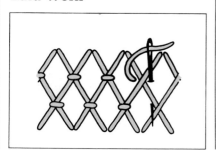

Feather Stitch

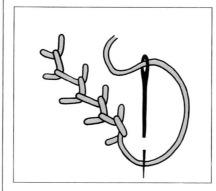

French Knot

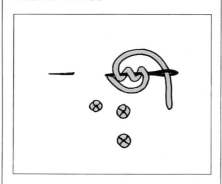

Outline (or Stem) Stitch

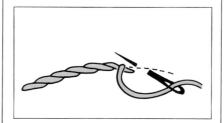

Long-and-Short Stitch

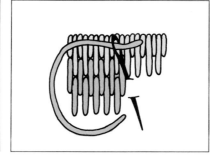

Running Stitch

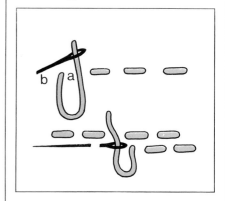

Satin Stitch

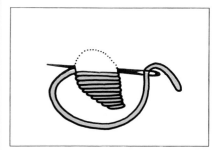

Seed Stitch

Straight Stitch

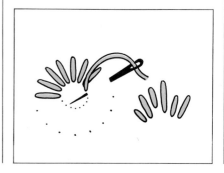

Basic Needlepoint Stitches

Bargello Stitch

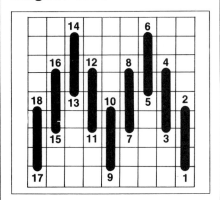

Basketweave Stitch

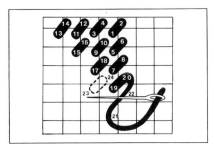

Continental Stitch

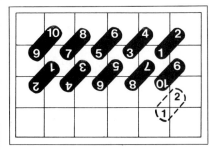

Cross Stitch

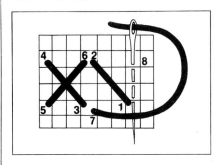

Diamond Eyelet Stitch

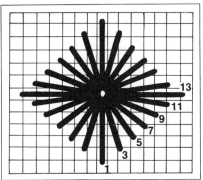

Mosaic Stitch

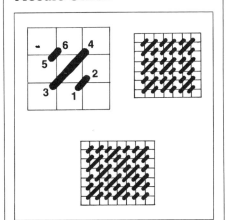

Smyrna Stitch

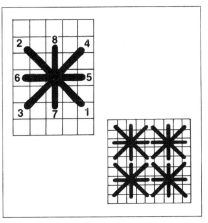

Slanting Gobelin Stitch

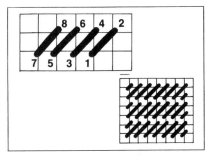

Straight Gobelin Stitch

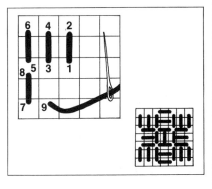

Upright Cross Stitch

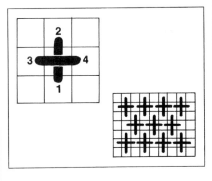

Waste Knot

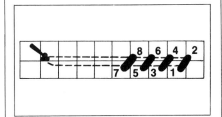

Designer and Photographer Credits

We are happy to acknowledge our indebtedness and extend our sincere thanks to all of the talented people who contributed craft designs and projects to this book.

June Alexis—doll, 90.
David Ashe—ornaments, 7; trees, 14; crèche, 15; doll furniture, 238; rocking horse, 240; blocks, wheelbarrow, cradle, 241; toys, 266.
Arlene Aune—wooden angels, 91.
Carol Austin—package wraps, 197.

Stevie Baldwin—wreath, 79.
Marie Bates—porcelainized flowers, 150.
Nancy Becker—marionette nativity, 218.
Judith Ann Benedict—crèche, 300.
Margot Carter Blair—lace ornaments, 163; lace boxes, picture frame, albums, pincushions, 166.
Morris Bober for Fairtree Gallery—wooden deer, 134.
Gary Boling—granny square stocking, 80; WELCOME rug, 152.
Kay Botkin for Glassart Studio—stained glass nativity, 282.
Noreen Boyd—delft ornaments, 148.
Charles Briarly—quilt, 239.
Patricia Burrets—paper flowers and wreath, 21.

Nita Cain (with Esther Thomas)—apple-head dolls, 196.
B. J. Casselman—foil and mirror ornaments, 132; white wreath, 149; stocking, 235; dollhouse, 244; hat rack, 261; doll, 265; straw nativity, 299; angel, 312; wise men panels, 313; straw figure with stars, 314; cornhusk tree, 329.
Lynn Hopkins Cipolla—schoolhouse block wall hanging, 89; log cabin ornaments, 93; baby basket (with Peggy Jester), 92; flower crocks, 151; velvet stockings, 234.
Michelle Clifton—ornaments, 199.
Gail Clingenpeel (with Lorraine Henriod)—portrait pillows, 152.
Coats and Clark, Inc.—tablecloth edging, 150.
Shirley Cooley (with Challie Reed)—stick reindeer, 261.
Council of 101—appliquéd banners, 309.
Joan Cravens—rose wreath, 77; stockings, 137; tablecloth, 146; picture frame, stockings, 147; stockings, 203.
Coleen Deery—macrame candle holders, 20.

Sherry DeLeon—bargello baskets, 30.
Penelope Douglas—angels, 220.
Phyllis Dunstan—spoon dolls, 9; tea party dolls, tea cozy, 205.

Linda Emmerson—stocking, 222.

Adele Franks (with Camilla Henneman)—wax dolls, 243.
Robert Furstenau—bunnies and bears, 261.

Rose Gerber for Monsanto Textiles—knitted stockings, 233.
Glass House Studio—angel, 317.
Kay Gleason—printed fabric, 11; printed paper and ribbons, 13; printed apron, pot holder, 14; printed paper plaques, 14; tin can lids, 132; bread dough crèche, 296.
Judith Gross—free-form needlepoint, 31.
Mary Grunbaum—quilted picnic basket, basket pincushions, 93.

Helen Hayes—wreath, 331.
Camilla Henneman (with Adele Franks)—wax dolls, 243.
Lorraine Henriod (with Gail Clingenpeel)—portrait pillows, 152.
Gladys Herndon—balsa crèche, 298; wooden trees, stars, wood-trimmed wreath, 326.
Susan Hesse—quilted farm scene, 90; quilted parlor scene pillow, 204.
Beverly Hettick—stockings, 199.
Linda Hicks—clay and yarn ornaments, bread dough ornaments, 132; Pysanky eggs, 132; yarn painting, 135; wrapping paper, 144; wooden candlesticks, 151; cookie puppets, 216.
Ellen Toby Holmes—ties, 26.

Susan Irish—ornaments, 200.
Rebecca Jerdee—banner, 21, 31, 303.
Peggy Jester—schoolhouse quilt, 92; baby basket (with Lynn Hopkins Cipolla), 92.

Alla Ladyzhensky—stockings, 12.
Jean Ray Laury—rag dolls, 242.
Ann Levine—stocking, 80.
Lion Brand Yarn—knitted wrap, 92.
Roma Livingston—tree, 328.
Jo Lohmolder (with Mary Spencer)—natural-dyed candles, 98; needlepoint sachet, 99.

We extend our thanks also to the following photographers, whose creative talents and technical skills contributed much to this book.

Larry Banner and Jack Burns Studio—127, 358, 364, 367.

Taber Chadwick—361.
Ross Chapple—88–91, 98–99, 166.

Mike Dieter—cover, 22, 160–163, 165, 330.

George de Gennaro—6–15, 20–21, 23–25, 27, 28–31, 40–41, 55, 60, 62, 69, 110–111, 119, 176–177, 180, 183, 187, 189, 192, 328, 346–347, 350, 354–355, 362, 368.
Al Gommi—65.

Jack, Jim, and Bill Hedrich-Blessing—47, 48–49, 123, 195.
Bill Helms—216–217.
Tom Hooper—222.
William Hopkins—26, 72–81, 92–97, 99, 120, 130–137, 144–152, 164, 168–169, 196–205, 214–215, 218–221, 230–235, 238–245, 258–267, 279–287, 296–301, 310–318, 324–327, 329, 331, 336–348.

Fred Lyon—116.

Vincent Maselli—44, 53.

Jimm Roberts—308–309.

William Sladcik—124.
Allen Snook—57, 67, 114.

Fritz Taggart—223.

William Wittkowski—302.

Recipe Index

A-C

Craft Index

In this index italicized numbers refer to pages with descriptions and color photographs of projects. Numbers that are not italicized refer to pages with project instructions.